Edward J. Tejirian, PhD

Male to Male
Sexual Feeling Across the Boundaries of Identity

Male to Male
Sexual Feeling Across the Boundaries of Identity

HAWORTH Gay & Lesbian Studies
John P. De Cecco, PhD
Editor in Chief

Male to Male
Sexual Feeling Across the Boundaries of Identity

Edward J. Tejirian, PhD

Harrington Park Press®
An Imprint of The Haworth Press, Inc.
New York • London • Oxford

Published by

Harrington Park Press®, an imprint of The Haworth Press, Inc., 10 Alice Street, Binghamton, NY 13904-1580

Cover design by Marylouise E. Doyle.

Cover photo © 2000 Steven Zeeland/Seadogphoto.com.

Library of Congress Cataloging-in-Publication Data

Tejirian, Edward J., 1935-
   Male to male : sexual feeling across the boundaries of identity / Edward J. Tejirian.
      p.   cm.
   Includes bibliographical references and index.
   ISBN 1-56023-975-1 (hard : alk. paper)—ISBN 1-56023-976-X (soft : alk. paper)
   1. Men—Identity. 2. Men—Psychology. 3. Men—Sexual behavior. 4. Homosexuality, Male.
5. Gender identity. I. Title

HQ1090 .T453 2000
305.31—dc21   00-027137

For Jeremy, Chris, and Scott

ABOUT THE AUTHOR

Edward Tejirian, PhD, has been a clinical psychologist and psychotherapist in private practice since 1976. Until 1997, he was Associate Professor in the School of Education, Department of Secondary Education and Youth Services at Queens College in New York.

Dr. Tejirian is Supervising Psychotherapist at the Institute of Human Identity, New York City, which offers psychotherapy to gay, lesbian, bisexual, and transgendered clients. He is also on the faculty of its postgraduate training program.

Dr. Tejirian is the author of *Sexuality and the Devil: Symbols of Love, Power, and Fear in Male Psychology.*

CONTENTS

If you bring forth what is within you, what you bring forth will save you. If you do not bring forth what is within you, what you do not bring forth will destroy you.

—The words of Jesus in the *Gospel of Thomas*
(From *The Gnostic Gospels,* by Elaine Pagels)

Foreword

The case histories told as stories in this monumental work reflect the release of passion and turmoil and pain and love experienced by Dr. Tejirian's students who were, or were hoping to become, secondary school teachers, as well as others. Ed gives us the accounts of his graduate students and others who had never allowed their sexual feelings and submerged dreams to surface. We also meet Clark and Seth and Kyle and Ron and Carl, who discovered that daydreams need not be night terrors. Throughout this work Ed examines the dry fears as well as the sexual pleasures we are all free to experience if we are encouraged and permitted to live open and joyous lives.

Professor Tejirian created this unique and sensitive view of human beings during almost thirty years of teaching in college as a clinical psychologist. He spent many hours beyond his classroom teaching, listening to and hearing the anxieties, pains, and conflicts his students (in our urban college) experienced while trying to live in the confinement of a frequently stifling code of acceptable behavior.

I was his colleague across the hall, sharing our confining offices with their poor lighting and dim hope. Ed's classes reflected his struggle to dig deeper into the human psyche and to discover the layers of feeling and repressed libido alive in the hearts and spirits of these students who were, or were about to be, educators themselves. To teach, he felt, is to seek to know oneself; without self-knowledge one could never become the teacher of others.

Beyond all the self-examination, we grow to understand the love we can develop within ourselves and to express our shared experiences. Ed reveals that all teachers, artists, writers, and creative individuals must understand their own sexuality if they are to live expressive and nonjudgmental adult lives. To be thoughtful adults we must be sexually alive and openly warm in all our human relationships.

As Ed writes, ". . . our culture's guidelines seemed to add to [Michael's] difficulties." This work shows us that we need to loosen our culture's chains if we are to live in a more loving and less angry society. Barriers, masks, and hidden emotions create a culture of hypocrisy, subterfuge, and rage.

The prisons warehouse angry human beings. Young men at Rikers Island prison in New York City are consistently tested by guards who mock their virility or sexual energy or needs. We will become freer when we can think and share our fears of sexuality and life. Ed's research and writing offer us hope for less frenzied lives, for less hate and hypocrisy, and for more joy if we permit freer and more honest sexual expression. He writes, "Dreams conceal, but they don't lie." This seminal work reveals that to be oneself is the only way we can be for each other. False identities do *not* engage us in reciprocal relationships.

Ed leads us finally into our personal search, a saga of a lifetime search for self. We encounter in this work a sensitive openly gay police officer who joined the "force" but never allowed himself to become an authoritarian person. In my own Rikers Island project, I was horrified to see young homosexual prisoners humiliated by staff, including "corrections" officers.

Ed had the courage and integrity to chair our department in an open and democratic way with grace and dignity. It may appear strange that academic life requires courage, but it certainly did. No college student passed through Ed's graduate course without gaining from his wisdom and his love of shared dialogue.

Regina Pomeranz Krummel
Professor Emeritus
Queens College
City University of New York

Preface

BIOLOGICAL ESSENTIALISM, SOCIAL CONSTRUCTIONISM, AND THE INDIVIDUAL

In their critique of biological essentialism and social constructionism, John De Cecco and John Elia set out the assumptions that underlie biological essentialism.[1] Among these is the assumption that sexual attraction is a purely physical phenomenon. The subjective components of sexual experience—emotion and meaning—are presumed to be by-products of the physical drive itself. The direction of that drive—whether toward the opposite sex or the same sex—does not originate in those subjective components, but rather is determined by physical differences between people who are accordingly categorized as manifesting either a heterosexual or homosexual orientation. In the most influential version of this theory, physical attraction only occurs between male and female. Consequently, when men are attracted to other men, it means that they have some critical, determining part of their physical makeup in common with women. A second version of biological essentialism—now no longer in fashion, but by no means defunct—is that everyone is biologically heterosexual but that various—usually unfavorable—factors have caused an individual's development to deviate from this natural path.

The social constructionist view takes the opposite tack, downplaying the influence of biological differences and asserting that cultural forms and historical forces are the primary determinants of how people experience their sexual desires. It has the real merit of taking into account the historical and cross-cultural evidence that biological essentialists tend to overlook—certainly, any attempt to understand human sexuality in isolation from a historical and cultural framework is incomplete. However, a cultural theory that does not take into account the fact that people are not only exponents of their culture

but, rather, always individuals in a potentially confrontational relationship to it is also bound to be incomplete.[2]

THE INDIVIDUAL IN PSYCHOLOGICAL RESEARCH

Much of the research on male sexuality has started by separating
men into two categories—"homosexual" and "heterosexual"—and
then hunting for statistically significant differences to justify the
categories. Generalizations about the etiology of "homosexuality"
usually follow, ignoring the data that show extensive overlapping
between the individuals in both groups. What has resulted is a set
of stereotypes that lay claim to objectivity even as they distort the
reality of what people are actually like.[3] What we have then is the
illusion of objectivity—of "science"—while the actual influence of
the researchers themselves on the "facts" discovered is unacknowledged and unexamined. Statistical tests of significance add a mea-
sure of mystification to the whole process while furthering the
illusion of scientific "objectivity."[4]

But the idea that, in psychology in general and the area of human
sexuality in particular, there can be some kind of purely objective
research that is not a process of dialogue—of interaction between
researcher and subject in which each affects the other—is itself an
illusion. Even with a standardized questionnaire given under rigor-
ously controlled conditions, the agenda is powerfully controlled by
the person who writes the questions. The less leeway the person
responding has to deviate from the list of alternative answers supplied by the researcher, the greater the possibility that the truth
about the person being questioned will be overlooked or distorted.[5]

Psychoanalysis—which is equipped with the tools to do justice to
the complexities of individual sexual life—was seriously hampered
after Freud's death by a cadre of revisionists who rejected Freud's
theory of universal bisexuality. They succeeded in stigmatizing psychoanalysis with a homophobia that Freud himself never shared.
But psychoanalysis is more than a theory of human sexuality. It is
also a theory of the mind and a method for its study. Freed from its
cultural blinders and homophobic biases, psychoanalytic understanding offers powerful tools for research into the problems and
perplexities of sexual life. Psychoanalysis understands that, behind

what is said, there can be much that is left unsaid. It understands that the mind can be divided against itself even as it recoils from the awareness of that fact. It understands that the mind has multiple avenues—language, dreams, art, and sex—through which it expresses what is important to it. Finally, psychoanalysis recognizes that, in spite of everything, to be truly and deeply understood is one of the most powerful needs of the human individual.

My work as a therapist as well as the research for my earlier book, *Sexuality and the Devil*,[6] has led me to feel that what is experienced at the surface of the skin in sex is connected to what is deepest in human emotion, as well as to the fabric of each individual life. More important, most of the people in this book intuitively agreed with this assumption. There is a long history—scientific and psychological—of telling people what their sexual feelings are supposed to mean. In contrast, even while acknowledging that everything that sex means to people might not be capable of being put into words, it seemed critical to allow people to speak for themselves in order to capture, as much as possible, the nuances and complexities of emotion and meaning embedded in their sexual experience. The more these nuances and complexities are stripped away in order to place people into categories for analysis, the further we get from reality.

The individual, therefore, is at the center of the research for this book and, much of the time, the voices of the people in this book are heard in their own words. There is a good deal of verbatim quoting, edited for readability, but never with the intent of altering meaning. Many people said things to me, shared feelings and thoughts with me, that they had not with anyone else. What they told me constitutes the hard data of the book, and the conclusions drawn stick close to these data. A fair number of people related dreams as well. In most cases, these dreams did not call for a great deal of interpretation. The manifest content usually revealed most of what was important.

By taking as its focus the subjective components of sexual experience—emotion and meaning—and combining it with analysis of the subjective experience of culture, this book aims to fill in the gap left by both essentialist and purely constructionist approaches to the questions surrounding same-sex feeling. In doing so, it aims to restore to individual men—and women—a place as spokespersons for their sexual lives.

Acknowledgments

Had I known how long the journey that this book represents would take, I don't think I would have had the courage to undertake it. However, undertake it I did, and I would like to thank those who, along the way, helped me to realize its goals. There are, first of all, the many men and women whose stories and portraits appear in its pages, especially "Clark" and "Zack"; Clark, for the courage to look unflinchingly into his heart and to say what he found there, and Zack, for his sensitive and generous spirit, and for staying the course until the end.

I want to express my deep gratitude to Regina Krummel—colleague, friend, and writer—for her support and unwavering friendship over the years, her willingness to read successive drafts of this book, and for her belief in what I was trying to do.

My thanks also to William Kushner, poet and friend, for his steadfast encouragement and literary advice. Thanks to writer and artist Ron Caldwell, for his willingness to think aloud with me about his relation as a gay man to gay culture, and for his willingness to contribute his own story to this book and to read sections of one of its earlier drafts. Dr. Kay Jackson was instrumental in getting me access to the institution where I met and worked with Clark. Thanks go to Caroll Hunter, who invited me to the meeting of the Gay Officers Action League, where I met Zack. I am grateful to my psychotherapist colleagues and friends—Jack Herskovits and Bob Hertz—for their friendship and support and to playwright and friend Larry O'Connell, for his. Finally, I thank Elli, life partner, travel companion, and friend, for listening to me over so many dinners, and waiting while I took innumerable pictures.

PART I:
ORDINARY PEOPLE

Chapter 1

The Inner Boundary

Much of the action of this book takes place at the "inner boundary," the point in the mind where individuals as exponents of their culture confront—or begin to confront—their sexual feelings as these emerge from the inner world of meaning and emotion. Situated at that point there is, for most people growing up in this culture, an inner boundary, which is an internalized replica of the external boundary that separates people categorized as "heterosexual" or "homosexual." Among other things, this book examines, in depth, what happens when the potential for individual same-sex feeling comes up against this inner boundary and the need to maintain a heterosexual identity.

The background for the present study was my earlier book, *Sexuality and the Devil*.[1] The first part of that book dealt with the analysis of a young man whose life experience and identity were heterosexual. His obsessional fear that he might be possessed by the devil symbolized an attraction to men that he could not accept. In the second part of the book, I also looked at male-to-male sexuality in two very different cultures—Greece of the classical period and the Melanesian culture area of the twentieth century—and at how each provided for the sexual expression of different but complementary aspects of male-to-male feeling. The Greeks stressed the ties of one-to-one love, with an emphasis on the expression of those ties between older and younger. The Melanesians focused on the ties that bound men together in groups and on rituals that drew boys and young men into the circle of male solidarity. Clearly, the potential for the sexual expression of feelings between men is a normal part of male psychological make-up, but—just as clearly—culture plays an important role in encouraging or prohibiting the fulfillment of that potential.[2]

For years, I taught the graduate adolescent psychology course in the School of Education at Queens College, in New York City. Starting in about 1994, I began to have the students in this course read *Sexuality and the Devil*. Since it dealt in depth with the development, life, and inner conflicts of one man, it fit well into the way I taught the course. I think the best way to teach psychology is to study individuals in as much depth as possible. Therefore, I had each graduate student do an in-depth case study on one actual person. Each case study was duplicated in enough copies for everyone in the class to read, which was conducted as a seminar in its latter half. By the end of the semester, each class member had read and discussed an in-depth study of thirty or more lives—both men's and women's. I think this method contributed to an understanding of psychodynamics in real-world terms while creating an atmosphere conducive to introspection and candor.

After the first couple of semesters of using the book in the course, I began to ask people to write their reactions to the readings. Not only did the book deal with the discovery of same-sex feelings in a man whose identity had always been heterosexual, it also dealt with how the religious condemnation of homosexuality had been medicalized and transformed into psychological terms by—among others—psychoanalysts who rejected Freud's theory of universal bisexuality. This analysis, as well as the cross-cultural material, appeared to raise the consciousness of both men and women with respect to the relation between culture and the potential for same-sex feeling.

If asked to place themselves in one of our cultural categories of sexual identity, most of the people in this group would have chosen "heterosexual." Although they were students, they were not the proverbial college sophomores. They ranged in age from their early twenties up to their fifties, with the average being late twenty-something. They were not selected for any special interest in sexual issues. They happened to take my course to fulfill the psychology distribution requirement for the MS degree in education. Most were already actually teaching, and the rest planning to, at the secondary level in a variety of areas—science, foreign language, math, English, art, music, social studies, or physical education. While all were, obviously, college-educated, that was by no means true for many of their parents, and they came from a variety of ethnic backgrounds.

Therefore, I was intrigued by the fact that the majority of both my male and female students agreed that bisexuality was a normal human potential. I was also struck by the fact that a number of them either hinted at or quite candidly told of experiencing some degree of same-sex feeling. They revealed these things in their "reaction" papers—written for my eyes only and returned with my comments and (of course) without grades. I was very interested in this unexpected development and, after a couple of semesters, added the following two paragraphs in my instructions for reaction papers, explicitly stating that people were free to say as much or as little as they wished on the subject:

At the bottom of p. 234 of *S. & D.* it says, "In my psychology classes, the subject of homosexuality provokes a great deal of animated discussion among students. In one class, after spending the greater part of the class in discussion provoked by questions and comments, most of it expressive of tolerance rather than condemnation, I asked them why, in their opinion, there was so much hostility directed at homosexual people. One young man, a physical-education major and from the same sort of background as Frank said, "I think because everybody, in the back of their minds, has felt something like that" [Frank was the man I had written about in *Sexuality and the Devil*].

In any discussion of human psychology looking inward is as important as looking outward. In reading and reacting to the material of these chapters, I'm asking you to reflect on your own inner experiences, and on your own observations about the people you've known, including, if you are already a teacher, the students you've worked with. To what extent does what the young man quoted above said resonate for you, however strongly or faintly? To what extent can you empathize with Frank's fears? How do you, as an individual confront and react to the goals and prohibitions of the culture you have been born into?

SAME-SEX FEELING IN HETEROSEXUAL
MEN AND WOMEN

I had a single class of thirty-five people in the fall of 1995—eighteen women and seventeen men. One woman was lesbian. Of the remaining women, seven gave evidence of some same-sex feeling. So did eight of the men. Thus, some kind of same-sex feeling was acknowledged by almost half of both women and men.

The spring of 1996 produced these results: Of twenty-two women, one was lesbian. Of the remaining twenty-one, five referred to some same-sex feeling. Of the ten men enrolled in this class, five acknowledged some same-sex feeling. Of those five, two had actually had some postadolescent sexual experience with another man, but did not consider themselves gay.

In the fall of 1996, six out of fourteen men acknowledged some same-sex feeling, including one with actual experience. Of seventeen women, two had some actual experience with the same sex, while three others acknowledged some same-sex feelings in waking life or dreams.

In the last semester for which I have data—the spring of 1997—five out of twelve men acknowledged some degree of same-sex feeling, while a sixth had an actual experience. Of seventeen women, six referred to some same-sex feeling.

THE TRUTH IS OUT THERE

In spite of the variability in percentages inevitable in groups of this size, I think consistency exists. Across four different groups over two years, about a third of seventy-four women and just under half of fifty-six men acknowledged some degree of same-sex feeling or had an actual sexual experience with someone of the same sex after the age of sixteen. Even though—starting with Freud—clinical experience and research have demonstrated the existence of same-sex feelings in people whose identities are heterosexual, those observations and data have typically been discarded, ignored, or rationalized away.

Almost half a century has passed since Alfred Kinsey shocked America by revealing what ordinary Americans told, when asked, about their sexual lives. Half of American men had experienced some degree of homosexual arousal, including 37 percent who had actual homosexual experience, after the onset of adolescence.[3] America has yet to assimilate these findings. For women, five years later, the figures were smaller but still impressive. The cumulative incidence of homosexual responses was 28 percent, with 13 percent having sexual contact to orgasm.[4] A realistic response to the results for both men and women would be to discard the rigid categories that had been constructed to sort and classify people as heterosexual and homosexual. But no. Rather like a virus that keeps mutating to fend off a toxic drug, the categories have simply redefined themselves.

The two Kinsey studies are probably still the best ever done on the subject of what Americans are actually like sexually. A more recent survey that did not have the methodological sophistication of those studies nevertheless turned up some interesting results. As part of a public health survey designed to provide information helpful in combating the AIDS epidemic, it took the unusual step of looking at same-sex *attraction* as well as homosexual behavior in large, broadly based samples of both men and women in three countries and provided some further statistical food for thought.[5] Men and women in the United States, United Kingdom, and France were surveyed. Numbers were on the order of 1,000 or more men in each country, and 600 or so women. Ages ranged from sixteen to fifty. Within each country, samples were stratified for geographic region and for metropolitan versus nonmetropolitan residence. Data were collected in face-to-face interviews and self-completed questionnaires. The data on sexual attraction and behavior were included in the questionnaires. The researchers felt that confining these questions about sex to the self-completed questionnaire would decrease the "potential for embarrassment," not only on the part of the respondents but, interestingly enough, for the interviewers as well. This method—and attitude—in comparison with the careful and sympathetic probing by Kinsey's trained interviewers, would suggest that the results are on the conservative side where the admission of socially touchy behavior or feelings are concerned. The questionnaire asked about actual sexual behavior with either or both sexes over the previous five years. In addition, it asked whether, since the age of fifteen, a person had felt any sexual attraction for—or actually had sex with—someone of the same sex.

In the United States, 8.7 percent of the men reported feeling some sexual attraction for another male without engaging in sexual behavior. The figure for the United Kingdom was 7.9 percent and for France, 8.5 percent.

For the United States, 11.1 percent of the women reported feeling some sexual attraction for another female without engaging in sexual behavior. The figure for the United Kingdom was 8.6 percent, and for France, 11.7 percent

For men, when some kind of same-sex behavior was added, the totals—including *both* attraction and actual behavior—were: for the United States, 20.9 percent; for the United Kingdom, 16.3 percent; for France, 18.5 percent.

For women, the totals—including both attraction and actual behavior—were: for the United States, 17.8 percent; for the United Kingdom, 18.6 percent; for France, 18.4 percent.

Only 1 percent of the men surveyed in all three countries reported having *only* a partner of the same sex in the previous five years. For women, the comparable figure did not reach 1 percent in any of the three countries.

The percentages of men who report having a partner of both sexes in the previous five years (rather than at any time in their lives) were: for the United States, 5.4 percent; for the United Kingdom, 3.4 percent; and for France, 10 percent. For women, the percentages were smaller: 3.3 percent for the United States, 1.6 percent for the United Kingdom, and 3.2 percent for France.

Another recent source of data about the relationship between categories of identity and actual behavior is the book by Weinberg, Williams, and Pryor called *Dual Attraction: Understanding Bisexuality.*[6] It is one of the few studies combining statistical analysis with in-depth interview techniques. In addition to studying those who identified themselves as bisexual, the authors gathered some comparison material on people who identified themselves as heterosexual.

About one-third of heterosexual men indicated having at least some degree of sexual feeling for the same sex. About 10 percent reported some actual same-sex behavior. Of the women, a larger proportion—about half—reported some same-sex feeling. However, only about 12 percent reported any same-sex *activity*, quite comparable to the men.

The authors also looked at heterosexual feeling and behavior among gay men and lesbian women, which is unusual. Like the heterosexual men, about a third of the gay men said they had some sexual feeling for women as well, with about 9 percent having some actual heterosexual experience—almost identical to the 10 percent of heterosexual men who had reported some homosexual activity. About half the lesbian women reported some sexual feeling for men—the same proportion of heterosexual women reporting some sexual feeling for women. About 10 percent of the lesbian women had crossed their "identity" lines to have sex with men, comparable to the percentage of heterosexual women who had crossed over to have sex with women.[7] This study was done in San Francisco in the 1980s and the self-identified heterosexuals were drawn from organizations that were rather like sexual "interest groups" whose purpose was to foster discussion and exploration of sexuality. The sizes of these groups were: heterosexual men, 84; heterosexual women, 84; gay men, 182; lesbian women, 93. These results for the three studies, followed by my own data, are summarized in Table 1.1.

I prefer to use the term "same-sex feeling" rather than "same-sex attraction" for my own data, because it is a broader term that is capable of taking in not only actual behavior and acknowledged attraction, but also inner meaning.

COMPARISONS WITH WOMEN

Although this book focuses on men, the data on women are a useful comparison because they demonstrate that the sexes are more alike than different in their capacity for same-sex feeling. The line between the emotional and the erotic is not stricter for men than for women. In fact, overall, men seemed to cross it more often than women—but they usually worried about it more. In line with the primary focus, the data on men are more extensive. For the most part they are based not only on what they wrote but also on one-to-one dialogues. On the other hand, women were, right off the bat, more completely up-front about their same-sex feelings in their written communications.

TABLE 1.1. Statistical Comparisons

Kinsey [1948 and 1953]

	Same-Sex Attraction	**Experience**
Men:	50%	37%
Women:	28%	13%

Three-Country Survey [N = 1,000 men, 600 women in each country. Study published 1995]

	Same-Sex Attraction	**Attraction or Experience**
Men:		
U.S.A.	8.7%	20.9%
U.K.	7.9	16.3
France	8.5	18.5
Women:		
U.S.A.	11.1%	17.8%
U.K.	8.6	18.6
France	11.7	18.4

Dual Attraction: Weinberg, Williams, Pryor [Data from San Francisco in the 1980s]

	Same-Sex Attraction	**Experience**
Heterosexual Men: N = 84	One-Third	10%
Heterosexual Women: N = 100	Half	12%
Gay Men (to women): N = 182	One-Third	9%
Lesbian Women (to men): N = 93	Half	10%

Tejirian: Graduate Classes CUNY [Age range of students from early twenties to mid-fifties]

Same-Sex Feeling [In actual numbers]

Fall 1995

Men: N = 17	8	
Women: N = 18	7	[Plus 1 lesbian woman]

Spring 1996

Men:
N = 10   5   [Incl. 2 with postadolescent experience]

Women:
N = 22   5

Fall 1996

Men:
N = 14   5   [Incl. 1 with postadolescent experience]

Women:
N = 17   6   [Incl. 1 with postadolescent experience]

Spring 1997

Men:
N = 12   6   [Incl. 1 with postadolescent experience]

Women:
N = 16   6

Sources: A. C. Kinsey, W. B. Pomeroy, and C. E. Martin, *Sexual Behavior in the Human Male.* Philadelphia: W. B. Saunders & Co., 1949; A. C. Kinsey, W. B. Pomeroy, C. E. Martin, and P. H. Gebhardt, *Sexual Behavior in the Human Female.* New York: Pocket Books, 1965; F. L. Sell, J. A. Wells, and D. Wypij, "The Prevalence of Homosexual Behavior and Attraction in the United States, the United Kingdom and France: Results of National Population-Based Samples," *Archives of Sexual Behavior,* 24(3), 1995, pp. 235-248; M. S. Weinberg, C. J. Williams, and D. W. Pryor, *Dual Attraction: Understanding Bisexuality.* New York: Oxford University Press, 1994.

Much of what has passed for research on sexuality—including the current revival of attempts to prove biological and genetic hypotheses—has ignored the effects of culture on sexual feeling and behavior even as it unwittingly incorporated cultural biases in its premises and methodologies. On the other hand, cultural theorists have had (for the most part) to rely on historical and literary sources and were unable to engage actual people in the kind of dialogue about their sexual feelings and experiences that I had the opportunity to do in the course of this study.

THE INSTITUTIONAL CULTURE

Culture is not monolithic. Ours is a culture in dynamic conflict. Late-twentieth-century America has been obsessed with sexuality. The obsession with sexuality—like most obsessions—reflects deep ambivalence and profound conflicts. The ambivalence and conflicts about sexuality have their roots in the religious traditions that have shaped our view of the world and our place in it. Although detailed historical analysis is not something this book will undertake, I think it is important for anyone doing research on sexuality in this country to be aware of the historical and religious context.

In the villas of Pompeii, buried beneath the ashes of Vesuvius in the first century C.E., the walls bear murals of satyrs and maenads making love. The erect phallus is freely depicted in painting and sculpture.[8] It is almost as if the burial of the city itself stands as a metaphor for the fate of the exuberant sexuality of the pagan world. After the conversion of Constantine early in the fourth century, the two religious systems, pagan and Christian, continued to coexist and compete for a time. However, under a series of Christian emperors, persuasion and imperial patronage favoring the new religion gave way to force in the form of an evertightening noose of legislation that, by a century and a half after Constantine's conversion, had effectively throttled the religion that had nourished and sustained the greatest empire that the world had ever known. Many of the pagan temples were destroyed, some by imperial edict,[9] others by organized Christian mobs.[10] The worship of the gods themselves was eventually forbidden and their images were ordered destroyed, although some, ironically, were allowed to survive as "art." At the heart of the new religion was a radical restructuring of the experience of the body and of its relation to the sacred.

The Metropolitan Museum of Art possesses two Roman sarcophagi from the late Empire that, when compared, graphically demonstrate this restructuring and tell of the profound upheaval that had begun to overtake the world of classical civilization. The first sarcophagus (see Figure 1.1) dates from the third century. On it, Dionysus is shown, seated on a panther. He is flanked by naked youths representing the four seasons. The second sarcophagus is from the fourth century. On the front of it, Christ is seated on a donkey as

FIGURE 1.1. Third Century C.E. Roman Sarcophagus

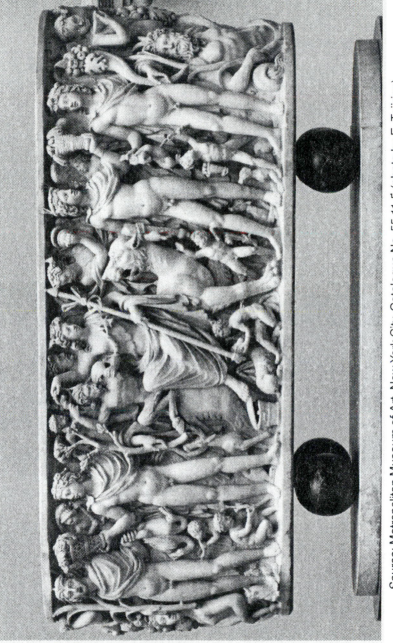

Source: Metropolitan Museum of Art, New York City, Catalogue No. 55.11.5 (photo by E. Tejirian).

he enters Jerusalem. Other scenes allude to events related in the gospels. However, one end of the sarcophagus shows two naked figures, carved in a rather primitive style, whose hands are covering their genitals (Figure 1.2). They are, of course, Adam and Eve. The later sarcophagus held the bones of a Christian; the earlier one, those of a pagan. More than a millennium and a half later, the dynamic conflict between the spiritual and sexual lives on, played out in the "culture wars" that began thirty years ago. From the responses of people in this study, it was clear that what some of them referred to as "society" is more accurately described as the "institutional culture"—that part of the culture controlled by our religious and political institutions. This institutional culture is not only opposed to homosexuality, it is deeply suspicious of the body and eroticism.

The fact that, when it comes to sex, church and state are still bedfellows is not merely an academic issue. For the men and women who spoke to me about their feelings, the relationship between sex and religions was not textbook material either. It was part of their lived experience. Having gotten beyond the terrors of adolescence, many looked back with amusement, some with anger and contempt, at the religious indoctrination about sex that they had shaken off. But this was less true where their same-sex feelings were concerned, especially for the men. Years of efforts by doctors and scientists to depict male same-sex feeling as pathological or deviant, backed up by the threat of social and legal punishments that are by no means a thing of the past, have made it much harder to throw off the burden of guilt and anxiety.

In contrast to the search for "environmental" causes for homosexuality, none of the men or women who confided their same-sex feelings to me attributed them to their environment—either social or familial. On the contrary, almost all of them experienced them in *opposition* to their environment—to "society" as some of them put it, and often to their families. They seemed to feel—and there is no reason to dispute it—that their same-sex feelings originated within their individual selves. On the other hand, the fear of these feelings was environmentally caused—they were clear about that. However, as research has abandoned the search for environmental causes, the fall-back position has become that same-sex feeling is biologically

FIGURE 1.2. Fourth Century C.E. Roman (Christian) Sarcophagus

Source: Metropolitan Museum of Art, New York City. Catalogue No. 1991.366 (photo by E. Tejirian).

caused—by a biology possessed by the minority categorized as homosexual. Ironically, the obsessive focus by religious leaders on homosexuality and the danger it represents seems to reflect exactly the opposite assumption. That is, since it is a temptation that everyone has to be warned against, it must be part of a biology that everyone shares. In fact, that appeared to be the direction that gay theory was heading in the latter part of the 1960s, according to Jeffrey Weeks, who commented, "The chief radical intent of the early gay liberation movement was to disrupt fixed expectations that homosexuality was a peculiar condition or minority experience."[11]

The things that the men and women in this study revealed to me confirm that the 1960s movement was on the right track. So too, I think, is Steven Zeeland in the 1990s who, in referring to "the myth of heterosexual purity," has been a spokesman for getting that movement back on track:

> Overlooked by almost all the parties to the gays-in-the-military debate is the reality that gay and straight service members do not comprise two species. . . . More accurately, they are all different, embodying a multiplicity of variegated and highly complex individual sexualities that are only crudely consigned to polarities of Us and Them.

and

> Unvoiced is the truth that homosexual expression is a natural possibility for men who identify themselves as heterosexual . . . [12]

Zeeland cites his research with men in the military to support this position. Based on data gathered on men in quite different circumstances, my own research strongly supports it. The extent to which both sexes were willing to acknowledge some degree of same-sex feeling really came as a surprise to me. But with few exceptions, I was the only one they told about these feelings. Their public silence demonstrated quite forcefully the extent to which the institutional culture has succeeded in imposing its version of "don't ask, don't tell" on everyone—thus keeping intact the myth of heterosexual purity and the dichotomy between gay and straight.

In a sense, the semester these students had with me was a temporary immersion in a different culture. In contrast to the negative attitudes toward homosexuality fostered by our controlling institutions, the reading they did, the class discussions, and the case studies they read and themselves did converged on a quite different view—one that regarded "heterosexual" and "homosexual" not as descriptions of conditions or labels for kinds of people, but rather as names for *ways of feeling* that are deeply embedded in the fabric of human experience.

SAME-SEX FEELING
AND "GENDER ATYPICALITY"

Much of the theorizing about homosexuality—including that underlying the search for biological and genetic factors—has focused on "gender atypicality," which casts same-sex relationships into a simplistic "heterosexual" model in which male and female are assumed to attract each other because they are opposites. In this model, the emotions of male bonding—which are acknowledged as powerful and even desirable in a whole host of other contexts—are, paradoxically, supposed not to express themselves sexually.

Zeeland's research on men in the military and my own with a quite different population undermine this belief. None of the men (or women) who disclosed their same-sex feelings to me would have been regarded as gender atypical. In fact, some would have been regarded as close to the cultural ideals for men or women. Their same-sex feelings did not appear to spring from a sense of being different from others of their own sex. On the contrary, women felt a closeness with each other *as* women. And a set of deeply affirmative themes that emerged in men's thoughts about sex with each other included friendship, brotherhood, love, and a sense of the sacred. Significantly, the way in which they most frequently experienced sexual feeling for another male was in relation to a good or best friend. The fact that, for both men and women, same-sex feelings appeared to embody bonds of identification as well as affection calls into question the idea that identification and object love are opposed, one that contributes to stereotyping sexual relations between men in male-female terms. It was clear that, for some men, this stereotype serves as a kind of cultural "bogey man" that makes them afraid to experience their own inner feelings for each other. What was astonishing to me was the degree to which men's same-sex feelings, as well as women's, could survive the enormous pressures of the institutional culture to emerge, not only in dreams, but in waking life as well. The conflicts they suffered along the way, the pressures they overcame—or in some cases, partially succumbed to—capture the contradictions of our cultural life and recapitulate its anguished sexual history. But it was deeply gratifying to see that once they were able to get past the judgments of the institutional culture—once they no longer were constrained to feel that half of the human race had to be off-limits for emotional and physical closeness—it was possible to see in both women and men a movement, even in the course of a fourteen-week semester, toward an integration of their same-sex feelings as a worthwhile and even enriching part of the self.

Chapter 2

Women at the Boundary

In the studies cited in Chapter 1, men disclosed more same-sex feeling than women in the two Kinsey studies, while women had the edge in the study by Weinberg, Williams, and Pryor. The Three-Country Survey was a toss-up. In my own data, while a greater percentage of men than women acknowledged some degree of same-sex feeling, women were initially more candid about these feelings. Their candor helped me to surmise that what was true for them might be true for men as well, and to offer men the gentle encouragement they seemed to need to talk about their feelings. In this chapter, I look at what women said about their feelings for each other—what they meant to them, the fears surrounding them, and their relation to identity—as a baseline for comparison with men's feelings in subsequent chapters. I also begin to try to put into place a broader psychological framework within which to view those feelings that go by the name of sexual attraction.

SEXUAL ATTRACTION AS AN EMOTIONAL RESPONSE

The psychological process that is sexual attraction has suffered remarkable theoretical neglect even though it is one of the most powerful experiences that human beings are capable of having. However, the underlying premise guiding this book is that the study of what is called sexual orientation is the study of one of the forms that sexual attraction takes. Sexual orientation—whatever the explanations offered for it—denotes the primary direction of sexual attraction. Sexual attraction itself is an *emotional response* to the image of the body. This chapter begins the exploration of that response. It also begins the exploration of a relationship that subsequent chapters will examine further—the emergence of that emotional response into consciousness.

Women were not without anxiety about their same-sex feelings. But most seemed capable of accepting an emotional response to the image of another woman without its being a threat to their sense of themselves as women. In fact, something like the reverse seemed to be the case. Thus, one woman said:

> Although I have never practiced homosexuality, I have always had curiosities. There have been moments where I wondered what it would be like to have a female lover. My intrigue has never dismayed me, as it might most. I have questioned myself as to why I might be attracted to another woman and my answer is that I have great admiration and appreciation for the inner and outer beauty of women.

Another woman, an artist, put it this way:

> I believe, as Freud believed, that there is a bisexual predisposition in all human beings. Whether or not these feelings ever provoke action is different for each person. Simply as human beings though, who can feel and love and admire beauty, it is difficult to imagine a person never being sexually attracted to someone of their own sex at some time in their lives. I know that there have been times in my life, once in high school for a favorite teacher/mentor and couple of times in college for fellow students, when I have felt something more than platonic feelings for another woman. It was alarming at first, that I could respond to another female in a romantic way, but in time I came to know these feelings not as a threat, but simply as part of being human.

She added, however: "I knew I was not homosexual though, which made having these feelings a bit easier." In other words, even though she had not been able to completely overcome the anxiety imposed by the categories of identity, she had not succumbed to their pressure by denial of her feelings. Now, some years later, the acceptance of bisexuality, not as an identity but as a normal predisposition, explained her feelings to herself.

AVENUES OF THE MIND

The mind takes various avenues to express itself. Language is the best known of these avenues. Dreams are another. The various forms of art are a third. The forms of sex—images and actions—constitute a fourth. Language, far more than dreams, is linked to life in culture, where sexual identity also resides. The waking self that we call "I" and that recalls the dream is not aware of having created it. But the dream is nonetheless a creation of the mind—of the brain, because the two are the same—which continues, during sleep, to express what is important to it in the images and words of the dream.

Even in waking life, the "I" with whom we consciously identify is not fully in control of our images. A story reported some years ago told of a certain sculptor who was having an exhibition at an art gallery in Tel Aviv. The sculptor was a Bedouin who had never had any formal training and who had begun to sculpt out of inner necessity. The Qur'an forbids the making of any graven images, and a strict interpretation of this prohibition would forbid sculpting the human form. Because he sculpted faces, his tribe severely censured what he was doing. He was quoted as saying that sometimes a face would take shape in his mind's eye. It might be disturbing, even terrifying, yet he felt driven to sculpt it. The face appeared unbidden in the imagination of the Bedouin artist in a manner essentially indistinguishable from a dream. The "I" with whom the sculptor identified did not wish this image into existence and sometimes feared the face he felt compelled to sculpt. But the mind expresses what is important to it, even when that is frightening or painful.

In its early days, psychoanalysis took the body as an important focus because of the fact that so many patients suffered from a peculiar kind of neurosis rarely seen in private practice today—conversion hysteria. A patient would appear to be suffering from a bodily symptom that, upon closer examination, proved to have no basis in any organic disease. A person might have "glove anaesthesia," lacking feeling in one hand. But this made no neurological sense since the arm to which the hand was attached was perfectly

normal. The symptom signified something quite meaningful—
the patient's conflicts that were too painful to think about in words.
In spite of the patient's attempts at repression, the conflicts that she
or he could not bear to put into words forced themselves upon her or
his consciousness in enigmatic and paradoxical bodily symptoms.
The mind, though divided against itself, nevertheless expressed
itself through the body. Like dreams, or the face that appeared
unbidden to the Bedouin sculptor, the images and emotions that
together make up sexual attraction also enter awareness without any
conscious sense of will.

IMAGE AND EMOTION

The relation between the sensory images of waking life and the
images of dreams, in works of art or in fantasy, was touched on in
an intriguing way in a recent *New York Times* article on the research
of neurologist Rodolfo Llinas of New York University. His theory
of how the brain works was described in these terms:

> The brain is an organ, and its function is to create images. At
> night, these images are dreams; during wakefulness, the images
> are modulated by the senses and represent the outside world in
> some very practical way that has been determined by evolution.
> A person's waking life is a dream guided by the senses. . . .[1]

In *The Power of Images* by David Freedberg, the analysis of the art
historian converges with that of the neurologist. Surveying the history
of human responses to images, primarily in the Western world, and
from the Renaissance to the present day, Freedberg concludes:

> . . . everything about the picture and the sculpture demands
> that we see both it and what it represents as a piece of reality: it
> is on this basis that we respond. To respond to a picture or a
> sculpture "as if" it were real is little different from responding
> to reality as real.[2]

The truth of his assertion is pretty forcefully demonstrated when
people are threatened with jail for showing images, as was the

director of an art museum in Cincinnati that put on an exhibition of photographs by Robert Mapplethorpe. The picture of a nude person can provoke as powerful a response in the brain and the body as a nude person actually standing in front of us. A painting or sculpture of a person and a real flesh-and-blood person standing in a room are *both* images transmitted from eye to brain. Intellectually, the mind knows the difference between a painting of a person and the actual person, *but the emotional response to the two can be exactly the same.* It is this sameness in the inner emotional response that gives the image in the picture its sense of reality. A major part of the study of sexual attraction in this book is the examination of that inner emotional response. Both the image of a flesh-and-blood body and the image of the body in a work of art can shake one profoundly by opening an avenue to emotions deep within the self. The memories of Julia, a young married woman, revealed how confrontation with an image—in this case, in a work of art—had done just that:

> Before I left for Europe, a three-year romance with my college sweetheart had come to a bitter end. It was a very painful breakup. Part of the reason why I pursued the overseas program was to move on with my life and escape those painful memories. That day in Paris I was traveling alone. In my guidebook an entire paragraph was devoted to the Rodin Museum. Best of all, admission was free for students. So, I casually placed the museum on my "things to see" list and off I went. Upon entering the museum, I remember how spacious it seemed. There were beautiful glass windows that surrounded the bright, white room. As I walked in, I was immediately drawn to this one sculpture, *The Kiss,* this angel white marble figure of a couple, their bodies wrapped passionately together in a neverending, loving kiss. It was beautiful. I was breathless. With my eye, I slowly traced the movements of each body. I explored every inch in detail. I found the piece so expressive. A limitless spectrum of feelings came over me. I was definitely aroused sexually. While looking at the sculpture, I continued the scene in my imagination. I could see the two beautiful bodies passionately making love, reaching orgasm, and gently falling asleep in each other's arms.

Never before had visual art moved me so. It was a wonderful experience. Looking back, I think I can now understand why these feelings were ignited. Many thoughts were drawn to the surface of my consciousness at that moment. Loneliness, desire for a man, fear of never being loved passionately again. I wondered if a man would ever kiss me that way. I wondered if I would ever share in love again. It had been over a year since a man had even held my hand. I was longing for the companionship of a lover and craved physical affection. *The Kiss* made me wonder, who was out there for me? Where was my life going and who was going to be there to share life with me? That evening I remember boarding the train for Vienna in tears, lonely, lost, and desiring male companionship in my life.

When reading the description for this assignment, I immediately knew what I was going to write about. I had never forgotten the impression of *The Kiss*. To really come full circle, I went to the library to find a picture of it. I needed to see it again and I also wanted to show it to my husband. Before I explained anything about its meaning to me, I asked him, "What do you see in this picture?" He said, "I see you and me." At that moment, tears flooded my eyes and I thought to myself, "Look how far you've come."[3]

At a time of crisis in her life, the image of the body in a work of art was an opening to an inner world of feeling that she was able to put into words for herself then and for me now. But there are many occasions when images stir feelings and engage the emotions in powerful and disturbing ways that can be put into words only partially, or maybe not at all.

YOUR BRAIN IS AN ACTIVE EXPLORER

When I was in graduate school in the late 1950s, the goal of "prediction and control" was still seriously advanced in psychology as a scientific ideal. For some, it was an article of faith that if one just could know "all the variables"—but of course one never did— one could predict and control individual behavior. There may be a few diehards who have not yet recognized this for the science fiction fantasy it always was. The premise was that who we are and what we do is determined by forces outside of our control. The end result of this picture was a self-contradictory conclusion: that you could control someone else's behavior but never your own. Research by a new generation of neurologists suggests a quite different picture of how the mind works—one that is both unsettling and liberating. It is formulating a picture of the brain—the mind—as a synthesizing, creative, and *initiating* organ.

In *Descartes' Error*, Antonio Damasio refers to the growing understanding that the mind is the sum of many brain centers that are in constant and dynamic communication.[4] Further, the brain, and therefore the mind, is itself a part of the body, connected with the rest of the body in a dynamic and ongoing interactive loop. At the same time, it is in constant interactive communication with the world outside the body. Neurologist Richard Cytowic says, "Your brain is an active explorer, not a passive receiver."[5]

There is no single place in the brain where "I" is located. The "I" of our dreams is as much a part of the brain as the "I" of waking life. Furthermore, neurological research seems to be leading us back to emotion as being squarely at the center of, and crucial to, all aspects of mental life, including decision making. Damasio has shown that damage to a part of the prefrontal cortex can severely compromise a person's ability to feel certain critical emotions. Even though intellectual capacities remain at preinjury levels, the person is unable to function normally in everyday life. This inability reveals something quite remarkable—countless decisions that we take for granted and appear to make automatically depend on an evaluation that is essentially emotional in nature. Accurate cognitive appraisal is not enough. Furthermore, these emotionally based evaluations need not be put into words—and may not even enter into consciousness—to function effectively.

EMOTION AS CHANGE IN THE BODY'S "LANDSCAPE"

Damasio arrives at what seems to be a biologically based yet psychologically sophisticated understanding of emotion that is directly related to the present study. It is an understanding of emotion as an alteration in bodily states:

> . . . the essence of a feeling is not an elusive mental quality attached to an object, but rather *the direct perception of a specific landscape: that of the body* [italics added].[6]

Damasio's understanding of emotion seems both apt and accurate when applied to sexual attraction. As the brain scans the parts of the image and assembles it, a connection is made between the assembled image and the emotional fabric of a person's life, past, present, and imagined. This meaning of the image for the person is signaled through the nervous system to every part of the body. The body literally "incorporates" this meaning in its organs, veins, arteries, and capillaries, in its hormonal reactions, and feeds these signals of bodily feeling back to the part of itself that is the brain—the mind—thus completing the emotional loop.

Here is the reaction of Michael, a man then in his early twenties who had, for years, been fighting his attraction to men—that is to say, his emotional response to them. It followed a confrontation by an older man who gently but frankly told him that he sensed that Michael, like himself, was attracted to men as well as women: "I was on the subway and I saw an attractive guy. For the first time in my life, *I let myself feel it*—I almost fell down, I almost collapsed. Had I not been holding on, I would have fallen down. . . . *it was so powerful!*"

Michael's reaction in the subway points to an important distinction that neurologists studying emotion have stressed,[7] which is that the biological or neurological processes that are the physical constituents of emotion are not always represented in consciousness, even when it can be shown that underlying emotion is influencing behavior. The wheel, it seems, has come full circle, as cutting-edge neurology lends support to Freud's assertions about the reality and importance of unconscious motivation. Michael (about whom I will say more in a later chapter) had come to understand that he had *some* feelings for men—an acknowledgment that itself had taken considerable time. Nevertheless, without realizing it, part of himself had not allowed the full force of that emotion into his consciousness. When he let down the barrier to its emergence, its power nearly knocked him off his feet.

SEXUAL ATTRACTION AS "MOVING TOWARD"

Much of the emotional landscape across which mind and body communicate remains terra incognita. The neurological mechanisms through which emotions that are felt in the body gain—or are denied—representation in the mind are still shrouded in darkness. Much remains to be understood about the neural connections among language, visual imagery, and emotion. But one thing seems clear, which is that the part of the self that thinks in language cannot choose what emotions the body will have any more than it can choose what to dream. Nor can it choose under what conditions or toward whom the emotions underlying sexual attraction will be directed. And yet, in a seeming paradox, the feelings of sexual attraction seem to be a movement outward—a "moving toward"—that comes from the self. I want to cite a striking incident that graphically illustrates this paradox. It was related by one of my students, a woman I judged to be in her late forties.

> Once, when I stood next to my soft-spoken supervisor, a handsome and charming man, as well as a devoted husband and father, far younger than I, his arm crossed my visual field. A sensuous pull *from my body* drew me into the charged air between my entire being and his luxuriously hairy arm, poised in space above a paper which he was writing on. Some powerfully magical force pulled me closer to him. A gray mass with black lines filled the void in front of me. I tried to halt myself before he noticed, but I didn't have control over myself. Instinctively, I averted my eyes so that he wouldn't notice my expression. I hoped, with an inwardly jarring fear, that I showed nothing. As the sickening fear began to recede, the lights brightened up again, and the room came back into view. *I could have sworn that I had moved toward him.*

In fact, she had stayed rooted to the spot!

Most people agree that there is a difference between admiration or aesthetic appreciation for someone's *attractiveness* and a feeling of *attraction* that is recognized as sexual. I think that the incident just cited reveals the essence of the difference. Sexual attraction involves a feeling of moving toward another with the aim of closing the gap between one's own body and that of the other and, ultimately, to touch it. In this incident the impulse toward movement that is experienced emotionally in sexual attraction was momentarily experienced as actually occurring in a trancelike hyperreality as—against her "will"—she felt herself moving toward his body. The "I" part of herself that looked askance at her desire for this much younger man said "no" even as another part of herself—the "inner I"—said "yes" and moved toward him.

Language is a modality well suited for the communication of ideas and for the expression of thought. Authoritarian systems have always aimed at controlling how language is used, not only to control what is said, but ultimately what is thought. One woman, Maria, recalled about her religious upbringing,

> Sex was dirty—that was all. The devil always tempted the weak person into doing or thinking impure acts or thoughts. It would never come from within since all Christians are "good" because they are in the likeness of God. An evil opponent of God had to be responsible for all transgressions. Sex, furthermore, was only to be used for the process of procreation. As a young adolescent, I was afraid to *think* about sex—I was afraid of having "impure" *thoughts* that I would have to confess to the priest.

It was striking that these lessons were taught—and absorbed—without the actual word "sex" ever being spoken aloud. It was assumed that these young people would *know* what they were not supposed to think about. The net effect, however—and this was surely part of the intent—was to control what could be *felt* as well as what could be thought. The control of images also has as its aim what can be imagined, thought, and felt. For this reason, authoritarians of every stripe have tried to control the arts and artists. In this country, the religious and political right has focused its efforts on censoring the image of the body. Much of this censorship has been justified on the grounds that it protects children. However, in all the years I have taught, not one of my students nor the hundreds of people on whom they did case studies told of being harmed by seeing an image of the body, even in what is called pornography. A great many, however, told of being emotionally traumatized or made to feel guilty and ashamed, as Maria was, because of their interest in their own bodies or those of others.

In any case, complete control can never be guaranteed because the brain not only responds to external images of the body with erotic feeling, the link between emotion and image means that the mind *creates* sexually charged images as well. These emerge both in dreams and waking imagination—for adolescents and even children, before they have had any sexual experience with an actual person. Dreams emerge from the world of inner feeling in a way that, to some degree, eludes the controls of culture. But, even in dreams, as Freud long ago pointed out, the part of the self that has internalized the prohibitions of the culture—the "cultural I"—is not entirely dormant. Nevertheless, dreams can tap authentic layers of individual feeling. Jung went further and felt that they could go beyond the life experience of any one individual and reach down into archetypes of the unconscious, to levels where culture had barely infiltrated. In any case, dreams were a place where women created and met images of each other.

Joanne recalled, "I have had dreams of being intimate with other women, but have come to accept this as a way *I can come into touch with my feminine side.*" What she said next was very interesting: "I am not embarrassed to discuss this with my friends or husband. I believe homosexuals act on their inner feelings eventually because, in them, these feelings, whether experienced in dreams or reality, are a lot stronger than in other people." She went on to relate how, one evening, she and a female friend who had also had dreams about women were talking about them with Joanne's husband, the friend's boyfriend, and a third man. She recalled:

> The men were very interested in what these dreams were about. However, when asked if they had had dreams of being with men, my friend's boyfriend said he could not remember having any, the other man first laughed for a while, then said of course he never dreamt or thought about another man in that way. My husband—who once told me that he had a dream

where he was almost intimate with another man (he was quite upset the next morning)—denied at first that he had ever dreamt this but then later said he *might* have had one dream about it. It was very easy for me and the other girl to discuss this, but predictably, the males were very hesitant and even hostile toward discussing their feelings about it. People tend to reject what they do not know about and are hostile to things they feel could threaten their identity.

Like Joanne, Celia had also created images of women in her dreams:

> I believe homosexuality is part of being human. *I am a hetero-sexual*, but I can admit that I have had dreams about being with another woman. I don't know why. I usually am with one other woman and we're "exploring" each other. Just when we might have "intercourse" I wake up. The dream doesn't "both-er" me. Most times, after breakfast, I forget about it. During the dream, I know I'm excited to be with another woman but *when I awake* the feelings and the desire are no longer there. Even though these "homosexual" dreams don't occur fre-quently, I've come to accept them. They certainly are balanced by dreams I have with the opposite sex. Again, I attribute my calm reaction to my upbringing [gay-tolerant] and the realiza-tion that they are a part of a natural fantasy—anyone's natural fantasy. I just choose to not let my dreams and thoughts affect my heterosexuality.
> Unfortunately, the culture I live in doesn't allow me or anyone else, to explore homosexuality or bisexuality. Yes, I might be comfortable with the idea, but for someone else. *I know that I would have a hard time crossing the line.* My parents might tolerate homosexuality, but again, with other people, not with their daughter. My husband might also be a problem, my job, my friends. . . . *I was brought up to be heterosexual and I am.* I am very happy to be *a married heterosexual.* I don't feel that I am missing out on anything.

I think that one can see in Celia's account the conflict between a movement of the "inner I" and the reaction to it by the "cultural I" that has to live within the boundaries of identity and marriage—"I was brought up to be heterosexual and I am." Although she says that she chooses not to let her dreams and thoughts affect her heterosexual life, those dreams and thoughts are not the result of choice. "Choice" is a deliberate operation performed by the "I" that thinks in language and that is not the part of the self that creates the images of dreams. But she does appear to make the deliberate choice not to move in her waking life—her life in culture—toward the emotional territory that those images point to. However, when a movement toward that territory suddenly takes a person unawares in waking life, it can be even more distressing than a dream to the "I" part of the self that lives in culture and has internalized its prohibitions.

Anna, who had a strict Catholic upbringing, recalled:

> I didn't see women as sexual objects until I was in my sophomore year of college. It was about the time that I began to feel comfortable with my body and my sexuality. College was the first time in my life that I was away from my mother's lectures on how sex was bad and I discovered that I actually enjoyed it.
>
> I remember during finals week I was pulling an all-nighter with a friend at her house. We had spent a lot of time together studying for this class and decided we needed some sleep. We both climbed into her bed together and I began to feel uncomfortable. This girl had done nothing to make me feel this way, yet for some reason I began to feel that she was attracted to me. I remember listening to her breathing because I was unable to sleep, and I felt a very strong attraction to her. For a short time, I wished she would wake up and *touch* me. After this incident, I remember having strong feelings of guilt, almost as though there was something dirty and evil about me. Then something strange began to happen. I began to shower three and four times a day and no matter how hard I tried I never felt clean.

Fearing she was "a lesbian," she started therapy. She found her woman therapist very helpful, and decided that she was not a lesbian. Rather, she said, "I am attracted to the beauty that all women possess. I am attracted to what I love about myself in other women—my capability to make myself look good, the way I look when I am dressed up, and how the shape and curves of my body are so lovely." For her, the solution to her dilemma was to see her feelings as connected—not with any one category of sexual identity—but with her identity as a woman, one shared with other women. This sounded a note that was a persistent theme in women's same-sex feelings.

Darcey touched on this note as well:

> At first, I found this assignment a bit difficult because it was asking me to express my inner thoughts or experiences about bisexuality and I wasn't quite sure how to do that. I began thinking about why it was that I felt this difficulty to express my opinion, and I realized that it wasn't because I didn't have anything to say about the subject. Rather, I've grown up in a culture *where "saying" anything is as taboo as actually "participating" in it.* I have at times said to my friends, especially after a break-up with a man, that I think lesbians may be right—women are more sensitive, they communicate more openly and they think alike, so there's more understanding between them. I realize that it is a more emotional definition than a sexual one. However, I've learned in this class that emotions and sex can't really be separated.
>
> Additionally, I have had conversations with both men and women about sexual thoughts toward members of the same sex, which usually resulted in a lot of denial: "I never thought about it," or "That's disgusting," and of course, inevitable laughter. However, I had the most honest conversation with my present boyfriend quite recently, while discussing this class. I asked him if he ever had a homosexual experience or just thought about it. He responded very openly and said that he never actually experienced anything physical with another man, but has had a few dreams where he is with another man in a sexual way (but he doesn't always remember the specifics). In turn, he asked me the same question.
>
> I too have never had a homosexual experience and although it only happened once I did have a dream about sex with another woman. It occurred about two years ago, with a

woman that I knew and admired. I did not admire her for her looks or intellect, however, but for her inner strength and the rapport she had with the men we both worked with. At the time, I was bartending and all the male bartenders thought they were better at the job than the females, except for her—she was considered to be at their level. She was about six years older than me, but I don't think her age affected the respect she received. Anyway, I had a dream in which she and I were together. It was very brief and never occurred again. Would I participate on a conscious level? I don't know, but I don't think so. I'm not sure why, except that I find men and not women to be sexually attractive. (Perhaps there are other reasons that I'm not consciously aware of?) In a sense, this conversation adds evidence to Freud's theory of "universal bisexual predisposition," stating that both men and women have bisexual tendencies in thought or action, or both.

The avenue between emotions and images is a two-way street. In the case of Julia, the image of *The Kiss* led to the inner world of feeling. In Darcey's case, the inner feelings led to the image. Judging from her remarks, those feelings included the sense of sharing with women a sensitivity, communication, and understanding that men might not have. At a time when she felt under siege by the men on her job, she created an image of sexual intimacy with a woman whose strength she admired and perhaps envied. Nevertheless, her ongoing need is for a primary relationship with a man. Therefore, it is the image of men that she finds sexually more attractive and toward which she moves. On the other hand, her present boyfriend appears to offer her some of the sensitivity and openness that she values in women.

Teri made explicit the connection between a sense of emotional compatibility with women and sexual feelings for them:

I was first introduced to bisexual and homosexual relationships in college. I played on the soccer team and knew quite a few athletes on my own team and others who experimented with men and women. I do admit that I was not aware that two of my very best friends were homosexual until they both slapped me across the face with the news simultaneously. At the moment of discovery I think I felt cheated and got very curious about the relationships they had. As for my own inclination towards homosexual relationships, they do interest me. The percentage of true matches, where both partners really complement each other, seem[s] to be much greater in homosexuality than in heterosexuality. There has never been a girlfriend of one of my female friends that I did not like. However, I probably can't even tally the number of boyfriends of my heterosexual friends that I feel are totally destructive, abusive in varying ways, and not at all right for the particular friend. There is a definite reason for this. Generally, growing up exposes one sex to very different circumstances than it does the other. This is not to say that all girls come out of adolescence into adulthood feeling inferior to the male sex, or unable to compete with anyone—male or female—in academics, athletics, or social functions. But they have been exposed to these issues in a way that men have not and cannot, unless they successfully disguise their body as a woman. Therefore, relationships between two women already have a greater advantage in communication and in an inherent understanding than opposite sex relationships.

Rona, who had an Orthodox Jewish background, echoed this theme:

All of my thoughts on marriage are based on the premise that men are inherently alien to women. I cannot deny at one time or another, having had romantic thoughts about someone of the same gender. When you have a strong friendship with a girl (and you've never dated a guy) you just entertain thoughts of what it would be like to live with her, or marry her. Not even the sexual aspect, just the companionship aspect. Of course, we would still both be girls. Why should one of us have to look all "butchy" just to be with another girl? I never understood that. I feel that American culture has done a number on human emotional potential as a whole. All of the capitalistic media [are] sex-based, solely heterosexual. AIDS was premiered as a gay man's affliction . . . when does it end?

The way in which friendship, the image of the body, and sexual feelings sometimes went together was mirrored in the light-hearted comments of another woman:

> I truly adored the slide, *Eternal Spring* by Rodin, that you showed. It was the most appealing image I witnessed that day. It was so sexy and alive. I visualized myself as the woman in the sculpture being so tenderly caressed and held by the adoring man. I admit there were moments when I was attracted to certain women, usually someone I developed a friendship with, but that does not mean I want to spend the rest of my life with a woman, because I certainly do not. However, a little fantasizing never brought me great harm so why should I be insecure about it?

In contrast, although Debra seemed at ease about her same-sex feelings, she was quite aware of the possibly negative reactions of others:

> I have thought of trying a same-sex partner. When I was much younger, I had a dream of making love with a female and I found it a comfortable feeling although I never acted on it. I woke up, thought about why I dreamt, it and then discarded it as unimportant. There was a period in my middle teens when I strongly disliked homosexuals, and it was around this time that, one day while I was alone in a whirlpool in a health club, a woman entered the pool and glided over to where I was sitting. Her body touched mine. I was very angry. Over the years my thinking has changed but I feel it has been strongly influenced in the early years by culture's and society's pressures. I wanted to fit in with my friends, and all of them were heterosexual. Later, I had gay friends when everyone else did.
>
> As I have grown more, read more, seen more, and interacted with more people, I have come to realize that one's sexual preference does not matter to me. *I believe that bisexuals and homosexuals are more in tune with themselves than heterosexuals because they have to look deep down and say it is what they are and then defend it to culture and society.* I believe that my potential *to be a complete female* is hampered by the

constraints of society. Sometimes I feel angry because I would have to orchestrate the opportunity to have a sexual relationship with the same sex, and my ability to feel pleasure and to experience the many dimensions of my body's sensual and sexual sides is diminished.

Barbara's same-sex feelings seemed more urgent and the question of identity and acceptance proportionately more acute:

Even though homosexuality and bisexuality are slowly becoming a part of our culture, there are many who view such a lifestyle with horrid disgust and label the participants of these acts as unnatural and immoral. I openly admit that I myself have had four homosexual dreams in the past year. When I had my first one I was shocked and embarrassed but I rationalized it, as I have done with the others. You once asked us if it is possible to separate sex from love, and with that one question I was forced to reassess my thought processes of the past. That is all I have been doing with all my relationships with men and women—separating love from sex. In my dreams, I'm making love to the faces of women friends, for whom in my life I have very strong feelings. They have [in the dreams] male bodies, however. This I attribute to the fact that I have a strong desire for intimacy with a male towards whom I [can] have a great depth of emotional connection, *as I do with my female friends.* I do not see that I will at any day soon act out my dreams. *I am a product and member of my society* and although I clearly express my belief that sex is the extension of emotions and desires, and that each individual has the right to express their sexuality and make their own "sexual object choice," *I hold that I am a heterosexual female,* who in the back of my mind and in the face of my consciousness and subconscious, has felt "something like that."

The meaning of the image that combines a female head with a male body has to remain uncertain. Her own interpretation might be quite right. Or, it might be an expression of her movement toward a fuller realization of a wish for a primary relationship with a woman—who might eventually appear in some future dream with a female body. In fact, in another communication to me, she alluded to explicit fantasies about a "homosexual lover." Thus, for Barbara the term "sexual object choice" might have been more than a figure of speech.

Carolyn, however went beyond thinking about it and actually moved into a sexual relationship with another woman. She did this with a female housemate who revealed to Carolyn that her attraction to women was more emotional than to men, and that she was bisexual:

> Because we were such good friends I felt very comfortable asking her all those taboo questions about female-to-female attraction. But, over the course of those few months, I realized my questions were for more than just data collecting. I was emotionally intrigued with this idea, for what I feel was the first time in my life. I was healing from the trauma of a previous male relationship. I began to be attracted to my roommate in a sexual way. I wanted to explore this side of myself. I was also shocked that I had these feelings for her and felt that if I did not explore this sexual attraction to her I would always wonder about myself and never be sure about my sexual preferences.
>
> After trying many sexual positions and actions with my roommate I started to feel uncomfortable with the whole thing. I started to feel less and less attracted to her sexually. My romantic attraction seemed to leave me as quickly as it came. During that time I came to a realization that I was not attracted to women, or I *could* be, but my main interest was in men. My encounter with a same-sex relationship was a real growing experience for myself.

Carolyn's experience further challenges the idea that sexual feelings emanate from a fixed and immutable sexual orientation.

THE INVITATION

Would Carolyn have moved into a relationship with a woman if she had not found herself living with a good friend who presented her with the possibility? It is difficult to say, but some other women also mentioned an inner movement in that direction after an invitation by another woman. The images of a dream are creations from within. But an invitation from the outside sometimes stimulated the emergence of emotions that, for the first time, went beyond the boundaries of a person's accepted identity. Sharon recalled:

> There was a woman I was working with. She was about thirty years old and we became very good friends. One day she opened up to me that she was a lesbian and although she didn't have a girlfriend then, she does date women. She told me that she was attracted to me. Until that time *I had never consciously considered a lesbian relationship, or even kissing another woman in a passionate sense. But after she told me that I often considered it,* although I never talked to her about it, and never told anyone at that time or for many years after. Nothing came of it, although we continued to stay friends for a couple of years after. The interesting thing is, I never felt ashamed of myself for having those feelings or that desire, although I never told anyone *because I was afraid of what they would think of me.*

Another woman, Laura, said:

> I used to have a boyfriend who would mention bringing in a third party (a woman of course) into our sex life. It was interesting that he would not even hear of bringing in another male, but another woman was fine. He had mentioned this quite often and my response was, "What if I like her better than you?" That put a damper on it for a while. On the one hand, I say it's okay to have homosexual feelings and I believe most people do, but won't admit to it because of other people's reactions. I fall into that same situation. *I don't know if I'd call myself bisexual* but I definitely appreciate the female body and sometimes feel sexual to other women. I think about these feelings often but have never acted upon them. I think it's all right to keep it as a fantasy. I guess I fall into the *same category molded by society* because if any of my friends or family found out they would freak out. I come from a Roman Catholic background but following it strictly went out the door with premarital sex. I have been hit on by several women, but one

time I was truly tempted. It was in Italy. This girl was beautiful and she looked similar to a female I had a dream about. To this day, I still think of that night and what stopped me from going with her. I must say I think it was because I didn't want any of my friends to know I had these feelings.

Although Laura had experienced same-sex feelings before the beautiful Italian approached her, she had no trouble rejecting her boyfriend's proposals. But the invitation from someone who look-ed—literally—like the woman of her dreams almost made her throw caution to the winds. Some other women, however, were interested in the idea of being with a woman and man simultaneous-ly. Melissa said:

> I believe we all have homosexual tendencies within us, but are too closed-minded to admit to them. I have often fantasized about being with my husband and another woman. I am ex-cited by both the idea of my husband being excited, and by the simple fact that a woman is more sensual and knows how to touch another woman more tenderly than a man. Women are much more open about these feelings and ideas than men are. My girlfriends will be very honest about their fantasies with other women. We are very sure of our identities, and we are not intimidated or threatened by our thoughts of other women. After all, our closest friends, that we share every thought with, are women.

This easy acceptance was in stark contrast to the wistful thoughts of another woman:

> I have always had the fantasy of being with my boyfriend in bed and another woman. I would never bring this up to him or any of my friends because they have such a closed-minded attitude toward homosexuality and bisexuality. I have the fan-tasy, but if I ever tried to have my fantasy lived out I would probably lose my boyfriend, friends, and anger my family. I guess that will be my fantasy forever. I heard from someone that it is good to have fantasies, so it won't be that bad.

A third woman related:

> Perhaps it is because I have never really been averse to homo-
> sexuality that I am able to relate to bisexual feelings in myself.
> While I never have actually had a sexual experience with
> another woman, at times I find the idea of it sexually arousing.
> Now I know this is going to sound like a common disclaimer:
> "I don't think I'm really gay." I have never really desired a
> romantic relationship with a woman. However, I do believe
> there is an intimacy that can be shared between two women
> that is different than what is experienced between a man and a
> woman. Having an intimate relationship with a woman is a
> common fantasy that both myself and my husband share. I also
> have had dreams [in which] I am involved with another
> woman. These dreams have never disturbed me—in fact, they
> have often been quite pleasurable. I think it is because I can
> accept that part of my sexuality and not deny it, that it has not
> been a source of anxiety in my life.

ADOLESCENCE

The fear of homosexuality is handed down from the top. Although the negative attitudes of the institutional culture have fil-
tered down to some children before adolescence, many are not yet
aware of the harsher realities of cultural life. But by the time adolescence has rolled around, the fear of it is well entrenched for many
boys and girls, making adolescence a time of terrified conformity.
One woman, now in her early forties and married with children,
recounted the progression of her feelings from childhood to the
present:

> I don't know if other people feel the same way, but I don't feel
> any shame in admitting that there were times when, as a child
> and then later in early adolescence, I was attracted to other
> females. There were many more instances where I felt at-
> tracted to boys and older men, but both inclinations definitely
> existed together. The first and most powerful feeling of love
> was towards my mother, whom I hoped to marry someday. I

can also remember having crushes on my older cousin and some of the more popular, pretty girls in my classes at school. Simultaneously, I was also attracted to boys.

However, the innocence of these early feelings gave way under the assault of social pressures by early adolescence:

After attending Catholic school for several years and becoming aware (via television, radio, and overhearing adult conversations) of the negative reaction towards homosexuality, I felt tremendous shame and guilt over any attraction I had ever had towards anyone of the same sex.

Despite these pressures, however, she was able to tell her mother about her fears:

My mother told me that it was natural and nothing to be afraid of. Today, I realize how lucky I was that I had a secure and open-minded parent to go to. Her understanding and calm attitude are the reasons I [am] able to discuss this now without hesitation or remorse. When I was eleven years old, however, I was filled with guilt and self-loathing.

As I grew up I can recall the nasty and vicious reactions that even a hint of homosexual behavior would draw from children who were my peers. There was nothing worse than calling someone a "faggot" or a "queer." In elementary school, the targets of this type of abuse were always boys. By the time I was in high school, however, it was clearly understood that if you wanted to survive socially you must never even suggest having a homosexual impulse to anyone. At this time, I can recall that girls were also now being targeted as different; some of the more masculine appearing or very athletic girls were being labeled "dykes" by other students. In the locker room you always had to avert your eyes lest you be caught "staring" at another girl. I think it is very important to realize just how powerful an influence an adolescent's own peers are. In my experience, admitting to being homosexual was equal to committing social suicide during the teen years.

In college, things lightened up considerably regarding the subject of homosexuality, for me as a woman anyway. I can still remember the guys that I knew being terribly negative and paranoid on the subject, however. These types of feelings had to come from fear, whether it was fear of being approached or, more likely, fear stemming from their own homosexual feelings.

In reflecting on what women in this chapter told me, I am struck by the fact that the degree of comfort or unease that a woman felt about her same-sex feelings did not appear to depend on whether they first entered awareness through dreams or in waking life. I am also struck by the fact that so many women accepted their feelings so well. Why didn't more women act on them? One answer was the social price they felt they would have to pay in the reactions of family, friends, or partners. For others, the need was simply not intense enough.

Although the "moving toward" that made them aware of their same-sex feelings was not a choice made by the "I" with whom a woman identified in her waking life, there was a clear exercise of choice in how far the exploration of those feelings would go. Carolyn decided to undertake that exploration. Had others followed her example and explored in their waking lives what they had in dreams, some might also have wound up doing what she did in the end—turning back toward men. Others might have discovered in those explorations compelling reasons to intensify their bonds with women instead. Still others might have tried to work out a way of living that would fulfill both sets of feelings.

As for an explanation of women's same-sex feelings as such, their frequency would indicate that they are simply part of the normal spectrum of women's emotional makeup. The question of why some women are more drawn to women, some to men, or some to both cannot be squarely addressed without considering the powerful social pressure to move in one direction and to avoid the other. But even if we could magically transform our institutions and remove the stigma that is now attached to same-sex feeling, I doubt we would be able to find any one "cause" that accounted for the same-sex feelings of all women. The same applies to women's feelings for men. As for the preference for one sex over the other, even if we put each individual woman's life history under a microscope, we would still be unable to say with any certainty *why* her emotional and sexual life moved along one path rather than another, though we might be able to trace the stages through which it unfolded.

There were, of course, other women who did not acknowledge any same-sex feelings at all, possibly for various reasons. Some might have been aware of them but simply did not choose to disclose them. Others might not have had any memory or awareness of any such feelings because they were not an important part of the body's emotional landscape and therefore did not generate the "moving toward" that constitutes sexual attraction. Thus, one woman said: "As a woman I find the female body a beautiful work of art, but seeing a nude woman does not generate the same feelings as seeing a nude man. When I see a nude man I want to touch and explore what I see. A nude woman does not arouse any desire to touch and explore." A third possibility is that the emotions were present but the avenues to consciousness—whether the consciousness of dreams or of waking life—were blocked by resistance.

This resistance, which Freud called "repression," has hardly figured in the research on homosexuality. I think this is because in the framework of the institutional culture, it was same-sex feelings that were seen as "abnormal" and therefore deserving of investigation, not the fear of them or the mechanisms for their denial. That resistance will, however, be the subject of closer scrutiny in the subsequent chapters on men.

Chapter 3

"Moving Toward" and Resistance

In this chapter, I want to begin look at the resistance that Freud called repression and—insofar as possible—to see it in operation. Seth and Will were among the first people with whom I spoke about the issues in this book. It was in my dialogues with them that I first saw the dynamic "moving toward" of men's same-sex feeling and the operation of the dynamic resistance that blocked it from progressing further.

SETH

Seth was in his early twenties and, though American by birth, had been in the Israeli army for a short time before injury forced him to withdraw. In a class discussion about the president's proposal to lift the military ban on homosexuals—which was still news then—Seth noted that in Israel gay men served in the military along with everyone else. Candidly, he said he understood the problems some people might have with this. Recalling an occasion when he thought that a certain man in the showers might be gay, Seth remembered feeling "queasy" when he felt when the man was looking at him. He could not explain why, nor was he saying that the ban should not be lifted. He was simply being honest in reporting his own experience.

In a follow-up conversation, he elaborated: "If I'm in the shower and I know someone in there is gay, the feeling is honestly that there is no difference between being in the shower with someone who is gay and a woman—not that he is actually a woman." When I began to ask him if he *had* ever been in a shower with a woman, he started to laugh. Of course, he had—with a girlfriend—and enjoyed it. Looking at these two situations, there was both a similarity and a difference between them. The similarity was that he felt that he was the object of sexual interest in both cases. The difference was that this feeling would be welcome in one instance and unwelcome in the other. Seth's feeling seemed very much related to the debate about whether men and women in the military should be allowed *openly* to acknowledge being gay. He said that if this man had done so he would have been *more* uncomfortable still, because he would then know for certain.

Seth was hard-pressed to explain why this would bother him more. But he remembered an incident in civilian life when he had felt a similar discomfort. He was in a shopping mall, and a clerk was looking at him with evident interest. Seth was quite uncomfortable and wondered if the man thought he was gay himself. That would bother him because, "The last thing in the world I would want is for someone to think I'm gay. And if he did think that, what is it about me that could make him think so?" On the other hand, if this man was merely attracted to him without assuming he was gay, that would still leave him feeling uncomfortable because, "He's a man and I'm a man—it's unnatural."

In light of what he had just been saying, I would not have been surprised at a flat "no" in answer to my next question. I prefaced it by noting that sometimes a heterosexual man could have a dream about another man or about men that was sexual, or had sexual implications. Had he ever had such a dream? With disarming candor he said, "Sometimes I've had a dream where I was hugging a friend real tight. *It was like the line between friendship and intimacy was blurred.* Some dreams I remember very vividly and clearly. Others I don't. I'd wake up in the morning after a dream like that and say, 'Wow, what was that all about? What *was* that?' "

I asked Seth what the emotion or feeling in the dream was like. He said,

> The emotional feeling—I guess it was just love for my friend—you know, brotherhood and whatever. But at the same time, in the dream *it was much more.* When I see my friends after they come home from college, it's always, "What's up?"

and a hug. When I got back from being abroad, everyone hugged me. But these dreams were, like, much more, like a *real* hug, like a *long* time or whatever.

Unlike some men, Seth had no problem acknowledging another man's good looks. He might feel envy, but nothing more than that. I asked Seth what he thought made a person gay—clearly, it was not only finding another man attractive. He said: "It all comes down to sex, to actual contact, usually what you'd associate with sexual contact, more than just hugging. There's a hug—and then there's a *hug*, there's even a kiss—and then there's a *kiss*." In the dreams that Seth told me about, it was just because the hug felt very close to a *hug* that he woke up asking himself, "What was that?" And that is a question worth posing—what was that? He himself said that it seemed very close to "intimacy" rather than only friendship. In this scene—and it had occurred in more than one dream—it was the long, intense hug that felt like more than friendship. It was close to what, by Seth's own definition, made a person gay. But Seth was *not* gay, so—again, to use his own words—what *was* that? Before trying to answer that question, I want to present some more of our dialogue.

I recalled that in one class I had asked students how many of them had wondered "what it would be like" to have a sexual experience with someone of the same sex. Quite a few people—between a third and half of the class—had raised their hands. I asked him if that question had ever occurred to him. He said, "Yeah, it has—very rarely. You know, as far as, like a kiss is a kiss . . . of course it would be a totally different feeling, having a guy's body in your hands instead of a girl's. You know, that's all really . . . that's the closest I ever thought about it." I asked him if an image occurred with that thought. He asked, "With that kind of thought—you mean like an image of a man or anything like that?" Was there even a vague image? I asked. "Just a basic guy's body, medium build, hair on the chest, really, because that's something . . . but no, nothing," he answered. Was Seth nervous about being questioned in this way? Perhaps, but it was the nervousness that a great many men with heterosexual identities might feel when asked that kind of question.

I asked Seth if having one sexual experience with another man would make a man gay. He said, "No, I don't think so." What, I asked, could the circumstances for such an experience be? He answered, "Maybe he was molested . . . or maybe he wanted to experiment and see what it would be like and actually had the guts to do it. . . . " But as for experimenting himself, the farthest he had gone was to entertain the fleeting image in his mind's eye that he had just mentioned. Otherwise, he said, "I would never experiment, no. I'm not curious enough." Seth readily agreed that he could love a friend, and that in the dream he felt a sense of intimacy, love, and closeness. What enabled him to express love for a *woman* in a physical, sexual way? He said,

> There's the urge to do it. You want to show the person that you love them and you are able to that way. And you want it and she wants it too. With a guy, it's not that you can't—you won't—you don't want to do it. On a mental level, there's a difference between love for a man and love for a woman. With a man, it's more like brotherhood. With a girl, you want to protect her, be there for her, guard her. I can have really deep feelings for a friend and love him as much as I love a girl, but the feelings are totally different. The thought of expressing it in any other way with a man—like to kiss him on the lips, use your tongue, or touch him in any other way—that repulses me and there's no question about it, it just does, bottom line, period.

Seth had been willing to be introspective and honest with me, and I appreciated that. I told him as much and said I was going to take advantage of it by asking him to push himself to the limits. What, I asked, made it so repulsive for another good male body like his own, belonging to a friend he was very fond of, to be in contact with his own body? He said, "It's just not attractive to me. It doesn't compare to if there was a really ugly girl. I'd be more willing to go with the girl. But," he added, "that might be a cultural thing."

"What happens," I asked Seth, "when you have a friend that you like emotionally and physically—that you even love—and suddenly that feeling of repulsion is right there when you come to this thing called sex?" Seth said, *"I can't answer . . . there is no an-*

swer." I said to him that I guessed there wasn't. It seemed he had gone as far as he could in explaining his feelings. But then he did go farther. "There are things you do with women and things you do with men. It's a different relationship and that's just not natural. Most people can't imagine anything more unnatural. You're talking about nature really. *What else is so unnatural?*"

Putting this question on the back burner, I want to look at the other one that Seth asked about the dreams of the intense hug between himself and a friend. What *was* that? The question was asked by the waking "I"—the "I" that lives in culture—and that Seth identified with. Nevertheless, the dreaming "I" that created this dream was also part of Seth—as much as the part of him that recalled the dream and wondered about it. Seth had said about women, "You want to show the person that you love them and you are able to that way." This seemed to be exactly what Seth was doing in his dream—showing his friend that he loved him. I suggest the following answer to Seth's question, "What *was* that?" Clearly, it was an emotion—love, a love that in his waking life he would describe as "brotherhood." But that emotion was stronger in the consciousness of his dreams than it was in the consciousness of waking life and it was moving toward an intensity of expression that had no parallel in waking life except with women. The intensity of the hug matched the intensity of the feelings. Knowing nothing else about the dreamer, how could one know if this was the dream of a gay man or a heterosexual man? One could *not* know. I think we have to conclude from this that Seth was in a space within himself common to *both* gay men and heterosexual men—a space where men experience powerful bonds of love and affection with other men. Sexual identities are bound up with life in culture, but in sleep the world of culture is more distant and the boundaries set by cultural identities less rigid. In his dreams Seth's mind could do what was, in fact, *natural* to it—create images that literally embodied his deep feeling for a friend and his desire for closeness with him. In doing so, he moved closer to the boundary between the heterosexual identity of his waking life and a realm of intense feeling for another man from which his cultural self automatically drew back.

Seth's background was Jewish. His home had not been religious, but he had been very close to his grandfather, who was Orthodox. His grandfather died when Seth was in his early teens, and after that Seth lost touch with Judaism. However, in his late teens, he went to Israel for a visit and " . . . it all came back to me—everything that he taught me as a kid—to be proud." His grandfather, he said, had been more of a father to him than his own father. The things he learned from him " . . . stuck with me and I'm hooked—the importance of Israel to the Jewish people." Israel made a lasting impression on Seth. He said, "I don't know how to put it. It was the first time that I saw Jews with guns! I had experienced a lot of anti-Semitism when I was younger. Most of my friends were Catholic and went to Catholic school. I don't know if they really meant it, but it was there all my life, jokes ranging from Jews being cheap to jokes about the Holocaust." It was important to Seth that in Israel, there was no need to deal with that. After 2,000 years, the Jewish people could have an army, control their own destiny. Seth's Jewish identity was very important to him, although it was more bound up with the secular life of the Jewish state than with religion as such, with the attainment of a nationhood on par with other nations. Parenthetically, he had noticed that his Israeli friends rarely talked about homosexuality, whereas in America it was a heated topic of conversation.

When I asked Seth to read what I had written about our dialogue, I included an analysis of the biblical story of Jonathan and David, from the first book of Samuel, that my conversation with him had prompted me to reflect on (it is contained in the Appendix of this book). Recent scholarship has rediscovered the deep vein of same-sex eroticism that runs through the world of Greek and Roman civilization, whose cultural heirs we are. Taken from a text sacred to both the Jewish and Christian branches of our religious tradition, the story of Jonathan and David is important because it is a story of same-sex love found in a sacred text from the *other* side of our civilization's cultural heritage—its Judaic side. Like the Song of Songs, this story is analogous to an archaeological artifact that links us to a past in which the idea of one God had barely cooled from the crucible of mythic imagination and in which the sexual and the spiritual were not yet separated by 2,000 years of Christian and rabbinical thought.[1]

The narratives of the Jewish Bible are not seen merely as history or myth. For Jews, Christians, and Muslims they are stories permeated with a sense of the sacred, of God acting *through* history, stories that have the power to shape and interpret experience down to the present day. If the sexual implications of the relationship between Jonathan and David had been acknowledged in the reading of their story, it might have shaped and interpreted same-sex experience quite differently from how it has been understood in both Jewish and Christian religious thought. It could have been seen to express loving emotion, consistent with qualities of male strength and courage and—above all—as meriting a covenantal sanction by God. There is no hint, in the original telling of the story, that Jonathan's love for David is unnatural, nor is there a suggestion that it detracts from the qualities prized in an Israelite prince and warrior.

I think the "queasiness" that Seth reported feeling in the shower was an emotional response to the recognition that his body could spark a feeling, not only in women, but also in other men. It occurred when his American heterosexual identity collided with the inner recognition of his body's potential as an instrument through which men could bond with each other—a potential perhaps realized 3,000 years earlier between the son of the first king of Israel and the young man who became his anointed successor. Seth was not displeased with the comparison.

WILL

Will was about thirty. Like Seth, his identity was heterosexual. Also like Seth, I met him at about the time when the president's proposal to allow gay men and lesbian women to serve in the military was being hotly debated. Will had served in the Navy as a junior officer some years before and recalled how the subject of sex between men had sometimes come up. I asked him if he would be willing to talk to me about some of his Navy experiences. I expected the focus of our discussion would be the observations he had made about the treatment of same-sex issues among the men he had served with. With his collaboration, however, our dialogue went well beyond these limits, and into himself. Will had served on three different kinds of vessels: a submarine, a frigate, and an amphibious ship. The personnel aboard varied with the kind of ship. On the submarine, people were better educated and much more tolerant. However, he said:

> I didn't know of any one who was a homosexual, but there was a lot of joking about it. After you've been under way for a number of months and you've been deprived of relationships with women, a lot of guys start talking about thinking about the guy next to them. It was mostly joking, but I always wondered how much *was* joking. . . . especially in a submarine situation . . . these guys are with you. There's no way to get away from them. There is a kind of attachment that develops, I guess. I myself never felt any kind of sexual attraction.
>
> It was mostly joking, like . . . "If we don't get a leave or port of call soon, God knows what's going to happen." If anything did happen it was very discreet and nobody knew anything about it, because it was taboo, *very* taboo. You'd be thrown out of the military if it was known and everybody realized that.

I asked Will how much the threat of being thrown out of the navy actually operated, in his judgment, to push the thought of anything sexual with another man out of men's minds.

> It was a big threat. In the military, every action you did, you were worried about the repercussions. It's an authoritarian situation, especially under way. It was always twenty-four hours alert, you had to be ready to go. You were deprived of most of your emotions at that time. It was pretty stressful. When you were off the ship, in a port of call, it was an entirely different situation, and you were out partying or drinking. It was a totally different world and it had to be because you had to relieve that tension and stress.

Will's reflections on the inhibiting effect of the official taboo against same-sex contact were striking. But equally striking was the absence of actual homophobia among the men. I mentioned the reports in the newspapers about men, from generals on down, talking about the discomfort that they would feel about being naked in the showers next to a gay man. His response was interesting. He said, "I think it's crazy, preposterous. There had to be a certain number of homosexuals, there had to be. If a guy was, you never really knew it." I asked him if he ever experienced a sense of tension or anxiety about being looked at. His response was, "No, not at all. That's why what's going on now is ridiculous. There's a certain amount of professionalism that's taught in the navy. You have to maintain that." But at the same time, the subject was the focus of a good deal of humor. While submarines had individual showers, the bigger ships did not.

> There would be talk about being careful, keeping your eye out—don't bend over if you dropped the soap. Your girlfriend would give you "soap on a rope" as a joke. It was like—"save yourself for me." It was just kidding around. I don't know of any guys being involved in relationships aboard ship because, like I said, it was such a taboo. If they did they were very discreet about it.

The references to sex that Will recounted contained echoes of Steven Zeeland's descriptions of the intense eroticism of the hazing ritual of "crossing the line" in the navy. It included seminudity and nudity, as well as simulated oral and anal intercourse.[2] This ceremony seemed quite deliberately to mock the line between "gay" and "straight" and, for a short time, to give men license to cross the boundary and do things metaphorically that could get them drummed out of the navy should they do them in reality. But the things that Will's shipmates said—and felt—also resonated with the now-suppressed sexual customs of American naval life of a bygone era as they were revealed in the diaries of Philip C. Van Buskirk, a young American seaman in the mid-nineteenth century.[3]

When I asked Will what he thought all the joking meant, his reply was, "I guess guys must have been feeling a certain attraction to other guys. It came up, it was discussed. Some guys would try to laugh it off, use humor to relieve the tension." Although the men actually serving could jest about the idea of same-sex feelings, the leadership did not think it was a laughing matter. The taboo Will referred to was imposed from the top down, and the threat of punishment was real if it should ever go beyond kidding around.

What is the effect on men when their religious, civilian, and military leaders tell them that, not only are homosexuals in the ranks a threat to "good order and discipline," but that they themselves will certainly be made uncomfortable by sleeping and showering next to them? The men are, in effect, being told that same-sex feeling and gay men are dangerous to them. It was on October 27, 1992, in the last days before the election that was to bring into office the candidate (Bill Clinton) who had promised to lift the military ban on gay men and women and a few months after the "family values" Republican convention and the hate speeches there that targeted gay men and lesbian women, that Allen Schindler was murdered by some of his shipmates. As the *Village Voice* reported it, "Schindler's attackers dragged him through the Albuquerque Park, three blocks from the U.S. naval base, then took him into a public toilet where they beat him and kicked him and battered his head against a porcelain urinal."[4] How different were the actions of these men from those of Nazi youth who were incited to mob violence against Jews by their leaders?

As a young officer in the navy and as a more mature man in civilian life, Will had no traces of the homophobic rage that had been unleashed against Allen Schindler. And yet, his heterosexual identity seemed an important part of how he saw and presented himself. He could surmise that, behind the joking and the humor, some men were feeling attraction to other men. However, he said that he himself had never felt it. While we talked about the explosive release, during liberty on land, of the pent-up tensions and stresses of life aboard ship, I recalled a bisexual acquaintance of mine describing how he and some sailor friends might wind up together in a hotel room after a night of drinking and a fruitless hunt for women. It was not unusual, he said, to find sexual receptivity among one of the group who could pretend, the next morning, that he remembered nothing. In response, Will said, "I never had any bisexual experiences myself. I'm not orientated that way. I'm heterosexual." While he didn't remember being looked at sexually while in the navy, he was aware that, nowadays at his gym, someone might be looking at him with interest. "It doesn't bother me, if anything it makes me feel a little . . . I guess flattered. If he finds me attractive, that's great—for him. But, hey, *I'm heterosexual, so it doesn't intimidate or frighten me."*

Even by the age of thirty, Will had not had many gay acquaintances or any gay friends. He said, "I was raised a Catholic, so homosexuality for me was evil—the Bible—you're going to burn in hell." But he did not hold those attitudes himself. He commented, "Sexuality is becoming political now. My view is that it's a very personal thing. It's nobody's business except theirs." I asked Will if he had ever wondered what it might be like having an experience with another man. My question brought up a memory of an event that had unsettled him many years ago.

> Right now, an incident occurs to me that happened many years back—at age eighteen. I was a senior in high school. It was St. Patrick's Day and I was with a bunch of friends and we'd all cut school to go into the city. It was me and a buddy and two girls—four friends. We were on Forty-Second Street in one of the peep shows. I was from Long Island and we were a little bit more sheltered out there. I put this quarter in and this movie was not what the blurb had said. It was a homosexual act by two guys having homosexual intercourse. I looked at it and I couldn't take my eyes off it and there was just like this interest in it. Then I wondered, am I homosexual or what? But it was interesting, almost exciting really. It was weird. I worried about myself after that. That was my first experience actually seeing sexuality between two men.

I asked Will if he could put into words at all what that first-time image did in terms of feelings or thoughts.

> My first gut instinct was slight repulsion, like wow! Then it was like, interest to see it . . . to see two men engaged in a sexual act and it looked like they were enjoying it. One guy was having sexual intercourse with the other guy—anal, from behind, and they looked like they enjoyed it. This was the first time I ever saw it, and they were enjoying what they were doing.

The thing that struck him so much that, even years later, he repeated the phrase several times, was that *they were enjoying it.*

The emotion evoked was, at first, repulsion that quickly gave way to interest and then to something quite like excitement.

A great deal of energy has been directed at preventing the overt display of male-to-male sexual imagery in mainstream print media and in film. I have already mentioned the attempt to jail the Cincinnati museum director who showed the Mapplethorpe pictures. In contrast to those incendiary photographs, a far milder picture appeared in *The New York Times* a few years ago. The occasion for this picture was the passage by the General Assembly of Connecticut of a statute outlawing discrimination on the basis of sexual orientation. The bill was sponsored by a thirty-four-year-old gay legislator, Joseph S. Grabarz Jr., who asked his colleagues to support the legislation, "even if it only protects me." His decision to announce his homosexuality publicly a few months before had played a role in the bill's passage. He said, "Legislators have said that knowing me has brought them to a better understanding and made them rethink the issue." When he first made his announcement about being gay, he kissed a friend in public, and the kiss was photographed. The picture shows two youngish men, wearing jackets and ties, embracing rather chastely and kissing gently on the mouth. One is wearing a baseball cap, adding a slightly rakish touch to the picture. If a man and a woman were kissing, it would be regarded as a sweet and modest gesture of affection. One state representative, however, saw this quite differently, saying, "He demonstrated complete disrespect for common decency. I can't tell you the disgust I had for it." A former political opponent said, "The picture is going to damage him more than his announcement. If a person was to come out of the closet, that is O.K., but the way he did it was unorthodox."[5] This was hardly a scene of sexual passion. It certainly was not obscene. But it was a signpost to the emotional and physical potential between men that exists beyond the boundaries set by heterosexual identity. Images are censored because they have the power to stir others to experience within themselves the emotions they express or to legitimize expression of those emotions. In that sense, an innocent kiss on the lips is even more dangerous than scenes of sadomasochism because more people can easily relate to it.

Could the image that Will saw in the peep show have had its effect without touching something that existed within him before he actually laid eyes on it? I don't mean that Will had a "repressed wish" for sex of this kind with another male. What I mean is that Will, by the age of eighteen, already had experienced firsthand the intense feelings that are embedded in sexual intimacy with another person. But both in reality and in imagination, these feelings had been limited to women. And yet, he had male friends with whom he had close emotional bonds. The image on the screen suddenly fit these separate pieces of his experience into a new configuration—a man having with another man the intense feelings of enjoyment that Will had experienced with a woman during sex. Somewhere there must have been an instantaneous and unspoken identification with one or both partners on the screen. That identification, and the accompanying emotion, frightened him and made him question his identity.

Although Will's professional life had to do with natural science, his view of sex emphasized the emotional side of it. He said, "It's really an unusual act to see two people having sex. It's incredible to watch it. For me, if two people are in love, and they're having sex, it's incredible, it's beautiful. For me, an R-rated movie is a lot more stimulating sexually than a really low-grade porn movie. What makes sex human is the emotions involved, the touching, the loving." I asked Will the nature of his response to the man's looks or physique in the scene of lovemaking in the kind of R-rated film he had mentioned. If a man were good-looking or well built, he said he often could feel envy. However, Will felt that, as a heterosexual person, his desire was fundamentally to be with a woman and that his heterosexuality must have some basis in biology. I asked him if he could, under any circumstances, imagine himself making love with a man. His answer was interesting.

No, but this is unusual—I've actually fantasized a woman making love to me as a man. I've never been able to realize it, but just to see how it felt . . . being a man, you're penetrating the woman, you're entering her. To be a woman . . . just to feel how it would be to be a woman, that sensation. I've thought about that. What does she feel, what does she experience, what are the sensations, the sensations at orgasm?

I asked if he had ever had a fantasy of that kind. "Sure," he said, "I've thought about it." I asked who would be the man in this fantasy.

> Usually the woman I'm involved with. She would be the opposite partner. Just to exchange the roles. Women can be difficult to understand. We're equal but different. Men and women have different experiences and handle emotions in a different way. Is that learned or biological? Sometimes you'll say something as a man and women take it a different way. Just to try to experience . . . women go through a lot of different changes in their body that a man doesn't go through.

If Will were gay, his statement about wanting to feel what a woman does when a man has sex with her would fit into our culture's stereotypes about homosexual men. But instead, Will's fantasy raises questions about the institutional culture's stereotypes of heterosexual as well as gay men, questions that will be explored in subsequent chapters.

In class discussions of the subject, there is usually general agreement that the fear and rejection of homosexuality are culturally imposed. But people who hold that view intellectually can find it hard—even in imagination—to cross the culturally drawn boundary. I asked Will if he could feel an internal, prohibiting boundary within himself. He said,

> It's got to be there. The majority of people have definitely thought about a homosexual experience—you have to. *Then you try to visualize it and there's a block*—I couldn't even see myself in that position. I don't know, *something just shuts off.* I have quite a few male friends that I love. If they were to pass away or get hurt, that would really affect me. But it's definitely a different kind of love than I would feel with a woman. Sometimes it's a stronger, closer love than I've ever had with the women in my life, because it's an unconditional love—a strong love but totally different. It's not a dangerous love. A

friend is a friend forever. A lover? I've had lovers that I'm closer to than any friend, but we're not lovers anymore and we'll never be lovers again.

I asked Will if, among all the male friendships he had, there was one person, or more than one, with whom love could be expressed in a physical and sexual way. He replied,

> Actually, it's a strange question, because with the whole issue of homosexuality coming up, I've probably thought about it with a good friend of mine, Mark. We have the same sense of humor, the same personalities, the same vision of life. People are on certain spiritual wavelengths or something. If anybody, this person would be the person I'd be involved with, because we have such compatibility at the friendship level. But then that block comes up and I think, *"What the hell am I thinking? That's crazy."* But yeah, I guess I have visualized it sexually but thinking. . . . this person, *if I was to be homosexual,* would this person be the one I'd be with? Yeah, I guess I have thought about it once or twice. But then, like you said, that block seems to come up.

It was interesting that, as Will recalled his thoughts about Mark, he said, "if I was to be homosexual." It almost seemed that he could not think such a thought as "a heterosexual," that to think it he would have to switch identities. At the same time, it was interesting that, although he was consciously intrigued by imagining himself as a woman having sex with a man, imagining himself as a *man* having sex with a man made him say, "That's crazy."

I commented to Will that, while we were talking about sexual orientation, we were also trying to explore the inner workings of a man's mind, with the all the complicated interplay of meaning and feeling going on there. In response, he said, "Let me put it another way. To be attracted to a man, I'd have to consciously imagine it. Whereas when I see a woman, it's instant. There's no thought at all. Where does that come from? Also, a woman's body is so much more beautiful than a man's body. But then again, if you look at some sculptures, like the *David*—it's a beautiful sculpture. Is there some kind of a sexual attraction there that we subconsciously feel?

Maybe. I don't know." I recalled his teenage experience on Forty-Second Street and how he began to worry about himself: "Questioning my orientation, sure," he said. What had he worried about?

> That I might be attracted to another man or just be aroused by it. But it *was* arousing, whether because it was so new . . . these two men were performing sex with each other and they were just as satisfied as a man and a woman. How? At this time, I'm at the height of adolescence, a time when you're totally pursuing the opposite sex. You want to see naked women, people having sex, then all of a sudden, you see a man and a man—like whoa . . . yet you don't look away. You're told by your society and your upbringing that you *should look away*. But this place is not a very classy place anyway, it's a peep show, so you say, "Aah, nobody else is looking," so you do.

Will's friend Mark was good-looking and, Will said, got lots of girls. He said, "We can talk just about anything. But there are certain things we can't talk about. Certain things like . . . seeing that pornography. If I told him I was interested in it, he'd probably think I was strange because he's from the same type of Catholic upbringing. His father was a cop, his mother a nurse—a typical Long Island upbringing, the whole bit. He knows I'm always thinking, but I wouldn't talk to him about that." I recalled that in the service people joked about sex. Could he joke about it with Mark? "Sure," he replied, "but yet, is there some type of subconscious . . . in that joking? There must be some kind of basis for that thought."

Men so frequently joke between themselves about homosexuality as a way of saying, "We don't really mean it." Yet Will himself was saying that *something* must be meant by it. But an attempt to go beyond the joke to find out what *is* meant can draw a blank. I said as much to Will. His next comment was interesting. "I've heard of instances of men being raped, and for me that would have to be the most horrifying. . . . I don't think I could ever deal with that, being raped. Just being violated in that way. I would kill somebody before they could actually rape me. I'd fight to death. I'd die first. I don't know where that would come from, but it's just there." The image of the homosexual rapist is at the opposite pole from the stereotype of the feminine homosexual. I think it is a powerful image in men's minds, though one that is generally suppressed and covered over by the less threatening feminine version. Will's spontaneous association of rape was an indication that, for men whose identities are heterosexual, one of the culturally determined meanings of "the homosexual" is the man who can victimize another man and reduce him to a state of feminine helplessness.[6] (This anxiety, and the defense against it, will be a major focus in the story of Clark in Chapter 8.) I said to Will that his reaction could not be only about the physical act itself since people perform that act quite voluntarily. He immediately agreed. "If two people are in love with each other it's a loving experience." But maybe, I continued, that was part of the fear in the military. Will said, "Women are raped in the military. When it's in front of you, you have to confront it. It's a lot easier *not* to confront, deal with things. The majority of people don't want to."

What, I asked, did people not want to deal with? Will answered, "I'll tell you. . . . the two interviews we've had . . . when I've walked out of here, I've felt very physically drained. It's a lot to come and confront what's inside here. It's painful and physically draining. That's why I still think there must be some kind of biological factor here." I agreed with Will that biology gives us the capacity to feel through our bodies. But I said to him that I thought sexual orientation comes down to the question of where a person finds emotional meaning and power. But fear and anxiety have enormous power too, and much more fear and anxiety are attached to homosexuality than to heterosexuality. If Will had seen a man and woman together as a teenager, he would not have worried. Will added thoughtfully, "Or two women either. That's strange. If it's so taboo for two people of the same sex to have sex together, why are men attracted to two women having sex?" And yet he felt that the majority of men would have watched the scene between the two men, just as he had. I agreed that a sizable percentage would have reacted with a mixture of interest and anxiety, but not with indifference. He picked up on this theme:

> People are driven to kill. Where does that come from? To see a guy beaten to death offends me more than seeing a guy having sex with another guy. You can't justify it. To be driven to that

just because someone doesn't have the same sexual orientation
. . . I don't know. Unless, subconsciously, there's some kind of
attraction he has for this man and can't deal with it because of
this block that's developed, and going into the subconscious,
the pain could drive him . . . this just came to mind now . . . he
can't deal with the fact that he is interested in knowing about
it. *That block is so strong that it's painful to try to confront it,
come close to it.*

I said to Will that if I should propose to him that he go home and
have a fantasy about a woman, or about two women, and bring
himself to orgasm, that would probably not be a difficult assignment. He laughed. "Not at all." But if I made the same proposal
about a fantasy about a man, or about two men, he would probably
have a different visceral reaction to it. "Absolutely," he agreed.
Somewhere in that visceral reaction was the block we had been
talking about, I said, although he certainly would not kill somebody.
Will then recalled the following situation in which he was the object
of a man's aggressive sexual attention. "Here's a situation—a guy
who is homosexual, who drinks and pursues men. Once he was
talking about me, about my ass and stuff. I was offended. I said,
'Get out, this is ridiculous.' I realized how a woman could feel
being harassed by a man. It's a strange role to be in. I felt embarrassed and angry—I was yelling, but I wouldn't hit him over the
head with a bat. But where does that anger come from? I should
be. . . ." Here, he groped for words. "Amused?" I asked. "Yeah," he
replied, "or something, but not angry."
    I asked Will about the feeling that immediately occurred to him
when I suggested having a fantasy about himself and another man.
He said, "I don't know. I'm always interested in going *beyond the
boundaries of the mind.* I never thought about it—now you're asking me to confront it. *I definitely have this headache up in here now,
thinking about this.* It gets your mind going." As I more or less
invited Will to approach the cultural and internal boundary between
heterosexual identity and same-sex feeling, even to imagine stepping over it, he actually felt pain. I said to him that, if there is some
kind of block within him, the pain he felt must localize it. *"In the
brain, in the mind,"* he added. Saying that the institutional culture

erects a barrier that separates same-sex potential from heterosexual identity might seem like an abstract statement. But Will felt that barrier in a very palpable way—it gave him a headache. It was an emotional—physical—reality.

Several times during our interviews, Will said that he "was" heterosexual. What did that mean? It seems to have meant a number of things. On the affirmative side, it meant that he felt emotionally and physically drawn to women. But it clearly meant more than that. I think it was possible to see this when Will talked about noticing someone looking at him in the gym shower. He said, "If he finds me attractive, that's great—for him. But, hey, I'm heterosexual, so it doesn't intimidate or frighten me." I think it makes sense to conclude that when Will initially said that he was not intimidated or frightened *because* he was heterosexual, what he was saying was that as long as he remained confident of being *only* heterosexual, he felt no fear. I think this provides some insight into the function of heterosexual identity in the psychology of men in this culture. The affirmation of heterosexual identity means a negation of the danger in the sexual potential between men.

Nevertheless, I think that, over the few hours I spoke with Will, a kind of movement was apparent. At the beginning, after he had told me about the sexual joking aboard ship, he said that he himself had never felt any kind of attraction. But as our dialogue progressed, memories and feelings emerged and began to coalesce into a theme that he himself could discern. As our discussion focused on the fragments of his awareness of the erotic potential in men's feelings for each other, both among his shipmates and within himself, a growing awareness seemed to take shape—an awareness of a place within the self where men's feeling for one another and its expression through the body could meet. Without putting it into so many words, Will did not relinquish his heterosexual identity. There was no need to, but he seemed to let go of some of the defensive parts of that identity. I think our dialogue provided a space relatively free of the noise and interference of our culture's preconceptions of male sexuality in which he could hear himself. By the end of the session, I think we shared a certain sense of deepening insight into the thorny issues we had tackled together.

SAME-SEX FEELING AND THE MILITARY

Around the time of my conversations with Seth and Will, the Senate Armed Forces Committee began hearings on the proposal to lift the ban on gays in the military, and an article appeared on the Op-Ed page of *The New York Times.* The article sought to explain the need for the ban. The authors were Bernard Trainor and Eric Chase—respectively, a retired Marine lieutenant general who was director of the national security program at Harvard's Kennedy School of Government, and a lawyer who was also a colonel in the Marine Corps Reserve. The article included a long quote by writer William Manchester, who spoke of leaving the safety of a hospital during World War II to return to his comrades in combat. Manchester was quoted as saying that this "was an act of love," and that if a man in combat lacked comrades who would die for him, or for whom he would die, he was "truly damned."[7]

Trainor and Chase commented, "Without any evil intention or misbehavior, gays would dissolve this intimacy and love," saying that the love Manchester described was not, and could never be, sexual. "With openly gay and heterosexual personnel together," they observed, "sexual tensions would fester twenty-four hours a day . . . ." They added that even unconsummated romantic interests would shatter the bonds of "unit cohesion."

And between whom would the feared romantic interests occur? They continue, "We do not argue that misconduct by all gays is likely or even predictable," implying that "misconduct" would be confined to or initiated by gay men alone.[8] However, the image of the gay soldier or sailor symbolizes a potential in men's feelings regardless of sexual identity. It was what the men aboard the ships that Will served on joked about. It was what accounted for Seth's dream. Toward whom, then, was the heavy taboo that Will spoke about directed? It seems to me that it was directed at the heterosexual men on board the ship just as much as at any closeted gay men. It warned them not to cross the line regardless of how much they liked their friends and no matter how much they longed for the human intimacy that sexuality embodies. There is something ironic about the fact that an enlisted man was routinely expected to have sex with a prostitute—quite possibly poor, desperate, and sick—in a foreign port of call, but would be expelled from service if he did the same thing with a friend he cared for. An officer's career would be destroyed.

The assertion that the open—as opposed to covert—inclusion of gay men and women in the United States armed forces would destroy "unit cohesion" was belied by a news report in *The New York Times* two months before the Trainor and Chase article. It was headlined, "Little Trouble in Canada When Its Gay Ban Ended."[9] The court-ordered end of the Canadian ban had occurred without incident. The ending of the ban in a geographic neighbor that in its English-speaking provinces is closer to us culturally than any other country in the world was, as the article put it, "a nonevent."

In an article that appeared about six months after the one that he co-authored with Chase, Bernard Trainor vehemently supported a Marine Corps directive saying that within the next two years the Corps would only enlist unmarried people.[10] (The Secretary of Defense soon rescinded this directive.) Trainor deplored the rescinding of it, arguing that young recruits were ill-equipped to handle the emotional conflicts posed by the demands of Marine Corps training and service along with the demands of a marital relationship. This seems to be an argument for an elite corps—like the Sacred Band of Thebes[11]—in which bonds of love tie men to each other, except that in Trainor's America this love can "never be [permitted to be] sexual." Attachment to a wife, it seems, would compete with the love these young men are encouraged to feel for—but never consummate with—one another.

Both of these articles reflect the denial of the widespread sexual potential in men's feelings for each other. However, in a paradoxical way, the denial also contains an acknowledgment. If it did not, what need would there be for the military regulations in the first place, or for the laws that still remain on the books in almost half the states of this country? At the level of the individual too, one can see both denial and acknowledgment. I think this was true for Seth. In spite of his insistence that sexual love between men was unnatural, it was he, not I, who initially discerned the sexual implications of his dreams. This was because, although one part of himself asked, "What *was* that?" another part of himself knew. In Will, too, one saw a denial succeeded by a growing acknowledgment. In both men, it was possible to see another kind of movement—even in the course of our brief dialogues together—toward a healing of the breach between the emotional self and the cultural self. The tension between these two parts of the self as well as the tension between movement and resistance continue as themes in the next chapter. In addition, another theme will begin to be more fully explored—the emotions and meanings embodied in the movement of men toward each other, a movement that has been the object of so much denial, anxiety, and—when the chips have been down—of punishment by the institutions of this culture.

Chapter 4

Men on Men:
Image, Emotion, and Meaning

The aim of this chapter is to continue the process of looking at the connections between men's bodies and men's minds that was begun in the last chapter. Starting with their own words, it looks at the emotions embodied in their movement toward each other and, where possible, the connections of this movement and these emotions to the fabric of their lives.

THE IMAGE OF THE MALE BODY

Several years ago, feature article appeared in a Sunday edition of *The New York Times* about the disparity between the frequency of male and female nudity on the cinematic screen—with female nudity winning hands down. The writer, a woman, cited different explanations. People are more accustomed to the vulnerability implied by nudity in women rather than men; audiences do not want to see male nudity because it is too private, less attractive than female nudity, and somewhat threatening; men film what men want to see; people are not conditioned to see men as beautiful. But the chief problem seemed to be showing the penis, and this alone was often sufficient to draw the dreaded NC-17 from the rating board of the Motion Picture Association of America. Suzanna Andrews, the author, concluded rather trenchantly: "On film, audiences have come to accept seeing women naked. They have also come to accept dreadful scenes of throats being cut, faces bashed in and bodies blown to pieces. In a movie culture in which almost everything else is shown, male nudity is still too scary."[1]

In view of the ambivalence about the nude male body, it is striking that the single work of art most frequently cited by men as well as women was Michelangelo's *David*. Fred related,

> In all my undergraduate experiences there is one picture in my mind that I will probably never forget. The image is a sculpture created by Michelangelo, *David*. There he was in all his splendor, looking as proud as a peacock and as handsome as any youth you will ever see. And there was his penis in all its glory. I was actually intrigued and perhaps even turned on by seeing this statue. I would never admit to it and open myself up to ridicule, but now after reading about Frank and Chapter 6 of your book ["The Artistic/Symbolic Framework"] I see that I was not being abnormal and that probably every other man that looked at it would feel the same. There is no doubt that this statue pulled me into the artist's reality and for a while I was actually in my own reality, and allowed myself to be turned on by the naked figure of a perfect youth. I also feel that the artist was turned on by the youth and wanted the observer to see what turned him on.

Fred's comment, "There is no doubt that this statue pulled me into the artist's reality," is a further tribute to the power that images have to open the door to an inner world of emotion. There seems to be little question that Michaelangelo, in his own inner world, felt sexually attracted to men and that his image of the "perfect youth" reflected this. But his artistry was such that he created an image that touches that place in others—men as well as women—where they are capable of feeling the same thing that he did. Fred—I think correctly—surmised that it was the artist's intent to do just that. And it worked for Fred. "For a while I was actually in my own reality, and allowed myself to be turned on." Not being naive, he understood that he ought not to publicize the fact that the image of *David* had opened a door into himself. But privately he was somewhat troubled because the door had not completely closed afterward. He went on to say, "Though I am happily engaged, I find myself conjuring up images of perfect humans, both male and female. They come up at any time of day—daydreaming in class, having intercourse, or dreaming during sleep. I've been very perplexed by my images and confused as to why I come up with them. I am very happy sexually and emotionally with my fiancée, yet I continue to go back to the images."

An art historian would point out subtle differences between the style of Michelangelo and the sculptural styles of antiquity. But there is an important similarity in their sensibility—an idealization of the male that incorporates strength, grace, beauty—and moral virtue. This was the sensibility that permeated the ideal of male-to-male sexual love in Plato's time. Thanks to Michelangelo, Fred had discovered something of that sensibility in himself and, thanks to my course, he could accept it as a normal part of his own feeling as a man. But he was acutely aware that he was not living in classical times. He went on to say,

> I truly sympathize with Frank's confusion and torment over looking at a male in a sexual way. I would be lying if I told you that I have never been in Frank's position. Everybody, regardless of gender, has looked at a close friend of the same sex with a little more than love, respect, and admiration.

Referring to a statement of mine about Freud, he continued:

> I do agree that loving a man emotionally is linked with having sexual relations with a man in a seamless continuum of emotional and sexual energy.[2] But this is where the restraints of society rein you in and cut off the sexual energy. *I do not have the courage to leave myself so open and vulnerable to the wrath of society.* It is both emotionally and physically dangerous. Emotionally I will be forever shunned by my own society and physically we all read the paper and know about the reality of "gay bashing." It would be much too complex if I had to think about having sexual relations with my best friend as well as my spouse. I can barely hold down a relationship with the opposite sex, never mind the same sex.

But it is clear that the personal challenge of having relationships with both sexes paled, in Fred's estimation, alongside the social difficulties. What Fred knew about himself he had kept to himself—until he told me about it. Clearly, however, he was not about to go

public with these insights. References to "society" and its intoler-
ance bring to mind Eve Sedgwick's observation that prior to the
reification of "the homosexual" there is a necessary reification of
"society" as being against it or him.[3] But "society" is not everybody. Like it or not, we live in a pluralistic society. The "society"
that is reified is actually those who control its institutions and have
the power to persuade, prohibit, and punish.

The legacy of centuries of moral condemnation and legal punishments has left its mark, as Fred's anxieties demonstrate. Although
he felt relieved by the assurance of the normality of same-sex feeling that he found in the pages of my book, his explanation of why
he would keep these feelings to himself reflected how our current
system of categories can create a vast gulf between inner reality and
public persona:

> One of the most dangerous and feared terms in our culture is
> the term "homosexual." *I can't think of any other word that is
> as loaded.* The mere introduction of the word within conversa-
> tion will either stop it or make everyone uncomfortable. All of
> a sudden everyone will think very carefully about what they
> say so that it is not taken the wrong way. As a teacher I have
> observed that being labeled a homosexual will start a fight
> among kids quicker than any other insult, including curses.

Fred had some awareness of his inner feelings. However, in his
conscious thoughts, he had not gone beyond visualizing perfect
male bodies to imagining himself with another man. But the potential for that kind of progression can be seen in the memories of a
patient of mine who recalled his early reactions to male bodies. At
about ages eleven to thirteen he began to notice and admire strong
men. He felt that someday, when he grew up, he would look like
them. He remembered one particular man, whom he used to watch
as he played softball. This man had strong, muscular legs, and he
felt he would have legs like those someday. When he began to
masturbate it was to the image of this man, although he did not
imagine him naked. Nor did he have the fantasy of having sex with
him or with any man for quite some time. When he was eleven, he
admired a certain champion wrestler. He thought that the wrestler's
wife must really like having sex with him. Later, when he did begin

to masturbate to images of people having sex together, these were images of male and female couples. It was only much later—when he was in college—that he could put himself in the picture with another male and explicitly imagine himself having sex with him. Fred had not gone that far. He could think about something with his best friend, but would not let his mind have the images, let it construct the visual fantasy. *"You're afraid to let your mind explore further,"* he said. In the confrontation between his inner emotions and culture, the result was a compromise. The inner boundary separating the sexual categories had been breached, but the fear of exploring the new territory beyond it persisted.

MEN'S FEARS

In looking at the emotions and meanings embodied in the movement of men toward each other, we also wind up looking at the feelings that drive them apart. Many of those feelings can be summarized under the heading of fear. Men appear to have some specific fears that women do not share. One man put it this way:

What bothered me about Frank's feelings were the similarities to my own. Recently a friend of mine told me about a "date line" where you hear messages from people and then respond. His exact words were, "There are some really whacked-out chicks who really just want to get laid. They're not all ugly either. The only bad thing is that there are some homos who somehow sneak onto the straight line. It's really sick, but they set it up so you can block out messages and shut the person off the line." He was experiencing anxiety at the mere voice of a homosexual trying to draw his attention. Keep in mind, these are messages sent out to everybody on the line, so it was quite impersonal. What was my response? "Good . . . I do not even need to hear that." After reading these chapters, *I have recognized how abnormal my discomfort toward homosexuality really is.* Despite recognizing this, I also know that passive homophobia is accepted in the heterosexual community and because of this *I find it difficult to motivate myself to change or explore these emotions.*

Watching [the television series] *Melrose Place* (is this another sign?) I became upset at my attitude toward the homosexual romance. I initially became uncomfortable, and then uncomfortable with myself for having these feelings of anxiety. The question I should now ask myself is why I get these feelings. Like most strong emotions, they are probably rooted in my past. I remember as a small child having a teacher who everybody thought was gay. Looking back, I realize that our framework for analyzing his sexual orientation was childlike, but his lack of authority was a startling contrast to the other fourth-grade teachers. I remember thinking it was strange that the children did not show this man respect. His style was such a contrast to my father's that I could not help but feel that a more effeminate style was not normal, or at least ineffective. Obviously, not all gay men display stereotypical traits, but the mere innuendo seemed to induce an immediate drop in status. So it would seem that *my symbol for homosexuality is weakness.* It is not a conscious thing, but I realize that there must be a reason for my fear of homosexuality. What I am left wondering is whether this means I have secret homosexual desires or whether the degree of homophobia is in direct correlation with these desires. In the past, I have discredited Freud, but I must admit, with a little introspection, I've been inspired into giving his thesis a second look.

Another man reflected on his own fears:

One can clearly see the homophobia prevalent in our society today. I accept homosexuals. I do not feel that homosexuality is a "problem" for men, nor do I view them as being "different" or "degenerate." Having had some gay friends I am comfortable making this statement. *However, I do follow our cultural norms* with respect to having a "phobia" of *being* homosexual. While reading this book *[Sexuality and the Devil]* I constantly found myself contemplating my own sexuality, the feelings and beliefs of my sexual choice. I have to wonder whether my feelings would change if our society/culture did. If homosexuals were the norm or at least not the object of prejudice, where would my feelings lie? I am reasonably sure I would not have any "fears" of being homosexual. These fears raise the question: what am I afraid of? I think the fear is of being *an outcast in society* rather than the fear of actually being homosexual. I am not quite sure what there is to be afraid of in being homosexual.

An example of this male "fear" occurred the other day in my school. We have school blazers that the students, male and female, are required to wear but are not allowed to take home. The blazers do not always get to their rightful owners and on occasion some students must wear another's jacket. One student came to me complaining that his was a girl's jacket due to the fact that it had only three buttons on the end of the sleeve and not four like the rest. He said he was being made fun of. *It is amazing to see how dominant cultural influences can be.* This student was lacking a button and was afraid of being labeled "feminine." His maleness was being attacked, or so he thought.

Not too long ago, I experienced the same type of fear. My friend and I went out for drinks. We decided to go to a bar that we had been to before but that was under new ownership and name. Our decision to go in was based on the fact that the place was crowded. Once inside, we ordered a beer and looked around to spot females. To our surprise the bar was packed with men, with the exception of a few masculine-looking women. We immediately came to the conclusion that this might be a gay bar. Needless to say we left after finishing our beer—quickly. We did not stay for a variety of reasons—embarrassment, fear of being "hit on," etc. The sad part is that we were not even 100 percent sure that it was a gay bar. The label of homosexual is a terrifying thought for many men—a fear that anything *remotely feminine* might cause him to be considered a homosexual. A ridiculous example of this might be the man who wears the color pink. It is not uncommon to hear jokes when a man wears this traditionally feminine color. No one wants to be labeled "different."

Men have more anxiety than the women about being categorized and have more categories to worry about: heterosexual versus gay—masculine versus feminine—strong versus weak. These are the polarities the mind is confronted with, and they group themselves as "heterosexual, masculine, strong" versus "gay, feminine, weak." Other words such as "outcast" and "different" also echo in the mind. The "I" with which one is consciously identified and that exists in culture turns away from the experience that might provoke the unwanted change in the body's inner landscape and the feared sensation of "moving toward" another man.

One man, Pete, told of confronting those reactions in his friends:

> In today's world it seems unacceptable for a male to view another male as attractive or good-looking. I myself have learned this through experience. Two friends and I were discussing actors and I commented on my opinion of Brad Pitt. I said I thought he is an attractive and good-looking man. My friends could not comprehend or accept my statement. In a typical male reaction they made fun of me and teased me for nearly two and a half months afterward. *I have come to the conclusion that society cannot accept the admiration of a male by another male.* I enjoy and prefer the female body and what it symbolizes to me, but I am secure enough in my manhood that I can admire or am able to notice an attractive male. I can relate [to] and understand what your former student meant in his statement. *Even the most macho or masculine guy, I believe, has had a homosexual thought.* I also feel this goes for women. It is almost unbelievable that men will pay to watch lesbians have sex, but want to bash homosexuals.

Pete and I had a follow-up conversation in which I asked him what he meant when he said that even the most "macho or masculine guy has had a homosexual thought." He defined this as the admiration or appreciation of the looks and body of another man. I asked him if the word "erotic" could be applied to that. He said some men had an "all-American" look, such as the young Tom Cruise. But about some others—such as the Spanish actor Antonio Banderas—he said, "If I were a woman, I would apply 'erotic' to that look."

I asked about his saying, "If I were a woman. . . ." What was that, what did that mean? He laughed and put it in the context of talking with friends. "I'm covering the back door by putting it that way, so they don't look at me and. . . ."—here he mimicked someone nervously edging away from him. When he challenged the friend who picked up on his comment about Brad Pitt—didn't his friend have to agree that he was an attractive man?—his friend answered gruffly, *"I do not look at guys."* I was intrigued, not only by Pete's frankness and humor, but also by the fact that he himself explicitly applied the terms "homosexual" and "erotic" to his reactions to certain men's looks. He recognized that the image could be an opening into an inner world of emotional and physical possibilities with men. His friend who said he did not "look at guys" recognized this too. Some men go so far as to say that they cannot even tell if another man is good looking. The man who had been dismayed by his anxiety that he had stumbled into a gay bar echoed the confusion some men feel about the meaning of their reaction to the male image when he asked, rhetorically, "If I think another man is good looking, am I bisexual?"

In a slide presentation about the image of the body, I showed the class a photograph by Jack Pierson (see Figure 4.1) of a naked young man in a hallway. One man later commented to me that he had noticed that some of the other men in the class actually looked away from the screen when that picture was shown. A religious student picked out that picture as particularly offensive. One of my woman students commented on the unease that looking at another male body can evoke in some men. She recalled, "While my two male best friends and I were at the gym, I remarked on another man's physique—that he had a really nice body, that it was not too 'buffed up.' One of my friends looked the other man up and down for a few seconds and said, 'Yeah, he has a nice, natural body . . . *not that I'm gay or anything.*'"

In Pete's sense of ease about his own response to the image of the handsome actor, he was like some of the women I have cited. Like them, he was implicitly acknowledging the connection between his own reaction and that of a gay man, without being alarmed about his sense of himself as a man, fearing he had to change his identity or give up his preference for women. But even with him—as with some of the other men in this chapter—a follow-up conversation was necessary to round out my understanding of what he meant, whereas the women more often laid it all out in the initial written reaction.

The thoughts of another man, John, illustrated the confusing tug-of-war that can take place within a person whose beliefs and ideology reject the condemning attitudes of the institutional culture, but who still feels the inner fears that have been internalized while growing up in it:

I grew up in a small suburban town where no one "came out." A cultural taboo definitely existed although I do not recall ever being *told* that homosexuality was bad. I do not recall thinking about it much at all. Occasionally while playing sports a teammate would get an erection in the shower and suffer the subsequent jokes of his teammates. Someone would make a homosexual joke but nobody ever truly believed that the unfortunate peer was really gay. After graduating and moving to New York I was chatted up by a man in a supermarket. I became flustered and left rather abruptly—not rudely but visibly shaken. Moments afterward I was bothered. Why had I acted in such a way? I had by this time developed a personal philosophy of live and let live as long as a person is "good" to others. Homosexual jokes that I had heard seemed goofy and tasteless and I had always registered them with the foolishness of ethnic jokes. This episode shattered my image of my own tolerance. I was upset by the come-on. It was a wake-up call for me and I have to admit I am still in the process of shedding my socialization. Over the past years, work and my social acquaintances have played a big role in this process. Many co-workers at my Catholic school are gay. The only difference I can see between us is the barrier always held up against them by society.

During this stage I thought about my own feelings about homosexuality. I always thought the stories of the Greek and Roman gods were cool for the fact that a god like Zeus could see the beauty in all living objects. It seemed to be liberating and opening that one could appreciate the beauty of all things without blinders. I guess for that reason I am more able now to say that I have had a few fleeting urges to kiss a man. These episodes were odd to me and *made me wonder at first if I was*

FIGURE 4.1. "Untitled, 1993" by Jack Pierson

Source: Whitney Museum of American Art, 1993 Biennial.
(Photo by E. Tejirian)

gay. I put it out of my mind but later on was better able to process it. I said, "So what?" My thoughts and urges are strongly heterosexual and other thoughts do not change that. One female friend tried to put me on the spot by saying that women often discuss what women they find attractive but men can't in regard to other men. She was surprised when I discussed a few names. It seems like such a silly thing to be afraid of doing especially if you are comfortable with yourself. I must admit that I am *not* fully comfortable with discussing some of the above lines, as evident in my actions while writing this on the subway. I found myself clothing my words so that the people around me would not get the wrong idea!

John's words reflect the fact that the memory of the gods of antiquity serve, in our cultural unconscious, as reminders that same-sex love was once associated with the sense of the sacred.[4] "For that reason," he is able to allow some inner emotions—still unspecified— to express themselves in the fleeting image of kissing another man. At the same time, the categories imposed by our contemporary institutional culture superimpose themselves. "These episodes . . . *made me wonder if I was gay,*" but, "my thoughts and urges are *strongly heterosexual.*"

ADOLESCENCE AND IDENTITY

Even more than for girls, the institutional culture has created anxiety for boys about their sexual identity. The adolescent peer culture, as a woman in Chapter 2 pointed out, has absorbed and transmits those anxieties. A graduate student who was a public school physical education teacher saw this in action among his seventh and eighth graders:

Many of the boys who are more physically developed and skilled are more inclined to show themselves off by being dominating against those who are less. During activities those boys would get picked last, ignored, or made fun of. I've heard many of these boys being called "faggot," "gay," or "gay boy." This has caused many of these boys to develop low self-esteem, a negative image of themselves, and a distaste for being involved in any type of physical activity. They are afraid to be ridiculed or harassed by the more dominating boys. I've seen these boys become less involved socially, where they would rather sit on the side and tend to their own little world. Other boys would go to the bathroom to change into their gym uniforms, rather than get changed in the locker room with everyone else, because they fear getting ridiculed or called "faggot." One day, we were doing cooperative games to develop the concept of teamwork and had to break up the class into groups of six or eight, with each group forming a circle and holding hands. You would not believe the number of boys that refused, saying, "I'm not holding hands with him; he's gay," or "Only gay people hold hands." Every year I come across a group of boys who refuse to play volleyball because they view it as a "sissy" sport that only girls play. Unfortunately, my school is in a district that *forbids the discussion of homosexuality*—the district that a few years back rejected the teaching of the Rainbow Curriculum.

In his comments, there is no suggestion that the boys who were picked on were, in fact, gay. They were simply the "carriers" for the anxieties of the group, which in turn reflected the attitudes imposed from the top by our religious and political institutions. Interestingly, the picture at the Catholic school where John taught was not as bleak:

The homophobia expressed by many of my students at the all-male school has caused me to be more vocal in its denunciation. Even though many of the boys are constantly hugging and touching one another as a means of affection, they still see homosexuals as somehow a danger to them. On the other hand, when confronted with a gay peer the guys have always been very accepting, unlike their statements.

Kyle, now in his mid-twenties, wrote about his own personal terror around his adolescent identity:

I remember growing up and having serious concerns about my sexuality. There were a few times in my early adolescence that I seriously thought I was gay. The particular school I went to was grade seven through twelve. If you wanted to be "cool"— and who did not want to be "cool"?—you had to have a girl-friend in the seventh grade. I had a crush on one particular girl. We had some classes together and got along very well. We used to talk on the phone till all hours, but that was about it. We never hung out. Once in a while we would go the mall together. At the end of each "date" came the awkward good-bye period. I know I felt very awkward and shy. It must have been at least five or six months before I got the nerve to kiss this girl, and that was a quick peck on the cheek. At about this same time, many of my friends and older teammates (I was on the freshman baseball team) kept nagging me as to how far I had gotten with this girl. They started poking fun at me, saying things like, "I bet you have not even made out with her." They were right—I had not. I wanted to but I just could not bring myself to be the initiator. I had dreamed about making out with girls, but had never actually done so. We brought up the issue of making out, in a roundabout way, and kind of decided we should do it. One day we stayed after school and talked for a long time. I then started walking her home. We got to the end of one street and stopped at the corner. My heart was pounding. I knew this would be the moment of truth. I went to kiss her passionately and did so for about three seconds before stopping and telling her that it just did not feel right. I felt horrible. We said good-bye and told each other we would see each other the following day. I think I cried all the way home. *I suddenly started having the feeling that I must be gay.* What other reason could explain it? Everyone made out with their girlfriends. Some were even having sex. I was mortified. What would I tell my parents or my friends, *who would totally abandon me?* I would be the laughingstock of my high school.

A second attempt with another girl produced the same result. A third try took place with an attractive girl who was two years older:

This would definitely make me cool. We hung out a few times but again, when it came time to say good-bye, I just could not bring myself to kiss her passionately. I was very distraught and again began to think that I was gay. *I think I may have seriously contemplated killing myself.* I thought if I told my parents I was gay they would disown me. Anyway, at this point I did not know what to do, so I just hid these feelings that I had. *Mind you, I did not have or feel any attraction of any kind toward men.*

The next time was in the ninth grade:

We started dating and it was wonderful in a special way. We had not yet kissed, but that did not seem to bother us; we were having a good time. It must have been a good three months before I got the nerve to give her a quick kiss on the lips. In the back of my head, though, I was thinking, *You must make out with this girl.* One night, however, we were in my house, watching television, with the lights out and the door closed. I had my arms around her, and then the most beautiful thing in the world happened. We looked at each other the right way, and it happened. We kissed passionately for at least half an hour. I felt wonderful and the best thing about it was that it happened naturally. I was so paranoid about touching a girl before this. However, this kiss opened me up. Fifteen or so minutes into it, I was feeling her breasts without even thinking about it. I just did it because it felt like the right thing to do. Things moved quickly from that point on. Within a matter of two months we were having sex on a regular basis. I no longer had those *scary feelings of being homosexual. I knew that I was strictly heterosexual.*

Kyle's memories demonstrate the way in which the prohibitions of the institutional culture are internalized and lived by young people. These prohibitions are not merely abstract rules. Rather, they can penetrate into the mind, take up lodging there, and cause real terror, even when the primary erotic "choice" winds up being the "right" one. Young people come into adolescence with a history of deep and even passionate same-sex friendships. As the body matures into a sexual and emotionally expressive instrument it is inevitable that, for a good many—both boys and girls—bonds of friendship would begin to be felt in the newly sexual landscape of the body in a newly erotic way. I think this is part of the explanation for the vehement denial by many early adolescents of any possible indicators of same-sex feeling in themselves and the hypersensitivity to any hints of it in their peers.

The culture of the Caribbean coast of Colombia, where Luis grew up, explicitly recognized this potential.

> I personally remember my high school years when we constantly called each other *mariquita,* which translates as "little faggot." Adults told us that we were in the "Dangerous Times," meaning that it was perfectly normal but that we really had to be careful, otherwise we will end up being faggots. I and, I am positive, other boys, were very anxious about that moment. So we tried to prove to the adults, to prove to our families, and to wear a persona on ourselves, so that we would not become *mariquitas.*

Paradoxically, however, there was a ritual that appeared to recognize the underlying sexual potential between friends even as it aimed to exorcise it by naming it. "We used to call our best friend *mi esposa*—my wife. Carlos was my best friend at the time. When we were alone or listening to music, he was Carlos. But in front of other teenagers I was almost forced to call him 'my wife' and vice-versa."

The fact that there was an element of force in this ritual indicates that one of its aims was to deny that true sexual feeling could exist between two people of the *same* sex by making each friend, in turn, call the other a woman. Luis seemed to interpret it that way when he said about it, "We were only victims of two thousand years of brainwashing, of a dictatorship perpetrated by one of the most abominable creations of man: the monotheistic religions." In adulthood Luis's sexual life has been exclusively with women. However, taking the course with me brought back memories of the acute conflict that he had felt, as an adolescent, between his inner feelings and the social persona he was forced to adopt.

I think that the issues discussed in these chapters are very provocative, and I also think that it made me aware of certain feelings that I had during adolescence—feelings I was even afraid of thinking of. Although I have never been a religious person at all, I did not escape that heavy moral crap. Every time I had a homosexual dream while sleeping, I woke up in a state of sheer panic. I was not haunted by religious paranoia since I was a consummate atheist already, but I really felt fear at the loss of status and the psychological and physical persecution I was going to put up with had I told anybody of my homosexual dreams and desires. I can really relate to Frank's experience. That is one of the most positive things about reading these chapters. They made me aware that there have [been] historical moments in which the admiration of the physical and even sexual beauty of the same sex, alongside the admiration of the beauty of the opposite sex, was quite acceptable. It is sad and unfair that during my puberty years I had to hide all my bisexual impulses the way I did, although my heterosexual fantasies were greater. But I do not deny the fact that there were a lot of homosexual fantasies. There is a definite bisexual component in all of us, whether conscious, unconscious, temporary, or permanent. We navigate a cosmological duality, especially when it comes to our sexual inclinations.

I think that Luis's comments highlight the fact that same-sex feeling is a powerful dynamic in Hispanic cultures, in the sense that it is deeply embedded in male feeling—both collective and individual. The exaggerated machismo pose is, I think, a reaction formation to this potential within the self, as is the exaggerated splitting of same-sex roles into "active" and "passive."[5]

As an adolescent, Kyle, too, might have experienced, across the landscape of the body, an emotional movement toward one or more of his male friends. But the memory of his terror demonstrates just how effective the socialization of our institutional culture has been. It also makes clear why the Religious Right objects so strenuously to any attempt to present homosexuality favorably or even neutrally in any educational context.

CULTURE—INTERNALIZATION
AND "DISIDENTIFICATION"

Throughout this chapter, a tension is evident between the inner movement toward the expression of same-sex feelings through the body and the prohibitions of the institutional culture. However, the strength and tenacity of these internalized prohibitions vary. Getting rid of these internalized prohibitions involves a "disidentification" with them and the development of an alternative set of standards for judging the self. For many of the people in this chapter, this process of disidentification had already gotten underway before they took the course with me.

Men and women in their twenties who recalled their fears about homosexuality as adolescents remarked on the change their attitudes had undergone in the interim from homophobia to tolerance where others were concerned. Tolerance in oneself is more difficult to achieve. This was evident in Jason, also in his mid-twenties. In spite of his intellectual formulation that same-sex feelings are a normal part of life, he appeared to become stalled in the process of his own disidentification. He had written,

> I find it interesting how many people would deny that they ever had any homosexual thoughts—ever. They clearly associate that having such a thought automatically makes them a homosexual. This is in my opinion a shortsighted and uneducated viewpoint. Everybody at some point in their life, even if for just two seconds, has had some kind of homoerotic thought. It's a natural thought, part of being human. You can't live in our society and not. What I find interesting in our society is that most people feel uncomfortable even talking about this topic. Nevertheless, we are absolutely surrounded by it and even crave it in our movies and media. In the last twenty-four hours, I watched a popular movie called *Threesome,* saw a Howard Stern show with a popular bisexual singer on it, and then watched a *Seinfeld* episode that dealt with two gay guys. I saw all this and was not even looking to find this kind of material. There can be no question that our society puts on one face that repudiates any homoerotic feelings and then quietly has another face that hungers for it.

It is at this point that I must say that I am a heterosexual person, although I do not know why I feel the need to assert this. I do feel, however, that anybody that has had any type of homoerotic feelings or thoughts need not be embarrassed or feel any guilt. Why should they listen to society, a society which in my opinion is the one that needs to change and is constantly changing?

Since he had emphasized that everybody had experienced some kind of homoerotic thought at some point in their lives, I asked Jason if he would be willing to tell me how he himself had had such thoughts. He mentioned a daydream, in which he would watch another man undressing, followed by an image of them both naked together. Then there might be some touching, but that was where it stopped. He said to me, "I ask myself, what would it take to try something with another man?" Friends had told him of being approached in a bar, but he thought that in such a situation, he would immediately say no. He had been in a threesome with a woman and a male friend. Nothing happened between himself and this friend, but he had felt a bond with him. He asked, "Why can't I just take away the girl and do something with the guy?" Trying to be helpful, I said that culture was very important. He said he realized this, yet he was willing to do things that went against culture in other ways. For example, some people thought he had been crazy to give up a very good job and go back to school. I asked him about the emotional tone of his daydream. He said that in it, the other man was both gay and rich and would be paying him to do something. But again, he said, "I ask myself what my problem is with actually doing something."

The meaning of having a rich gay man pay him to have sex is not clear. It may be a way of rationalizing the experience, even in fantasy. On the other hand, and I think this is more likely, it may be an expression of the wish to be *desired* by another man. There was a kind of stubborn courage in Jason as he tried to understand the block within himself. The block came up in imagery, as well as any contemplated deed, because he was aware that he stopped his daydream—significantly—right at the point of touching. Although he was willing to talk to me about these feelings, it did not seem all that easy. His conflict seemed to mirror the two parts of our cultural conflict and was reflected in the two parts of his written statement. The first part—"I must say that I am a heterosexual person"— seemed to be saying that his identity in culture was the sticking point. On the other hand, the second part—"I do not know why I feel the need to assert this"—seemed to be rebelling against the demands of the institutional culture. The conflict could be seen in his fantasy, where he was aware of stopping himself from going further with it. Fred had said, "You're afraid to let your mind explore further." For Jason, as for Fred, shutting down the fantasy kept the full force of his emotions out of consciousness.

IDENTITY AND THE DIVIDED SELF

Although anxieties about same-sex feelings are imposed from the top down, the pressure of these feelings, pushing up "from below" as it were, can generate anxiety in the "I" that lives in culture and needs to retain its heterosexual identity for survival. For Anthony, as for others cited in this book, it was the "dreaming I" that expressed his same-sex feelings in images of the body. The first of these occurred when he was seven or eight years old.

> There was a girl in my class, Jeanne, who I liked for several months. One night I had a dream about her—it was one of my first sexually oriented dreams I can recall. When it came time for Jeanne to take off her pants, my dream quickly turned from erotic to nightmare. Jeanne's private parts had turned out to be a penis in my dream. The next day in school I could not even look at her because the dream was so real to me that it had completely turned me off to Jeanne. I still see her and until a few years ago, I was not able to look at her as the attractive young woman she is today. My first explanation for this dream is guilt. I have very strict Catholic parents who had sheltered me from everything they believed a seven-year-old boy should not see or know about. I honestly think I did not know what a female's genitals actually looked like completely. I knew nothing of what existed besides the pubic hair. (Why didn't this image come to me in my dream?)

Anthony's shocked reaction to his dream would appear to be evidence of the extent to which, as a young boy, he had already internalized the prohibitions of the culture as these had been handed down by his parents. Now, as a young man, he said,

> If it is implanted in one's genetic makeup I cannot allow myself to completely condemn homosexuals. However, I cannot deny the sick feeling I get when I see two men (and oddly, not women) hold hands or act affectionate in public. I do not know why two females do not upset me (rather, I actually think it is sort of erotic) but it is like night and day when I compare male and female homosexuality.

What he said next, however, might provide the explanation for the discrepancy in his reactions to men and women. "Looking inward at my own experiences with the subject, I know that there have been some very odd dreams I've had about my male friends but to my conscious knowledge there was never any homosexual activity involved."

In a follow-up conversation, he said that he had had several dreams in which he and his best friend since kindergarten were naked together. Though willing to talk about it, he appeared uncomfortable and it seemed that some reassurance was in order. I told Anthony that a number of other men had told me about a sexual image or feeling involving a best friend. He then related that he had been out, not too long ago, with a group of friends, including a brother-in-law whom he had initially been unsure about, but whom he had come to like very much. Impulsively, he threw his arms around his brother-in-law and gave him a kiss on the lips. His girlfriend, who seemed surprised at this, asked him, "What did you do?" He replied that he was simply expressing his feelings about what a great guy his brother-in-law was. I again reassured him that it was natural to the human mind to express feelings of affection and strong friendship for another man in terms of the body, and that these could coexist right alongside a man's feelings for women. He seemed relieved and grateful for this reassurance.

For Anthony, as for others, the prohibitions of the institutional culture act like a knife, cutting the self down the middle and producing a sense of alienation from parts of one's own self. It is striking that this had already occurred by the time Anthony was seven years old. It is quite likely that the image of the girl with the penis was a replacement—in response to these prohibitions—of the image of the same male friend who appeared in his dreams later on. When the prohibited movement toward another male appears in the conscious-ness of dreams, the "cultural I" can experience it as alien, even in a dream. The "sick feeling" that Anthony experienced when he saw two men holding hands was a reminder of those parts of his own feelings that were alien to his cultural, heterosexually identified self. In contrast, seeing women together did not provoke the same feelings of uneasy identification.

MOVING TOWARD FRIENDS

It was striking that when men's feelings were focused on one particular man, it was almost always a good or best friend. The fact that it was Anthony's best friend who was naked with him in his dreams indicates to me that it was from that place within himself which could feel love for another man that the impulsive kiss he planted on his brother-in-law's lips emerged. Another man, Miguel, said in one of his writings to me,

> I believe that everybody has homosexual tendencies. I believe it is possible and perhaps even quite normal for a totally physi-cally heterosexual individual to fantasize and be turned on by a member of the same sex. It only becomes a problem when the individual who becomes turned on by someone of the same sex begins to feel ambiguous about his or her sexuality as a result. I would not share these feelings with members of my own family because I come from an Hispanic background and in my culture homosexuality or anything that vaguely re-sembles it, is as a great, big, gigantic NO-NO. I, however, do not have a problem with these fantasies or feelings when they occur because I am very secure with regard to my sexuality. Besides, I crave women so much that I probably would not get along sexually with a man anyway.

In a follow-up conversation, Miguel said that he did notice and admire good-looking male bodies in ads and on television, as well as noticing men on the street who were good-looking, slender, and muscular. He sometimes had a fantasy of being with someone, and when I asked him for an example, he mentioned a man who was very close, "like a brother, a good-looking, clean guy," whom he thought about in that way a couple of times. However, he did not broach anything with him. Again, Miguel's comment about the taboo on homosexuality in Hispanic cultures is commonplace. However, although I have nothing like serious statistics to offer on the subject, the impression gained from the men in my classes from Hispanic backgrounds is that awareness of same-sex feeling within themselves is no less prevalent than among non-Hispanic men.

BISEXUAL IDENTITY

In contrast to Miguel's implication that same-sex feelings were all right as long as he held onto a heterosexual identity, Hank, in his first reaction paper written for me, described himself as bisexual:

> I have always believed in a bisexual nature in men and wo-men. Even when I was a child, the thought of a muscular man with a beautiful woman would get me horny. This thought did not bother me; I attributed my reaction (an erection) to erotica in general. I believe in the beauty and sexuality of both men and women. The poet Walt Whitman wrote extensively on the beauty of the human body—both male and female. While most critics deem him as homosexual, I believe his poetry to be an illustration of bisexuality, or simply an appreciation of physical beauty with regard to both sexes. The ancient Greeks were similar in that they saw sculpture as a way to idealize the human body.
>
> To me, bisexuality is an appreciation of the body and mind of both sexes. It is an attempt to amalgamize masculinity and femininity. Unfortunately, our culture is not that of ancient Greece. It is a common belief in our society that a human being is only heterosexual or homosexual. I believe, as does Freud, that biologically we are all bisexual. However, I think our culture plays a large part in repressing that desire for us. While I choose women to be the main object of my sexual

desires, I do have intimate, caring relationships with my male friends. While in this culture I can be labeled as heterosexual, I feel that my true nature, as is everyone's, is bisexual.

This paper was written about halfway through the semester. At the end of the semester I asked Hank if we could have a talk about the thoughts he had set down for me. The childhood arousal that he referred to had occurred at about the age of eight. Although he had considered himself bisexual even before taking the course with me, reading my book had relieved some of the "pressure" he had felt about it. His fantasies were 99.9 percent about women, but he recalled one that he had had about a man: a well-built, muscular man was lying on top of him, and then, just at the last instant—before orgasm, I presumed—he thought the image changed to a woman. He said that he guessed he was being "submissive" in that fantasy. But coincidentally, the night before our talk—which we had not planned in advance—he had the following dream:

> A well-built, good-looking man was after me, and I'm trying to get away. Then, suddenly, the scene changes and this man is having sex with an Indian (from India) young man. The young man is bent over and the other man is having anal intercourse with him. He's looking at me meaningfully.

In the scene of intercourse, the good-looking man was now naked, whereas previously he had been clothed, as was Hank. "But," he added, "I killed him. At the end, he got hit by a train." He thought the man in the dream might have had something of himself in him. He recalled that the man had a "washboard" stomach, and he was working on achieving that at the gym. He also worked part-time with foreign students, some of whom were Indian. But he felt that he could definitely not do what the man in the dream was doing. What he *had* thought about doing was hugging someone, maybe kissing him on the mouth. About the image in the dream, he said that his feeling about the anus was that it was "dirty, cankerous," though he had not realized until that moment how negatively he felt about it. But paradoxically, he said he loved women's buttocks and found the idea of anal intercourse with a woman appealing. As we talked about this further, he said that his doing it to a man might be a possibility after all, but having it done to him seemed quite unacceptable.

Male-directed feeling, even in a man who accepts his same-sex feeling, can still involve conflict. Even though anal intercourse is a primal modality in male-to-male sexuality, the cultural anxiety attached to phallic penetration of one man by another is not easy to overcome. (In other cultural settings, this is not necessarily so. A colleague who, some years ago, was in the Peace Corps in Kenya said that, among the Kikuyu, reciprocal anal intercourse between male adolescents was common.[6]) Hank said that oral sex was easier to imagine being associated with a loving feeling than anal intercourse. For anal intercourse between himself and another man to occur, there would *absolutely* have to be love between them—a statement that interpreted the meaning of his dream. In the dream, the man was making love to another man—a surrogate for Hank, at whom the man was looking meaningfully—but through a modality so stigmatized by the institutional culture that the lover had to be "killed off." At the same time, the man had the "washboard" abdomen that Hank was working on for himself. There was something of Hank in this man too, performing the male-to-male sexual act that he had such mixed feelings about.

A bit over three decades ago, a well-known study comparing the life histories of heterosexual and homosexual men stated that rejecting or distant fathers were more frequently found among the homosexual men.[7] This idea seemed to get into the popular culture, so much so that it has sometimes been cited by my students. However, the same study commented on the very low frequency of warmly related fathers among the heterosexuals too, a finding confirmed by the case studies done by hundreds of my students over the years and generally ignored in the comparisons between gay and heterosexual men. But in contrast to so many men, Hank had very good feelings about his father, who was a construction worker, very masculine, but also very romantic and warm. He kissed and hugged Hank often, and at moments when his father had been especially proud of him, Hank remembered seeing tears in his eyes. Even though his father was of the "old school" in which "gay was gay" and "straight was straight," he felt he could tell his father anything. Hank had a girlfriend whose brother was gay. She would encourage him to kiss her brother, and he did. And when a gay man seemed interested in or attracted to Hank, he felt very flattered. Hank had the example of a warmly affectionate father who expressed his love for his son in physical terms. I think that the example of a warm and loving father helped Hank to feel for other men in these terms too, perhaps even by the age of eight, and that this sense of warmth and closeness constituted an important meaning of his attraction to men.

THE CLASS SUBCULTURE

The class I taught was, in a sense, a kind of subculture that was free of the judgments of the institutional culture. The book students read, the case studies they themselves did, and the approach I took seemed to create an atmosphere where feelings and thoughts could emerge into awareness in a new way. One man mentioned how taking the course had spurred a positive movement in himself.

> The material presented in these chapters has confirmed many ideas that have been floating around my head for quite some time. It also seems our class discussions have been something of a catalyst to crystallize these formerly fragmented ideas— namely, that people have the potential for both homosexual and heterosexual feelings for others. The extent that everyone "in the back of their minds" has felt homosexual feelings is dependent on many factors—primal, cultural, and personal issues. At the personal level, I have experienced both homo- sexual and heterosexual feelings. *Homosexually, it seems that I have complied with our societal mores—very much a hands- off policy.* Heterosexually, I seem to play by society's rules as well. Through it all, I do not wrestle with conflict or turmoil. I think the simple fact that I acknowledge these feelings is enough.

For another man, Jack, taking the course prompted him to notice a response to the image of the male body that, it seems, had pre- viously escaped awareness:

In my life I have been affected by my culture in every way. I guess that is an obvious statement and yet until this class I never really examined that fact. I have recently noticed something about my feelings of attraction to people of the same sex. This has only recently come to my attention while attending this class and reading your book. When in public places, I check people out as they pass by my field of vision. I have noticed that not only do I look at women's buttocks as they pass by, but also men as well. I immediately find myself looking around to see if anyone has seen me looking. I have also seen the majority of other people around me doing the same thing regardless of their gender.

He went on,

Another idea that comes to mind is that, once in a while, when I am with a friend I wonder if they have sexual thoughts about me. I find that if they did, it would really bother me. For instance, my best friend is a very sensitive person and although we live in separate cities we are very close friends. Sometimes when we get together we will talk about something very personal to him, which will make him upset and cry. I feel like I should hug him for consolation and yet I feel weird in doing so, so I never do. Something inside me feels it would be embarrassing to me. When he tells me he loves me I feel weird about that as well. He is a good-looking male with lots of girlfriends and we have known each other most of our lives.

I truly feel that I have no desire to be with anyone of the same sex. As you may recall from my last paper, I wrote about how I would be quite bigoted about homosexuality, basically because of the obnoxious femininity many homosexuals display in public. I associate this behavior with my own thoughts or feelings about someone of the same sex and that is probably why I am so against the idea of those feelings. I sometimes even feel strange giving my own father a kiss instead of a hug. This class has been helping me to see a different perspective on this whole topic. Maybe I will be a little more respectful of these kinds of feelings in the future because I will understand

where my feelings stem from. Growing up in this culture is
definitely a huge part of that.

There is good deal of food for thought in what Jack said. He
makes it clear that his anxiety about the possibility of same-sex
feeling in himself stems from negative cultural attitudes reinforced
by his association of it with a certain kind of femininity that is
incompatible with his sense of himself as a man. However, taking
the course with me prompted a reevaluation of those feelings and,
with it, a movement toward an awareness of something about his
own response to men's bodies that had been previously unnoticed.
It was a striking demonstration of the way in which culture can raise
the threshold of consciousness so that not only emotional, but even
visual responses escape awareness. And, although he does not make
the connection directly, a link between these visual responses and a
set of ambiguous but unsettling feelings about intimacy with men—
that he had been aware of but not dwelt upon—is strongly implied.

Trying to relate what Jack said to categories of sexual identity
would only confuse his efforts to be honest with himself. What Jack
has said here may not be a precursor to having a sexual relationship
with his best friend, but it may be an opening to a greater freedom
and pleasure in the intimacy of his male relationships.

In their study of men and women who identified themselves as
bisexual, Weinberg, Williams, and Pryor found that attraction to the
opposite sex generally occurred first, with same-sex attraction occurring a few years later.[8] The mean age for men's first conscious
sexual attraction to females had been 12.8 years, and to males, 17.1.
For bisexual women, attraction to males was felt at a mean age of
10.8 years and toward females at 18.5. The reason for this discrepancy, which also describes the experience of some of the people in
this chapter, is probably the terror that the institutional culture imposes on adolescents, and even children, about same-sex feeling,
and with which, in turn, they terrorize one another. The sharply
demarcated categories of gay and straight intensify the fear about
letting their minds stray over the culturally drawn line. For some
people young adulthood brings a greater capacity to stand apart
from their peers and to think for themselves. And those who go to
college can find their cultural, intellectual, and sexual horizons

expanded, both through the curriculum and through campus life. Many form close new friendships, intensified by the proximity of dormitory living. Minds seem to be opened even as emotional bonds with both sexes are formed under newly found conditions of freedom and at more mature levels. Under these conditions the internalized taboos of early adolescence can give way.

An awareness of same-sex feeling can emerge then, for the first time, and it is possible to see a process of movement taking place over time, as the capacity for peer-independent thinking grows and fear lessens with exposure to new ideas and realities. In Charlie, now in his mid-twenties, this movement had begun in his undergraduate years and culminated in a new and easygoing self-description as bisexual by the end of the semester with me. Speaking of his awareness, as an adolescent, of gay sexuality derived from the media on one hand and from his visits to Manhattan on the other, he said, "I remember thinking to myself that it was not what I considered 'normal' but I did not think it was wrong. Also, it did not make me sick to my stomach like my friends said it did. But I pretty much kept my thoughts to myself through high school."

During his first two years at community college, Charlie met and spoke to some gay people about their sexuality, the first of whom was the mother of his then-girlfriend.

> I mostly asked my girlfriend and her sister about their mom and I felt really comfortable in their presence because they were open and honest. Overall, I was not very surprised but in the same respect relieved with knowing that homosexuals were "just like" heterosexuals except for the obvious difference. My friends would dehumanize them and, sadly enough, I actually needed proof to validate what I thought to be true.
>
> Before meeting the second openly gay person, I had a homosexual dream. I don't remember any details but I do remember waking up and thinking, "What the fuck, I'm gay!" Looking back it was a little disturbing but very humorous because I was in a psych class at the time and two days after the dream my teacher told us that, almost certainly, everyone has or will have a homosexual dream in their lifetime, but they

may not remember or acknowledge it. I remember letting out a big sigh and then smiling for the rest of the day.

From the next person, a gay male friend with whom he spoke to at length,

> I learned a lot and my new understanding made it difficult to be around my friends. The same is true now but to a lesser extent because I realize that they are ignorant and closed-minded when it comes to people being different than they are, especially in terms of sexuality and race. The main problem is their religious beliefs, which I also rationalized out of my life, like a bad habit. You do not need religion to be moral. At this present time I have become more open to bisexuality. I have never felt the desire to have intercourse with a male but have thought of kissing one of my friends at my under-graduate school. I feel really close to him and respect him a lot because he loves everyone and accepts everyone, even the people I feel like punching in the face because they are so ignorant. I remember saying to myself, "I could kiss Tommy" one day as we were sitting around talking. *I consider myself to be bisexual because I love both males and females,* and if I ever feel like being physically close to a male and he's open to it I will do it. I would not have oral or anal intercourse because I have no desire to do so. To date, I have never considered anal intercourse with a female either and have never wanted a woman to "go down" on me because for some reason I find it degrading. I wish things were different in this society and I try to be open with myself with my feelings and with other people. I am constantly thinking and will continue to expand even if I am going against the grain.

Although he had just said that he did not desire to have inter-course with a male, he also mentioned two very recent dreams.

> I was being chased by a bunch of hoods. They finally caught up with me, but then we all just played music together.

and

> I was having intercourse with a Hispanic guy from the back.
> We were both naked. I was dominant, but the feeling in the
> dream was not that of being domineering or aggressive.

Running from dangerous men is a common theme in men's
dreams. In men whose identities are heterosexual it can express the
"lethal" threat posed by the sensed sexual potential in their relations
to men (as it did for a patient of mine whom I will discuss later in
this chapter). In spite of the genuine movement that had taken place
within Charlie since high school and his openness to a sexual relationship with a man, some residual anxiety is evident in the first
dream. But even here movement takes place, and the danger is
defused. He and the "hoods" who had given chase wind up playing
music together—that is, being emotionally expressive and "in tune"
with one another, corresponding to his adult sense of what a sexual
relationship with a man would be. After the danger in the first
dream is resolved, the second takes him further. And here the "inner
I" is a bit ahead of "waking I." In his waking thoughts, he does not
feel the wish for anal intercourse, perhaps because this mode of sex
between men is so heavily freighted with our cultural obsessions
about power relationships in sex, as his use of the term "dominant"
seems to imply. But his feelings in the dream are neither domineering nor aggressive. In waking life, he has already moved across the
inner frontier separating cultural "gay" from cultural "straight." The
dream he creates takes him more deeply into the realm of male-to-
male feeling, where the physicality of intercourse is one of the
primal modes through which that feeling is expressed.

The institutional culture has made contact with another man's
penis a cultural symbol for the loss of masculine strength—and, of
course, for femininity. But for Charlie, as for Hank and other men
who spoke to me, once the internal barrier to male-to-male sexuality is breached, the image of intercourse seems to arise. I think that
Jack found himself looking at men's buttocks because anal intercourse is built into the structure not only of men's bodies but also of
men's minds as a prime avenue through which emotional intimacy
with another man is realized.

A pair of vase paintings, done by two different painters in Greece of the classical period, both in the latter half of the fifth century B.C.E., testify to this. In each, an act of penetration seems about to take place. On one vase (see Figure 4.2) a youth is sitting in a chair that is slightly inclined backward. He is naked and his penis is erect. A slender young woman has her hands on his shoulders, and her

FIGURE 4.2. Young Man and Young Woman on Greek Vase, Fifth Century B.C.E.

Source: Staatliche Museen zu Berlin, Preussicher Kulturbesitz: Antikensamm-lung: F2414. (Photo by Maria Daniels.) Reprinted with permission.

right foot is on the seat of the chair. She is about to straddle him and, evidently, to lower herself on his erect penis, as they are gazing into each other's eyes. In the other painting (see Figure 4.3) a naked youth leans back in a chair, his penis erect. He is wearing a headband with tall spikes. His companion is another young man, wearing the same headgear, maybe indicating that they had been to some sort of celebration or party together.

His left foot is on the seat of the chair. In his left hand he has a staff, which he may use to steady himself as he prepares to straddle the body of his friend and—evidently—to lower himself on his erect penis. An older man and a woman seem to be watching this encounter.

THE EMOTIONAL FABRIC

A major theme of this book is that sexual attraction is connected in important ways to the underlying fabric of emotional life. I think that the experiences of men reported in this chapter permit us to see that emotional bonds between men are a strong part of that fabric. Brad had made some rather cryptic statements in his first reaction paper. He said that, in his view, men's heterosexuality had to do with jealousy of what women had and the desire to possess it through sex with them. Men's homosexuality, on the other hand, was a response to a felt deficiency and the desire to compensate for it through sex with another man. I asked him how these things applied to his own experience. He said that he did envy women's capacity to carry a fetus inside of themselves. On the other hand, he said that in sex men were in a more "giving" role. But sometimes in making love with a woman he would reach a high point, and it just seemed that there could be something more—he was not sure how to put it into words. He hesitated, saying, "Maybe something . . . spiritual?" In high school Brad had gone out with girls and had sexual experiences with them short of intercourse. He then went away to college. In his first year there he had gotten on the Internet. He found that people could sometimes be rude and unfriendly, but that people on the gay line were usually pretty nice. He and another man got into an ongoing dialogue and, he said, *"I kind of fell in love with him."* He said that after a while, "We would sometimes talk dirty." This aspect of their electronic relationship eventually cul-

FIGURE 4.3. Young Man and Young Man on Greek Vase, Fifth Century B.C.E.

Source: Collection of Sir William Hamilton, British Museum, London. (G & R): Vase F65. Reprinted from: Catherine Johns, Sex or Symbol: Erotic Images of Greece and Rome. Austin: University of Texas Press, 1982. Reprinted with permission.© the British Museum, British Museum Press.

minated in an on-screen (verbal) fantasy, in which Brad came to orgasm imagining himself performing oral sex on the other man. They talked about meeting but never did. There was some sense that he—or they—feared that the reality might be disappointing.

Prior to this—I think it's quite accurate to use the word—relationship, Brad had never had any sexual experience or felt any attraction toward another male. But subsequently he did have something of a sexual encounter with another man. While he was working in a house, painting, the phone rang and someone was moaning at the other end. It happened several times, and finally a woman's voice came on and started talking "dirty" with Brad. A bit later it was revealed that "Danielle" was not a woman, but rather Donny, a man Brad had known somewhat in high school. They eventually got together. Donny gave him a massage. At one point he asked Brad if he could kiss his neck and Brad said no, adding that if he had not asked but just gone ahead and done it, it would probably have been fine. Donny also asked to perform oral sex on him. All this happened when Brad was between girlfriends. Brad had no special feeling for him, and they did not seem to have anything else in common. He thought that the main thing was the fact that Donny desired him. Brad had some concern about its becoming public if he did anything with Donny. In fact, he would be worried if any of his sexual feelings about men became public knowledge. He did not let Donny perform oral sex on him. In retrospect and even now, he had some fear that if he became sexually involved, he might start to like it, which could threaten the life he had planned for himself—including being a father, since obviously neither he nor a male partner could, as he put it, bear children.

In solitary sex, Brad found that sometimes a woman would come into his mind, sometimes a man. He might have a fantasy about going to a bar and picking up an attractive woman and coming back home and discovering it was a man. His images included oral and anal sex, both ways. When I asked him what this meant emotionally, he again mentioned being wanted or desired. As for performing oral sex on another man, he thought it would feel good to make someone else feel good. He had no particular sense of seeking a relationship with another man, however, nor did he see that happening in the future. Currently he had a girlfriend, following the breakup of a previous relationship of several years. They had been exploring some new sexual and emotional possibilities with the aid of a good book.

In class, Brad had said very little during the whole semester, and even in a one-to-one conversation, his style was somewhat subdued and reserved. But I was struck by one image that indicated an ability to be in touch with the deeper currents of feeling in himself. He recalled how, at college, he would sometimes sit in one of the connectors linking two of the campus buildings and just watch people walking through. The experience was one of simply looking at life and of "embracing" it. I think this embrace included both the men and the woman who were part of that life.

Brad's initial interpretation of the meaning of homosexuality as a response to a felt deficiency and the desire to compensate for it through sex with another man is a reflection of one of the institutional culture's conceptions of male homosexuality. However, his first sexual experience with another man began with an electronic *verbal* exchange. What, then, was the meaning of his same-sex feelings? He already had given a couple of answers to this—the pleasure in feeling wanted or desired, and the pleasure of making another man feel good. However, there was, I think, another answer in a memory that came back in the course of our second session. He had a very close friend in high school who, like Brad, was going away to college, but not to the same one. The day this friend was leaving, everyone was saying good-bye to him, and when it came to Brad's turn, he began to cry. A few days later, when Brad was leaving for college himself, he cried again at the thought of leaving his parents' home, and he attributed his reaction to his friend's departure as an anticipatory reaction to leaving home himself. However, their friendship had never been the same since.

I think this piece of information was like a missing piece in a puzzle. An emotional connection between this friend and Brad had been disrupted by their going off to separate schools. I told him I did not think it was a coincidence that he had developed an emotional connection—electronically—with the man on the Internet. The key was the *connection* between himself and this other man. He had not fallen in love with him because he had seen him in the gym and envied his build or admired his looks. And certainly falling in love with someone goes beyond "dirty talk." That was merely a way of heightening the connection between them, of making it more intimate, as the emotions that the body is capable of expressing were drawn into their dialogue and eventually, through orgasm, into the coupling that each, sitting alone in front of a computer screen, imagined with the other. Ironically, they never met because of the fear that what they had had might be spoiled. What was there to be spoiled?

The emotions that underlie the imagery of sexual attraction are often masked by the sheer impact of the visual in that experience. But, in this instance, the *absence* of the visual image lets us see the emotional basis of their relationship. It expressed, through the imagery of the body, the need for the male-to-male bond that was disrupted as Brad and his high school friend went their separate ways. The experience of this bond could account for his saying, "I kind of fell in love with him." The sexual connection between them was the container for an emotional and spiritual bonding that he did not want to risk spoiling.

NEW MOVEMENT

Brad allowed himself—as Fred and Jason had not—to move toward creating an actual fantasy of sex with a man. It not infrequently happens that a gay man does not allow himself to acknowledge his suppressed feelings for men until his late teens. He has to "come out" to himself. I do not think this was happening to Brad. Rather, for Brad, a new movement had taken place within himself as a consequence of this experience in his late teens. He had done what so many men are afraid to do—he had brought together the physical in the sense of the sexual and the emotional in relation to another man—and maybe the spiritual that he sometimes found himself reaching for in sex with a woman. He had experienced a fulfillment that remained potentially powerful for him and to which he returned in fantasy. And it is significant that, when he fantasized, images of reciprocal oral and anal intercourse emerged in his imagination, indicating again that these are primal modalities in male-to-male sexuality.

Did Brad have an inordinate need for an emotional bond with another man? I do not think so. Nor was his family experience one that conformed to the popular cliché about homosexuality being linked to a missing or rejecting father—both his parents had always been loving toward him. I think the simplest and most accurate reading is that a set of circumstances, accidental in a way, confronted him with an opportunity that he took instead of recoiling from it. A curtain was lifted from a realm of feeling and, in spite of his culturally induced anxiety, he could not and would not draw the curtain across it again.

In Jeff, another man in his mid-twenties, the emotional bond that energizes men's sexual feelings for each other was even more transparently clear—and to himself as well. He reminisced about the best friend of his adolescent years, a boy from a large, well-off Italian family. "I would spend days at a time with them, lounging in their game room, eating dinner with them as a family member, swimming in the pool or Jacuzzi, or bouncing up and down on their trampoline located in a backyard the size of a football field." His friend had two older brothers who, naturally enough, had a lot of influence over him. One of the memories Jeff had of this friend was of his homophobic reactions.

> He was sure to denigrate "fags" at any or all costs, swiftly and viciously, as if his life and honor depended on it, which was to some extent true considering the influences that his older brothers had upon him. Well, one day I can remember that, after he had said something, I looked at him and I silently came to the realization that the reasons behind these utterances were fear. He was afraid of admitting that he too could possibly feel these feelings, that he too (and his damn brothers) were cowards who had to express their deep emotional fears with violent responses. In fact, another memory just came to me as I am writing this. His eldest brother told us a story of how he was hit on by a gay man. The victim in question commented on how handsome he was. He said that his response was total silence, but that he had then turned around and "cold-cocked" this man, or hit him, without any warning and seemingly without remorse.

Somehow, the adolescent Jeff realized what lay behind his friend's homophobia and the brother's violence. These memories served as a lead-in to another memory from a later period in Jeff's life—college.

I have never had a *physical* homosexual experience. I say physical because I did have an experience which *bordered on an edge of some place I'd never been.* It was very close to a homosexual experience, not so much because of what happened, but rather because what happened afterwards was what I felt would happen if it *had* been physical (you'll see what I mean). I was a junior in college, about the time that the Oliver Stone movie, *The Doors,* came out. And it just so happens that a lot of psychedelics were being passed around, to coincide with the retro-hippy phase that everyone seemed to be going through with the advent of the movie. So one night my roommate and I spent the whole night tripping on high grade acid— clean, lean, and crisp. It was like tasting a fine wine or seeing opera for the first time. It was so good that we were able to stand in a crowded house full of screaming fraternity party goers, with music full blast, and enjoy ourselves—actually hold a conversation. If you have ever tried the pseudo-psychedelics of the eighties you would realize just how hard this is to do!

The whole night passed and we ended up at around three in the morning, coming down, but not "crashing." I had decided to make some tea, and scrounged up some strawberry jelly and toast. As we played in our silent, darkened living room, his girlfriend broke our spell by coming into the house. She was pretty intoxicated by this point, which was a very different state of mind from the highly cerebral state we were in. And when I say, "broke the spell," I mean it. There was a lot of sexual electricity in the air, mostly coming from me because I had the hots for my best friend's girlfriend, which he knew and she certainly knew. As I stood on one side of her, and Larry stood on the other, one of the strangest occurrences of my life happened. It was like Larry and I used Meg as a sounding board to "touch" each other. *Our minds touched.* It was a dizzying experience, very hard to describe but not unpleasant.

Sounds like strange science fiction, but it was real, just as authentic as anything Asimov could write. *I have never been this close to another human being in all my life. It was exhilarating, exciting, and definitely sexual.* I'm pretty positive that Larry never had a homosexual experience either, so he was very aware of the implications as well as the fall-out.

We verified, as best we could, what had happened, the next day. We *very* gingerly touched upon what had happened to us the night before. When we asked Meg about it, she said she was totally unaware of what had happened between us, a fact that Larry and I found hard to believe. It was *so real*, it was as if someone had slapped you, yet Meg had not noticed, which adds weight to my usage of her as a sounding board, really a grounding for floating electricity. *It was such an intense moment that, four years later, I still get excited about it, although I must say that this is the first time that I have actually written about it or told anyone about it in detail.*

The day after this happened, and indeed for many weeks after, there was an uncomfortableness between Larry and I. We really only discussed what had happened in the vaguest of terms, because we were both so blown away by it all. For two friends as close as we were (and still are) to have a strange air about them for so many weeks points to a significant event. We were both very afraid—afraid of the implications of the situation, afraid of a lessening of our friendship, and perhaps a little afraid to admit that it was so pleasurable. *I know that one of the reasons that I have never had a homosexual experience was precisely the outcome of that night.* The uncomfortableness of the feelings that I had, as well as the thought that *perhaps there was no turning back once this particular road was taken* are definite roadblocks. I can say that I do not have a desire to sleep with Larry when I am with him, which is probably mutual, and that has helped in keeping and cementing our friendship. *I suppose that my reactions to society's prohibitions to homosexuality are deeply embedded. I accept the feelings because they are latent.* If they were more apparent, then I would be angry, probably frustrated and scared shitless. If they were overwhelming feelings, *so strong that I had no choice in the matter, then . . .*

Jeff recounted that the following day Larry said that things had happened the night before that they had better not talk about. Why not? Jeff said that they were part of a tight circle of friends, in which everyone knew everyone else. It would have been difficult, Jeff thought, to keep it from coming out. Like Brad, he too feared that it might be a road from which there was no turning back. At the same time, he feared—as did Larry, I think—that it might change their relationship for the worse. I was the only person Jeff told about that night and the feelings surrounding it. He said nothing to his current girlfriend because if they broke up, she might say something about it to someone who knew him or Larry.

But what is the "it" whose secret the friends felt they had to guard, even from themselves? Trying to explain it further to me, Jeff copied an excerpt from the novel *Dune*, which describes a ritual in which one of the characters, Jessica, is made into a "Reverend Mother" through ingesting "spice liquor." Jessica's sensations after taking it are described in the following terms—"The stuff was dancing particles within her, its motions so rapid that even frozen time could not stop them. Dancing particles. She began recognizing familiar structures, atomic linkages. . . . " Jeff's comment about this passage was, "Here she [Jessica] is able to handle the drug. We were not." A few paragraphs later, there is a further description of Jessica's experience—"And there was another psychokinesthetic mote within her awareness! Jessica tried to reject it, but the mote swept closer . . . closer. They touched! It was like an ultimate simpatico, being two people at once: not telepathy, but mutual awareness. With the old Reverend Mother." Jeff wrote in the margin here, "This is what I was trying to ascribe it to. But it was fleeting [for him and Larry]. This is drawn out."

It seems that the LSD created a kind of isolation chamber of lucidity around the friends, and within that isolation there was a heightened awareness of the "two-ness" of their friendship. This "spell" of isolation was capable of shutting out the music and tumult of a raucous fraternity party. Alone in the darkness later, the spell continued to hold until Larry's girlfriend interrupted it. There had already been a powerful emotional electricity between the two friends, but an electricity that had been felt intellectually, cerebrally. But as though combining with the sense of erotic potential that Meg's presence had introduced into the air of their isolation chamber, this current now surged between them and took on the character of a sexual experience. The core of this sexual experience—and what made it sexual—was this emotional current. The effect of the drug, the intensity of that evening, the isolation of the early morning, and the arrival of the woman they both had erotic feelings for all contributed to allowing the intensity of their feelings for each other to come through with unusual clarity. When Jeff said "our minds touched" he may have intuitively put into words what sexual experience at its most powerful is all about.

Jeff's recollections and feelings again show how, in sex, the body clothes the mind, is its instrument and its mirror. What Jeff has described is sexual desire *in statu nascendi*—in the process of being born. But it was a process that both friends tacitly agreed they had to abort. In the culture of which they were a part and among their tight circle of friends, there was no place for that kind of relationship between heterosexual young men. Not talking about it also helped, because language can bring it into that world of culture where the sense of identity exists.

But Jeff and I *were* talking about it in this world, the world of culture. I asked him, if something physical had occurred with Larry, would it have changed him in any way? He replied, "I think it would have made me a little lighter in the loafers," meaning it would have made him slightly more feminine. This comment seemed to reflect the cultural interpretation of the meaning of such an experience. But I think a better indication of that meaning was the dream he had just the night before our conversation. In fact, it was a nightmare:

> I dreamed that my brother was in a plane that crashed somewhere in the Midwest. I was distraught, crying. I woke up and went back to sleep and the dream continued, with the same feelings.

This was one of his two older brothers, the one who had been especially good to him and to whom Jeff felt especially close. Larry had also been a "brother" in the fraternity to which Jeff was pledged. (Another resemblance between Jeff's brother and Larry was that they were both very good looking.) In our culture, men are accustomed to talking about loving someone "like a brother." In Roman sources, "brother" appears as a term that is understood to mean "lover"—of either a woman or another man.[9] One man, who had talked with me at some length, could not get in touch with any feeling for another man that he could identify as erotic. Yet, a month before the first of our two meetings, he had the following dream:

> I was with a woman, and then she changed into a man—it was my brother and he was naked. He was coming at me and I said, "No way, get out of here, you pervert."

The intensity of an actual brother-brother relationship can generate a good deal of love as well as anger—in other words, the kind of ambivalence that can characterize passionate, erotic relationships. And the life histories of men, both gay and heterosexual, are not infrequently characterized by brother-to-brother sexual play, both before and during adolescence. Seth had spoken of the feeling for the friend he hugged tightly in his dream as "brotherhood." The double meaning of "brother" from Roman times continues, but now only as an unconscious double entendre.

Jeff's brother had either just had an operation, or was about to—I'm not sure which—and Jeff suggested that this might have prompted the dream. On the other hand, he had just been reexperiencing some of the emotions he had felt with Larry that night four years ago. The nightmare was a dream of loss and grief over loss— and it had to do with a brother he loved. Was the dream about his fear of losing his loved older brother? Was it about a more deeply buried but not necessarily less powerful feeling about Larry? Was it about some sense of loss in that relationship, as they both retreated from the intensity of what they sensed could happen between them? Jeff's reference to becoming "lighter in the loafers" seemed to have to do with cultural stereotypes of "feminity." But the dream provides a different perspective on how Jeff might have changed if he had done something sexual with Larry. I think he would have loved Larry more, perhaps even fallen in love with him, and probably feared losing him. In that sense, Jeff might have become more "feminine"—feeling love for a man, and being afraid of losing him, just as a woman in love with a man might feel. The need for love and the fear of losing it are common to both women and men. But as another man pointed out in his writings to me, "The concept of love between men is something that our culture is not completely comfortable with. It is acceptable for a man to remark on the physique of another, but not acceptable to be in love with that man." I think the operative phrase here is "to be in love." Being in love means "loving" *plus*—loving through the body—and that is what Jeff and Larry sensed that they had approached that night.

SPIRITUAL CONNECTIONS
AND THE SENSE OF THE SACRED

Brad had talked about looking for something missing, perhaps something "spiritual"—that is, something beyond the physical as such—in his sexual experiences with women. I think something was also implied in the excerpt from *Dune* that Jeff compared his experience to. In speaking of Charlie, I remarked that a common theme in men's dreams is being chased by another man or men. A man that I saw in therapy had a series of "chase" dreams, in which the pursuers were rarely seen, although he always assumed they were male, as they proved to be when they finally became visible. After some months, however, the following dream occurred:

> I'm sitting in a chair, in front of an open window. A breeze is blowing; the curtains are billowing in toward me. There's a presence behind me, and suddenly there is a hand on my shoulder. I turn around and see a man, standing right behind me. I'm startled because this seems like a sexual thing.

The man in the dream was tall, rather handsome, a little older than himself. When we spoke about it a week later, he recalled that the figure of the man was surrounded by a kind of whiteness or light. He was a striking figure, "almost godlike." The feeling was of being cared for, protected. In his waking life my patient could not conceive of anything sexual with another man, nor did he usually turn to men for emotional closeness and understanding. He had a

father to whom he had once been very close but who had disappointed him severely in adolescence, and who was now ill. He was,
of course, in therapy with a man. But there was no male friend with
whom he felt a strong bond or kinship. Team sports had once played
a very important part in his life, but they seem to have provided a
place where he strove to excel as an individual, rather than to form
strong bonds of friendship. Nonetheless, the man in the dream was
my patient's creation—it was he who gave this figure both a kind of
spiritual luminosity *and* a possibly erotic intent.

As his need for a spiritual and emotional connection to another
man moved toward expressing itself through the body, the "I" with
whom he was identified—that exists in culture and has a heterosexual identity—was not equipped to deal with this movement. Instead,
this inner movement was met by fear and countered by flight—the
literal image in his and many other men's dreams. I think that my
patient felt the need for a spiritual bond with a man. But because
this spirituality moved toward clothing itself in flesh, it also was
felt, deep down, as an erotic possibility. It was probably no coincidence that, in the same session that this dream was reported, he
related a second dream in which he was alone with a woman who
was on a bed, with the idea that they were going to "fool around." In
the dream, he wondered what point that would have. As we talked
about the first dream, he commented—with some irony—that it had
seemed perfectly "normal" to have men chasing and shooting bul-
lets at him in his dreams, but that when a man was being tender or
caring it was disturbing! Nevertheless, his need for a spiritual connection with a man was just as unconscious with respect to his
waking thoughts as any movement toward an erotic experience with
a man. The erotic side of this potentially two-sided experience
remained totally incompatible with his sense of identity. If he
should have sex with a man, he said, "I would not know who I am."

This story has an interesting follow-up. My patient had been a
student in one of my undergraduate classes before he began therapy
with me, and he took my graduate class a couple of years after
terminating. I had the impression that we had not satisfactorily
worked through his feelings and fears about men. I was surprised
and gratified, then, to have this response from him in one of his
reaction papers:

In exploring this aspect of my life [the potential for same-sex feeling] I am fortunate to have had help in sorting out my feelings on the subject (most notably, you!). If you had asked me this question say, ten years ago, my immediate reaction would have been to proclaim myself a healthy and exclusive heterosexual. I would not have had the capacity to look at the other side of my psyche. Although I enjoy sex exclusively with the female population, I can now acknowledge the fact that I have strong affectionate feelings for other males. I would think of this as a sign of weakness and abnormality in earlier times, but have accepted that strong feelings towards men are natural and fulfilling. The fact that I do not feel the urge to express my affection in a sexual manner does not negate the strength or power of that feeling to other men. Just like I do not have sex with every woman that I have an affectionate feeling for, I do not express my feelings with men in this way.

Married now, he told me that he had recently gone on a week-long vacation with a good male friend and enjoyed it very much.

Terry, too, was in a committed relationship with a woman. However, he dwelt on the deeper meaning that sex with a man could have for him:

Almost like *friendship* would be a really good part of it, someone who was a lot different, that could show me different things. I can picture it in my mind better than I can verbalize it. The person would be very quiet, they're a very cool headed person, who sort of enjoys life in a lot of ways. You want to find out why they enjoy life that way and become part of that. And someone *who is almost larger than yourself*—things just happen in their lives. Some parts of their life are a little more *magical* than my own, *mysterious* to me. That would kind of be an attraction. Sometimes I read a book about homosexual characters who have these wild sexual encounters and I think, "Wow, that was pretty sudden." *Maybe there's something in me that I repress the way most men do.* I do not really know what's missing but I feel there's something missing that would make me want something like that.

My life was [once] kind of magical. In the twelfth grade, I went from living a horrible life, and suddenly these magical things were happening. Now I feel the magic is falling down. I'm looking again for that magical thing that happened. I had not felt good about myself, was sexually repressed. I forced myself to do things differently, I met my girlfriend, met friends with different lifestyles. It opened my mind. It was something in the air—a special feeling. If we went to a gay club, just to see the openness of it seemed fabulous. For me, it was my own personal renaissance. There were things I did not know I had in me—it was the period of art, I did some writing.

I asked Terry about the idea of repressing something in himself, ". . . the way most men do." He went on, *"Even imagery in your own head.* It's taboo in our society—to have an *image* of that, it's disgusting, bad, something not even thinkable. I was like that, I could never imagine things like that." Was he aware of a tendency to suppress an incipient image?

Yeah, *I think I switch it off.* I turn away from it. I do not know exactly why. For example, one of my friends was sleeping over. He wanted to jump into bed with me instead of sleeping on the floor. I found it flattering but, "I'm in a serious relationship—thanks, but I think you'd better go to sleep." I wondered what it would be like but it scared me. I think the actual experience would scare me, the physical skin contact. With a woman, I could imagine it better, like a friend. All right, there's contact, fine, but it's like magnets, positive and negative. In my mind, I know there's nothing wrong with it, but just the contact, like the virgin who is terrified of losing her virginity. I could picture it in my mind, but when it almost happened, it was something different.

I asked Terry about what the meaning of something sexual with a man might be for him. He said,

With friends, I'm not sure if I'd be comfortable. That's a very heavy question. There would be a lot of expression. You would express feelings, *but in a really different sense than just male-female.* Almost like women are different from men in so many ways. Like with a woman, you're having sex, and it's over and it was great, and you get that sexual energy out and it was fine.

Terry then recounted an imagined scene to me.

Being at a club, taking some ecstasy, meeting someone interesting—a quiet, handsome person, dancing with him, rubbing up against him, going to the bathroom or finding some place to talk. Going to a hotel or something. Taking our clothes off, holding each other, just laughing, having a good time, not taking it too seriously. I think I'd like to masturbate the person, or use my hands. Do that for a while and make the person almost ejaculate and stop. Do it again and then stop, like torture the person a little bit. Then, just relax for a while. Then, going down on the person and having him go down on me. Just enjoying it in a light kind of way. You do not necessarily have to ejaculate, just enjoy the play of it, the tease of it. With a man . . . even though you prefer women more than men . . . it's something like a *brotherhood* sort of thing. *Doing something sacred with someone who is not just this sexual outlet.* It would be more something of your own—it's hard to explain. I do not know, I guess it's not just curiosity, *it's a need to express something.* As in the *Kiss of the Spider Woman,* Raul Julia gives in—there was a need in him to *express love* for another man.

With Gary, the elements in the feelings for each other of which other men in this chapter have spoken—a loving bond, the relationship to a best friend, and the potentialities of the male body—converged in a way that was both emotionally powerfully and physically expressive. Yet again, the first year of college brought with it expanded horizons.

College was a great awakening for me. I felt that I belonged. Whereas I attended an all-boys high school, now I was at a coed college. I began to talk about how I felt about myself. I felt safe as others did the same. Meeting people and discussing emotion was new to me. I felt very attracted to those people who shared themselves with me. I met a friend during a laundry room discussion and became closer with him than with any other person, before or since. *I felt a love for him* that I had not noticed before.

When they first met, Gary had a girlfriend and his friend had also been dating women. He recalled feeling that the relationship would have been perfect if this friend were only female. But then the friend revealed to Gary that he was gay.

When he wrote to reveal that he was attracted to me I threw away the letter unopened because I was afraid to acknowledge his and my sexuality. When he revealed verbally how he felt, our relationship became strained. *I was not able to accept my own feelings.* My initial reaction was knee-jerk. I backed away and we did not speak for more than two weeks. I then ignored his revelation. Later we addressed it and left it as: he was gay, and I was straight and flattered.

Nevertheless, a reciprocal desire began to take shape in Gary's mind, and he found himself fantasizing about his friend. At the same time, the closeness between them was regained. "About half a year later we had oral sex for the first time. I was wracked with guilt, not because I had cheated on my steady girlfriend, rather because I thought I had done something wrong, that something was wrong with me." At a purely physical level, there was also a problem. Although his friend was handsome and had a body that was otherwise attractive, he was hairier than average, which was a turn-off for Gary. Nevertheless, although Gary has continued to date and have sexual relationships with women, he and his friend have repeated their sexual encounter a number of times over the space of several years.

I asked Gary if he could say anything about the special quality that the maleness or femaleness of the other lent to the experience. His first response was that, physically, he felt a greater attraction to females, so he imagined that being with a male would not be as satisfying in the long run. However, another factor seemed to be even more important than the sex of the other person. Speaking of his friend, he said,

> It was all a matter of the chemistry between us. We were spending a lot of time together—and *revealing*. I think there is a lot of power in revealing. When you reveal yourself to someone, you come close to them. Or maybe it's vice versa, when you feel close to someone, the more you feel you can reveal. It was the first time I was opening up. I'd gone to an all-boys Catholic school and there was not a lot of revealing of how you felt; it was very superficial. This was a kind of awakening—now I can reveal myself, now I can be with all sorts of people.

He continued,

> Most males do not hold an attraction for me, and one reason is that they're not emotionally open or available. That's one of the reasons why so many close friends have been females. Initially I taught in an all-girls Catholic school, and they really expressed themselves. Now, in public school [where he was then teaching] the ones who will talk more are, again, girls. In that respect, maleness is not a turn on at all. They do not express or reveal themselves. They are not thinking about much and if they do—obviously they *are*—they are not revealing it. They're really cheating themselves and the people they're with. So, that's one thing about females that is an advantage over males—they reveal more. But strangely enough, when they're in a relationship with you, they reveal less! They stop revealing. With the one male I was with, that was not true. He revealed more, and that was great. I really enjoyed that. Once you get to know someone, they can become so attractive to you. It's their personality, *how you feel when you're with them,* the chemistry you have. If you're opening yourself up to them, *why not open yourself up sexually to them?*

The depth of feeling Gary had for his friend persisted to the present. I asked him about the components of that feeling.

It's strange, when you think why you love someone. If it's an action, if you took it away you'd still love them. If it was their appearance, you would still love them, but I guess those are the only things you can talk about. But he revealed things to me. He questioned me. I really like that, and do not get that enough. He questioned things I said—"Why do you think that?" He had a genuine interest in me. I found that warming. Why do you love your parents? They have a genuine interest in you. They really want you to succeed. I'd never been in love with anyone. Here was a person very interested in my success, very outgoing themselves. He spurred me, thought I was really great, but did not idolize me either. One of the problems with women was that they idolized me, and if you idolize someone, they're untouchable. He showed attention to me, one of the first times anyone did. In high school, there was no best friend who called me every day. He'd come by every day and say, "Let's do something." I thought that was great. Somebody actually wanted me in their life. I felt very secure, very warm about it. It seemed to last forever, thinking about that first semester. I felt very strongly about him, not thinking that I loved him yet, but within a month—when he invited me to his mother's wedding—I remember having really strong feelings, and that was September or October, so it was not very long at all.

For Gary the power of the emotional bond nurtured by mutual revealing seemed to be an essential component of sexual feeling. Gary had grown up "oriented" toward women, as had Jeff, Brad, and Charlie. At a point when people seem to be more open—the college years—a friendship developed, became strong and emotionally compelling. What would have happened if his friend had not been gay? Quite possibly nothing explicitly sexual would have happened, as with Jeff and Larry. There are no conventions whereby men whose social identities are heterosexual can move to a sexual consummation of their feelings for each other. As was true for many of the people I have cited in this chapter, a door had been opened for Gary; an inner boundary that had hitherto closed off a realm of emotional and physical possibilities had been crossed. He had indicated to me that sexual preference was, at this point in his life, an issue for him.

Where was he on that issue?

> I don't know. I don't feel particularly satisfied with the quality of my sexual experiences with the women I've been with—maybe because I was not really in love with them. At the same time, I don't feel really satisfied with the experience of being with men—I don't know why exactly because in some ways that arouses me more. Maybe because it was a different experience—sort of like the first time you had sex, it was extremely arousing. Being with a man, because it's so infrequent, maybe is along the same lines. But I don't know, being with women sometimes is just blah, it's just not there, not exciting. I feel burned out on sex, have no interest in it sometimes.

I asked where Gary found his thoughts and fantasies going.

> I don't have a lot of sexual fantasies just now. I think more about doing things, writing things. [But if he did have a sexual fantasy or daydream?] With women. Sometimes I think of a relationship, what it would be like, where we would go or what we would do—a good deal of that, more than having sex. Going places, doing things, having her next to me in my house, talking. That dominates more than having sex. Or sometimes the idea of having sex right *there* [when with a female friend] or something. But the more *intense* fantasies I have, and they're very infrequent, once a month or once every two months, are with a male—always with my friend. One of the persistent ones involves a shower—having sex in the shower, and having him enter me. I don't know why showers exactly, but that's one I have over and over. The fantasy lasts longer than the ones with women and it's much more intense. I'll get much more aroused.

This had never happened in reality. Sometimes, as in the fantasy, he felt it would be fulfilling, while at other times the idea was almost like a turn-off.

The interpenetration of bodies, by whatever means, has force and power that seem to transcend male or female roles, that go beyond anatomical ease or difficulty. In relation to a woman, the man is most commonly the entering person, whereas with another man, there is a greater potential for being entered. I said these things to Gary, and they seemed to touch a chord.

> I sometimes think I want to experience the other end of that. If I'm with my girlfriend, I'm always inside of her but she's never inside of me. I wish that it could be reversed. I wish I could feel like how she feels about it. Not because I want to experience things from her side, I guess, but because it seems like an enjoyable experience. It seems like that's inside of you, *within* you, not outside of you.

Gary's friend had only performed anal intercourse on someone once and had not found himself particularly drawn to it. I asked Gary what its meaning might be for him. Was it about feeling the maleness of the other person?

> I don't know if it's maleness—it's just having a person inside of you, male *or* female. I have not actually fantasized about it too much, but what if my girlfriend had a strap-on or something like that? Maybe that would be all right. I do not think it's about being male. The other *person* is now inside of you. Everybody else can be outside of you. Everybody in the whole world is *outside* of you, but only a few people are going to be *inside* of you. *In a way if they're going to be inside of you spiritually, now you can complete it and you can have them inside of you physically.*

I have said that much of what people told me in their writings and in our private dialogues was not revealed in the class or anywhere else. Gary reflected on this fact.

> Here's the thing, though. Most people do not know that I've had that experience. You have these things inside of you and when would they come up? When would you speak of them? I'm not particularly trying to hide them, but when would they come up? I dated a girl for a year before I told her I was adopted. It just never came up. So when would it come up?

"Yes, I've had sex with that man over there." It's a strange thing. Am I not saying it because I have a problem with it or am I not saying it because there's just no occasion for saying it? In college, before we were even involved, there were people writing things in the hallway and in bathroom stalls about us—that's the mentality that's out there. It's just a nuisance. They're not going to benefit, and you aren't, so why have them know? But there have been plenty of times when I *wanted* to tell. You've had this experience and you haven't told anyone—*no one,* you know. . . ?

People are forced to keep secrets—"don't ask, don't tell"—and so the falseness of our categories remains unchallenged. One of the costs of this imposed silence is a distortion of social reality. But one could infer from Gary's vehemence—"You've had this experience and you haven't told anyone—*no one*"—that secrets can exact a personal cost as well, in not permitting people to be themselves when with others. Secrets can also be corrosive in relationships, which may be why Gary did tell the woman he had recently begun to see.[10]

Chapter 5

Heterosexuality
versus Moving Toward Women

As the institutional culture has constructed it, heterosexuality is the polar opposite of homosexuality. Whereas homosexuality results, by implication, from "gender nonconformity,"[1] heterosexuality has simply been regarded as the natural unfolding of feelings by men for women or vice versa. However, it is clear from what both women and men have revealed that, for many, heterosexuality—as *we* know it in this culture—is the net result of a combination of inner conflict and conscious, self-protective concealment. The concept of masculine identification seems aimed at buttressing this one-sided version of heterosexuality while denying the potential for same-sex feeling in the male self. Thus, heterosexual men are supposed to have achieved a state of masculine identification that results in their exclusive attraction to women. In fact, masculine identification—both as core gender identity and as value placed on one's own sense of maleness—is characteristic of the great majority of gay as well heterosexual men, just as it was for the men in this book who disclosed their same-sex feelings to me.[2] But the stereotypes about heterosexual men help to perpetuate those about gay men. Looking at the feelings and thoughts of individual heterosexual men is a step toward the deconstruction of both sets of stereotypes.

Comparing the three men in this chapter helps one to see that no single set of behaviors or personality traits characterizes all men who are designated as heterosexual. Rather, what they had in common was that each of them moved primarily toward women in their search for emotional and physical closeness with another human being. This comparison also demonstrates that the formulation masculine identification leads to heterosexuality is one that does justice neither to the range and complexity of men's identifications nor to the range and complexity of the meanings that a man's attraction to a woman can signify.

NICK

Nick was a man in his mid-twenties who responded to my invitation to talk with me about what it was like growing up as a sexual person in this society, with the understanding that we would talk about imagery of the body and about heterosexuality and homosexuality. For Nick, fantasy was an important part of his sexual life. Two main themes ran through Nick's fantasies—bondage and anal intercourse. He dated the beginning of his interest in these themes from a summer at camp during his early teens. It had been a "renaissance summer" of learning about sexual things. He and his friends had a counselor who was very open, and they could ask him about many of the things they were just learning about. He and his friends also had access to some sexually explicit magazines, where they found one image that intrigued them all. "This woman was dressed in sexy clothing, lingerie and everything. Her hands were tied above her head and this guy was having sex with her. I noticed we were all looking at that picture all the time and I wondered, 'Wow, will I ever do that?'"

Nick thought of sexuality as central to his life, and central to his sexuality was an attraction to women. He said that as soon as he got to know someone, he would speak of his fantasies, hoping that she would be willing to do the same. Issues of masculinity and femininity were important to Nick. He said that he had absorbed his awareness of what a man is supposed to do in sex from "everywhere" —friends, videos, parents—in other words, from the culture. He said, "I guess there is sort of a set pattern, and it's I as the male tending to be more—not too much—but a little more dominant in the relationship, and that's the basic set pattern. *It seems that's how you go about things.*"

The actual bondage scene that Nick and his girlfriend might act out was entirely consensual and fairly uncomplicated. He saw it as a fulfillment of a mutual fantasy. He described how it usually occurred with one girlfriend.

It wasn't too involved. She had stockings and she preferred that to rope because that might cut in. We'd just start out kissing, and regular foreplay where she would have an outfit on and after we got to the bed, there would be something to tie on to, within the first ten or fifteen minutes of foreplay. Then, if there's clothing, undressing goes on, then lovemaking. It's not a very intense thing with whips or anything extra, or legs being tied down—just the arms. About fifty percent of the time she would be facing me and fifty percent lying on her stomach.

At first, Nick said, when the idea of anal intercourse came up, it seemed weird. But then he saw it in magazines and:

My buddies and I got kind of fixated on it. It was like a group thing. And from an early age on, it seemed like this was okay, a fun thing to do together. So it was okay with women, but not when you applied it to homosexual people. Even with some of my straight friends, if that comes up, it's like, "You weirdo, you homo. . . . " I'm like, "What are you talking about?" If we agree, it's just another form of sex between a man and a woman. The ones that have done it and enjoy it agree and the other ones that don't want anything to do with it—like the anal area is just taboo for some reason. Even if they agree with me, there are some insecurities against letting it be known that it can be enjoyed between a man and a woman. Most of my close friends talk about it just like the time of day. It's just a healthy thing, but for some people there's a taboo.

Nick said about himself, "It's in my nature to push boundaries. It's not like being a pioneer. It's that you're doing something more special and you have more variety—maybe it gives me something more to offer a girl, some more options and wildness. I think of myself as somebody not really inhibited. And if I can find a girl who enjoys it the way I do, it's even more special." With respect to bondage, he remarked that some of his female friends saw it as demeaning. One went so far as to accuse him of being afraid of women. When he protested, she insisted, "I don't care. You're still sick." Although he defended himself, inwardly Nick did wonder to himself if he had some kind of insecurity. But he said,

> When I've asked girlfriends [if they] like it, they've said, "I love it." They like the feeling of being overpowered, subdued, seduced, all in one—in a pretend sense. And I like to do those things, to temporarily take control for the five minutes leading up to it and it's like a whole mixture of those feelings—the one person wants to give herself up, the other person wants to take her over, but it's not really taking over . . . but maybe it is . . . that feeling of being in power—*I've got the most manly feeling you can have at that moment and she's got the most feminine— of helplessness—and at the same time loving it.*

Males, from adolescence onward, confront the myths of masculinity our culture has constructed. The image of a man having intercourse with a bound woman that so captivated the adolescent Nick and his friends was about power, an issue with which the culture confronts young males on one side or the other of the border between childhood and puberty. One of the primary ways in which this issue emerges at puberty is with respect to the image of the body, and especially its power. In high school Nick had been thin and had lost a couple of bad fights. He put himself on a weight training schedule and spent two years working on his body, with a good deal of weight lifting. At the time of our interviews, he was feeling content with his physical self. Most men I have talked to have been concerned about how their bodies look and how strong they are. I doubt that Nick's anxieties in this department were any greater than those of the average American male. But his weight training was clearly about his power and strength as a man.

The image of his own body could also be part of the erotic excitement in a sexual situation with a woman. He mentioned a girlfriend who had bought huge mirrors for her apartment.

> We could actually see both sides and it was just wild. She'd move in a certain way and I realized she's looking in the mirror, and we never really talked about it, but we definitely knew what was going on. So that's a key element to the erotic,

definitely. I'm looking at the whole thing, sometimes just her, sometimes myself. Yeah, I do both, I look at both.

In looking at his own reflection, he felt, "Self-assurance—okay, I'm here, like a grounded feeling, this is me, this is what I expect to see, good, like all systems check." Many, if not most people, are drawn to watching others have sex. And yet, our culture is deeply conflicted about this, and this conflict fuels our thriving pornography industry. For Nick, the ultimate closeness he sought had a twin focus—on his partner as a woman and on himself as a man. The response to himself was part of the erotic charge of the situation.

Anal intercourse between men and women has an ancient lineage. But as Nick pointed out, some of his friends, both male and female, were uneasy about it. I asked Nick whether some zones of the body were prohibited or more dangerous than others. He replied, "That would be *the* zone, even with women, because either you're very open sexually, and creative with ideas, or else you're just raised in a conforming mode where all that's acceptable is basic missionary styles and one or two positions, and that's it."

In light of what he had just said, his response to my question about whether any girlfriend had penetrated him anally was unexpected.

> Absolutely not. It's weird. I once had a girl try to put her finger up my butt. I didn't particularly like it. It was, "What are you doing? Get away." And she was laughing. I guess that would be a taboo area. I guess I've been so conditioned to think it's okay for a man to do this for a woman, but it's not okay for this to be done to a man. *Most boys are taught all your life that it's okay to like girls, to pursue them, go out with them, but it's not okay when two boys go together.*

It seemed paradoxical that something that a woman was doing to Nick would have a homosexual meaning. I said as much to him. He went on, "In some weird way it does. It's saying, no, I'm not homosexual; it's like, 'What you are implying?' even though she may be implying nothing." When he had anal intercourse with a woman, he did not feel it compromised her femininity at all. On the contrary, he said, "If anything, it enlarges her femininity within her sexual arena." Women with whom he had done this agreed. Nick said that most of his friends shared his feeling that allowing anal penetration even by a woman implied something homosexual. "Friends of mine say, 'I wanted to do this, this, and this, and she said, I want to put my finger up your ass, and I said, no way.' And they're like, 'What about you?' And I said, 'No way.' "

Carrie, one woman I interviewed, had tried anal intercourse with her boyfriend, but it had been too painful for her. But she had done to her boyfriend what Nick and his friends would not allow. She said, "I don't think it had ever happened to him before, because it was like, whoa . . . but now he loves it. It stimulates him—how could it not? The same for me." With respect to her feelings about doing this, she said,

> It excites me. I don't know—I never really thought about it. It just happens. Honestly, you know what? Because sometimes I know it hurts him a little bit . . . this is probably a little sadistic . . . the more it hurts him, the more I continue. But I know he likes it. He would make me really stop if it really, really hurt him. I'll touch him then go deeper and deeper—I don't go that far—because I know it hurts him a little bit and that's exciting and *I'm in a lot of control there*, because I watch his face and I see it. Usually the guy has the control, but now I can have a little control and do something to him that he was never aware of happening to him. I don't think anyone has ever touched him like that before, because of the way he acted when I first did it. I like that—something he never had before—and I felt special too.

Carrie's boyfriend was opposed to anything sexual with another man, but he was able to enjoy this. She herself liked the implied reversal of the power balances in their sexual relationship, and maybe he did too. Nick did not seem prepared to accept that kind of reversal, explicitly associating it with homosexuality and even more strongly with femininity.

At the same time, Nick clearly thought of himself as an uninhibited person and certainly not a bigoted one. When he was younger, he had felt revulsion toward homosexuality. But in his late teens, while doing construction work in Manhattan, he worked with designers, which was the first close contact he had with gay people. Once, he was treated curtly by an establishment from which he was supposed to pick up some parts. He was not dressed well and was basically ejected from the premises. The well-known designer he was working for—a gay man—called up and spoke to the people and when Nick returned, "They treated me like gold. I had a new feeling about gays. This guy is just like I am, *he obviously holds a hell of a lot more power than I do* and he helped me out." He saw condemnation of gay people as a narrow-minded rejection of a minority in a culture where homosexuality was taboo. He cited a philosopher who said that many people had a deeply repressed homosexual potential that led them to a strong counterreaction to the homosexuality of others as a way of denying it in themselves. "A lot of people can't deal with the feelings that they have inside—it's 'Oh no, that couldn't be me.' I think this is a major problem."

In spite of an intellectually open-minded attitude, emotionally, Nick himself had a "that couldn't be me" feeling about same-sex attraction even though sexual imagery with males had sometimes occurred in his thoughts. These images were both anal and oral.

> One was with me on the bottom, which is like abhorrent and also, what it would be like if, instead of my girlfriend, it was a guy on his knees in front of me, so to speak? Those are the two images I can remember. Then there's this one movie that my friends were watching and I came in at the middle. And this guy gets into trouble and they make him work for them as a homosexual prostitute. I remember walking in and [saying], "What are you people watching?" He's on his knees in the bedroom—a guy standing in front of him. That's in my mind, maybe because it's something I've seen in the last year or two years, on TV. Those are the kind of images.

What happened when Nick saw himself on the bottom? "I try to imagine how would it be if I let some guy do to me what I do to some of my girlfriends. It's really a thought that turns me off, you know. But I can't deny ever thinking about it, because I think everybody thinks about it." Although it was not entirely comfortable for him to talk about these images, he tried to be candid in his responses to me:

It's mostly a fleeting thought. I remember once in high school some guys were talking and one asked, "Can you imagine that?—I don't know how girls do it, give blow jobs, can you imagine that?" I remember the whole group going quiet for a second—it's going through everybody's mind at that moment. The others, I can't remember anything but fleeting thoughts that just popped in, like when I walked into that movie. There are other instances, but fleetingly so.

When he was on the bottom, was it an actual image? He said,

It's kind of murky, but yeah, I'd have to say so, not as clear as day. Somebody about my size too, or maybe larger, doing the same thing, the same way I do with a female. With my girl-friends it's been lying down, always a prone position. If I pictured it in my mind, me doing it to a guy, it would be the same way, so it's just . . . they're both prone.

In his imagination, both he and the other man were nude. But the image did not remain very long. "It totally turns me off. It's a repulsive image to me, and while it's something that I know goes on—*it's not me.* I couldn't imagine enjoying something like that, and I still have a hard time understanding how people enjoy that or why they do. It's simply that they do. But I know for me it's completely repugnant."

And yet, Nick had estimated a third of the population, of both men and women, had repressed their homosexual potential, certainly not less than a quarter. Of those who have come out as gay, he said, "I think they're only a small portion of those who have that tendency or feeling." Freud would have agreed with Nick's analysis. About his own feelings, he said, "I never even considered it for myself, so there's no inner taboo." Yet once again, his emotional response to the images his mind created directly contradicted that, as did his statement, "If I started thinking about it, some guilt would come up."

Nick had no problem acknowledging deep bonds to male friends. But as for anything sexual with a man, he said a number of times that he had been "conditioned" against it by his upbringing—not that he was explicitly warned against it, but rather that his female-oriented interests had been so obviously encouraged. In a way, then, he could recognize the effect of conventional attitudes on his feelings. But his own rejection of homosexuality seemed to go beyond a simple conditioned rejection. About why he could not feel sexual attraction to a man, he said,

> I can sort of explain it. With a woman, you realize that I'm going to be a little more dominant—like in foreplay, it's fun and both accept that. But with a man, I'd say no, *because a man would assume a female role. It would be like I don't respect this.* "Listen, you're a man—act like one." I accept two women together. I feel that women were more meant to be the receiver and man gives to them, like it was set up that way— whoever you want to say, God or the cosmos, but two men, it's just innately not meant to be.

How much of his feeling of repulsion had to do with the sense that a sex change from male to female would be taking place? "Not just that part, but the other guy, the masculine part of it, like—where is your mind, why don't you just go find a beautiful woman, or any woman? *Obviously you're capable*, so what's the attraction to a man? It works both ways. *I'm repulsed by both of them.* I realize it's going on, there's a reason for it, but. . . . "

I had asked Nick about dreams in which a man might have appeared in a situation that was sexual or could have a sexual connotation. The only one he recalled having was the following:

> There was this big guy—someone we all respected—and he had a woman's dress on. It was a shock.

It is clear that, for Nick, dominance and power were critical components of masculinity, of what a male person ought to be. When the gay designer demonstrated his power and exercised it on Nick's behalf, it actually raised gay men in the estimate of the nineteen-year-old Nick because the man had shown that, while being gay, he had the kind of power that Nick saw as an attribute of masculinity. The image of the big man in a dress combined two things in a way that could only be paradoxical—size, a symbol of masculine power in a man he also respected, and women's clothing, symbolizing submissiveness, something he found contemptible in a man. It seems that, in spite of Nick's feeling that it was in his nature to push boundaries and his condemnation of public homophobic attitudes, he had a visceral rejection of male homosexuality because, deep down, he saw the power—and hence the masculinity—of one or both partners compromised.

This visceral rejection existed right alongside a directly contradictory intellectual stance that regarded homosexual potential as widely prevalent. And when he gave his thoughts on adolescent sexual development, he said,

> Especially when you're younger, everything is developing—that's one of the main things that drives people to it, the sexual drive. Whether you can satisfy that early on the normal way—with girls—that will be a part of determining which way you're going to go, because *it is in everybody's mind, I guess, but more repressed.* I had no trouble. I was very successful. I remember having sexual drives at seven years old. I had a girlfriend in second grade and from then on I always loved girls. If you can never get together with a girl, the sexual drive is so strong that it will turn people the other way [to homosexuality]—no doubt about it because they need contact. *If you're not successful,* good at the game, then you are more likely to go the other way.

In a reversal of what some women feel, Nick remarked, "It's harder for men to start over and get women than it is for women to get men—this we know." Nick's theory seemed to acknowledge a universal homosexual potential in adolescence, while attributing a homosexual outcome to a failure in power—the power to attract women.

I remarked that success or failure did not, in actual fact, seem to play a role in sexual orientation. Rather, it was emotional need. If he had an emotional need for a man, without fear of its negative meanings, the ability to relate to the body of another male could exist even for him. He said, "I don't think so. I just can't imagine it. I've been close, bonded with friends, but I can't imagine what would drive me to that emotional need that would make me *cross that line.*" Nick meant the line between masculine and feminine even more than the line between heterosexual and homosexual. The structure of men's bodies and the histories of men's lives converge to ensure that the symbol of anal penetration has, between them, a deep and primal significance that is woven into the very structure of human experience. On the other hand, it may be a link to the female universe through a discovery of something enveloping and dark in one's own body, female in the sense that the earth is almost always personified as female. Nick seemed to want to experience that universe, but through the body of his girlfriend only, never through his own. For Nick, an ultimate meaning of "feminine" was helplessness and, for that reason, he had to deny any woman entry to his body and to reject homosexuality, which he associated, not with male-to-male bonding, but rather with female powerlessness.

TONY

The thing I find attractive is when I can see a bit of myself in the person—in the eyes. I can see a lot of the same emotions I feel in myself when I have that connection. That's when I feel the most intimate with a person. I have a strong need to find someone that I'm completely compatible with—emotionally and sexually. In terms of pure sexual arousal, it's hard for me to separate the two. I don't have many one-night flings. I look for a monogamous setup. That's what really drives me. It's not a physical thing. But the eyes are my big thing. If they turn me on I'd be very attracted. But it's very much the inner self I'm looking for—a kind, good person, someone who could understand the things I've been through and empathize with pain that I've felt. The whole soul mate cliché—that's what I look for. I would want to marry somebody spiritually compatible.

In sex, Tony looked for, "A sort of unification—two people coming together. Reaching orgasm is definitely a part of it, but I really enjoy pleasing someone I'm with. I'm not sexually selfish. Totally feeling *at one* with the person is the height for me."

Tony was about the same age as Nick and, like Nick, identified himself as heterosexual. But his thoughts about his own relation to women and to the feminine seemed rather different.

I grew up *very* close to my younger sister. Now I'm very close to my older sister. *I'm closer to the women in my family than I am to the men.* But I've achieved an understanding with my father and forgive him for the things that happened. I was closer to my older brother through baseball, but we've drifted away somewhat now. *I always felt that I identified with women very well.* I'm a very sensitive person. I've learned to control that in a more positive way for myself because it was a big problem growing up to find women I was compatible with, because I was *too* sensitive. I came across too strongly and they were turned off or intimidated by that. At fourteen or fifteen most women are not looking for a husband, they're looking for someone to have fun with, and a lot of times I came across as being too serious. I've often felt very empathetic with women's issues and problems and related to them very well. On the surface, I'm a macho person, *but underneath it all, there are a lot of feminine qualities that I have.* The woman I'm seeing now, on the other hand, is a feminine person who has a lot of male qualities. One of the things I like about her is that she is strong, has a backbone—not that I equate women with weakness.

While he admired strength in women, he also said,

One of the qualities about women that I like is the softness, the tenderness. When I had what I called homophobic tendencies in my life—because I say that I identify with women very well—not to say that homosexuality is a pure expression of wanting to be a woman—but it's interesting how I identified with it in a certain way and also feared it in a certain way.

Tony seemed to be saying two things—that he identified with women, yet had once feared homosexuality, which evidently had some sense of a female identification for him. He recalled an incident when, at seventeen and a freshman at college, he saw a poster for a gay campus organization and said "faggots" out loud.

A girl looked at me and said, "You're kidding, right?" I stood back and asked myself, "Yeah, why do I feel that way?" I felt very inadequate at that time. All the males in my family have struggled with weight and I was the heaviest I'd ever been. I dieted and lost sixty pounds. It seems fairly obvious now— when you feel so low. . . . When I look at how my view of homosexuality has changed, *it seems so blatant to me now that men who resent homosexuals are repressing their own homosexual fears or tendencies.*

Tony was speaking from personal experience. He recalled being quite homophobic in high school, but prior to that—at age thirteen or fourteen—he remembered a friend he grew up with and was very close to. At that age he recalled feeling "some level of attraction to him." Tony was brought up in an Italian family to be "very macho." Nevertheless, the males in the family kissed each other and, to this day, Tony said he will still kiss an old friend hello. He said, "That's where it gets confusing to me. I don't know if I felt a sexual desire for my friend or not." But I think he now recognized something sexual in those feelings because he had never disclosed them to anyone before our interview.

Quite honestly at this point in my life I'm very happy with women. I really would not want to experiment. There *was* another time with a friend I grew up with. I was in his house and he said, "Pull down your pants and show me yours, and I'll show you mine." We were six years old and his mother walked in and freaked out. He grew up to be a very sexual person—he lost his virginity much earlier than my other friends. He was with a lot of different types of women, including sleazy women. He was into exploring his sexuality and I wouldn't be surprised if he told me he had been with a man, because he's a very exploratory kind of person. I saw him a few months ago and kissed him hello—I think that's a very healthy thing for guys.

I try to be honest with myself about it. It's very hard to be objective. I really can't look at it as a repressed sexual desire— I could be wrong. I would never have imagined myself with two earrings six or seven years ago. The eighties were such a macho era when I was growing up. Now you see guys with long hair, earrings.

Had Tony ever wondered what it would be like with a man?

> Yes, I have actually. After taking your class, because the issue
> was so prevalent in the class, I remember one day trying to
> imagine what it would be like to have sex with a man—not
> really fantasizing about it but wondering, what would it feel
> like? It was a strange feeling. Then again, there are some men
> who don't express feelings of homosexuality, but get aroused
> when a woman does things anally to them. I don't know what
> that all means. For me that's also an area that could be arous-
> ing. But not as arousing as the phallic.

About the strange feeling he had when he tried to imagine what it
would be like to be with a man, he said, "I remember laughing.
*I was almost trying to make myself feel like what it would be like to
be a woman.* Like if I thought of a man having sex with me—then I
would feel like a woman—a woman being penetrated by a man. If it
was happening to me, it would be like what a woman would feel
like, what I'd *suppose* a woman would feel like. These are things I
thought I'd never say in my life." he laughed. But about penetrating
a man, he said, "I couldn't. Maybe it goes along with fact that I
don't fantasize a lot about penetrating a woman. I fantasize about a
woman performing something on me."
Tony had mentioned a woman putting a finger inside him.

> It's difficult to say. I haven't experienced it very much. It's
> very sensitive, but in a different way. Like my mother used to
> take my temperature rectally—it's almost a feeling of violation
> a little bit. If a woman does oral sex on me, I don't feel
> violated at all. But like in someone taking your temperature, or
> at times when I've done it myself—it's a feeling of almost
> treading areas that are taboo, really being violated in a way,
> but at the same time arousing. *You might make an analogy
> between a person's butt and the dark side or zone of their
> psyche, the forbidden area that's taboo or off-limits*—but it's
> not something that's *particularly* arousing to me.

Tony's sense that there was something dark and forbidden about
anal penetration was similar to Nick's, but his reaction to it was not.

Before our next interview, Tony began to get sexually involved with the woman he had been getting to know. He said,

> Last time, I said I see a lot of myself in someone. It was interesting, the first time we had gotten intimate, that was exactly the feeling. At the moment almost, of orgasm, I had this tremendous . . . it was this image in my head. It was very strange. It was like an image of myself—of her and myself just completely together. *I saw my own image within an image of her.* It was very strange. And it was the first time I had an orgasm with her. She was using her hands and then as I was— I've never been able to tell a girl that I was about to have an orgasm—I told her I was going to, and she put her mouth on me. It was amazing.

As he ejaculated into her mouth,

> That's when I had that image—that wild image—in my head. I was looking up. I thought about it afterward and I thought, oh this is perfect for what I had been discussing with you. It just came into my head.
>
> *It was a feeling that inspired a visual image.* It was very bright—like a fiery bright . . . almost like when someone flicks a light on in a dark room and you get light in your eyes, like a red, bright light. I just saw myself with her.

If he were trying to paint that image, how would it look?

> I do paint. It would be a lot of red, sort of like—this is going to sound like something you hear on those "psychic lines"—sort of like a doorway, with a blast of light coming through, red, yellow, white light. And this image of me and her together, but it's interesting because I was like out of my body looking down at me. *I guess if I could paint myself as a woman, that would be how I would do it.*

"So," I said, "you're kind of looking down, but you are no longer visible, it's her that you're incorporated in?"

"Yeah," Tony answered, "It's all her. I don't get many images like that. It was a bizarre experience for me. The whole thing happened in my car, which is kind of bizarre in itself. It was one of those freezing cold nights. I didn't expect it. That image stirred up a lot of feelings about what I was saying—*unity, closeness.*"

Tony told me a few things about his family history. He had two older brothers—one "good" big brother and one "bad" big brother. The good one was much older, and it was he who introduced Tony to baseball. The younger of the two brothers, who was still older by nine years, adopted a sadistic attitude toward his little brother. A traumatic incident occurred when Tony was only ten, the memory of which he actually recovered a good many years later. His brother had been slapping Tony, saying, "I'm going to make you a man." His older sister tried to stop him and the brother turned on her instead, and beat her. Tony summed up the effect that he thought this brother had on him.

> Growing up with someone that I had such an aversion to would, I'd have to say, make me want to be closer to females. I grew up more sensitively. I didn't want to be violent. I reacted to everything that he did and did the opposite. *That seemed very consciously like a motivational factor to identify with women.* He was this horrible, disgusting thing that abused me, and I felt women would never abuse me—women would take care of me.

In the sexual part of a relationship with someone he trusted, the adult Tony said about his feelings, "It's always a feeling of security or safety. I feel completely secure and safe with the person. It's a primal, nurturing, 'taken care of' kind of feeling. I feel totally secure when I'm intimate with her."

The institutional gender system assumes that identification with women leads to sexual desire for men. With characteristic insight, Eve Sedgwick questioned this assumption when she referred to the "slippery slope between desire and identification."[3] For Tony, identification with women was not associated with attraction to men, but on the contrary, it seemed to be a key part of his attraction to women. Sex with women seemed to be a way of getting closer to them and feeling that closeness more intensely. These feelings existed right alongside his sense of himself as a man. Nor was he immune to the anxieties that men feel about masculinity. He told me about an incident and its aftermath when he was in college that seems to have shaken his self-confidence in that respect:

> In my junior year, there was this girl. She was on the bitchy side, but she was a lot younger and looked up to me. I felt I'd be in charge, but the first sexual experience was really bad. She completely dominated it. I didn't really want to have sex at that time. It's almost like she forced me to—it was almost the equivalent of rape, emotional rape. She threw me down, and got on top of me—I had a condom, and she took it and threw it away. I wasn't even fully aroused and we had sex. It was short and then it was like, "Okay, put your clothes back on." It was a typical male stereotype. I felt very strange after that and the second time we tried it I was completely not aroused. If I'm with a girl I feel very close to I get very aroused very easily. I don't have any qualms. If I'm with a woman I don't feel close to, I have a severe problem physically with being able to perform physically.
>
> We tried it again and there was no arousal. I remember crying—it was a severe feeling of stress. At the beginning she was understanding, and then she completely turned to the opposite. The second time I failed, she asked, "What's wrong, has this happened before?" But you could see a part of her that was like a man—"You're not satisfying me, so screw you." She turned on me very quickly and started to see another guy behind my back. There was this devilish quality, like, "Yeah, well, you can't perform. . . ." I felt really insecure about that for a very long time. I really felt like there was something wrong with me and actually did start seeing a social worker because of my experience with her. I was really deeply depressed by the end of that semester. I told him I was having these feelings of almost uncontrollable rage with this girl. When I'd see her I wanted to physically hurt her. I felt very inadequate after her. I didn't have sex with anyone until my senior year.

As we talked about the stress men experience over "performance," Tony said,

There's a tremendous double standard about that. It's almost accepted if a woman can't reach orgasm, but if a man can't it's almost a disgrace. But then if he does too quickly, it's a disgrace also. Between ten or twenty minutes—then it's great. But if he takes too long . . . it's crazy when you think about it. Let's say you have sexual intercourse with someone for an hour and you never reach an orgasm—then there's something wrong with you. But if you reach orgasm *after* an hour, then you're incredible because you lasted an hour!

In contrast to Nick, the image of himself as a powerful man was not particularly important to Tony, although it is clear that he was not immune to the power issues involved in cultural definitions of masculinity. There was little fear of homosexuality in Tony and, at this point in his life, not much interest. It was the image of the woman he was drawn to, not the image of the man, neither his own nor another's. The striking image that burst into Tony's consciousness when his girlfriend brought him to orgasm in the car that night was a synthesis of image and emotion that, in a flash, captured the quintessence of what sex with a woman meant to him—ultimate closeness through identification.

RUSS

In Russ's feelings the themes of masculine and feminine, of heterosexual and homosexual, also interacted in ways that do not conform to the stereotypes of the institutional culture. His earliest sexual memories had to do with his fascination with girls. About the female body, he said, "Girls have penis envy. I had vagina envy, almost." His interest in girls remained strong during his grammar school days, and he recalled being yelled at for spending too much time looking at them. Although he went to an all-boys high school, Russ was an adolescent during the late 1960s and early 1970s, a time he remembers as one of sexual openness and experimentation. Skinny dipping in mixed groups and couples having sex in the same room were among his memories. Although he had never liked his looks when he was younger, Russ grew into a tall young man with a lifeguard's build and, although he was shy about initiating conversations with girls, he found that they would approach him. From his teens onward, he had many sexual partners. Both then and now Russ has always been very careful to make sure that the woman is satisfied and has an orgasm. He said that he had acquired a reputation for this. "Girls came up to me in my early twenties. 'Oh, I heard you're wonderful in bed—would you have sex with me?' Word would get around—it was great. I'd make a girl feel good about herself too. I was romantic and giving and made her feel like a queen. I'd go out with married women whose husbands didn't make them feel good."

Whatever his motivations, I think it would be fair to say that Russ was quite capable of fulfilling the role expectations for heterosexual males. However, he did not share the contempt for homosexuality that some of his heterosexual contemporaries displayed. Russ grew up in what can best be described as a tough, working-class neighborhood in Brooklyn. Some of his friends had been arrested for "fag bashing," but he himself never understood this or participated in it. On occasion, he had asked people why they did this. Speaking to me, he quoted them as replying, "I dunno. They're faggots," as if it was self-evident that this would be reason enough. He even knew of one family in which the sons learned that behavior from their father. It seemed to constitute a sign of manhood. However, his own experience with gay men while growing up was good. He was befriended, in the sixth grade, by one of his teachers, a Christian brother who he understood to be gay. He took Russ to the opera and the ballet. "It was almost like he was dating me." But nothing sexual was ever broached. In the eighth grade, another priest took him and some of his friends under his wing. He was progressive and assured the boys that there was nothing wrong with masturbating. Russ said that he and this man, whom he assumed was gay, were still friends. Their swimming coach was also homosexual and, although he had the boys swim in the nude, Russ never heard about any impropriety toward any of them. Closer to home, Russ's next-door neighbor was married with two children, and he was known to have his boyfriend visit every weekend. When Russ was around seventeen or eighteen, there were two male teachers who lived together, and Russ and some friends would hang around their apartment. These men were good-humored and intelligent and everyone enjoyed their company. He said about gay people, "So at a young age I saw them as regular people. People who have never been exposed have a fear of the unknown. But I had gay teachers who were out of the closet in high school."

With Nick, the contrast between his liberal attitudes in the abstract and his profound rejection at the concrete level was particularly striking. But Russ had acknowledged the sense of a sexual potential between himself and another man. Initially, he put it this way: "I never felt there was anything wrong with being attracted to a man. I just never felt anything. I always felt that if I were attracted someday, I would give it a try." I asked Russ if he could describe the imagined scenario for the homosexual experience he had sometimes thought he might have.

> Someone I felt very relaxed and at ease with, not something planned, very spontaneous. There wouldn't be kissing involved. But dancing—that image just popped into my mind— slow dancing even and caressing. Anal sex never, for some reason. I don't know why. Even with a woman I never enjoyed anal sex. It would be more mutual masturbation, stroking. Maybe some oral sex—I couldn't rule that out. Somebody with a nice body, somebody attractive, soft skin, with more feminine qualities, never one of those macho leather guys. There would be more of a romantic quality.

But in reality, the closest he had come to sexual contact with another man was in threesomes that included himself, a woman, and a male friend. I think that the experience of two men and one woman is a way for two men to be sexually close, as it was for Jason, without actually having sex with each other. A friend of one of my students had once told him about meeting a girl he had known in high school and going back to his apartment with her and the male friend he had been out with. They had sex with her in turn, but for him, the intensity of the experience had been with his friend, not with the girl. In reminiscing about it he had said, "Afterward, I felt like we were blood brothers." Although Russ participated in this kind of trio about five or six times, he said, "There was never any contact between me and the other guy. *It was very strict, rigid boundaries.*" At that time, he was aware of finding excitement in seeing the woman's excitement. "It was watching her get pleasure from two guys."

It is also striking that Russ did not absorb the homophobic attitudes that characterized some of his friends and acquaintances. What were the critical factors? Having gay teachers he liked? The fact that no homophobia was expressed in his family? Russ's background contained some interesting contradictions. Although he was raised in a Catholic home and went to Catholic grammar school, the atmosphere around him was not hostile to sexuality. He was aware that his father had a collection of *Playboy* magazines and said that his mother read pornographic books. He was later told by friends of his parents that they had always had a good sexual relationship. He also recalled hearing them making love through the partitions of their country house. Was it the general era of liberality he grew up in? Probably all of these factors were important.

But something else cannot be discounted—his own individual response to the conditions and circumstances that confronted him. Russ repeatedly made reference to how the "forbidden" could be erotic. He said, "Maybe the forbidden thing made it more exciting, breaking new boundaries. Maybe that's what it was—*crossing new boundaries,* which is why I always thought that maybe, someday, I'd have a homosexual experience." Nick had also spoken of himself as "pushing boundaries," but it was clear that those boundaries were definitely more circumscribing for him than they were for Russ. As far as having an erotic dream that included male images, Russ said,

> I can almost visualize some kinds of images, but it's hard to tell because I don't know if they're dreams or memories of real-life experiences. I was on the swimming team as a teenager and we all swam naked. When you think back, you kind of picture men's butts and things like that. The only thing that comes to my mind is stroking the back of a man and just running my hand over his butt.

He assumed this image was a recollection from a dream.

At this point, Russ added a further observation about himself that opened a new avenue in our dialogue.

I have a hard time with masculine and feminine. I'm very feminine inside. I'm sensitive and cry at movies. I believe in reincarnation and think I was a woman in the last couple of lifetimes. I feel closer to women, though I have a lot of male friends. But I'm more comfortable around women. I like romantic music. I don't have a lot of macho attitudes. In my early twenties, I'd go out with mascara on to clubs. It was more of a joke. I'd stand there talking to a woman and they'd ask, "Do you have mascara on?" I felt comfortable enough with myself to do something like that. I liked shocking people. I always felt a feminine side to me. It wasn't that I wanted to be a girl, but sometimes I think I would have been happier because I thought they had less problems, maybe didn't have to prove themselves, didn't have all that pressure to prove that you were macho. I'm talking about my late teens. In my early teens, I was just preoccupied with having sex, trying to have a girlfriend and all that. As I got older, I started thinking and tried to let myself go. I started cooking, going to the ballet and museums, breaking away from the "just hanging out" mentality.

I asked Russ with whom he would have sex if he were a woman. He said,

I was never able to actually picture it. I assume I'd be a heterosexual woman because I'm heterosexual now. I've never gone so far as to visualize myself as a woman being made love to by a man. I just assumed it would happen. I do have a more feminine side than most guys I know. It doesn't bother me—I enjoy that part of me. If you resist it, you end up unhappy. If you let yourself go with it and enjoy that side of yourself, you'll have a much more enjoyable life.

But the reason why I wanted to be a woman wasn't sexual. I wanted to be a woman *because they were more open than men, could express their feelings more.* It was more on an emotional level that I wished I was a woman as a teenager. There were no sexual fantasies at all. I wanted to be a woman so I wouldn't have to hold back my feelings and I could have someone to take care of me. Even though I don't like anyone taking care of me as a man, as a woman I might allow that. It might be nice.

When I was a teenager, I thought that it might be nice too, to have someone protect you. I had a very violent childhood as far as gangs and things like that. I got arrested for murder when I was in my twenties—I didn't do it. It was a gang fight and I got off. Another time I was arrested for beating up a guy pretty badly. I never felt that I was really tough even though I was able to beat anybody up. I never got beat, never lost a fight. I was always a big kid and in good shape. I wasn't going to let myself get hurt, but I never liked fighting, and yet you were expected to because it was a violent neighborhood.

I hate that I let myself get forced into those situations where you had to do it. You couldn't get out of it. I think that's another reason for having these feelings of wanting to be a woman. The guys in my crowd never really talked about their feelings either, never really opened up, and I always felt that I had a lot to open up to.

I guess my feminine side came through because some people have thought that I was gay. The macho guys in my neighborhood were never going out with girls a lot. They were so busy being macho [that] they were stupid about it. It was a turn-off for many of the women. For me and a few other guys like me who were always getting the girls, the macho guys said we must be faggots. They never carried the thought that far as to why we had all the girls.

I said to Russ that the way in which some men experienced the relation between masculine and feminine seemed full of contradictions. Some men wanted to be very close to femininity by touching a woman, having sex with her, but—paradoxically—feared any aspect of it in themselves. In contrast, some men dressed as women and adopted female mannerisms and sought to be close to the maleness of another. I mentioned these two ends of the spectrum, and Russ replied, *"Or guys like me who feel a feminine side and still look to a woman."*

What was the meaning of sex with a woman for Russ?

This may sound corny but *I feel almost like I become one with them.* As I said before, I like to please a woman, so with oral sex I always make sure that they have a couple of orgasms even before I start. I enjoy that closeness where you feel like you rise up and all of a sudden you come together and you're one. *I don't think you can get any closer than that.* You get inside them almost and *you feel like you've become one with them.*

He said about the moment of orgasm, *"I feel a oneness with them. I don't feel like a separate entity."* About sex with a man—which Russ had never, in fact, had—he said, "Yet—I imagine it would be the same closeness if I did. I don't think it would be that much different as far as the close feeling if you let yourself go. If you hold back, or are nervous and fight it, it wouldn't work. If I was going to go that far, I would let myself go. It would be for nothing if you didn't."

About what made Russ move toward women sexually, he said,

I'm attracted to the feminine qualities, which is why I let myself have them—because I'm attracted to that in women. It lets me actually share in those qualities when I'm with that woman. I don't find that many masculine qualities attractive. I find them to be more necessary. That's probably why when you look at the male, you wouldn't want it, because those qualities don't attract me. More than the beauty even, more than the physical aspects, *it's the essence of what makes a woman* that I find attractive—that's why I could never be with a woman who wasn't feminine, as opposed to masculine-type women. I grew up with some like that. They're very attractive physically, but they've never done anything for me sexually.

Russ made it clear that it was not qualities of feminine beauty—skin, hair, eyes—that would attract him to a man. He said,

It's not even the image, it's the qualities—which made me think that if it were a guy who was feminine, I'd find that more attractive than the masculine kind of guy. There is a difference between being a sissy and having feminine qualities. I would find a guy like that, who was open, and soft, and receptive, and caring. I find *that* attractive—a guy who's open, honest, a person who'd let his feelings out, cry at a movie. Those are the things I associate with myself too. So maybe it's an ego thing.

Some girls in the group would enjoy me because I wasn't macho. But some would turn off—"He's a faggot." They wanted that tough guy and wound up marrying one too—the kind that slapped them around.

ONENESS

Freud observed that in the condition of being in love, the normally firm boundary between self and other—the "love object"—is abolished: "Against all the evidence of his senses, a man who is in love says that 'I' and 'you' are one."[4] Russ said, about his experience with a woman at orgasm, "I feel a oneness with them. I don't feel like a separate entity." From this perspective, she could be said to be entering him as much as he is entering her. The temporary loss of a sense of separateness was just as dramatically true for Tony, who saw himself fused into the body of the woman. If male and female are regarded as opposites only, this sense of oneness can be experienced as paradoxical or even threatening, as it was for Nick. Of the three men I have so far discussed in this chapter, Nick most needed to keep the sense of himself separate from the sense of the woman he was with. Yet, at the same time, even he seemed to be entering into an emotional bond and, through that bond, forming a unit composed of twin poles—masculine and feminine—welded together by the erotic current between them. He said,

> You transcend everything else—all your surroundings. It's just you two—you're close as two people can get and all of a sudden it's real, so everything else at that moment can be real or not real and you don't even care, because now you've transcended all the hang-ups you may have had, or problems, or bills you needed to pay—it's all left behind. For that moment, you're just living your fantasy and when you're living your fantasy, it's incredibly satisfying. It's compelling just to get to that point, and you've shared it with your girlfriend, you love her—it's a combination of mutual trust and fulfillment, like only we two know about this and the fact that I made it happen. So it's like a transcending kind of thing. I lose myself in it, but together with somebody—it's not something you

want to get lost in alone—you want to be connected with your
girlfriend. Just you two in that space for that time and it's your
private thing. And it's happening, the fact that I have this
knowledge inside, "I actually got to do this." That's how it
used to feel—it still does. You come home, you're smiling,
you're glowing. I did this, it happened, it's great.

But even as he said of the orbit he formed with his girlfriend, "I
lose myself in it," he found it important to assert the distinctiveness
of his male self. Ironically, then, for Nick, more than for Tony or
Russ, a kind of inner union with the masculine was *erotic*—just as it
is for gay men. But he had to experience the union with the masculine only within the boundaries of his own body, never through union
with the body of another male. The image of himself in the mirror
was erotic, but not the image of himself with another man. When a
girlfriend wanted to put her finger inside him, his sense of union with
the masculine in himself was threatened, because letting her do it
implied a femininity in himself that he could not accept, along with a
closeness to a masculine other that he could not accept either.

Although our religious tradition and scientific folklore see only
the attraction of opposites as "natural," in the material I have so far
presented in this book, it is possible to see that, psychologically, a
sense of sameness or identification can attract just as powerfully in
male-female relationships as in male-male or female-female relationships. Of the three men depicted in this chapter, Nick's approach to
sex most closely conformed to the institutional culture's model for
male heterosexuality—a dualistic relationship in which clear boundaries are maintained between a self experienced as masculine and
powerful and an other experienced as feminine and submissive. But
Nick also revealed both the fear of femininity in the self and the fear
of homosexuality that is a consequence of that model. The image of
himself with another man was a kind of emotional and visual thinking out loud—a "what if "—focused on the emotional possibility of
bonding with a masculine other. But, for Nick as for many men, the
socially constructed heterosexual role leaves no room for this. I think
this situation gives rise to a paradox in the feelings of many men.
Sharing a valued sense of maleness is a basis for bonding with
another man. But in a system of thought that specifies that the only

conceivable form of erotic bonding is between "opposites"—masculine power and feminine submissiveness—the sense of masculinity of one or both male partners is bound to be endangered as one or the other feels forced into a "feminine," and submissive, role.[5]

Other cultures, however, can offer psychological insights that our own traditions neglect or deny. In contrast to our tendency to polarize feminine and masculine, one of the most striking images in Hindu religious imagery is that of the incarnation of Shiva—one of the three major gods in Hindu thought—as Ardhanarishvara—"the Lord whose half is woman" (see Figure 5.1). In this incarnation, the single form of the deity is divided down the middle, the female breast on one side, a masculine chest on the other side of the body's midline. In Hindu thought, divine power may manifest itself in male or female form, but at the same time, there is a sense in which the power of each is completed by the other. In the incarnation of Shiva as Ardhanarishvara there is no tension of opposition between male and female. Each is distinct in the divine body but, at the same time, it is understood that, at the deepest—or highest—level, male and female are manifestations of an underlying unity into which each is dissolved. This seemed to be close to the model for how Tony and Russ experienced *their* heterosexuality. Associated with it was a recognition that their primary attraction to women was not threatened by a possible sexual potential in their feelings toward men. The dream in which Nick was shocked to see a man in a woman's dress expressed the fear of a feminine component in the male self. However, this dream could be seen not only as a fear, but also as a recognition—not understood by his waking self—of the deeper psychological reality of which the image of the "Lord whose half is woman" is a collective symbol. If this affirmation could somehow be integrated into the consciousness of his waking life, he probably would—like Tony and Russ—still seek fulfillment through bonding with a woman. But the image of the male-to-male bond would, I think, no longer be surrounded by an aura of dread and symbolic emasculation.

FIGURE 5.1. Shiva Ardhanarishvara: "The Lord Whose Half Is Woman"

Source: From the collection of the St. Louis Art Museum. Indian, twelfth century, Chola dynasty. Reprinted with permission.

Chapter 6

Emotional Paths

If "the heterosexual" is a stereotype that fits the ideology of the institutional culture, is the notion of a fixed path of gender development that eventuates in heterosexuality also part of that ideology? The fact that Colin and Alex came to their heterosexuality by radically different developmental paths adds to the evidence that it is.

COLIN

Colin grew up in South Africa. But his religious environment that he was surrounded by in his formative years was not conventional. His mother was interested in Hinduism early on, and then switched to Christian spiritualism, including working with mediums. Referring to Frank, the man I had written about in *Sexuality and the Devil,* Colin said,

> From this vantage point, I can only empathize with Frank's fears to a degree. I grew up believing that the soul is neither male nor female. *I believe that "God" is both sexless and all sexes at the same time.* Our "earthly" sexuality is just a product of our human bodies' genetics and accompanying constructed social environment. Thus, although I subsequently acknowledge whatever sexuality exists within me, I do not really question it, but instead try to accept it and allow it to manifest itself in whatever way it does. In short, I do not think that Christian monotheistic images of evil and good ever haunt me.

Although these views might owe something to the religious milieu in which he was raised, a powerful strain of individuality was also evident in Colin.

Beginning as a baby and continuing into young adulthood, I used to have a series of repetitive dreams of an adult man who would come to visit me in my dreams. Although he never verbally communicated with me, he nonetheless sent me various images. I understood him to be a *guide* and, at the same time, *another incarnation of myself.* Thus, regarding my own response to images of the body, I have always wanted to be the same as the man that visited me in my dreams. The man in my dreams became the ideal male that I wished to emulate. Not only do I judge myself against the ideal male of my dreams, but I also judge all other men and women, that I have come into contact with, against this same ideal as well.

This male image was about six feet two inches—willowy but also muscular. Sometimes he would have clothes that appeared "sprayed on," revealing all of his musculature. At other times, he would have Eastern, or Indian, clothing. Colin understood this man to be a spirit as well as an incarnation of himself. At some point, Colin also realized that, although his body had a male form, this figure was "bisexual" in the sense of being both male and female— as Colin felt he himself was. This spirit-incarnation gave Colin the understanding that *he should not be assimilated into the culture and ways of thinking that surrounded him.* Later, I will return to this spirit-incarnation of Colin's, but here I want to point to the striking parallel between it and the incarnation of Shiva as "the Lord whose half is woman"—an image that Colin might or might not have known about in his childhood.

Somewhat later and in his waking life, Colin was struck, as others discussed in this book were, by one of the artistic master-pieces of our own civilization. "The first work of art that had any kind of arousing 'sexual' effect on me probably was Michelangelo's *David.* I wished to have a physique similar to David's, probably because I both found his body so attractive, and at the same time thought that his (my) body would be attractive to other people as well." In Colin's school, sports were compulsory, and in the course of playing various sports, he had a lot of physical contact with males. He said, "Thus I assumed I must have formed most of my sexual imagery based on male images. As a result, the first time I actually had any 'sexual' physical contact with a girl, at about the age of twelve or thirteen, I was stunned by how fatty, soft, and unmuscular they are. It pretty much disgusted me. I couldn't believe it, and it took quite a while to get used to their morphology." However, he did get used to it and had girlfriends all through high school. He would not have intercourse because he refused to risk creating another human being until he could care for it responsibly. Some girls were intrigued by him for that reason. On the other hand, he had no problem with other forms of sex, including oral sex, which were pleasurable. He said that he had the usual "homosexual" interactions that heterosexual men in the South Africa of that time did—the "patting on the bum" that was common in sports. In that connection, he commented on the irony of the homophobia that was especially prevalent among the "jocks"—who were, incidentally, not necessarily either the best athletes or the best sports.

As an adolescent he found that he could feel attraction for boys as well as for girls, and as an adult found both females and males sexually attractive—although usually gay rather than heterosexual males. He considered himself bisexual, although he had never had any actual male-to-male sexual experiences. Now, in his late twenties, he had been married for eight years and for that reason would not consider a sexual relationship with a man any more than he would with another woman that he found attractive.

Obviously, Colin is an unusual young man. His worldview, while drawing upon elements of Eastern religious thought, nevertheless seems like a highly personal synthesis that has enabled him to transcend many of the cultural constraints of the larger societies— his homeland, Britain, and the United States—in which he has lived. These constraints include the categories of sexual identity and gender that can have such an intimidating effect on feeling, imagination, and thought. He explained his heterosexuality in the following way. "I'm straight because I'm living in a culture where that is the norm and expected. I assume that if I lived in a society where you were expected to be gay, I would be gay."

But even as he acknowledged the influence of the wider culture on his sexual life, he had a sense of inner freedom with respect to his sexual feelings that is clearly unusual for men who have grown up in it.

ALEX

In contrast to Colin's Eastern exoticism, Alex's sexuality had a kind of plain vanilla quality—which is not to say it was bland, but rather that the path to his heterosexuality seemed to conform much more closely to the route our culture envisages for men. His earliest memories of what he could now describe as sexual attraction were from the age of eight. "I liked being with them [girls] or the attention they gave me. We didn't do much but when I wasn't with them sometimes I found myself thinking about them. That was the attraction. Usually just thinking about being alone with them, and kissing, and things like that, although I'd never done it before. That was really the extent of it."

He remembered his friendships at that age with both boys and girls, with girls having a slight edge. One of his best friends was a neighborhood girl he had grown up with:

> I had lots of interests—baseball, stickball, sports, football, soccer. I went to the park regularly with friends, and played stickball, Wiffle ball, even with my father and brother. With girls, or with the larger group on the block, we would sometimes play fantasy games, for example, the "Six Million Dollar Man." I'd pretend to be the bionic man, role-playing like that. I always had an interest in horror films—Frankenstein, Dracula, Wolfman, cowboy films too. I also had an interest in "phenomena"—Bigfoot, the Loch Ness Monster, UFOs. A big game too, would be to hang out late—until nine o'clock, when it was dark. We would think, "What if there was someone watching us?" This was with both boys and girls, but a lot of it was with my good friend who was a girl. With the bionic man thing, she might be the bionic woman. Or you would make believe you were part of secret agent service—girls would play that role as much as boys.
>
> With boys there was physically more of a rough playing around. Emotionally, there was caring and friendship, but I wasn't as open with them as with girls. Now, I have very close friends that I can be very open with, but even now, generally speaking, I do tend to be more open with women. At least, there's more of a comfort level there. [Earlier] I would have

liked to be alone with them. I thought about kissing them. There was a *deeper feeling*, a desire to be more with them—when I was in these moods—than with guys. I can think of a few girls in elementary school that I liked. I was more "touchy-feely" with them too. A guy you might jump around with, play football with. I remember wrestling and things like that—who knows what that means at a subconscious level? But with women, I'd like putting my arm around them, a more gentle approach, and I'd enjoy doing it.

What emerges from Alex's reminiscences is a picture of a child who had friends and enjoyed playmates of both sexes. But his feelings toward girls were already being distinguished from those toward his male friends in a number of ways. He would daydream about being alone with a girl. Emotionally, these daydreams included a greater openness and a deeper feeling than he had with any boy, a feeling that seemed to move toward expression through the body—putting an arm around her, kissing her. Although on balance, he recalled sharing more interests and hobbies with his male friends, emotionally he referred to a greater openness with females.

It's even true today, partially—*initially*—not once I get to know a person. I was probably more revealing about my feelings, like being more upset about something, feelings that at that age, I guess, are more restricted among the male group—I don't want to get mixed up with labels here like "the masculine side" or "feminine side." I said something about that in one of my papers and you made an interesting comment: "Why do we have to associate those sides with sexuality?" I really don't but sometimes you can't escape that when you use the label. But for those feelings—that might be attributed to a quote-unquote "feminine side" that men don't usually tend to reveal—like being very upset because a pet or a family member died—I was probably more revealing of in front of a girl, rather than a guy.

In thinking about the relation between sexuality and emotion, it was interesting to hear Alex's recollections about the relation between emotion and the physical in his relationships to boys and girls

as he was growing up. He had mentioned wrestling with a male
friend, but putting his arm around a girl. That particular gesture did
not come up with another boy. He described the emotional meaning
embedded in it.

> Closeness, a bit of fantasy—being alone, doing things in pri-
> vate, where she is the main focus of my attention, or me of
> hers. Then, just the physical attraction. I might not have
> known much about sex, but there was the desire to hold her, to
> kiss her, even if it didn't happen. [With male friends] it was
> just playing around, your adrenaline was rushing, it's fun
> wrestling, letting go of everything. We used to have a lot of
> wrestling matches in the backyard or in school. It was a differ-
> ent feeling, you didn't have that feeling of necessarily wanting
> attention. It was just a matter of having no boundaries set upon
> us. If someone gets hurt, no one is going to tell us to stop. You
> can run around, destroy things while you're doing it. It's a
> form of closeness, I guess you could say, because I wouldn't
> have felt so comfortable wrestling with someone I didn't know
> as friend. But when I was wrestling with a boy, I didn't feel the
> *emotion*—maybe it's a hormonal activity or something like
> that—the *desire*—it's very hard to describe. My hand around a
> girl—there might have been some anxiety there—but it was a
> relaxed, soothing, comforting feeling. A different kind of
> adrenaline rushing through your system, where your heart
> beats a little faster, and it's kind of like a high. There's a great
> difficulty putting a word to it. I remember how I felt, the
> *physical* signs, my heart rushing and so on, but I can't think of
> a term that could describe the feeling. It's kind of mind-bog-
> gling—*there are no words.*

I said to Alex that, although it was not his word, the image of his
putting his arm around a girl brought the word "tenderness" to
mind. He said, "I think you're right, I do. When I was with a girl,
along with that, there was a feeling of 'Wow, I'd like to have or do
this again!'—whereas when I was wrestling with a boy, that wasn't
there. I felt in a much more tender, sensitive position with a woman.
Maybe the sense that my feelings were better absorbed, more appreciated."

The terms "masculine" and "feminine" did not mean a lot to him. He said, "I recognize what would be a feminine trait in a man or masculine in [a] woman, but I think we all have many of the attributes labeled masculine or feminine in each and every one of us." He added, "Generally I don't see myself as having masculine or feminine sides. I see myself as one entity." But although his masculinity was not an issue for Alex, it was important that he be the focus of a woman's attention as well as she being the focus of his.

> I'd like to think that there's something in me that she's never experienced before or that is unique to her or that really appreciates. But initially and strongly it's a sexual thing. I think of her attention to me in my physical appearance or my performance during sexual intercourse or something like that. You want her to know your body as well as you know hers and to appreciate it, as well as vice versa.

In a sexual relationship, the sense of a woman's "femaleness" coupled with the sense of his "maleness" could sometimes be erotic, without having the intense meaning that it had for Nick.

> It's not consciously true all the time. The idea of me being a male, whatever that represents, and her being a female, whatever that represents—and that's hard to describe in words—is definitely part of it sometimes. Some of the things I'd tend to attribute to the male, or to the masculine side, would be the attribute of power or dominance. When I did play the dominant role in intercourse, there was more a sense of "I'm the male and she's the female." But I don't always feel I'm in a dominant position, or that either one is. And there are times when the woman has been in the dominant position and that literally becomes part of the turn-on.

Zack, a gay man about whom I will have a great deal more to say later, had said to me at one point, "I'm attracted to myself." I quoted this to Alex and asked him if he would say that about himself. "In a way yes, I'm attracted to myself. I can understand that. It's hard to describe what that means. . . . I feel confident in myself, proud . . . yes, I see myself in an attractive aspect. I guess you can say I'm attracted to myself." Alex had male friends and recognized a special dimension in these relationships.

> In male friendships, interests parallel. There is something about men and what they represent, so that most men like to have male friends, and don't only want female friends. With male friends there's a certain bond there that might represent something. Maybe because you see someone as you see yourself. Now you're interacting with some [one] who is the same as you, the same initial group, of the male species.

THE ONE-TO-ONE BOND

Nevertheless, there was a dimension of closeness that he did not seem to need to experience with a man—an intense, one-to-one bond. That desire was directed toward a woman. Hence, it was the image of the female that he felt himself "moving toward." It was a female that, from the age of eight, he had fantasies of being alone with. This seemed to be the core of his attraction to women, rather than to men. Not needing that intense, one-to-one bond seemed to explain why he did not feel attraction to men. When I expressed this to Alex, he qualified what I had said further.

> I can only say that those feelings and desires just aren't there to trigger something with males as they are with a woman. But furthermore, feelings of *dis*attraction are there with a male, and I don't know where they might come from. I could simply say I'm not attracted to a male physically, but I could also say that I'm—not repulsed, that's ridiculous—maybe *repelled*, like in a magnet—to feeling that way about another male.

"To *feeling* that way," I said, "that's an interesting term." He started to correct himself, but I told him not to take back what he had spontaneously uttered.

> *Feeling* that way, yes. Feeling a sexual attraction, a desire to be with male as I am with a woman. But I *don't* mean "feeling" that way, I mean "sexual attraction." I'm pretty objective,

really. I can kid around with guys, joke, but I don't feel that attraction, and even imagining it, imagining the attraction and thinking about being with a man as with a woman, I feel repelled, "disattracted."

As Alex spoke of this, he seemed to separate feeling from sexual attraction. I think this reflects the split between sexuality—conceived of as physical only—and feelings that is part of this culture's thinking about sexuality.

Having in mind Colin's description of how he had initially felt repulsed by the soft bodies of girls, and how some women had told me of their initial shock at the sight of a penis, I said to Alex that, with someone of the opposite sex, there is, on the face of it, a greater difference between one's own body and the body of the other. Conceivably that could give rise to a feeling that the other is alien. But with one's own sex, the similarity is there to start with. From that perspective, I said, it was almost more difficult to understand logically the feeling of "disattraction" or of being repelled by one's own sex. He agreed. "It is. Because when you asked, I could truly say that I feel attracted to myself. But it's ironic, because I sincerely feel that I'm *dis*attracted to another male. It's a paradox."

Alex readily acknowledged that he could look at and admire another man's looks or build. He knew when a man was attractive, but when it came to moving toward him to feel—using Alex's word—with him what he felt with a woman, the sense of disattraction arose. Could it be, I said to him, that the body of the man was not the problem, but rather that the issue revolved around feelings, that there were certain emotions that he wanted to have with a female member of the human race, and not with most male members of the species? He asked, "You want to know why that might be?" Then went on,

> Honestly, I don't know that it's an intimidation in feeling. I just know that there is something, a desire there that I feel I might want to experience with a woman that I don't want to experience with a male. A range of feelings—closeness, tenderness, openness—I'm tending to focus on the sexual side because that's where the difference lies, in that sexual aspect and, of course, the whole range of emotions that go with that.

> They're so hard to describe—those feelings. Whatever that
> feeling is, my desire is to share that with a woman. That
> feeling can only be attained through a woman. Like there
> really is no option, I wouldn't have that same feeling, that
> same high with a man. So then, the question almost answers
> itself.

The cultural prohibitions against homosexuality probably played
a role in Alex's sense of disattraction toward sex with another man,
even though he was not homophobic. But if sex expresses the need
for emotional bonding, then his disattraction to sex with a man
could also reflect the "mismatch" between the body of a man and
his need to experience that emotional bonding with a woman. A
young woman told me of another kind of mismatch—her marriage
to her kind and loving husband. Try as she might, she never enjoyed
sex with him very much and finally had to acknowledge the need
for a woman that she had tried to suppress, and to leave her marriage. Even when the sex of the partner is "right" but the emotions
are not, sex can be a problem. More than one man has described
having trouble coming to orgasm with a woman he did not have any
feeling for.

Alex was one of the last people I talked to in my research for this
book. Because he also had just completed my graduate course, I felt
able to run past him some of the ideas I had been formulating. I said
one school of thought would say that, from boyhood onward, Alex
had been forming male identifications and was, as a consequence,
attracted to females. But looking back at it, did he think that his
initial attraction to females depended on the sense of himself as a
male, or did he think that his attraction to females was an independent dimension of feeling? He said,

> I'm more inclined to think it's a more independent circum-
> stance, or choice. There were periods when I was younger
> when I had many female friends. There were some periods,
> not very long, when I was not hanging out with other males
> from school, but I still was involved with female friends. *So
> there were periods when male bonding was not in place, yet I*

still found myself attracted to women. I think it's more of an independent choice, if choice is a proper word to use.

One could think of Alex's heterosexual development as moving toward a female—a "moving toward" whose aim was the experience of one-to-one closeness to a girl and later to a woman. Initially, it expressed itself in a feeling—wanting to be alone with a girl, wanting her attention—and then moved toward expressing itself through the body, wanting to put his arm around her and to kiss her—wanting to close the gap between his body and hers. He was hard-pressed to find a word for the emotion embodied in that wish. It seemed to be defined by imagery and movement rather than language. However, he agreed that "tenderness" might describe it. It was only later, as the changes of adolescence worked their hormonal magic of physical amplification on these emotions, that this "moving toward" expressed itself in the fantasy of seeing a female nude. When I remarked on this sequence of psychological events to Alex, he agreed that it was definitely true.

COMPARISONS WITH GAY MEN

The first part of Andrew Sullivan's *Virtually Normal* is an account of the emergence of his male-directed feelings. He recalled one of the earliest stirrings of what he called, looking back at them, "homosexual emotions":

> I remember vividly—perhaps I was five or six—being seated in the back of a car with my second cousin, a tousle-headed, wide-grinned kid a few years older, and being suddenly unwittingly entranced by him. It was a feeling I had never felt before, the first inkling of a yearning that was only to grow stronger as the years went by.[1]

> Looking back, this inchoate ache was all that I knew of the homosexual experience. But I knew also, because of the absence of any mention of the subject, because of the lack of any tangible visible reflections of it in the world around me, that there was something wrong with it.[2]

> Maybe I should be clearer here. The longing was not sexual. I
> was too young to feel any explicit sexual desire. I had no idea
> what an expression of sexual love might be. So far as I can
> remember it, it was a desire to unite with another: not to
> possess, but to join in some way; not to lose myself, but to be
> given dimension. At the same time, I also had fantasies of
> being part of some boys' gang, or a rock group—some institu-
> tion that could legitimately incorporate the half-understood
> half-felt emotions that were filtering through my system.[3]

Eventually, the longing for physical contact emerged into his
awareness and became more intense and explicit. But it seems to me
that it was the longing for an emotional tie that preceded and gave
shape, direction, and meaning to the longing for the physical. Although he had female friends, and his first "explicit sexual fond-
lings" were with girls, he recalled:

> . . . I had no longing to unite with them, didn't even want to
> talk to them much. I preferred hanging out with boys, traipsing
> through the neighboring woods with them, forming secret
> clubs, cycling around nearby lanes, playing childhood chase
> games (and in much of this, I guess, I was indistinguishable
> from any other boy). I was, in other words, virtually normal.[4]

Eventually, the pressure of the wish "to unite with" another male
became inescapable and, as it did, the mind created images of the
body—as it inevitably does—to clothe that wish.

I see only a few differences in Andrew Sullivan's account of his
homosexuality and the same-sex feelings of men who identify
themselves as heterosexual. But these differences have little or
nothing to do with the quality of the feelings. The primary difference is one of timing—the emotions he described began earlier than
they did for the majority of the heterosexually identified men. The
other differences are in intensity. His feelings for girls—or later on,
women—never matched those for males in their intensity, and his
feelings for men had more urgency than did those of most of the
men in Chapter 4. What Andrew Sullivan and the men in Chapter 4
seemed to share was the deep emotional tie with another man that
moved toward expressing itself through the body.

The parallels between the sequence of feelings described by Alex and those described by Andrew Sullivan are striking, down to the age—eight—at which the first inkling of what Andrew Sullivan labeled "yearning" was recalled. Alex's wish to be alone with a girl was an expression of the desire for the one-to-one bond that was later to find embodiment in explicit sexual desire, just as Andrew Sullivan's yearning toward his cousin was an early harbinger of his later sexual longings. If it lacked the imagery of the kiss that was present in Alex's fantasy, it was, perhaps, only because, as he put it, there were no "tangible reflections" of that imagery in the male-to-male world with which he was familiar. For both Andrew Sullivan and Alex, these memories were their first recollections of the emotional "moving toward" that would guide the trajectories of their sexual lives. Although both boys had male friends, the sense of their own masculinity did not seem to consciously enter the thoughts of either boy as the basis for his feelings. For each boy, the focus of that movement was on the other person rather than on the self—a male person for Andrew Sullivan, a female for Alex.

Writer Ron Caldwell has written of his experiences in *Boys Like Us* when a collection of coming-out stories by gay writers.[5] Coming when they did, the series of dialogues between Ron and me were particularly helpful as I was trying to formulate some of the key ideas for this book. As part of those dialogues, Ron described his memories of the process of "moving toward" that culminated in the recognition that it was men who would be at the center of his emotional and sexual life. As with Andrew Sullivan and Alex, his sexual orientation had its origins in an "emotional orientation." Like many boys, his earliest memory of friendship involved another boy. Although his memories included friendships with girls, the most emotionally vivid memory of his early years had to do with other boys:

> At the age of two, Barry was the first playmate I had and at thirty-three years old, I still remember being in the room with him, and being interested in him, probably no differently from the way that all children seem to be fascinated with each other. Whether that has any sexual component or not, I don't know. If I move up in time, I can remember us being encouraged to play with each other while our mothers talked.

In school there was one girl in particular, a kind of tomboy, and then another girl I played Barbie dolls with. Then—having normal workaday friendships with other guys, being in a little group of four or five, nerdy, witty little guys who were always chasing girls and kissing them, competing with each other but really being quite close.

At the age of seven, these happy memories of bonding with his male friends were interrupted.

I feel if I'd stayed in Houston, I would have been okay—not that I would have been straight—but we moved away from this extremely prosperous neighborhood in Houston to the boondocks, and I never recovered. From then on, I felt like an outsider. I started searching for this one friend that would save me, love me, and wouldn't think I was a misfit—I'd find some boy that I thought was really special. As I got a little older, they got better and better looking. By the time I got to high school it had a huge sexual component. And then I'd go to Boy Scout camp, and there were naked boys all over the place.

By the time Alex had entered early adolescence, he was aware of the sexual nature of his responses to girls' bodies. These feelings were not hard to understand because they were synchronous with cultural expectations. On the other hand, a boy's understanding that he is having sexual feelings about other *males* may dawn considerably later, since it is out of sync with the expectations he is taught to have and, until very recently, with publicly available models for romantic and sexual love. His confusion can be compounded by the double message he sometimes gets from the culture and his peers—"boys don't feel that way—but *you* do." This accusation can add further incentive to distance himself from these feelings as well as undermining his sense of himself as a male. Ron's early adolescent years reflected this confusion.

I don't know. I can't believe that things can be that unclear. I'm sure I was fantasizing about guys when I was masturbating at the age of thirteen or fourteen . . . it's pretty foggy. I had these romantic feelings for girls—I always wanted to have a

girlfriend too. My fantasies about them would be very complicated, and very domestic, and hardly sexual at all. Even when
I was going out with girls in college, I don't remember fantasizing about them, though when presented with one in the
flesh, I was perfectly happy to have sex with her—and I don't
remember fantasizing about men while I was doing that.

It seemed that though he liked the company of women, could
daydream about them, and enjoyed sex with them, it was the image
of men, I remarked to Ron, that ultimately had the power to fire his
imagination. He agreed.

Yeah, definitely. As far as I remember about having clear fantasies, I would fantasize about couples. But someone pointed out
to me—at twenty or twenty-one—that I was really thinking
about the man. The watershed was when I was going out with a
woman and fell in love with a man—that was the last time I had
a relationship with a woman. Before that, the interest in another
man fell under the rubric of friendship, and the desire for that
was very intense on my part. If I look at it from where I am
now, a huge component of it was physical attraction. I can trace
that back, and it becomes more and more vague as I go further
back. But I can never remember a time when I wasn't possessed
of some kind of interest like that—in another man—*and in
having him intensely focused on me and interested in me with
the same kind of passion that I had for him.*

As in the case of both Alex and Andrew Sullivan, the trajectory
of Ron's emotional life began with the emotional bonds of friendship. As he got older, he had playmates of both sexes, just like Alex.
But of the available bonds with boys or girls, he found himself
looking to reinforce, deepen, and extend the bonds with boys,
whereas Alex did this with girls. For both Alex and Ron, as brain
and body began to mature at adolescence, the emotional need for
closeness and bonding—to girls for Alex and to boys for Ron—was
automatically linked to images of female and male bodies. The
"sexual orientation" of each—heterosexual for Alex and gay for
Ron—was simply the awareness of this link.

In contrast to Alex, Andrew Sullivan, and Ron, Colin early on identified himself as both male and female—as he had identified the spirit-incarnation of his dreams. But like Alex, he was conscious of his own body and wanted it be an attractive male body in the same way that Michelangelo's famous sculpture was. The only man Alex felt attracted to was himself. But Colin, who was, like Alex, a well-built and good-looking man, could sense an attraction to other men as well. Hence, he considered himself bisexual. However, he was to all intents and purposes as heterosexual in his life as Alex, since he sought emotional satisfaction in a one-to-one bond with a woman. Andrew Sullivan and Ron Caldwell sought it with a man.

A careful look at the lives of individual men will reveal no fixed path of development that could be said to characterize all heterosexual men or all gay men—or all bisexual men. Nor is there any factor that can reliably differentiate the men our culture has categorized in these ways, except for the difference in the emotional bonds that each moves toward strengthening. And the movement along these differing emotional paths is not a conscious decision of the "I" that thinks in language, but is rather a movement of the "inner I"—a movement that reflects an interactive relationship with the world, not a reflexive response to any given set of life circumstances or to any roll of the genetic dice.[6]

PSYCHOLOGICAL ROCK BOTTOM

In noting this inner movement—whether toward male or female—we may have reached the limits of explanation because we have reached psychological rock bottom, which is that we are programmed biologically and emotionally to move toward other human beings. The end result of that movement, touching—coming into contact with the body of another—is the logical fulfillment of that emotion, which can sometimes be described in words, but sometimes only in terms of the body. "It's mind-boggling," Alex said, "there are no words."

Our religious, political, and even scientific institutions have asserted that to move toward another of the same sex is "against nature"—or, as Nick said, "like it was set up that way—by whoever you want to say, God or the cosmos . . . ." But an unbiased examination of individuals' emotions and lives leads to a quite different conclusion, which is that both male and female are emotionally compelling in their own right. Like twin stars, each emits a light and a beauty that is capable of eliciting the emotion in both sexes that seeks expression through the body and in the "moving toward" that we know as sexual attraction.

Chapter 7

Identity Crises

In this chapter, I look at three men who, in different ways, crossed the identity boundaries set up by the institutional culture. This crossing went beyond fantasy or experimentation as each passed through a series of emotional crises at different stages of their lives. At different stages and in different ways they found themselves moving toward one sex or the other. The concern with identity—imposed from the outside—complicated but did not measurably help them in their search to understand their own experience or find emotional fulfillment in their lives. It merely added another element—an identity crisis—to the emotional problems they were trying to solve.

JOHNNY

I met Johnny about a year before his release from the treatment institution where he had served sixteen years for rape.[1] During the latter part of his sentence, he had begun to work very hard in the therapy programs offered by the institution. It was clear that he had thought long and hard about what had led him, as a very young man, to commit the crimes that had resulted in his imprisonment. Now thirty-six years of age, he had virtually grown up in jail. Facing the prospect of a much-longed-for release, he was honest enough to recognize his anxiety about leaving a place that had become the only home he had known for over a decade and a half. He was grateful for the help he had been given and was determined to make a decent life for himself. He said, "If I do it again, I deserve all the time they give me and don't deserve to come back here."

As a mature man of thirty-six, Johnny condemned what he had done as a youth and felt deeply for his victims. He had also struggled very hard to understand why he had done those things in order to make sure that they would never recur. He recognized his good fortune in being at an institution dedicated to protecting the public he might otherwise be a danger to by helping him to change those dangerous elements within himself. However, I did not initially ask to talk to Johnny because he had been convicted of rape. Rather, it was because his therapist told me that, in the course of therapy, he had come to feel that he was bisexual.

Johnny was the youngest of three children in what could be accurately described as a seriously dysfunctional family. His mother chose to leave when he was eight years old. For a long time, he did not know where she was. His father, who did know, would not let him see her until Johnny was in the hospital five years later, almost having been killed by contact with a high-tension electric wire. His father was an alcoholic who, ironically, never missed a day of work. He was also punitive and beat his son without restraint until Johnny stopped showing any reaction. For a while, his father was also in jail. During that period Johnny was taken care of by his grandparents. The grandparents came from the South, and his grandfather liberally enforced biblical morality with a switch. By age ten or eleven, he discovered an antidote to his unhappiness in solitary sex. "Anytime I felt down or depressed, I'd go masturbate. I got all my pleasure from masturbation. When my father was away, I got into his movies and magazines. These were just stag magazines, not bondage or anything."

At age sixteen, a significant event occurred in Johnny's life. It involved his stepbrother, who was in his late twenties, the son of his father's second wife:

> I was laying in bed one night and I felt him nudge the bed, I guess to see if I was awake. I played asleep. What he did was to get in bed with me. I was awake, but I was very afraid of him. He got into bed. He lay down in back of me. I was facing the wall. He started fondling me. He put his arm around me. He had pulled my underwear down. While he was fondling me, he moved my leg up and stuck his penis in my butt. It

really didn't hurt the first time. At one point, there was fear, but when he started masturbating me and fondling me, it started feeling good, and that that's when I started to relax, to like it. So I figured, what the hell do I have to be afraid of? Once I started to relax, that's when he started to penetrate me, and it really didn't hurt. Initially it did, but very brief[ly] and after that I started to enjoy it. While he was doing that he was still masturbating me. I'm pretty sure he came the first time and so did I—that just increased the guilt even more. There was one time he allowed me to do it to him. *Out of all three or four times there was not [a] word spoken.* I used to talk to him before this. From the first time, to the present day, I've never spoken one word to him, nor him to me. Once it happened the first time, all communication stopped. I had seen him at my father's wake in eighty-four or eighty-five and there wasn't anything said then.

There was a couple of times after the first time, when I actually laid in bed awake, hoping he would come back over. I didn't attribute it to being intimate or anything like that, but through that there was a part I was getting fulfilled—something I wasn't getting fulfilled in the rest of my life—that softness, the attention, the care, because through that there was a feeling that he cared. Even though I knew that it was wrong, in another realm it was still nice. I never thought of having sex with my father, but it was like part of something I wished I was getting from my father—the tenderness, closeness. I never got it from anyone, unless I did when I was younger and I don't remember.

Until this happened, Johnny's sexual fantasies had been about women only. However, the first time he himself performed intercourse with anyone, it was not with a woman, but his stepbrother. This too happened in silence.

He went through the regular routine of getting into bed, but this time, he got me to roll over first, then he rolled over, and positioned himself to the point where I didn't have to do anything. He was laying on his side, and slid closer to me. Once I was in, I started to make the regular motions. Through all that

there was not a word spoken. I still wonder about that sometimes. . . .

Although no words were spoken, Johnny felt something was being
communicated to him. He felt that

> . . . he cared, liked me. It was the hugging that went on in the
> process. He didn't just lay behind me and fuck me and that was
> it. The one time he masturbated me to orgasm. The other
> times, he would have his arms around me, like holding me.
> That contributed to the good feelings—the holding I never got
> from my father. I don't remember, before the past couple of
> years, hearing my mother tell me that she loved me. Some-
> times that's still a surprise when I hear her say it on the phone.
> I never remember hearing my father say that. . . .

When Johnny first told me about what happened with his stepbrother, he referred to it as a rape. It is true that he felt some fear at
the beginning. But fear did not seem to be an important factor later
as he lay in bed, hoping his stepbrother would come to him again.
Many gay men report that their earliest sexual feelings and fantasies
are directed toward males. In contrast, during masturbation Johnny
had peopled his inner world with females. Like most boys growing
up in this culture, however, he had been exposed to and internalized
the fear and condemnation attached to homosexuality. From his
grandparents he had learned that it was immoral. "You aren't supposed to enjoy things like that—you'll burn in hell." Johnny's
grandparents were not Catholic, but it is striking that these were
precisely the same words that Will had used in describing what his
Catholic education had taught about the penalty for sex with another man. I asked Johnny if he had any concept of bisexuality back
then, or were people simply straight or gay? He said, "It wasn't
'gay,' it was people were 'fags' or 'homosexuals.' They were dirty.
As soon as it happened, I went right into it. I was dirty, no good, a
fag, homosexual. People like that were people you didn't care for.
They were sick, demented."

When Johnny says that he and his stepbrother had no communication, he meant, of course, communication in words. But everything he says about the experience confirms that communication of

a very powerful sort passed between them. It was communication through the body, in the language of the body—"there are no words," Alex said. Yet, what did it mean that, after the first encounter, not a single word ever passed between them again? It seems that they had done something unspeakable. It could literally not be spoken about because the only words they could use were ones that their culture gave them—"fag, dirty, demented."

In my conversations with Johnny nothing emerged to suggest that he had been unknowingly repressing a "homosexual wish" that was somehow cordoned off from consciousness. Nonetheless, he was aware of a boundary—an external, cultural boundary. He had understood the language of contempt and derision that people used to talk about those who crossed it. And now he had crossed it. After the encounters with his stepbrother, he began to have a recurrent dream:

> I don't remember what the person was doing, but I was fighting to get up. There was a feeling of someone holding me down and a feeling in my body, like jerking, trying to get up. But I couldn't wake up.

The imagery of the dream graphically captures the conflict that Johnny was feeling about what had happened to him. In the dream someone is holding him down, and that someone must have been his stepbrother. But the other force holding him down was Johnny's own feelings—the part of him that, as he lay in bed, wished his stepbrother would return.

Until that time, during solitary sex, he had imagined being with a woman. But the experience with his stepbrother opened a door for him—a door to a place within himself where men could find intimacy, consolation, and closeness with each other. Once opened, the door was left ajar. Had he not found the emotional part of the experience fulfilling, surely he would have found a way of avoiding any future sexual encounters. But—paradoxically—Johnny's culture characterized what he had found with his stepbrother in feminine terms. Thus, Johnny could not avoid seeing what he had done in those terms.

As soon as I started to enjoy it *I felt I was more of a woman than a man.* That's where a lot of conflicts came in. I thought that, just in walking down the street, people could pick that up. What reinforced that was being picked up by a man in a sports car. I thought that, if he didn't see it, he wouldn't have tried to get me in the situation. At first, he just wanted directions. He asked if I would mind showing him the way. I got in. He didn't touch me in the car, but talked about a friend who had an apartment that we could use. I don't recall if the conversation turned sexual or not. But once we got to the apartment, it became sexual. I really didn't know what I was doing. He was masturbating and when he got ready he told me to put my mouth over his dick. When I did, he ejaculated in my mouth and that didn't taste good at all. So, when he was getting ready to leave, I spit it out behind the radiator. I'm pretty sure that I ejaculated in his mouth too. That experience left me feeling even more that someone could just look at me and think that *there's* a person who's having sex with other men. That bothered me for a long time.

Following the episodes with his stepbrother, he had his first intercourse with a woman just before his seventeenth birthday. Although before his stepbrother the images in his fantasies were only about women, he now found that the image of a man would come into his mind sometimes, and he would try to push it out. In spite of himself, he would think of penetrating his stepbrother while his stepbrother was inside a woman or having his stepbrother penetrate him. Every time he imagined such a scene he would feel like "a piece of shit, different, sick, special." He thought no one would understand. He would ask himself, "How can I be here having sex with a woman and thinking about a man at the same time?" Sometimes he would go away and cry by himself. If he cried in front of others he would have been called "sissy, fag."

The experience with his stepbrother was one that he had never had before or even imagined. It pulled his emotions along as it connected with the fabric of his life. It took Johnny to a place he had never been before, a place of special feeling and meaning. It was an experience of the body that took him to what he now saw had been a sacred place. Almost twenty years later, he said, "Even though me and my stepbrother didn't have any communication or anything like that, he was fulfilling something in me . . . at the time I didn't know what. And even though it was in a sexual way, he was paying attention to me, *he was showing me almost what I considered a sacred part of life. It's something that everyone in life doesn't share. I look back and see it that way now.*"

In common usage, "taboo" means forbidden, but in the Polynesian culture that gave us the word, it connoted the sacred as well, the sacred that it was forbidden to approach. Johnny said that his stepbrother had shown him a "sacred" part of life, in the sense of being both sacred and forbidden. However, in the world that Johnny and his stepbrother knew, only the forbidden part was spoken aloud or thought about in words. The sense of sacredness was expressed through the body and experienced through the intensity of arousal and orgasm. They had no words to speak about it, and perhaps none to help them think about it—even in the privacy of their own minds. Nevertheless, although between them the language of the body could not be translated into words, the ecstasy of the flesh in orgasm appeared to signify to both man and boy some deeper ecstasy of the spirit.

CARL

The relation between emotion and image, the relation between the need for love and sexual attraction, and the meaning of identity and the capacity for movement across its boundaries converge in Carl's history. Carl was in his mid-thirties when I first met him. He had been married for more than ten years. Yet he spent three years—between the ages of sixteen and nineteen—in a relationship with a man eleven years his senior. In his early years he recalled, as had Alex, having some sense of attraction to girls. "I have a distinct memory at about five, playing on the block. There were two girls about my age. They did something, like they stuck their backsides out. It struck me very powerfully. But it was only some years later that I said 'Wow.' I remembered that dance, or whatever it was. I could say it was sexual, in retrospect."

He also remembered a fantasy that he had about one particular girl when he was seven years old. In it, the town they lived in was flooded out and he was alone with her in a kayak, playing the role of her protector. The feeling in this fantasy was that of "an embracing, a closeness." Later he would be able to put the word "attraction" to this feeling. Similarly, he had a certain feeling toward some of his male friends between the ages of nine and fourteen. "A sense of wanting something that I didn't know what it was exactly. A wanting and a curiosity. It certainly wasn't verbal. In trying to relive it, seemed almost physical and located in my chest . . . very amorphous."

However, at age eleven he had an experience that was both explicitly sexual and very frightening. "I had been in bed at the time just ruminating, when suddenly out of the blue this struck me—it was overtly sexual, like being hit in the face with a sexual picture—very explicit." The image that struck Carl—and he quite deliberately chose "struck" to describe the quality of the experience—was that of a man, his church choir director—naked. Instantly, there came the thought, "Oh my God, I'm homosexual." And on its heels came another thought, "I can't be." Carl had learned about sex with the help of books supplied by his parents, and by the age of ten he felt the wish for sexual intercourse with a female. This wish, though a bit precocious, was something that was consistent with the conscious sense of "I" that he had already formed. The image of his choir director was also his creation, but because the "I" part of himself that lived in culture already understood its prohibitions, it had the quality of coming to him "out of the blue"—from outside himself. At the same time—and this seems significant—his first ejaculation, somewhere between ages eleven and thirteen, was through a nocturnal emission. The dream image that accompanied it was that of "a beautiful mermaid in a glittering sea."

Carl's first sexual experience with another person was not by choice. As with Johnny, an older stranger in a car stopped Carl. He explained that he was lost.

> I helped him find the street. He invited me in and bolted the door. I assumed that my life was being erased at this point. But I was instead accosted and orally sodomized. I thought I was

going to be decapitated, so it was something of a relief that he just wanted sex. I was given a lift back and a five-dollar bill for my trouble. I tried to talk about this violation with my first girlfriend, but she was too busy praying during a church service.

Although he was very upset about this experience at the time, he later realized that every time he put on the pants that he had worn on the day of that incident, he would feel some sexual stirrings. At the time, he did not realize the connection. As an adult Carl felt that this incident had not had any long-term effects. He said, "It was traumatic at the time, but it has very little bearing on what I am today." But another incident was more significant. The choir director whose image had so suddenly appeared to him was a man between thirty and forty. Carl said that this man had become something of a father figure to him. But he was a kind of accepting and permissive father that most adolescents do not have.

He made himself very available. He was willing to sit down and listen to my problems. He let me smoke and smoked with me, and he made coffee for me. At the time I was stealing records, and I was able to bring them over, tell him about it, and play them. He was a very accepting and open kind of guy. A year or two into this relationship, he stood up and embraced me, which was atypical. He said, "What's the matter, did you think I was going to touch you?" He made it almost a challenge to accept—"What are you afraid of?"—and at the same time, "How dare you be afraid?" It was a very subtle thing. It led to his fondling me. I'm not sure about the specifics, but he fondled me, took out his penis, and tried to masturbate me while he masturbated himself. He was unable to bring me to orgasm, but he had an orgasm. I think that happened one more time and I just stopped going there.

Carl was fifteen at the time. At first, he saw this incident as "par for the course, like this is what's happening." He also realized that he was not the only boy who had been approached in this way, because the choir director told Carl that "'So-and-so' liked to get high while I played with his penis." In retrospect Carl felt taken advantage of and told some of his choirmates about what had happened, with some sense that what had been done to him was not proper. But, he said, "He [the choir director] was very charismatic, affable, ebullient, very beloved by the congregation. My choirmates literally said, 'No, it didn't happen.'"

Home life was unhappy for Carl. He was the firstborn of three in a marriage where the parents had stayed together solely "for the children." He took the brunt of much of his mother's unhappiness, with his father usually backing her or being harsh toward Carl himself. At the age of sixteen, Carl met a man of twenty-seven, Al, through a mutual friend. He took an interest in Carl at a low point in his life.

> I had taken an overdose of aspirin before moving out with him. He came, took me out, talked with me all night. Much like the choir director—he was concerned and everything. He made me feel complete in a way. I didn't have much love in my family. The idea of love helped me transcend that and to become a different person in a sense. It was a very powerful feeling. The first thing good about it was its reciprocity. There was something coming back at me. I had gone out with a girl for a month at fourteen, but she was kind of cold and strange. He was really interested in me, showed a lot of concern.

This love and concern seemed to draw forth a powerful response from Carl. But there were some paradoxes in Carl's feelings. Al had an extensive collection of male pornography that Carl enjoyed, and he thought a lot about men sexually. But in spite of his responsiveness to male images, he did not want to be a gay male. He told himself, "I'm a heterosexual person, but I'm in love with a man." Al was African-American, worldly, self-assured, and attractive. But the relationship was not without its problems. Al could be physically abusive, especially when he drank. Between four and six times during each year they were together, he would fly into a rage and pummel Carl. He was also "uptight" sexually. Mostly, sex was mutual masturbation, with some oral sex, and occasional anal intercourse, always Al performing it on Carl. He would never let Carl penetrate him. However, the side of Carl that was drawn to women remained.

> I remained interested in women and I began to fear that I'd die without ever being with one. I had this intense longing and the sense that I was not going to be with them. I started hanging around with some heterosexual guys nearby. They had female pictures on the walls, and magazines. I was attracted to that. I would see their girlfriends and be envious. I went out with a girl one time, even though I was in middle of this. I wanted to be with her, but ended up going back with Al for another year and a half.

While he was still with Al, Carl met Michelle, the sister of a drug dealer they knew. Michelle was twelve years older than Carl.

> I was struck by her. She was overweight and, in hindsight, not particularly attractive, but at the time I found her very attractive. Sexually, I fell in love with her. I became sexual with her and was with Al at the same time. After the first time we had sex, she threw her husband out the next morning. Within a couple of months, I was living with her. I really enjoyed the heterosexual sex. She let me have as much as I wanted. I was having sex with her five times a day for some months, but that was not the only reason I was in love with her. It was more conventional, easier to understand emotionally. I was never comfortable in a romantic sense with Al, even though I had romantic feelings toward him. Much of the time, our relationship was not a lot different from a heterosexual male-to-male relationship. We hung out, rode around. Maybe because of the lack of societal roles, there was not much of a way of expressing love. It was much easier being with a woman—flowers, walking down the street, holding hands.

When I asked Carl to compare the emotions he experienced with Michelle in sex with those that he experienced with Al, he said, "They were much more fulfilling, much more exciting with her. Most of the sex between Al and me was mutual masturbation. I always felt like it was not enough. If he'd let me penetrate him, I'm not sure if that would have fulfilled that need. It might have been closer but I think I really needed to be with a woman." As for Al penetrating Carl, he said, "It was a small component, sometimes very exciting, sometimes very painful, so it had its own pluses and minuses, but it really only represented a tenth of the sex. But overall it felt unsatisfying, whereas this [sex with Michelle] felt liberating almost."

Carl's relationship with Michelle lasted about three years. She told Carl that anytime he wanted to be with a man, it was fine with her. But he said, "No, I don't want that anymore." During the time he was with her, he occasionally thought about a man and mastur-bated, but rarely. After the relationship ended, Carl moved to anoth-er state and for the next year, although he didn't have sex with anyone, his thoughts and fantasies were exclusively about women. He then met the woman who became his wife. Things clicked between them and they soon got married. In the thirteen years since his marriage Carl has had no other relationships with men. He was very attracted to one man in a college class, but his attractions have otherwise been directed almost exclusively toward women. A re-cent fantasy involves two lesbian women: "Being with two women who were being sexual with each other and being able to be sexual with them at the same time would be my ultimate fantasy."

I asked Carl if he had any thoughts on explaining to himself the attractions he had felt over the years. He said,

> I always thought that part of it had to do with availability. If I'd been sexual with a girl, I never would have gone out with a guy. The way it happened—going into his [Al's] home with no livelihood—probably kept me there longer. Probably being sexually molested and hit upon by the choir director . . . it left me more open to doing something like that. In sense, a barrier had been broken. I'd done that kind of sex, so it wasn't such a leap. Why was I attracted to those girls at age five? I couldn't say, I just was.

Early on in his parents' marriage, Carl's father had proposed "swinging" with other couples as a way of dealing with his marital dissatisfactions. Even before he understood this, Carl had sensed a certain sexual tension in the air when another couple had stayed overnight in his home. So maybe this subliminal awareness had moved him along the path of expressing his emotional needs sexually more quickly than he otherwise would have. But it does not explain the fact that both males and females were the objects of those needs. Although it is altogether possible that the naked image of the choir director was partly in response to some sexual "signals" the latter was sending out, it was also—at the very least—an indication of Carl's inner responsiveness to those signals. But the amorphous feelings in his chest signifying that Carl wanted something from his male friends around early adolescence certainly came from himself.

Like so many adults who engage adolescents sexually, the choir director, like Johnny's stepbrother, was unable to understand the full range of emotional needs of a boy of fifteen. His sexual fondling was exploitive, clumsy, and isolated from the caring components of the relationship that Carl had previously valued. Speaking of it, Carl had said, "That's not what I was there for, you know?" The relationship with Al was much more of a total package. But although Carl was genuinely in love and erotically drawn to him, Al was also too limited emotionally for the relationship to be truly fulfilling for Carl. The first wet dream he remembered was indicative of the other theme in Carl's emotional life—his connection to a woman. His fear when he was with Al that he would die without ever being with a woman signified not only his disappointment with Al, but also a real urgency about making that connection.

Was Carl "really" heterosexual all along? Or did he "become" heterosexual while he was with Al? If we tried to fit the facts of Carl's life into our cultural assumptions about different "kinds" of people, we would have to say that Carl was heterosexual from ages five to nine; then became bisexual until the age of fourteen; homosexual until the age of eighteen or nineteen; and that he finally became heterosexual—more or less—until the present time. But this chronology seems to be somewhere between cumbersome and absurd. I said, at the end of the last chapter, that human beings in both their male and female embodiments were emotionally compelling in their own right and capable of eliciting the emotion that can cause—in both sexes—the "moving toward" that we call sexual attraction. Although his earliest memory of attraction was to girls,

Carl subsequently found himself having some strong but not clearly articulated feelings toward boys. The naked image of the choir director and the mermaid in the glittering sea were telling him—and they tell us—that he needed something emotionally from a man, as well as from women. He might have especially needed something from a man at the point in his life when he moved in with Al. Had an older woman intervened at that point, would he have moved in with her? Possibly. Perhaps he left Al because, flawed as the relationship was, he had gotten what he needed from him. Or perhaps he left him because Al's limitations had made him feel that a man could not fulfill his needs well enough. In either case, he turned back to a woman to get what he needed emotionally as a young man. It seems to me this kind of explanation fits the observed facts of Carl's life better than the insistence that he be placed in some fixed and permanent category of sexual identity.

MICHAEL

Although individuals are exponents of their culture, they are not simply clones coming off the cultural assembly line. Each person remains, at the same time, an individual in a potentially confrontational relationship with his or her culture. Michael found himself in a confrontational relationship with not one but two cultures as he crossed and recrossed the cultural boundary dividing heterosexual from homosexual. I encountered in Michael a person who was not only sensitive and open, but also unusually gifted in his ability and willingness to put into words the feeling components of his sexual experience on both sides of the cultural boundary. More than any other person I have spoken to, he throws into sharp focus the painful dilemma a man faces when he is caught between powerful need for individual emotional fulfillment on the one hand and self-realization through participation in a deeply felt cultural tradition on the other. Like Seth, Michael was Jewish, but in contrast to Seth the focus of his Jewish identity was religious.

I met Michael by chance at a meeting run by a bisexual organization. Part of the purpose of the meeting was to try to demonstrate to those attending it that bisexuality really did exist. And it was clear that there were as many skeptics in the ranks of the gay audience as there are in the population at large. People lined up to say a few words at the podium, and Michael captured my attention when he questioned the meaningfulness of the bisexual category in a provocative way. He said that he was not sure that he could say he felt bisexual, adding, "When I'm with a woman I feel heterosexual, and when I'm with a man I feel homosexual." At the end of the meeting, I approached him and said I was doing research on some of the sexual issues discussed that evening and asked if he would be willing to speak to me. What follows comes from our dialogues.

> I'm not sure I could have articulated things when they were happening. I remember feeling uncomfortable in gym during high school, and I felt uncomfortable with girls. There was some kind of unspoken fear. I knew everyone had that, so I didn't feel unusual. I made a lot of excuses about why I didn't take a certain girl into the woods at camp. I was thirteen and she was fourteen.

Michael's first experience of physical closeness with a female was a little bit later, when a girl he knew invited him to her house, where she taught him how to kiss. But she did not touch him otherwise. He said, "It didn't do anything for me. It was interesting but it didn't feel good." Michael was keenly aware of his Jewish tradition. His grandfather had died at Auschwitz. By age sixteen he was in the process of connecting himself to boys and girls of traditional backgrounds. He decided to become Orthodox and it was during his sixteenth summer that he adopted the religious prohibition against physical contact with women. "No doubt," he said, "it put the whole issue of sex on hold." He would nevertheless date, but these relationships would go nowhere. In fact, he had a two-year relationship while in college, but no touching occurred until the end—by that time he was twenty. "I told myself that it was her and that I was not attracted to her."

Up until this age he had no awareness of any attraction to males. His first experience with another male person occurred in Israel, where he had been studying for two years. It was a deeply spiritual time for him. He even stopped masturbating for a period of three or four months. He used to go the Turkish bath, a place that was frequented both by men who were gay and men who were not. It was the custom for people to sometimes massage each other, and one day a man offered to do that for him.

> All of a sudden he started to put his hands in places that were a bit unusual and I got an erection while I was lying on my belly. He told me to turn over. I didn't know what to do—I was caught. He saw it and covered it with a towel, but he continued and I came eventually. I was embarrassed but I couldn't stop it. I came back a few weeks later and a young Arab boy started playing with me and I willfully played back this time. I felt terrible. I identified it not so much as attraction but being sexually deprived in other ways. I was and was not conscious of it.

Attraction to males was to prove to be an important part of Michael's sexual life, yet he had not been aware of that up until this point, his early twenties. He had never masturbated to images of men, nor was he conscious of looking at men in a sexual way. As an adolescent, he reacted to male bodies with discomfort rather than interest.

> I remember feeling uniquely anxious in the locker room, particularly when one fellow came in because he was stocky, well built, and muscular. It was about the time when I was becoming religious—age fifteen or sixteen. I went out with girls and almost nothing happened. A number of girls wanted a relationship with me and I didn't know what to do. So I didn't do it.

Michael sensed he was feeling *something,* but he could not recognize what that was. Although he had consciously taken on the religious prohibition against touching women, the unconscious prohibition against touching men was even more powerful. Somewhere he sensed the impulse toward movement when confronted with the reality of the male other, but all that was in awareness was the sense of anxiety that intervened to suppress the impulse to touch. The meaning of the incident at the Turkish bath, in which another man had touched Michael's body, remained unclear to him. Consciously, he responded to what the man was doing to him, not to the man. And when, shortly after, he allowed himself to be drawn into sexual play by the Arab boy, he still could not quite admit to himself that sexual attraction to the boy was involved or acknowledge the emotional power of the body of the male other. Perhaps, he thought, it was just "sexual deprivation." However, the resistance to this acknowledgment soon broke down, but not the conflict about it. He recalled an "eye thing with a young soldier who began to proposition me." His response at that time had been, "I could, but I'm choosing not to." Michael knew that people could feel attraction to both sexes, but neither his American background nor his Jewish training offered any models for dealing with this dualism in himself. Michael remained conflicted. He eventually returned to the United States and took up both a secular job and a position as an Orthodox rabbi. He had some occasion to deal with homosexuality because a gay man in his synagogue came out to him, but the whole concept remained distant from him personally. He continued to date, as always, and got as far as lying next to a woman in his underwear. He got an erection but felt guilty, and nothing more happened. He cared about the woman a good deal, but he just did not feel anything physical with her. "I set up the romantic circumstances all the time and then nothing would feel."

It was at about this point that he met Josh. Josh said to him, when they met, "I want to tell you one thing—when I was single and before I got married I had some relations with men, and you seem to me like you could also be kind of bisexual or have ambiguous sexuality." Michael said, "It blew me away. My jaw dropped. He asked, 'Am I right?' Later, as I was going home, I was on the subway and I remember seeing an attractive guy. *For the first time in my life, I let myself feel it—I almost fell down, I almost collapsed. Had I not been holding on, I would have fallen down. . . . It was so powerful!*"

At age fifteen, the muscular body of the boy in the locker room had an effect on Michael, but he could not identify what it was. Some years later, in Jerusalem, he came to recognize that his emotions were stirred by the body of another male, but he still could not allow himself to experience the full intensity of those emotions. Josh's shrewd insight broke down the last of Michael's resistance—"For the first time in my life, I let myself feel it." The image of the body of the other, the feelings that surged through his own

body, and the complete recognition of those feelings all came together.

A week later he took a step that he had not dared to take before.

> I was out with a group of people. There was a woman who had
> been pushing for something with me for some time, but I said
> no to her and put her in a cab. I bought a hat because I wasn't
> going to the Village with my yarmulke on and went to a bar. I
> was just capable of doing this—drunk enough to be able to do
> it and not drunk enough not to be able to. I picked someone up
> and brought him back to my place with me. *My first sexual
> experience with a human being.* It wasn't wonderful, but it was
> done.

It was different from the experience in the Turkish bath in Jerusalem because this time he was consciously experiencing his own
feelings in relation to another male. The following summer Michael
returned to Israel and had an experience with a woman.

> I said, "Listen, I've never had sex with a woman and I just
> have to." She had pity on me and said okay. It also wasn't
> wonderful—it was okay, but I couldn't keep an erection with
> her. I came back and something began to happen between Josh
> and me, and it became a five-year relationship . . . in which
> time I was dating because I wanted to be married and he
> wanted me to be married. In the initial year we fell in love, but
> as I failed to get married, it became harder and harder to have a
> relationship and have it make sense. I couldn't justify it. It was
> codependency. He was wonderful, but I was angry because
> you never have the person but they have you. But I still was
> very much loved and in love, and I couldn't run anywhere. I
> never fooled around all those years except three or four times,
> where I had an orgasm but never really had sex. I was dating
> two women, one who broke up with me and one religious one
> who wouldn't touch me. I was so upset with the closed doors
> in my life. I went to a bar and picked someone up. I'd taken
> some condoms and had borrowed an apartment in Manhattan.
> We went back there and I put a condom on the guy. In my
> ignorance, because I was never part of the gay community, I

used baby oil. The condom broke and I'm HIV positive. I never did anal intercourse with anyone except Josh before then, never. That was two years ago. It was too much for Josh to bear.

There was a period of anger, but I told one of the women who had pulled away. For the first time in my life I was honest with a woman about being bisexual—and now HIV positive—and I fell in love, madly, wonderfully in love with her and her with me. Sex was wonderful, with all the precautions in the world. I loved it because I was honest—I wasn't hiding anything. I discovered that the things that had gotten in the way of my loving a woman were the deceit and fear of rejection, the lying and knowing that I could be found out and rejected. Once I could tell about it, I could feel loved, and once I could feel loved, I could love back. She is not the most beautiful or intelligent woman in the world and it didn't matter anymore. Loving replaced all the fear. I actually fell in love. It was wonderful. The emotional connection was wonderful. And intercourse was riveting. It was wonderful to feel myself move in and out of her. It was exhilarating. I felt like I'd joined humanity and now was part of the way the world worked. It was an incredible experience. And the sex—it was a wonderful feeling of moving together, almost dancing together, sexually. It was fueled by an incredible sense of closeness and the feeling, "My god, this woman loved me to do this with me." *The resource of that loving was so powerful. It was the most incredible sexual and emotional encounter of my life.* It lasted two and a half months, until she couldn't handle it.

Deborah had lost a parent in her teens and could not face the prospect of losing another person she loved. By the time that Michael and I were talking about it, the passion he had felt for her had cooled to something closer to fondness. But when Michael fell in love with Deborah he also plunged across another inner boundary—one that had until then separated him from women. His description of the emotional and physical whirlwind he experienced is indistinguishable from the exhilaration that might be felt by a man who had nothing except heterosexual experiences in his life. And yet, he opened his second interview by remarking, "I wanted to tell you at this meeting, 'Listen, I lied. I'm gay.'" Even as he disclosed this urge to confess, he added that he had said this to himself a hundred times and still knew that it was not true.

Michael was trying to make sense of what had happened to him emotionally, but our culture's guidelines only seemed to add to his difficulties.

> Being next to a woman feels right in a way that being next to a man does not. Like I've joined some natural chorus and I can't even describe it. I've known several gay men who had successful sexual lives with women. But what they couldn't do without was having a male lover. It didn't necessarily mean that they weren't happy in their marriages, but if they had to either/or it, they wound up defining themselves as gay and *shaping a deeply gay identity.* I wonder if many gay people are really bisexual and it's not possible, so they make choices. And the gay community is a powerful identity builder.

Michael's speculation that some people who called themselves gay might really be bisexual was an interesting reversal of the more common idea that people who call themselves bisexual are, in fact, "really" gay. There is a powerful cultural imperative to define oneself, even when it is against a person's will to do so. In contrast, I spoke with a young man who had gone through what proved to be a brief homosexual period during adolescence. It ended and a few years later he married, but wound up feeling unhappy with the choice he had made—not with her gender, but with her as a person. He was dating at the time I interviewed him and was very interested in developing a serious relationship with another woman. However, he mentioned a man at his workplace who was probably gay and who might be attracted to him. I asked him if he would ever consider a relationship between himself and another man again. His reply was candid. He said, "If I said no, that would be a limitation. Why limit yourself?"

But Michael seemed to have some very powerful reasons to limit himself. He asked,

> Does bisexual mean someone who has not yet chosen a full-time lover, or someone who is open to different possibilities?

My parents only know about my sexuality and the HIV for the past six months. My mother still thinks it's a perversion. What shall I tell my brothers? That I'm gay or bisexual? As a rabbi, people would say, "That's very nice, but get married." I didn't explore my gay identity until I became HIV positive. I had a lover, but that wasn't exploration. That was just getting love, affection, and physical satisfaction until I got married. Being bisexual was a way to say, "Yes, but I'll be getting married." It was a way of hiding the dynamics of the problem. But it seemed too painful to be suffering from this gay disease and not be gay. "Oh my god, you got yourself zapped and for what, just another flavor?" It was easier to say, "You're gay and that's why this happened to you." Political identities are different from real ones. You make alliances with people that you share political aims with, but I have no community in terms of "sexual preference"—neither a heterosexual nor a gay community. I feel much more that I belong to the heterosexual community as unmarried and single. And people will be happy to see me as the heterosexual guy who is unmarried because he just can't work it out, and "That's all right, we love him."

I remarked to Michael that it was hard to consult one's inner feelings unfiltered by a set of definitions and expectations. Michael replied, "Is it ever really possible? Do you really think it's possible to have no glasses?" I said that I did not know. But perhaps it was a question of degrees of freedom. "That I'll buy," he responded. "You can make the lenses a little bit less distorted. Even if we got get rid of our Western glasses and I got rid of my Jewish glasses, and we got rid of the various social stereotypes, you'd still have to get rid of English because English itself makes predispositions." In my interviews with Michael, as in all the interviews I conducted for this book, I found it necessary to allow myself to be a participant in a dialogue, to an extent that I had not been accustomed to in my role as therapist. Venturing into unknown territory as I felt we often were, I allowed my thoughts to emerge spontaneously and found myself sometimes putting certain ideas or questions into words for the first time. Maybe, I suggested, it made more sense to try to be transcultural, as it were, to get beyond culture. Let us say, I pro-

posed, that there was this great theme in human history and in
human nature, which is men's affiliation and bonding with one
another. This theme could be interpreted and expressed in different
ways. It could be expressed in emotional terms, in emotional and
physical terms, or in emotional, physical, and sexual terms. I said
that the male-directed part of his sexuality could be viewed, at this
historical moment, at this pinpoint of time, as an expression of this
theme, one that swept back through thousands of years, to Jonathan
and David and well beyond.

Michael was struggling to reconcile two great components in his
life—the sexual and the spiritual. But Michael's spirituality was
deeply embedded in what he termed the millennial Jewish tradition.
And this struggle of his enriched the context of our dialogue, taking
it beyond biological or environmental reductionism, or the dogmat-
ic moralizing in which so much thinking about sexuality is stuck.
Growing out of this context as they did, my comments struck a
responsive chord in him and Michael replied,

> That's a lovely thought. I need ways of sanctifying what it is I
> discovered in myself without completely obliterating the cate-
> gories of sanctity that I'm comfortable with, that I've grown
> with. I'm drawn to something transcultural and that is in deep
> tension with a deeply cultural, deeply parochial life that I also
> cherish. But I don't think that any one cultural referent owns
> God. I see the Jewish people as a people that became an
> interlocutor with God and God refers to them as "Thou," even
> though they are all individuals. So I stand in for the eternal
> Israel, as every Jew does, and the children after me will do the
> same. Your comment—about being part of the sweep of explo-
> ration of how men are loving to and connected with other men
> in sexual and nonsexual ways, and how this is one dot of light
> that expresses it—that resonates for me and I like it.

And then he recalled how, that weekend, he had spent time with a
fellow rabbi, a new gay man he had met, and a woman who was
interested in him. He had been, consecutively, Michael the rabbi,
Michael the gay man, and Michael the heterosexual, all in the same
weekend. "Here my three identities converge. I'm [a] rabbi on
Friday and Saturday with my rabbi friend in my Orthodox commu-

nity. I'm with my newly forming gay friend, and I'm with this woman who clearly wants a relationship that is more than platonic and is open about that. When I was going through it I clearly felt comfortable and uncomfortable in every place." Later, he was telling a friend about these events and said, "In retelling it, I wondered about the great pleasure I take in being all these things. It [the weekend] was a way of saying, 'Damn the society that makes me limit myself and not participate in all these different places.' "

The theme of identity kept reappearing in our discussions. Three levels of feeling seemed somehow related to this question—the social, the emotional, and the physical. Which of these defined his identity? I asked. Michael replied, "If it were physical, there is no question but that it would be men. If it were social, there is no question but that it would be women. And as far as the emotional goes, it's a toss-up because I have different, powerful, wonderful emotional connections to both men and women." The relationships with both Josh and Deborah were now over. Passion had cooled to friendship. A new relationship with a somewhat younger Israeli man, Gil, had become part of Michael's life. They were separated by time and distance, but they considered themselves lovers.

It seemed impossible to stick a single, exclusive identity on Michael. The person he called "I" seemed to be a spectrum of potentialities for feeling. He had lived with men, women, a mother, a father, and all those had left their traces in him. When he was with Gil certain elements of him coalesced, came together. With Deborah, certain elements of him came together and coalesced around that experience with her. As he had described these experiences, some parts of them were different and some the same. The configuration was somewhat different with each. Each configuration had two poles. He and Gil formed one set of poles and he and Deborah the other. Currents passed between him and Gil when they were together and between him and Deborah when he was with her. "So," I asked, "how can we say, 'you're this' or 'you're that'? When you're with him you're 'this,' when you're with her you're 'that.' " Michael answered,

That's what I told you—that's how our conversation began, remember? I said, when I'm with a man I'm homosexual and when I'm with a woman I'm heterosexual. When I'm with Gil, it's not helpful to think that I could be with women, and when I'm with Deborah it's not helpful to think that I could be with men. The truth is that it doesn't happen. When I'm with Deborah, I have no interest in being with men. When I'm with Gil I have no interest in being with women.

It was his Jewish identity that was most precious to Michael. And the following remarks reflected that powerful urge to integrate the person he was in the present with the past from which he felt himself to have sprung.

Part of the Hebraic genius was to see that the many gods are one and that it is damaging never to see them in their diversity and never to see them in their oneness. That's why they're called Elohim, which is plural—that's the name of God. And yet it's one. To be able to put together that divine wholeness is not easy. If you look at the Hebrew texts, God is not one in some absolute sense, God needs to be made one. There's work to be done in uniting the divine fragments and making God one. The prayer said every day ends with, "On that day the Lord will be one and His name will be one." As if to say, he's not yet. The implication is that this is not a won battle, that God himself is seeking to shape a single self out of the diverse elements. It's there but it needs support. That's one picture of what the biblical task would be—to help the Divine seek that unity. Seeking unity for me has been extremely important.

I think it was helpful to Michael to relate his inner struggle over the seeming paradoxes in his own nature to the implied paradoxes in the divine nature. And it was illuminating to me. I found in it another reminder that people's attempt to understand their sexuality cannot be isolated from their need to find meaning in their lives. And for many people, the need to find meaning in their lives requires some sense of a connection with the sacred, whether this implies an organized set of religious beliefs, or simply the existence of an enduring and transcendent reality, named or not.[2]

PART II: CLARK

Chapter 8

"A Man Like Myself"

When I met Clark, the identity that he was struggling with was not one that had to do with his sexual preference, but quite another one—that of rapist. Clark had been confined for six years, four and a half at the treatment center where I met him. He was thirty-two years old, a high school graduate, the divorced father of a little girl. His worst brush with the law before his arrest had been a traffic ticket, yet his crime had been a serious one—aggravated rape. He was a large man, six feet two inches, dark skinned, with broad shoulders set on a lean but muscular frame, and with biceps that reflected the many hours he put in at the gym. Clark referred to himself as black rather than African-American and his story follows his usage. But I could not help but think that his overall look—nose slightly aquiline, the shadow of a beard that just barely outlined his mouth and chin, his size and bearing—could make him a fit subject for the portrait of an African prince. I think my impression reflected the rapport that, early on, was established between us. Even in our first session, Clark seemed candid and forthcoming, rather than defensive. Plus, he showed evidence of an engaging sense of humor.

SEXUAL IDENTITY

Before his arrest, Clark had thought of himself as purely heterosexual, without being at all homophobic. His movement into sex with men had been gradual, and not without mixed feelings:

> For the first six months or so that I was incarcerated I had no thoughts of sex with men. This did take some time, especially once I got in this setting here and I saw how open it was. I got

propositioned a lot, right out the door. At first, it was, "No, get away from me; I'm not into that." But being taken out of my natural environment—you know, women, for a heterosexual male—after a while, looking at a *Playboy* or *Hustler* and masturbating, you sort of want that ultimate, *which is meeting flesh to flesh. But I needed those feminine qualities*, as I see in a woman, which naturally arouses me. I don't want no big, hairy, musclebound man like myself. That's not going to arouse me. Those feminine qualities were important. If I didn't see them, I wasn't aroused. We have some of those in the building—the street term for that would be "flaming." All of their qualities are like a woman and I found myself being aroused in their presence. There was one occasion when I was propositioned by one and my first reaction was "No, get away from me." But a thought process takes place. Out of curiosity, I was wondering: "What would it be like? Can I accept this? Oh, I can't do that." Then over a period of time, I came to terms with myself. I'm going to take the guy up on his offer the next time. I found the things that had made me reluctant to do it the first time—*I was able to block out*. I didn't want to look at no man's dick and balls, at his hairy face—that's what I didn't want, and I was able to block out that this guy has got the same thing that I've got. I was able to block all that out and during the course of sex, *fantasize in my mind that I'm with a woman.* A whole complete process has to take place and before you know it I'm aroused and we're having sex.

PRISON CULTURE
AND THE HETEROSEXUAL ROLE

Although the expectations and prohibitions of our institutions effectively prevent people from exploring emotional and physical possibilities with people of the same sex, the one place—ironically—that people are relatively free to explore some of those possibilities is behind bars. The culture has, in effect, changed. The prison culture says that it is okay to explore. There are, however, anxieties and contradictions in how it does that, as illustrated by what Clark said.

I came to the institution where Clark was confined because I wanted to look at how people actually underwent the experience of movement from previously exclusive heterosexuality to prison homosexuality, at the interaction between cultural and psychological change. Clark was in an institution for sex offenders. I had intended to go to an "ordinary" prison for this research. However, I was steered to this institution because it had a large psychology staff and was receptive to psychological research. As it turned out, this accidental choice worked to my advantage. In ordinary prisons, a system of roles and definitions about who does what to whom seems to protect the sense of the heterosexual identity of some men even as their behavior crosses over the boundary. Ray, another man I interviewed for this book, told me that his brother had been in jail for a short time some years before. Recalling what his brother had told him, he said to me, "You have guys in jail always doing it and they don't consider themselves gay. And I don't either. My brother was in jail and he said there are a lot of guys in there who want it. He said that as long as he didn't let anyone penetrate him and as long as he didn't suck anyone else, he saw nothing wrong with it." By restricting his behavior to the "masculine" role, his brother foreclosed—in his own mind—any question of losing his heterosexual identity. In the institution where Clark was, however, the treatment staff strongly felt that if a person was having sex with another man, he had to be willing to accept the fact that he was at least bisexual, not heterosexual. In an institution where men were confined for rape or sex with minors, consensual homosexuality was seen as unproblematic. The problem, however, was the failure to acknowledge it as part of oneself. This kind of denial, it was felt, could contribute to either heterosexual rape or acting out with children as a substitute for the unacknowledged homosexual feelings.

So, in our first interview, Clark said to me, "You can call me bisexual, homosexual, or whatever you want—but I call it adjusting to my environment. I've been taken out of my natural environment, where females were available." Recognizing the staff position on the identity question, he was prepared not to quibble about labels, but without being defensive, he seemed to be also saying that his homosexuality was a pragmatic adaptation to the situation in which he found himself rather than an integral part of his personality.

THE FEAR OF DOMINATION

Clark said he had adjusted to his environment in prison. But this adaptation was not simple. In adapting to the absence of women and needing more than just fantasy and solitary sex, Clark turned to males as the only available partners for the "flesh to flesh" meeting that he described as "the ultimate." Yet their very maleness was a serious problem. Without considering his problem more closely, one might think that it was only the internalized cultural prohibition that was operating. But his problem had another dimension—fear of domination. There were, he said, some gay men in the institution who were as big as he was or even bigger.

> And that's intimidating to me because of the fear that they might try to overpower me or penetrate me or get me to do something to them. You see, I'm not aroused by sucking them off, I'm only in it for my pleasure. I don't know what they get out of it, from sucking someone's dick. And that's what I fear. *It would make me feel like I'm being dominated and that's one of my worst fears.*

He related this fear of domination to an abduction in his childhood. Clark had grown up in Chicago and moved east at the age of ten. He told me of an incident that, in his own words, traumatized him when he was nine years old. He was accosted on the street and pulled into a secluded area by an adult, who forced the terrified boy to perform oral sex on him.

> At that time I guess I was pretty slender, and thinking about it now I'd say he was late teens, early twenties. My initial response when he grabbed me was that I was scared, terrified. He wasn't a big guy but I was scared. He told me to come with him and I knew that if I didn't do what he said he would hurt me or kill me. Growing up in the inner city of Chicago in 1968-1969, I'd seen a lot of violence, a lot of brutal shit. I was always conscious of it. At this point I was scared because this guy had me. I said to myself that I better do as he says so he'll let me go. All I wanted to do was go home. I pretty much gave in to his demands, and I had to suck this guy off. He ejaculated in my

mouth and everything. I just wanted to get it over with as soon as possible. He didn't talk very much, didn't say a lot. He just pulled his penis out and said to suck it. I did until he was satisfied. He let me leave and I went home. I was so scared that I don't know what I was experiencing. I just remember wanting to go home. I never told anyone because I was so embarrassed. The reason I didn't was that I felt I could have done something about it like screaming or hollering.

Young though he was, he had already heard his aunt use the term "cocksucker" in tones of contempt, and now he felt it applied to him. For more than twenty years he had carried his secret, never telling even his parents. It was only at this institution, in a therapy group, that he had finally revealed it.

Clark told me about another instance of sexual abuse. Incredibly, it happened for the first time—because it occurred about a dozen times in all—the very same week he had been abducted. He had a babysitter, a seventeen-year-old girl, who would take him into the bathroom, where she took off his clothes and her own. She would play with his genitals and put his hand on hers. Or she would take him in the bedroom and make him perform oral sex on her while she masturbated him. He did not find this the least bit pleasurable—in fact, it was very unpleasant. "I looked at her like a mother figure. When I refused to go along, she told my mother I had been playing with the burners on the stove and my mother beat the shit out of me."

And yet, in spite of his childhood trauma and the fear of domination, he acknowledged, "You see, deep inside, I believe I'm capable of that but I don't allow it to happen. I'm capable of engaging in a full relationship. It's something I fear because in a lot of relationships the sex is mutual. Both males usually do for each other. I'm only one-sided. I'm just passing through. I'm not stopping my car and turning the engine off." Although he had been traumatically abused by both a man and a woman, Clark went on to have sex with girls and women. It was only the abuse by the man that he felt he could not get past. The explanation for the different outcomes has to lie with culture. Clark had plenty of encouragement from his peers and the society at large to have sex with females, while the reverse was true when it came to males. His aunt's contemptuous epithet—"cocksucker"—said it all.

THE IMAGE OF THE MALE BODY

Although Clark had begun to have sex with males, his reaction to the male image had some paradoxical elements. Unquestionably, a shift had taken place in the image of the male for Clark. Before his confinement, the male body did not have an erotic quality for him. He said, "If it was well-conditioned, well-shaped, pretty much put together, I would admire that. That would be as far as it went. I don't remember ever being aroused by looking at the male body. When I came here it was a little different. I was looking for the *opposite* of a masculine body." But by the time I began to speak with Clark, certain qualities of the male body *could* have an erotic aura for him, although he said that 99 percent of his fantasies were about women. For Clark, as for many men in prison, the male body was split into "safe" and "dangerous" zones. A man's buttocks were in a safe zone as a focus for erotic feeling. But the same man's genitals were definitely in the danger zone. Clark said of one man, "I guess you can say I fantasize about having this guy in my room in the missionary position and fucking him in his ass. But what destroys this is that I know this guy and he's going to want to get his shit off too, and I can't do nothing for him. I have an attraction to him and I want him, but he's not fucking my ass. I'm not going to suck him off."

Tony had said, "You might make an analogy between a person's butt and the dark side or zone of their psyche, the forbidden area that's taboo or off-limits." For Nick, that area had been very off-limits even to his girlfriend. This split in the body image appears to reflect a split in the mind as well, a psychological splitting in one's own masculine self, a denial of some part of the totality of the feelings of which, as a man, one is capable. The half that is denied is identified with the person who is penetrated—orally or anally—and identified with the feminine. The other half, the part doing the penetrating, as well as the feelings that accompany the act of penetration, form part of one's masculine identity.

I told Clark about how, among the Sambia of Papua New Guinea, preadolescent boys learned, from their fathers and uncles, that they had to regularly perform fellatio on the adolescents so that, by ingesting semen, they too could grow up to become men. What had been so traumatic for Clark at age nine was a valuable ritual that enabled a boy to become a man in another culture. I asked him, if our culture at large were more open to men having sex with each other as lovers or friends, would that help him in any way? His answer was ambiguous. "No, it wouldn't help because the childhood trauma would just stick with me." But then in seeming contradiction he added, "If I was a kid at that time, and you know how boys sometimes experiment with sex, and they might suck each other off or something. If something like that would have happened, I wouldn't have that blockage."

When men appeared in his dreams, it was in the context of sports.

> But nothing erotic, which is something I fear. I'm afraid of that—I don't want to lie to you—of actually dreaming about sex with a man—and I'm not talking about a man sucking me off or me fucking him, but me doing something for *him*. As a matter of fact, the other day I was drying my ankles after a shower and one of my buddies came in the room and stood right about there when I was bending over. I saw his legs thrusting forward like that and I asked him what the fuck he was doing. He said he was only playing around, that he was just kicking my leg and he couldn't understand why I was getting all shook up about that. Later I told him not to worry about it, that it was only a childhood experience I was reacting to. It goes to show you how sensitive I am about it.

One could see Clark struggling to keep his head above water in the cross-currents of at least three conflicting cultures. The first was the culture of the wider society in which he had grown up, in which all same-sex relationships had a taboo quality. Even without having been traumatized the way Clark was, Will had felt a palpable block in the form of a headache when he thought of something sexual with another man. The second was the culture of the prison which said that, in jail, men do that—but with certain role restrictions. He had found a compromise position in dealing with these conflicting cultures, a position where *he* would always be the penetrating party in any sexual exchange with another man. There was a third cultural current, however—the therapeutic culture. The therapy staff ran a program in sex education. An important part of this program was the assumption that homosexuality was not inferior to heterosexuality. The therapeutic culture placed a premium on honesty with oneself and on self-knowledge when it came to matters of sexual orientation. Denial and repression were seen as likely to lead a person to recommit his offense. The therapeutic culture was not supportive of the kinds of rigid role distinctions that are so pervasive in run-of-the-mill prison situations. Since most of the men in the institution had been arrested for either rape or offenses against minors, consensual relationships between adults, particularly where these were affectionate and mutual, were seen as signs of movement toward a mature and healthy sexuality. In fact, the insistence on a one-sided "dominant" role could be seen as the unhealthy perpetuation of a "rape dynamic" transferred from women to men.

MOVEMENT THROUGH STAGES

I remarked to Clark that Freud felt that everybody had some homosexuality in their unconscious. Clark said,

> The way I see it, some people like myself do have hidden tendencies. Then you have some who have tendencies that are strong. It's like in those magazines I used to read. There would be ads from black couples looking for other black couples where it would say the wife was "bi" and wanted to indulge in sex with another woman. In order to put an ad like that in there, you have to have a strong feeling that you want to be with another woman. *When I was in society, I didn't have that feeling* but once I came in here and was taken out of my natural environment they sort of came to the surface. It's like a process has taken place and I had no problem letting a guy suck me off. *I'm like working my way through different stages.*

Clark said that he felt that he had "hidden tendencies." Had he not been arrested and put in a prison environment, these hidden tendencies would probably never have been allowed to emerge to the extent that they already had when I first met him. Clearly, it was the prison culture that permitted and even encouraged it. The therapeutic culture also played an important role. And now, our dialogue was providing a forum where Clark could continue to think about these and other issues in his sexual life. Clark had already, in prison, stepped over the boundary set by his heterosexual identity before I met him. But he had only one foot over the line. However, he had come up against this boundary at age twenty-three or twenty-four, well before his arrest:

> I had a friend who was gay. We were real good friends and we established a good relationship with each other. I remember one day he went with me down to the lake to throw the line in the water. I remember it was hot outside and taking my shirt off. He started looking at me and said I had the kind of body he wanted. Before this time he had mentioned to me previously that he wanted to suck me off. He told me he could [do] it better than any woman and that he was the best, but I told him no. This day, I took my shirt off and I was sitting there fishing. He started waxing my car and I told him he didn't have to do that. I walked over there and he started looking at me and I guess he got all excited and aroused and was getting aggressive about giving me a blow job. At first I was fighting with myself about whether I should or not. Because of the way he was talking I had actually gotten an erection. *My body responded and I was wondering what the hell was happening.* When he started getting aggressive about it, then I got angry and that erection just deflated. I just decided I wasn't fucking with that guy no more. I always wondered what would have happened if he hadn't got so aggressive. *He was getting close to me, touching me,* and I wasn't used to that. It turned me off. I was intimidated and got angry. Funny thing about it though, I had an erection when he was just being verbal about it. All the things he was saying sounded good, but when he started walking towards me that turned me off. But he was a good friend until then.

Like some of the people I have discussed, Clark had been affected by this invitation—and like some of them, frightened. The incident damaged their friendship.

I let him go after that. I had put up with a lot of teasing, ridicule, and criticism from friends because of us hanging out together. You know how ignorant people who don't really understand can be. We were just friends, looking out for each other and that was it. The guy shared some deep feelings with me. I would ask a lot of questions about his childhood, what his brother and dad had done to him. He had been married previously and had four kids. He was in his mid-thirties. I was really curious and I asked a lot of questions about why he liked men.

Although Clark never had sex with this man, a fantasy about him entered his married life.

At the time I had recently been married, and my wife questioned me about us being friends, him hanging around, his motives. I didn't know that women had certain fantasies. She questioned me about whether I was having sex with this guy. She told me that she'd actually like to see me screw this guy. I was shocked. She just wanted to watch. I thought about it. I already knew the guy wanted to suck me off, so I knew I could get him to come over, but I didn't want to do it. My initial reaction was that this was a crazy fantasy. I could have done it if I wanted, I just didn't want to. (She later told me she wanted to watch me have sex with a white girl, but she backed off *that* real quick. Having sex with a man was okay, but having sex with a woman wasn't.) She pretty much dwelled on that, watching me have sex with another man. During sex I would tell her how I was fucking this guy. She'd really get aroused by this. It became a regular part of our sex life. It got to the point where the fact that I could be with a man didn't bother me so much anymore. As I'm telling her stories about screwing another man, I look at her face, and she's getting more excited and I'm getting more excited. It was good for both of us.

His wife opened up a realm of sexual imagery to Clark that he had not even contemplated before. It reminded me of something I was told by a man I used to see in therapy some years before. One day, his girlfriend said to him that she would love to see him with another man. He had never entertained the thought before and, like Clark, was taken aback at first. However, he found himself drawn into the fantasy and, as with Clark and his wife, this fantasy became a regular part of their sex life. In that instance, however, the primary exciting image was him performing oral sex on another man. With both Clark and my patient, it seems that a kind of permission was granted for a same-sex fantasy in the reassuring context of a relationship with a woman. However, although my patient and his girlfriend made their fantasy a reality once, he never went on to pursue any other sexual relationships with men. Unlike Clark, the culture surrounding him never changed in a more permissive direction. Nevertheless, prior to his arrest, a male never appeared in Clark's fantasies except in that one situation.

RELATING TO A MAN—AS A MAN

Clark had initially maintained that it was only feminine characteristics that he could find attractive in another man. But the maleness of another could be arousing in one way: " . . . the fact that I've got another man down there sucking on my dick. That arouses me, *that I can dominate this guy,* not only in a physical way, but in a sexual way." It was ironic that the very thing Clark feared happening to him was erotic when he was doing it to another. This was, I think, because a man's domination of another man is perfectly consistent with our culture's definitions of masculinity, in which one man wins what the other loses. But several months later, Clark moved beyond the safety of that position to the recognition of something else. He said, "What's even more exciting than that is the mere fact that *another man is attracted to you.* That's somewhat erotic to me. It's beyond flattery. It sort of hits you in a different way. I can say now it's something I can appreciate more than fear. I just can't find the words to describe it right now."

This remark related to a question that had begun to emerge in my dialogues with Clark—could he relate to another man as a *man* rather than as a woman substitute? He had started off some months previously by saying that the other person had to be a very feminine male, indeed that he had to see him virtually as a woman even to let the other perform oral sex on him. When that restriction was relaxed, another condition was initially laid down—that the other person had to be gay and have feminine qualities. But then he agreed that a man could be masculine in his actions, as long as the physical type fit the specifications of being slender and smaller than himself. Finally, he agreed that being gay could also go by the board if he was the right physical type. I know from experience that, no matter how careful I might try to be in exploring the boundaries of a man's sexual imagination, I cannot make him go further than he is at least inwardly prepared to go. I had no idea what to expect with Clark and, by accident or luck, I met in him someone who was also inclined to test and to push his own boundaries.

"I SEE MYSELF"

"When I see a masculine body I see myself," said Clark, "and that's a turnoff." Yet, he had come to feel that the male gender of the other person had an appeal in its own right, which was something of a paradox. I know that deep down inside there are other attractions I have yet to explore. That's why a lot of your questions are hard for me to answer, because there are a lot of things I haven't engaged in yet, so I can't speak about them right now. I can only give you thoughts, how I might react. I think if I had the opportunity I would really learn a lot. In order for me to go that far, to put my mouth on his penis or let him penetrate my rectum, I would have to have some deep emotional feelings. There's got to be some bonding there, some caring there, the same feeling I have for females. That I haven't had the chance to experience yet. There are a lot of unanswered things about me.

He had begun to look for some of those answers in the weeks between our sessions with one man with whom he had a steady sexual relationship. He related:

> During the course of sex this thought came across my mind, that maybe I should reach around and jerk him off. The thing about it is that when I touched his penis I didn't lose my erection, and I thought about that for days. That's when I said that I'd like to have him for a couple of hours and experience these things. He has hair on his chest but that doesn't bother me much. When we're having anal intercourse, I'm kissing him on his neck, licking him on his earlobe. I kissed him and I never kissed a man in a passionate way before. It felt good. *It was like, what's hap-*

pening here? This isn't what I thought it was. This is okay. They have to have that profile, that petite physique. That's one of the main qualities that would keep me going.

THE AESTHETICS OF FEAR AND POWER

I think one cannot explain aesthetic preferences beyond a certain point. But one thing that went beyond aesthetic preference was the fear of domination, which seemed to be involved in Clark's requirement that the other person be "petite"—small. When I said to Clark that as he developed more confidence and self-esteem it might stop being an issue, he said, "You could be right—maybe I would lose that over a period of time and perhaps engage in sex with someone that's a more masculine type." As a child of nine who didn't have a choice, he had had a very frightening and out-of-control experience. As a man twenty years older and more in possession of himself, what did he really have to fear? I didn't see anyone being able to force him to do anything. Clark said, "Like you said earlier, that's tied up in those old fears. I think you have a good understanding of what I feel."

I had not planned to see Clark for more than a few sessions—perhaps half a dozen at the outside. But the issues in his life seemed both important and challenging, and he himself was so willing to explore them with me that our work became quite open-ended. Although my aim was primarily research, it converged with Clark's aim of self-understanding. He seemed genuinely interested in the possibilities of movement within himself and in his life. Thus, in our eighth session, he said, "I've never been able to sit down with anyone and share deep pain, deep emotional thoughts. Now I feel like I can do that. This is kind of new for me. Before it was all anger, rage, hollering, fussing, cursing. I don't want to do it that way anymore."

MALE BONDING AND SEXUAL LOVE

I recalled that Frank, the man I had written about in my earlier book, had said, "You don't love a man—that's wrong—you love a woman." Clark said, "I've had guys in here that I love, care about, although it's not sexual." Could he imagine sex with one of them? "No," he replied, "they're too masculine—*as myself.* We do have that male bonding, *but it's not sexual.*" Here again was the great paradox in male-to-male relationships in our culture. The sense of shared maleness—"male bonding"—is experienced by the "I" that lives in culture as *the* obstacle to a sexual relationship. On the other hand, the feelings of the men I talked about earlier in this book indicate that the sense of identification and sharing is especially likely to account for the "moving toward" by the "inner I" that results in a sensed sexual attraction between oneself and another man.

Trying to explore this paradox with Clark, I asked him if he knew a man that he liked who was masculine in his mannerisms and build, while being good looking and smaller. A person did come to mind. Could he imagine something intimate and sexual with him? He said, "Intimate, no. Just raw sex, yes. You see, intimate means you're *passionate*—the touching, the kissing, the caressing. *He reminds me too much of myself,* but he's got a nice butt on him. I wouldn't mind fucking him." I had, in the past, talked with Clark about what I termed "body parts"—about the splitting of bodies into bits and pieces. So he knew what I meant when I laughed and reminded him, "body parts." He laughed too and said, "Yeah, exactly, body parts. It's like a woman with nice, big, firm breasts. You want to touch them, but that's all you see, not even her face. You're asking me if I could be attracted to someone as myself, not so feminine. But that's how it would end up being, just raw sex—no emotions, *no feelings of love.*" Even though before his arrest, Clark had thought about sex with his gay friend, the male body had not really taken on erotic qualities for him until he was confined. Initially, however, he had to see the woman in the man. But now, partly as a result of our conversations, he had come to acknowledge his ability to respond with erotic feelings even to the body of a masculine man—to a point—the point of saying, "He's got a nice butt on him—I wouldn't mind fucking him."

I said to Clark that, judging from what he had been saying, to have such a fantasy about a man he saw as masculine, he would have to imagine feelings of closeness, intimacy, or even love with him. Maybe then he could have a fantasy where the focus was two people together rather than "body parts." He replied, "I'm going to try that. It's going to be interesting because I never did it like that. It's like going out, holding hands, the kiss on the cheek. It's the buildup there. I didn't do it like that, I went straight to the sex parts."

AN EMOTIONAL MILESTONE

I had begun my dialogues with Clark in late April or early May. Our ninth session took place in November of the same year and proved to be something of a milestone. The discussion began by Clark reminding me of the suggestion I had made in our last session—one that I had frankly forgotten about—that he might try to have a fantasy about sex between himself and another masculine man.

> I had started going through the fantasy with this guy, built like myself, in bed. The first time I did it I went straight to the sex and I didn't really feel anything—just empty, nothing there to move me. Then I tried a different approach. I started off with the basics—touching, caressing, the slow approach. I was getting aroused, but here's the problem—I ran away from it. I cut it off, I rejected it. It came on kind of strong. I asked myself that night, "Is it true that I'm capable of holding a full-fledged homosexual relationship?" *For the last week or two, I've been trying to reject it, wipe it off.* The way I view homosexuals, I did cut it off because it's bad. Do I really feel that way or is [it] for other reasons? But I did find it interesting, and very powerful.
>
> We're lying down in bed, touching. He's white, medium build, slender-like. We were caressing on the neck, the earlobes. We were touching—the buttocks, penis area. I didn't even make it to any anal penetration. This is just foreplay. And I imagined what it would be like—his mouth being on my penis. And this is where it really picked up and started getting strong. As the fantasy was going on, I imagined what my mouth would be like on his penis and I didn't get the reaction I thought I would. It became even stronger—and that's when I cut it off. Just visualizing me sucking him off, I was fully aroused. It sort of shocked me.
>
> The minute I cut it off, I was reiterating in my mind the first time you and I had talked about this. I thought maybe this guy

has got a point here—there's a lot of truth to what he's saying. *What I was feeling was real*—and what I usually feel when I fantasize about *women*. It was very erotic, strong, passionate, the same type of thing as if I was engaged with a woman—*it scared me.* It was kind of hard because I had to fantasize about somebody masculine, like myself, and I wasn't used to that. I didn't think I could feel that way towards anyone like myself—someone masculine. It's unbelievable, interesting, what I felt from this fantasy.

Suppose he had not stopped himself? I asked. Where would he have gone with it? "I don't know. I think I cut myself off from some valuable information about myself. I'm going to try to get back to it and see where it goes." Why did he cut it off? "I don't understand. Why did I do that?" What, I asked him, was erotic about taking the other man's penis into his mouth?

His response to my putting my mouth on his penis—his liking it—was the core of the arousal. He was erect. It was pleasing to him and that, in turn, was erotic to me. Compared to the sex I've had with men, it was quite different. *I put myself in the position of giving rather than receiving pleasure,* and that's something I've never done by choice, anyway, with a man. That was a big step by itself. At the beginning, I was saying I don't think anything is going to happen. I can only say I was shocked, surprised—this is very deep. We talk about hidden tendencies—*I didn't know that the tendencies I have could go that far. It took me three days to get relaxed.*

About the emotions involved he said,

The feelings were strong, passionate, erotic, like with a woman. When I was fantasizing about the kissing, it was two aggressive males. When I say passionately, I mean vigorously, *with a lot of meaning behind it.* It wasn't soft, tender—it was very hungry-like—not barbaric, but strong. *I didn't think I could ever feel anything like that*—that I could get aroused to that point. On a scale of one to ten, this was eight and a half, almost nine. But not only once—I can find myself doing it in the middle of the day, with the TV on, the tape player going, and it will cross my mind. And I can visualize that fantasy in the back of my head—to that point where I left off—with my mouth on his penis. I keep replaying it over and over in my head, but I keep cutting it off and asking myself, man, *what does this mean?*

Did he have any sense of what it meant? He said, "For the same reason that I cut this off, I'll never be able to have that kind of relationship till I understand it, get to the bottom of it. I don't really know what it is. With other males, my thing was to outdo, outpower, and outshine. To be with another male like myself in a sex act—putting myself out there, vulnerable, I'm not used to that." I said to Clark that, in this fantasy, he had removed a barrier. One of those barriers had been the formula, "I'm looking at a woman, not a man." He had let that go. Now he was looking at a man, not a woman, and then he let that man be a man, with a penis and an erection, and that seemed important. In reply, he said, "Let's go back to my past—adolescence—the way my brain was conditioned to being aroused by the opposite sex—that barrier is a thick barrier." Yet, I said, he was not putting it back up. He said,

> I'll have to let that fantasy go all the way. The person had to be smooth, without much hair. I felt I was cheating, but then I said, wait a minute, people like different types of masculine men. Why did I cut it off? A male's mind has been conditioned to the opposite sex with a minimum of sexual attraction to other males or with other males restricted to effeminate ones. Even when I got here and got aroused by other men, I think I crossed a barrier then, because there was a time when I wouldn't allow myself to go that far. I'm going to have to go back in there—it's just another barrier I'm going to have to cross and see what happens. I really wanted to talk to you first, before I let myself go back into this type of fantasy. I'm going to try this again.

Clearly, Clark wanted to talk over what had happened to him and to understand it and, of course, I did too. The first and most striking thing about the experience was the tremendous power of the *image* —the image of himself putting his mouth over the erect penis of another man. The analogy that comes to mind is that of splitting the atom. One does not know the power of the energy bound there until it is released. When that image formed itself in Clark's mind, he was shaken. It took him three days to get back to himself. He said, "I keep replaying it over and over in my head, but I keep cutting it off and asking myself, man, *what does this mean?*" I was as interested in the answer to Clark's question as he was. Yet, the very question confirmed that it did have meaning for him. It seems important that he felt nothing when, as he put it, he went "straight to the sex." It seems equally important that feeling began to build as he backed up and started again, but now more slowly, with caressing, and kissing that had *"a lot of meaning behind it."* Again—what was that meaning? I think there is a significant clue in his saying, "I had to put myself in a state about this person that I really loved, really had strong feelings for." This was, however, not easy to do. "To be with another male like myself in a sex act, putting myself out there vulnerable—I'm not used to that." The feeling that Clark allowed to infiltrate his fantasy seemed to gather intensity until the point where he imagined, *"His liking it. That was the core of the arousal."*

STEPPING OVER THE CULTURAL BARRIER

Echoing what he seemed to be saying, I repeated that it was when he imagined loving this man, feeling close to him, that . . . *"I was able to feel something,"* Clark finished. Six months ago, I said, he could not have let himself feel that. He said, "No, because you kept asking me this question about guys around here I was close to. Was it possible, was I capable of having a relationship with them? It was a different kind of love, a friend love. We were close in other types of ways—that's what I was trying to explain to you." But at that point, I started to say, he couldn't let himself imagine . . . *"Imagine, that's right,"* he agreed. I continued that he could not let himself imagine making love to another man. "That's right—exactly," he agreed. *"And that was that barrier that I stepped over."* He added, "You can love a person and it doesn't have to be sexual. It's different when it's *intimate* and I can distinguish between these two."

It is striking how his words echoed Seth's, who told about how, in his dreams, the line between "friendship and intimacy" had been blurred. I'm also reminded of Will asking himself, "Are you crazy?" when he found himself momentarily thinking of the possibility of sex with his friend. He came up against the very barrier that Clark said he had just stepped over. I think Clark's metaphor of "stepping over" a barrier should be taken seriously as a metaphor of movement. He stepped over the barrier that separates one realm of potentially loving feeling—friendship—from another—intimacy. He also stepped over the internalized cultural barrier that separates men from each other. As we explored these things, I said that an important difference between having a close friend that he loved and having sex with him was that, in sex, he was bringing his body into it. His response was revealing. He said, *"You're giving yourself to somebody, physically—and mentally.* If I'm going to do that, deep down inside I must have some strong feelings for the other person. This is my buddy and I love you and I'll do anything I can for you—rather than just 'this is my buddy.' *It's two different types."*

Along with and through the physicality of what they were doing, there was a powerful emotional connection between Clark and the imagined other. These were the potentialities that both Will and Seth must have sensed in their relationships with friends and from which they recoiled. When Michael finally allowed himself to step over the barrier that Clark referred to, he was nearly overwhelmed by the intensity of the feelings he discovered there. All four of these men felt the taboo with which their culture surrounded that experience of intimacy. For Johnny and Terry, that experience of taboo also had an aura of the sacred. For Clark, confronting the taboo was a major step in a process that had begun before we met—a process of transformation of his feelings and of himself.

Chapter 9

Movement into New Territory

The fantasy of having sex with another masculine man occurred after about six months of our work together and appeared to be something of a culmination or—perhaps—a fulfillment of a direction that our dialogue had taken soon after the first session. It marked the opening of a new realm of feeling and potential experience. Initially, Clark had told me that virtually all of his fantasies prior to our first session had been about women. But he now told me,

> Let's say I'm masturbating and fantasizing about a girl and *right in the midst of a climax or ejaculation, a male will pop into my mind.* This happens occasionally, right in the midst of an orgasm. It would go from one fantasy to another, and all of a sudden I'm fantasizing about some guy sucking me off or me fucking him—at the moment of orgasm! Before even speaking to you this would happen. I used to say to myself, "What the fuck am I doing, man? What the hell is going on?" It never happened on the outside. It happens quite frequently. I never looked at it. I think it involves the fantasies I have, involving male and female. I think it reflects on that. I didn't lose my arousal or erection. *Why would it come up like that?*

To Clark's question of "why would it come up like that?" I said that somewhere within himself, he must have already been having some powerful feelings about another man and, even though he did not start by thinking about them, when the orgasm came up the images that went with those feelings came up too. He said, "That's exactly how it happens. Do you think I ought to let go? Do you think I'm holding off? *I'd like to take it as far as I can and not be afraid."* What was that fear, I asked? I was surprised at the answer. *"Being emotionally attached—not being able to be with that person, being in a position where I can be hurt."* This was quite different from the fear of domination. Clark had mentioned seeing how, in the institution, men in relationships could not find the time or place to be together, and about seeing the pain that this inflicted. He did not want to experience that pain. It seemed that the possibility of a relationship with a masculine male might have more emotional intensity than one with a "feminine" man, and more potential for hurt. He had said, "A fantasy about a masculine man like myself—I cut it off. It was a very powerful thing. *It was new territory."* Even though Clark had been having sex with men for some time before I met him, the "new territory" was the place where, as a man, he was meeting another *man.*

Clark was in the early and still tentative stages of exploring this new territory. Nonetheless, he was determined to do it. He said,

> We've got to talk some more because this thing is really on my mind. I want to do some research here—*reaching new depths, new territory.* I want to explore to see what it means. A heterosexual male, put into an institution won't, overnight, just start having sex with other males. A lot of things are hidden inside. Some of these things are coming out. Put it this way, as far as giving, it hasn't been a problem, but being receptive is another thing and I want to explore that some more.

Clark was not only exploring his capacity for sexual feeling for men. He was simultaneously exploring a whole different way of relating his emotional needs to others. Dominance—of which the rape was the most destructive expression—was designed to conceal his sense of powerlessness—from himself as well as others.

THE RAPE DYNAMICS

The dynamics of rape were not on the research agenda for this book. However, in the course of our more than three-year collaboration, I was able to get a clear understanding of those dynamics, and

I think not mentioning them at all would be a significant omission. Initially, I didn't see a connection between the two themes—sex with men on one hand, and women and rape on the other. But Clark linked the new feelings he was discovering with men to overcoming the destructiveness in his past relationships to women. It was becoming clear that what he wanted from men included intimacy, closeness, and love. He had wanted those things from women too, but other feelings had complicated and masked that fact. In one of our earlier sessions, Clark talked about how sex with women had often been a kind of performance.

> To me it was to prove to them that I was this good lover, and I was going to fuck the shit out of them. That was my attitude. I was going to rip their guts out, take this dick and fuck the shit out of them. I wasn't satisfied until they fell out, were unconscious or just couldn't go anymore. After I saw them in that state, I knew I had done my job. *That's* the way you're supposed to fuck women.

The complex of feelings underlying this scenario had its beginnings in his childhood in the inner city of Chicago.

> When I first started to go to school in Chicago, inner city kids were very aggressive, and I found myself getting my ass kicked by females and males in my class, in the third and fourth grades there. *My mother said I had to start protecting myself and fighting back.* I did and I developed a reputation at a very young age that sort of got out of hand. When girls made fun of me or my clothes, I'd sock them in the mouth, guys too.

At home, his mother did not believe in sparing the rod. Even though he said that he usually deserved them, he added, "Those beatings would be considered child abuse now." But worse than her strictness was the feeling that he had been deprived of part of his childhood and adolescence.

> I remember as a kid being very angry with her because at this time I had three younger sisters from her second marriage and I didn't grow up the kid I should have grown up. I spent more

time being like a parent to my brother and sisters than actually being a kid. I remember not being able to participate in things like karate and basketball because I had to stay home and baby-sit. I'd feed them, bathe them, and dress them. I couldn't even go down to the lake to go fishing, something I really liked to do, because I had to stay at home. It was kind of rough.

At about that time, he remembered being afraid of females. "I felt, 'They're out to get me, out to hurt me.' This wasn't the case but that's what I remember." He reacted to this with aggression—it was also one of the reasons he would hit girls. With the onset of adolescence, Clark started to look at girls differently. "Let's just say that the fear faded, and now I wanted to touch them. I would go to extremes to do this. When they refused to let me touch them, I'd beat them up." Although the fear Clark had felt for females was no longer in consciousness, the anger he felt for them seems to have remained and now had a new stimulus—their rejection of his desire to touch them. This set of reactions proved to be the prototype for the rape that would eventually result in his arrest. He continued to be something of a behavior problem in junior high school, and his parents had to go to the school frequently for conferences with the principal because of his violent behavior. "I don't think that even then they knew what was happening to me, why I did what I did." But the aggressive behavior stopped by the time he got to high school, from which he graduated. He was a good football player and he could have gone to Kentucky State. However, he could not qualify for a large enough stipend because his family income was too high. He wound up going into military service instead.

SEX AS DOMINANCE AND PERFORMANCE

In reflecting on his early aggressive behavior, Clark offered an explanation for his violent assertions of dominance: *"It made me feel secure. Once I established that I didn't feel fear."* The performance-driven sex with women that he described also had its origins in fear. It began in his senior year of high school with his girlfriend. One evening, after studying together, he left her house and on the way home remembered that he had left something behind. When he returned, he found her having intercourse with another man. He was devastated and left. Afterward, he kept asking himself if this man were a better lover, had more money, or a bigger penis. This incident had an enduring impact on him.

> I told my cousin what happened and he said I was too soft, too gentle. "You've got to tear that pussy up." After that time, every time I had sex, I felt, *"I'm going to punish this pussy, I'm going to hurt this pussy, I'm going to tear this girl up, and that will never happen to me again. No woman is ever going to do that to me again, ever."* From that day on, every woman I had sex with, *I was punishing with my penis.*

This exaggerated and fear-driven sexual performance converged with the way that, years before, he had learned to use aggression and dominance to make himself feel secure. It also fanned the flames of his early adolescent anger toward females.

> After that day, I didn't look at them as soft, tender creatures. I saw them as sexual objects. That describes how I went from making love to fucking, brutal, sadistic fucking. This isn't about love anymore. I'm trying to validate myself so I can feel good about myself again. It's one thing to have someone tell you your girl is messing around with someone. But to actually *see* it. . . . She told me three weeks later, "I was seeing him before I was seeing you." But it didn't stop how I felt about myself. Every time I had sex with her after that, I wanted to hurt her.

And in fact, he did.

> The next time we had sex, I was screwing her doggy style. *"I'm going make you love . . . you're going to take this dick and you're never going cheat on me again, you slut."* I was saying all these things in my mind. Suddenly she screamed out from one of my thrusts, got up and went to the bathroom. When she came out she told me she had a small cut in her vagina. I felt I had given her what she wanted, sex rough and

hard. When I saw that look of pain in her face, I got aroused. After that, if I didn't see that look I thought I wasn't having sex right. I felt like I had to win her back sexually. I had to show her I was this good lover. It became an obsession. I saw her for another four or five months and then we split up after graduation.

A bit more than a year into our sessions, Clark remembered the first time he had let another man in the institution perform oral sex on him.

That's how I started off with the sex acts. The first time, there was this guy—he was on his knees and he had his mouth on my penis. I wasn't responding with pleasure, if he'd looked up into my eyes. My jaw was tight, I was jackhammering his mouth with my penis. Although that might have been the way he liked it, what I was feeling inside was not pleasure. I wanted to hurt him, degrade him. That's when I first realized what I was doing, because I felt guilty, remorse over why I did that. The next day, he wanted to do it again. I said, "If I let you do this, I'm going to do nothing except victimize you." He said, "Oh come on, it won't take long."

Since then, Clark had come a long way. He never wanted to go back to that place because it was in that place that he committed the rape that had resulted in his arrest. The rape was a crime that he himself described as "heinous." It was, however, the culmination of a long history of deep ambivalence toward women that began with his mother. Clark had been in the Army for a while after his graduation from high school. However, he was given an early, though honorable, discharge because he could not be offered the training program that had been specified in his enlistment contract. He was living with his parents again when an incident happened that convinced him he had to leave. He had a few friends at the house and one of his younger sisters was making a pest of herself. He shooed her away and his mother got angry with him. A couple of words were exchanged and his mother hit him on the forehead with a small bottle, opening a gash that required five stitches. Clark drove himself to the hospital emergency room and his mother neither expressed remorse nor apologized. He said about his mother, *"That was the first time I ever felt like physically punishing her."* Soon after that, he borrowed some money from his uncle so that he could get his own apartment. He asked his girlfriend to live with him and when she said her parents would object, he told her that he loved her, let her know that he wanted to marry her. He said, *"I was afraid of being alone.* I had this apartment two weeks before I got married. I would never go there to live until she came to live with me."

Clark turned twenty-one the month after the wedding. His wife was two years younger. They had been going together for about a year. In less than six months Clark was having sex outside his marriage. They separated for two months when his wife caught him with another woman. After coming back together, there was a brief period of smooth sailing but then things between them began to go downhill again. They separated again and this time Clark went back to live with his mother for about six months. He was working steadily, but he said, "My mother wanted more money for living there, so she threw me out. I stayed with my wife at her parents' house and she became pregnant." Rather than making an active decision to reconcile, it seemed that, once again, problems with his mother pushed him into his wife's arms. "We moved out and the baby was born after two months. My routine became sincere and honest, *but it was like the power shifted to one side.* I felt so guilty for what I'd done in the past that I owed this to her, to let her do this to me. I said, 'Who's wearing the fucking pants around here; what's going on?' We never shared emotions."

The most important—but unfortunately unrecognized—clue to the meaning of Clark's crime presented itself in a series of disturbing, recurrent dreams.

> Before I committed my crime, I was experiencing some unpleasant dreams, dreams of extreme violence against females. It was always a white woman in my dream. The first couple of times I woke up in a cold sweat. I was worried and asked family members, my brother, cousins, and friends whether they had them and if it was normal. They said it was normal and not to worry about it, but to me I felt like it was telling me something.

I remember a woman being in front of me—this is a white woman with blond hair, a beautiful, attractive woman—begging and pleading not to hurt her. Then I would commence clubbing her with whatever I had in my hand—all over.

No sex was involved in this dream. In fact, in no way was it erotic. The woman was fully clothed. There was no sense of sexual arousal; no sexual acts were being performed. What he could not understand was why these were *not* sexual dreams. He said, "I don't understand. This is the kind of woman you want to dream about having sex with, not beating her up." In fact, the image of the woman in these dreams did have a history in Clark's life.

THE TOP OF THE LINE

Growing up, in school, in the service, fellow employees I worked with, they always seemed to talk about one particular woman. Even other women I've had relationships with seem to talk about just one particular woman they'd like to be—or on the males' part to have sex with—this blond-headed, blue-eyed girl. This was the top-of-the-line, like a top-of-the-line car or top-of-the-line liquor.

This was the woman of his dreams—figuratively and literally. Speaking of the woman he raped, he said, "She looked just like this. She was gorgeous."

Well before the rape, Clark had also had fantasies of "rough sex," grabbing a woman by her hair, forcing his penis into her mouth. These did not become elaborated into fantasies of rape until about two years after his marriage. That was a rocky period, marked about a year later by the loss of his good job when the steel mill closed. Although his employment situation eventually improved, the rape ideas never went away. And then the violent dreams in which he was beating a beautiful woman began. They went on until about a year before the rape. About the time they stopped, a more elaborate rape scenario emerged in his mind. "I fantasized about taking this woman, keeping her in my own little personal chamber or room, where she would be my toy to do what I want to do with her. To see her fearful, begging and pleading aroused me a great deal, made me feel powerful.

"The night I raped, I thought this woman [his wife] doesn't love me for me. Whatever happened to me?" And—significantly—"Who's the boss around here?" But at the time, there was no connection between those feelings and what he was about to do. "That night the thought just hit me. When I walked in the store she was there and she was by herself—and she was blond. I said, *'This is what I want and I'm going to get it.'* "

THE TWO EMOTIONS IN THE RAPE

The rape appeared to bring together two very different emotions—intense need and intense anger. The intense need was seen in his desire to touch and be accepted by the woman he idealized. The intense anger was expressed by the dreams in which he was beating up the same woman. The piece that was missing from his memory of those dreams was supplied in his waking thoughts—that this woman would dismiss him with contempt—"Get away from me, you black scumbag motherfucker."

THE RAPE

In one of our sessions, Clark mentioned that in one of his group meetings they had been discussing the sequence of arousal in rape. The therapist asked him to talk about his own, and I asked him to repeat what he had said. In the following discussion, Clark was trying to be candid as well as introspective. In recording it, I kept in mind—and I hope those reading these passages will as well—the admonition of a nun whose personal calling was to try to save people on death row from execution. She said that one should not judge a man by the worst thing he had ever done.

> When I abducted my victim, I didn't have an erection when I was looking at her and thinking how I was going to get her with me. It was just my heartbeat, with the adrenaline flowing. But once I captured her and was going to have sex with her, I had an erection. Once I had her in the car with me and had total

control over her, overpowering her, I had an erection. I hadn't even touched her, looked at her naked or anything and I got an erection. I'm driving and I've got a screwdriver—she probably thought it was a knife and she was totally in my power and that felt good. The sex was just putting the icing on the cake.

After he stopped the car, he ordered her to remove her clothes, while he still remained clothed.

It feels good—I was still aroused because I'm the boss now. [As she was taking her clothes off] it's like opening up a present on Christmas morning, looking at all the goodies. This is the contents of the package, what I've worked for. *I want the very best—this is the top prize, the ultimate woman.* I kept saying to myself, during the rape, *"I've got the very best. You think I'm not good enough for you, huh? You think I don't deserve you? I'm going to show you I deserve you."* I finally got this woman I desired. I felt a wave of excitement that was indescribable—unlike having normal sex—it was more intense, more arousing. I found myself being more aroused than ever before. I never lost my erection over the course of an hour and a half. I kept saying to myself, *"I finally got this woman, so this is what it's all about, so this is it."* I even took time, while she was laying there in the front seat of the car, and just sat there and looked at her. I guess you could say I was admiring what I had there, almost like a hunter looking over his kill. Then I would commence raping her. I had three orgasms altogether.

The intense idealization he felt toward the woman of his dreams was striking. The contrast between those feelings and the next few lines is equally striking.

My attitude and thoughts were very domineering. *"I'm going to make this woman do some of the most despicable, horrible acts I can think of."* These things were going through my head—what am I going to do first? Am I going to penetrate her rectum first? Am I going to have her give me a blow job first, penetrate the vagina first? At the same time, the excitement, the arousal is still hot, very hot. First thing I was going to do was to penetrate her rectum, but I didn't. I made her give me a blow job. Then I penetrated her vagina. Then I made her suck me off again. I took my shirt off. I never fully removed my pants. I was saying things to myself, like *"You think you're too good for me? Won't allow me to touch you, look at you!" Cursing her out under my breath, "Who do you fucking think you are, bitch? You're going to take this dick and you're going to love it."*

The language here was strikingly similar to the language he had used in talking about his girlfriend in high school. *"You're going to take this dick and you're never going cheat on me again, you slut."*

At one point, when I had her sucking me off, I grabbed the back of her head and thought, "This woman did this shit before. She knows how to suck a dick; she'd done this before." I could tell this is no work of an amateur, because she was fully cooperating with me. I said to her, "You done this good." She said, "Thank you, you're the first person who ever told me that." I thought, *"You slut."* Down deep inside, I told myself, "You're not this princess, this goddess, you're not this pure type of woman that I said you are." Immediately, I turned her on her back and jackhammered the pussy.

Why he had taken his shirt off? He said, "Funny you brought that up. When I had fantasies, thoughts about raping, I always visualized my dark skin against her white skin. Even when I had her in the missionary position, I actually looked at the color contrast. That's why I did that. *I wanted to feel my warm skin against hers."* This last phrase struck me. It seemed out of place, a tender feeling paradoxically surfacing in a torrent of anger and abuse. Something else was paradoxical that he noticed as well. After he ejaculated twice, his excitement was falling, not because he had already had two orgasms, but because she was putting up no resistance. "I wanted her to resist, in a verbal way, and I wanted to say, 'Shut the fuck up.'" He found it even more disconcerting when, during intercourse, she held onto his buttocks and moved with the rhythm of his strokes. "I got a little confused. I'm saying to myself, *'Is she enjoying this? This isn't the way it's supposed to be.'* When I had my fantasies I expected them to be frightened, terrified. And I expected her to say things to talk me out of it." When she participated, his physical arousal did not diminish, but his mental excitement did. *"It was like somebody just changed the script."* When he realized that she had performed oral sex before, he was angry. "To show you how distorted my thinking was about that type of woman, I didn't think they did those types of things, that they were *good* girls. In my mind, they were pure, the top specimen of women." Supposing she had said to him that she had always been attracted to his kind of man and would not have minded dating him, why did he have to rape her? "I would have felt bad; I would have probably stopped. It would have got under my skin and I'd say, 'Shut the fuck up, I don't want to hear that shit.' Or, 'You're just saying that so I won't rape you.' I might even have slapped her. I don't know—I would have been angry."

REJECTION IN RAPE

I said to Clark that the whole rape seemed predicated on the assumption that the woman he desired was going to reject him. *Rejection was an indispensable element.* He replied,

> You could take two white women, looking the same, one driving a BMW, looking very nice. The other, driving a Chevy and wearing jeans and sweatshirt—I would have no trouble going over to her. The first one—her attitude, her nasty-type disposition—that angers me, because I think she's looking down on me, thinking I'm a piece of shit—"You're not worthy of being in the same room with me. You black scumbag, motherfucker, get away from me." That's how I perceive her—which is very distorted. Let's say she didn't have a BMW or Jaguar—it's the attitude. The woman in the store, I'd seen before. I thought she had a nasty, uppity disposition. It triggered those thoughts. It goes even back to women who are dominant—that attitude. This is a whole different arousal pattern from being in a rela-

tionship. With my wife, I didn't have to jackhammer the pussy—we made love.

I told Clark about a case study one of my graduate students had done for me, on a young woman who looked very much like Clark's blond, blue-eyed ideal. Her mother had died when she was seven, and two years later her father began forcing her to perform oral sex on him. Sometimes, after it was over, he would hit her. She left him at age fourteen, lived with a friend and the friend's mother for three years, and then went out on her own. Shortly after she left him, her father departed from town and she never heard from him again. Now, in her early twenties, she would perform oral sex on men she knew casually, for drugs. In her waking life, she offhandedly acknowledged the connection between sex and drugs but discounted any between sex and love. Yet, she had a dream in which she was performing oral sex on a man who beat her up and left her for dead. The dream, in this instance, was the interpretation of her waking reality and explained its meaning. She was recreating in her waking life the scene of degradation and hurt at the hands of her father, because not only had she not gotten over it—that was where she still was.

Clark asked, "Are you saying this applies to me?" I said to Clark that he was not only degrading the woman, he was recreating, in that rape scene, a scenario of rejection—his own, one that already existed in his head. *"Get away from me, you scum."* This had to be very painful coming from a woman who occupied such a lofty pedestal in his mind, but in the rape "script" in a very ironic way, that was what he was seeking. He recalled, after the rape:

> I pulled up in this mall parking lot. I was on the verge of striking again and I found one. This woman pulled up in a black Jaguar—blond-haired, gorgeous. You know why I didn't attack her? As she pulled up and I'm looking this way at her through the driver's side, she got out, she said, "Hello, how are you doing? Nice out today." I said, "Yeah, it is." That killed it off—just nothing. The whole bottom came out. I said, wow, she's nice, not like the rest of those rich, stuck-up bitches. She talked to me, said "Hi," smiled. I felt like a piece of shit.

Her friendly words eliminated her as a candidate to play the role the script called for. *His* role was clear—to be the "black scumbag motherfucker"—the despicable rapist. When he said to himself that he was going to make the woman he abducted perform "the most despicable, horrible acts" he could think of, they were despicable and horrible only because, in her eyes—and at some deep level, his own—*he* was. Otherwise, they were the same acts lovers might perform. Yet he was determined to get close to her, even though she despised him, to make her feel his "warm skin" against hers, to make her take him into herself, at any cost—to her or to himself. Clark said, *"I've actually turned down sex from the type of women I raped.* They weren't very rich, but they were decent women and I turned down their propositions." These women would have accepted Clark, but his rape was not only about the need for acceptance—although it certainly was that. Nor was it only about anger, though it certainly was that. It was also about his own rejection.

Was there, in addition, a racial component in Clark's crime? This is a difficult question to answer. It was present in the epithet he imagined being hurled at him, "black scumbag motherfucker." But class seemed to be more of an issue than race, since he had found a fair number of white women who were attracted to him, including even the "jeans and sweatshirt" counterpart of the "high-class" woman he felt he could never have. He certainly was not unaware of latent or overt prejudice in this society but did not appear to feel that he had been a victim of it to any significant degree. Plus, his own attitudes were racially tolerant. And yet, he said that he had always visualized his dark skin against her white skin—as well as "I wanted to feel my warm skin against hers." My feeling is that, although the cultural meanings of race and status were in the background, they had become assimilated to the primary—and deeply personal—meaning that the rape had for Clark.

REJECTING THE RAPIST MENTALITY

But now, Clark wanted to erase all vestiges of a rapist mentality from his relationships, which held true for any relationships he might have with men, who, for the moment, were the only people available for emotional and physical closeness. In his daydreams now, he thought of someday having a situation where he could be living with both a man and a woman. He visualized the three of them in bed. "Touching, caressing, engaged in full oral and anal sex, just relaxed, no sneaking. Everything is right there, just a comfortable setting." When Clark mentioned this daydream to me, it had been about five months since that first breakthrough fantasy, and he had continued to move in his feelings and thoughts since that time. I think that what was going on was not the uncovering of previously repressed wishes. Rather, it had the quality of a thoughtful, deliberate—and new—movement. This movement involved not only getting closer to men, but also allowing different feelings into his sexual life—whether in imagination or reality. He again described how sex had been a performance for him. But now, he could imagine having emotional sex with a man—with a masculine man, as well as with a woman. I remarked that the fear of dominance, once such a powerful block, seemed to have evaporated. He said, "It's the trust thing. When you love somebody that goes with the territory. *What made me feel secure all my life was to frighten, intimidate. 'You're not going to hurt me.'*"

As for the emotional qualities that he imagined would characterize a one-to-one relationship with another man, he said, "Very much the same as having a friend you dearly love, or even having a girlfriend whom you love—people that you like a lot. I've had friends like that on the street—you care for him, like him, only this time there would be a lot of *intimacy* instead of just a regular relationship." When he was on the street, I asked, was there a barrier to how intimate or close he could get to another man? In his reply, he made an interesting distinction. He said, "In a group sex setting, there was not, but when we were alone, there was definitely a barrier." In other words, the emotions of the one-to-one bond are the more dangerous. But that bond was the one that he wanted to explore now. As he did that, the culturally induced split between emotional bonding and sexual feeling began to be healed. As that happened, he could let himself think more and more about the possibilities inherent in the body for the expression of intimacy with another man and, quite naturally, his mind began to dwell on anal intercourse.

Although the institutional culture has linked male homosexuality with feminine identification, as Clark explored the dimensions of relating to another masculine man, he was not changing his own sense of gender. And as he was able to let go of the fear, he no longer had to make his partner into a woman either. When he imagined oral sex with another man in the mutual "sixty-nine" mode, he remained as firmly grounded in his own sense of masculinity as ever. The same thing was true as he began to think about experimenting with anal penetration.

It was around this time that Clark began to look around for someone with whom to experience some of the things he had been thinking about. He spoke of experimenting with one particular man. He described his feelings toward this man as "Just wanting to get close." But this wish to get close was now finding expression in physical imagery. He said, "I mean physical, imagining having sex. The full sexual act, penis to penis, mouth to penis, the whole nine yards. My arousal kicks in when I do this now. It's amazing to me. I don't understand it, but I'm not afraid of it." When he caught himself casting sex with him into the kind of "performance" scenario that he now believed had marred and distorted his relationships with women—"Sexually dominating this guy, fucking the shit out of him, make him scream and holler—I'm like, 'no, wait a minute.'" With women, he said, "It was crazy—I just changed the whole intimate thing to a performance thing." He didn't want to do that anymore, with either women or men.

But even before Clark and I began our sessions, deeper emotions would sometimes creep into his encounters with men.

> Sometimes it would get so deep—say a guy was giving me a blow job—I would respond, with touching, massaging his back, his neck. I was responding and in turn they'd respond back. I told myself one day—after all the talks we had I was doing a lot of thinking—if I went that far I could go a little farther, see what it's all about. It's not just a learning experience, *this could be a part of me.*

As with Johnny, the process started with an experience of the body, and that experience led him to a place within himself, a place of feelings. When he thought about sex with a man now, he told himself, "I'm going to open myself totally. This isn't about me performing, trying to be Mr. Joe Macho king—it's getting myself to a relaxed stage and letting things take their course." But the emotions in the imagined scene seemed every bit as important to him as the acts themselves. He thought of, "Being embraced—the hug, not so much the oral or anal sex, just the embrace, the touch—that right there is more arousing than the fantasy of the sex act to me. My skin against his skin, my chest against his chest, *the warmth of the skin.*" Speaking of a man that he formed an interest in, he said, "The other day I saw him naked and saw his buttocks but that was not the main thing that turned me on. I have this thing locked into my head right now where I want to lay down in bed next to another man. *It's not just sex.* A couple of years ago it might have been like that, maybe a hit and run. Going in there, bang, bang, boom and then I'm gone." A year previously the masculinity of the other person had been almost an intrusion, something he would rather not know about. "Now," he said, "that fear is no longer there—it's turned into eagerness, something I want to attack, to pursue this now." A year before he had said that the only thing he found erotic about having sex with a man was dominating him. In striking contrast, he said, "Right now the thing that strongly drives me is the closeness, the touching, even the fact of rubbing two penises together—it's erotic, it would move me, so it's totally different."

"I HAVE A CHOICE"

I said to Clark that some theories talked about repressed homosexuality. But it seemed that what had been repressed or stopped in him was a kind of movement. As the block was removed, he began to move toward another man, toward exploring a whole new realm of emotion and physicality. "Yeah, I'm not afraid anymore. Before, males weren't in my fantasies when I masturbated. And now I have a choice." He did not really have a choice before?

> *Right, there wasn't a choice.* When I first came here and certain guys propositioned me, the first thing that hit my mind was my friend back on the street, that day he was waxing my car, and he was propositioning me. During the sexual act, I

didn't see a male image. But when you and me first started working and I was going through the fantasies, *I saw a male and that's when the fear hit. Now, I look at the whole body.* I'm working the fantasy. I'm naked, he's naked. I'm trying to work this out. I'm like, it's a male's face, a male's body. *I go all the way with it now.*

I had interviewed Will shortly before this session, and I told Clark what Will had said about feeling a block, literally in his head—in a headache. He smiled.

He said he was getting a headache, huh? I can identify with that. I guess he was rejecting it. In a way, you want to look at it, you want to feel it, but then there are other things going through your mind rejecting it. That block is a whole lot of things. Fear is the main core in that block, but a lot of other things too. Image has a lot to do with it—how people see you, what they say about you. Plus your own views about homosexuality, how you see it. Is it a 'No, no, it's not supposed to be like that"? Once you understand it and you know what it means, that blockage goes away. But speaking for me, fear was the main blockage. I like my own attitude. I'm taking all this macho-ness, all this imagery, and shutting it off to the side. I'm not going to do this thing as a sexual performer. This is for me, I want to see what I feel, what I'm going to get out of this."

AN EXPRESSION OF LOVE

He recalled how he thought that a woman only liked him for his body, was not interested in his thoughts, his goals, or how sensitive he was. Looking back, he had remarked that it all seemed rather sad. "My attitude now is to enjoy it. *It's an expression of love, you know.* If you know somebody likes you, loves you, cares about you, it makes you feel good inside. You don't feel empty, alone—somebody is there with you. It makes you feel secure. That's the best way of describing the feelings." About the man he found himself attracted to, he said, "There's something about him that strikes me as nontoxic, a pureness, innocent—like a fresh spring leaf." But as yet, nothing had actually taken place between them, nor was he certain that it would. However, he did continue to have an occasional encounter with his long-standing sexual partner. But he saw this man as quite feminine and, while Clark liked and respected him, he really wanted to have an experience with somebody more like himself—the very thing he once rejected.

Nevertheless, it was with him that Clark felt he broke new ground in the exploration of male-to-male sexuality. In one of their encounters,

> He reached down under there and started licking my anus—yeah. I found that quite pleasurable. I felt that I was right on the edge. I had that feeling of like a semi-orgasm that was constant. You know, when you're right on the edge of having an orgasm and where it's really intense—an intensity that's long term, constant. I found my body going into a nervous frenzy. He did that first. If you measured my erection on a scale of one to ten, it would have been a ten or a ten plus—ultimate stimulation. I must have been off in [a] twilight zone somewhere. I didn't know it was that pleasurable—I had no idea. Now I'm thinking about somebody penetrating me. Maybe it's not as painful or bad as I thought it would be. Somebody entering my rectum, and I'm thinking, wow, maybe this is one way you could get a person relaxed, open up, open the door for other things, other sexual acts. I was open, just open—I learned quite a lot. I think this opens up the door. I feel my courageousness has increased and you could say it's stimulated me to do more and see what happens. I wasn't afraid of anything.

About this encounter, he said, "It was unlike anything we had done before. There was more feeling." The rigid zoning of the body, which had once served to protect what he had come to see was a false sense of masculine identity, had been erased. It was a protection he no longer needed, and he could allow the primal modalities of male-to-male sexuality to assert themselves.

CHANGE IN FANTASY LIFE AND IDENTITY

At this point, the content of his fantasies had shifted toward a preponderance of male imagery. Now, he said, his fantasies were probably 80 percent about men and 20 percent about women. Reflecting on these changes, he said,

> I was thinking all the way back to day one and how far we had gone with this thing. No doubt about it, I'll openly admit to myself, sure, *I'm bisexual.* And neither one of my patterns conflict with each other. One doesn't cancel the other out. They'll intertwine, with the men and the women, even with sexual fantasies. But they don't clash, they just twine together. That tells me I'm comfortable with this. Those barriers, those walls you mentioned are no longer there.

This was quite different from his breezy acknowledgment, at our first meeting, of, "You can call me bisexual, homosexual, or whatever you want—but I call it adjusting to my environment."

Even though the culture of the institution in which Clark was confined lacked the extreme differentiation of masculine and non-masculine roles found in some ordinary prisons, its categories of thought still reflected some of this kind of role-playing. Clark was a bit dismayed to realize that some people tended to typecast him as the super-endowed "stud." At this point, he had little patience for this role. In addition to making him feel used, doing that would simply be replaying his rape dynamics. For some months now, Clark had been getting to know a second man with whom there was an obvious mutual attraction. This man had had some relationships with women, but his predominant orientation was to men. He fit the general profile that Clark was looking for now, someone masculine without being macho—a distinction he had come to draw. He had a dream about this man, Alan:

> We were laying down on the bed, side by side. He was saying something about liking to be kissed. All I could see was the upper part of our bodies.

A few days before the dream, Alan approached him in the laundry room and said, "What a handsome man you are." Clark responded by kissing him on the neck, which Alan liked. About the dream, he said, "As a teenager, I would have dreams like that with women, with more taking place, eventually resulting in a wet dream." In spite of the performance-driven aspect of sex with women, the capacity for tenderness and the desire for intimacy had never been lost. In the dream, he was kissing a man in the same affectionate way that, in dreams, he had sometimes kissed women. Describing his last sexual encounter with his customary partner, he said his excitement was not about the anticipation of receiving oral sex or his performing anal intercourse, but " . . . just the fact of two warm bodies touching. That closeness, embracing meant more to me than anything. It was not just sex, that's what I'm trying to say." More and more now, his thoughts turned to experiencing these things with Alan.

MAKING LOVE WITH A MASCULINE MAN

It had been almost two years since our first meeting and about a year and a half since that first breakthrough fantasy in which he imagined himself with a masculine man that Clark finally had the experience, in reality, that he had come to want so strongly. He was with Alan. It turned out to be a landmark experience, and I want to let him describe it in his own words:

> It was quite an experience. The excitement of the thing in anticipating it was kind of overwhelming. We went down to his room and were there for an hour and a half. We started off by hugging, embracing, kissing. The foreplay went quite a long time before engaging in anything as far as oral or anal. Then it just seemed so smooth, and gentle, sensual. We were touching each other all over, stroking, a little kissing on the neck and body parts—I was so excited. Our penises touched and that was sort of arousing in a way. We were picking up the pace. We lay down together on his bed. He got on top of me. He started kissing me from here all the way down, my legs, all over. I just sat there and absorbed it. Once he got down there, he performed oral sex on me. Then I did the same thing to him—all the way down, a slow-moving process, *a love-mak-*

ing process. When I got down there, I had no problem with his penis. But the weirdest thing happened to me. I've been trying to put it into words for a week. I haven't been able to figure it out yet, but let me try. It was not unpleasant. *I felt like I conquered something.* Did you ever do something, fix something, and then say, "there . . . ?" It was sort of like "there," sort of like something left me, lifted off my back, and I had this weird, comfortable, contented. . . . I can't explain it. I was sort of relieved in a way.

After I did that, after I was giving him a blow job, he kept pushing me back. He liked it, enjoyed it, I could tell by his response. But I don't think that's what he really wanted me to do. He said, "I want you to fuck me." So I did. The first time, it was hard to get in, then he did something and I was able to penetrate. He seemed to really enjoy that. It was what he really wanted. Then, after I ejaculated, he lay there for a moment, and I explained to him that this was new to me. He understood and said, "That's good; you should do what you want to do." We lay there, and we were still touching. And here's the thing—he wanted me to screw him again, so I did. After, we lay there talking and held each other. It was okay. I had to pause after the first section, so to speak, because it was sort of overwhelming. I felt very comfortable, just mellow, relaxed. I even noticed my behavior in the past couple of days. I haven't gotten angry, even out on the softball field.

I recalled the fear of domination he used to have. He said, "Maybe I just conquered it, I don't know." An indication that he had was the fact that Alan did not conform to the slender, petite body type that Clark had earlier insisted was absolutely necessary for him to be able to have sex with another male without fear. Clark described Alan as average in height and weight. "I'm taller, leaner. His legs and behind are a little bigger. My penis is fatter and slightly longer than his, but in a limp state, his seemed to be slightly bigger." About taking Alan's penis into his mouth, "It was no different from kissing him, or licking, or touching any other part of his body. That really shocked me. I didn't have any hang-ups, get sick or anything, and he seemed to enjoy it." He added, "Anal sex crossed my mind, and I thought he might ask to go inside of me." Although Clark was prepared to accept this, it did not happen. However, Alan did insert his finger into him, and that he found erotic. He remembered how one of his therapists had once said that he had to deal with the issue of his childhood abduction and molestation. "I think she was saying I was still holding that and walking around with it." Maybe now he was not, I suggested. "Maybe I'm not," he replied.

He went on,

> I was sitting there on the edge of bed, laughing, shaking my head—that feeling of relief, joy. It felt good—I couldn't even exactly explain it to him. I told him how, in the past, I'd victimized other guys in the building, how my rape qualities had come out. "But," I said, "Things are little different right now. You know that I like you a little bit and have certain feelings towards you. Right now, I'm dealing with that."

What were his emotions?

> Very strong, powerful, toward him during the acts themselves. You know, when you. . . . I'm not going to say "love" . . . when you like somebody. I guess you could say love . . . it was that type of feeling that overwhelmed me. It fucked with me, man, so to speak. It sort of knocked me on my knees. My rape qualities didn't come into play. It had meaning, there was something there. It was giving *and* taking. I felt very strong caring for him. I'd been looking at him for a long time. The attraction was there. When I went into his room, I went in with a great deal of respect for him, as opposed to the past. *The real Clark was in that room, having sex.* The gentle, the kind, passionate, affectionate person that he can be—that's who was there. It just felt like something I haven't had in a long time— since I've been locked up.

Ironically, this first experience with Alan was destined to be the last. Alan was leaving the institution in a few days, having completed his sentence, and circumstances did not permit them to get together again. Clark said,

> Talking about feelings between us two, emotions could build up. Becoming attached—I could see that happening very easi-

ly. The day before he left I remember saying to myself, "Well, he's going and I don't know if it's good or bad. I wouldn't mind doing it again. Wow—maybe I'm attached a little bit or feelings are starting to grow. Maybe it's good if he is gone, maybe not; I don't know."

I said to Clark that, although both his gay friend and his wife had brought him closer to the inner boundary internalized by men in our culture, it was when he came into the institution that he began to discover, beyond that boundary, a world of men that had always been there but that he—interrupting me, he completed the thought—" . . . *never dared to go.*"

COMPARISONS WITH WOMEN

I asked Clark about the difference between sex with a woman and sex with a man. He mused,

> Women, to me, are more moody. Emotions fluctuate, all over the place—it's hard to read them. But looking at my male friends, they're the same most of the time. They aren't hard to read—you can see how they're feeling. Sometimes I can't connect with women because I don't understand where they're coming from. I can identify with males more easily than I can with a female. Speaking with another guy is easier for me.

It was very interesting that Clark did not respond to my question by comparing men and women sexually, but rather in terms of the *relationship* with each. I tried to narrow the focus by asking him about the difference between making love with a person who had a male instead of a female body. He said, "When we had sex, it was strong, powerful, pretty much the same emotions and feelings that go with a female—*the same thing.*" But he could put his finger on one difference. "*This time I didn't feel like I wanted to dominate the whole situation. I stayed equal with him. None of my rape dynamics came into play.* I didn't have the need for it." In looking back over this conversation, I have the impression that the question of how it was different to be with a man, compared to a woman, was *my* question. Clark was much more struck by how it was not different. The difference that was important to him was the difference in himself—the difference between the angry, defensive, desperate rapist and the warm human being who was no longer afraid of his own feelings, who could use sex to love and give instead of to dominate and take.

MALE TO MALE

Nevertheless, Clark was able to draw some comparisons between women and men in an erotic sense. He said,

> It's like two male bodies, two erect penises touching each other, when you embrace. It's different—hard to put into words. With Alan in this room, when we were taking our clothes off, from the moment that we were touching and kissing, the excitement level went from zero to sixty in two seconds, without even any touching yet, just getting undressed. Then it goes even higher, once you start touching and embracing. To me, it's different. I didn't want to dominate him in a rape-type fashion, but you could do it in a healthy way. Even when I lay on my belly and he was on top of me, I felt no insecurities.

Was there, I asked him, something particularly powerful or unique about being with a person whose physical being was like his? "Yeah," he replied, "that's it—you may have just said it right there. I was going to say that, but I didn't think it made a lot of sense. Looking at another male—*male to male*—right in front of you, *that's* a difference." The wheel had come full circle—the maleness of the other that he once had to block out had become central in the experience of making love with Alan. When I said to Clark that it seemed that half of the human race was no longer off limits to him for emotional and physical closeness—it was with Clark that this phrase first occurred to me—he laughed and said, "I don't know what kind of answer to give to that."

RAPE DYNAMICS—DISSOLUTION

Clark had made a second and unsuccessful rape attempt. In contrast to the first time, the woman he selected resisted and kept on resisting even after he pulled out the razor he intended to intimidate her with. Although he had not planned to use it, in the escalating violence, he cut both her and himself. However, when he saw the blood, excitement drained away.

> It was a turn-off, it stopped me. I didn't want that to happen, I swear I didn't. *I don't even like thinking about it, it's something out of a horror movie.* I immediately stopped. I drove around for about two days, making contact with nobody. I couldn't believe what I had done. I kept saying, "That isn't the way it's supposed to happen, that isn't the way it's supposed to happen."

Although consciously, the weapon was there to make her comply with his sexual wishes, unconsciously it was a symbol of his deep anger. His nightmares of beating a beautiful woman were not dreams of sadistic excitement, but of pure rage. However, when the second time, reality overtook his nightmares, he was severely shaken. Shortly afterward, he went to a wooded area and tried to hang himself because he felt he was out of control and could not bear what he was becoming. But someone saw him and called the police. He was stopped before he could succeed, and he confessed what he had done.

Even before I met Clark, he had been working on understanding what had led to his crimes. Just before the encounter with Alan, Clark had told me about a dream he had about a recently released inmate who was just recommitted because, in a dispute with his wife, he had threatened her by putting a gun in her mouth. Clark knew him and had talked to him. In the dream, he said:

> I confronted him and had sad feelings. I was so mad, I wanted to sit there and cry.

I think the anger in this dream was toward himself as well, as were the tears. I did not say this to Clark at the time, but about two months later, and after his sexual experience with Alan, he related the following two dreams:

> The first dream involved my therapist, Jane, me, and four or five other group members. She had us all in a room with a blackboard. She had graphs on the board, that had to do with us raping, and our victims. Her behavior was very aggressive as she was writing stuff down on the chalkboard, explaining it. When she stopped, one guy got up and ran out the door and I stood there, and I was crying, very emotional about what she said. A couple of other guys had their heads down. I was feeling. . . . I don't know whose pain I was feeling—my victim's? The whole room looked different, with lights in there.
>
> In the second dream, I was in a parking lot, in a car. There were lots of other cars there. I was driving around. I'd pulled over and this little white girl, around five, maybe six, had on a yellow jacket and blue pants and she was lost and crying. I put her in the car with me and we were driving, and she was saying that she was hungry. I looked for money in my pocket, and I only had two dollars. I went to one of those convenience stores. She jumped out of the car and we went into the store. I saw one of my friends and he asked, "Who is the little girl?" I said, "I don't know; she's lost. I'm trying to find out where she lives, where her parents are. She told me she's hungry so I'm going to buy her a hot dog." There was a hot dog stand in back. She was running around the store, and I bought her a hot dog. My friend kept saying, "Where are you going to take her?" I said, "I don't know; she's lost—a little white girl, she's lost." I remember paying the guy and getting some change. It was sunny out that day. I remember feeling sorry, and taking care of her. It was sad.

These dreams were, I believed, connected. Over the past two years, he said, he had many emotional dreams in which he was feeling sorry, feeling pain for someone. The first of these two dreams brought into focus, for the first time, the object of his pity—his victims. Clark had, in our sessions, frequently said how sorry he was for what he had done. But I think this dream was important in testifying to the genuineness of his remorse. Dreams can conceal, but they don't lie. The second dream was not at all clear to him. However, I think it is possible to understand it. In this dream, he returned to the scene of the rape—he had abducted his victim from a convenience store. Like his victim, the little girl was white. But instead of giving her the blond hair and blue eyes of the woman he raped, the dream transposed these significant colors to her outfit— a yellow jacket and blue pants. Now he was seeing the woman he hurt as a little girl, rather than as a "high-class bitch." She was a human being, vulnerable, and he was taking care of her, trying to make up for what he had done to her. Clark had three sisters whose care he had been very much involved in and whom he loved. He said, "When I woke up I felt like she was one of my sisters and I was taking care of her."

TWINNING—MALE SELF, MALE OTHER

Clark had initially said, "When I see a masculine body I see myself, and that's a turnoff." In a paradoxical way, the masculine other was the "evil twin" of Clark's own sexual self. One of the reasons he rejected a man like himself might have been because he could neither trust nor like what he saw in himself—those parts that he called his "rape dynamics." He himself attributed this fear to his childhood abduction, which was certainly part of it. But I think his personal life history only heightened the sense of badness that this culture's institutions have projected onto the male sexual self, along with the love for another like oneself. Thus, it was no accident that Frank, whom I wrote about in *Sexuality and the Devil* selected the devil to symbolize the man he unconsciously wanted a sexual connection with—and love from. The demonization of sexuality in general and male sexuality in particular—through its association with the symbol of ultimate cosmic evil—was already firmly in place by the early Christian era.[1] Frank had feared that if the devil possessed him, he would "make me his slave, kick me around, humiliate me." This was remarkably similar to Clark's fear of being dominated in sex with a masculine man.

Men's fear of homosexuality is, then, a fear they have been taught to have of each other. Nevertheless, in striking opposition to what they had been taught, the most powerful theme in the same-sex feelings of the men I have discussed was the sense of shared ties to other men *as* men. Those who gave voice to their same-sex feelings seemed able to overcome—though sometimes only partial-ly—the cultural sense of dread that is projected onto the masculine other. They did not therefore have to see the men they were drawn to as feminine. Gert Hekma proposed that, in the nineteenth centu-ry, characterizing homosexuals as the third sex was attractive to some because it reduced the image of the "sodomite" from a power-ful seducer to a nonmasculine man who could not threaten the virility of "normal" men. It was a nonthreatening representation of the homosexual for heterosexuals.[2] I think that the scientists—and they are overwhelmingly men—who have been proposing that same-sex feelings are indicative of a feminine component in men's mind's or bodies are engaged in the same kind of denial and for the same reasons. Behind the mask of the feminine gay man looms the shadow of the masculine other, the demonized twin of the male sexual self.

It is significant that, as Clark let go of the protective persona of masculine dominance and came to value the warm and loving emo-tions of which he was capable, he came to like and trust himself more. As he did that, he was also able to move toward another man like himself—to see him as a man, and to experience with him the emotions of the male-to-male bond that are at the core of men's same-sex feelings. Clark said he had conquered something in mak-ing love with Alan. I think it was the fear of the image of the male twin that is both a reflection *of* the self and a completion *for* the self. It is an image that is profoundly important to male experience. The fear of that image is what a boy developing as a gay man in this culture must also confront and conquer. How one man did that is the subject of the next part of this book.

PART III:
ZACK

Chapter 10

Cultural Confrontations and Identity

This is the first of three chapters about Zack, a gay police officer whom I met at meeting of the Gay Officers Action League, where I was introduced as a psychologist interested in speaking with gay men working in law enforcement. I met Zack about a year after the president's attempt to lift the ban on gays in the military. Among the unacknowledged aims of that ban were not only the social and psychological isolation of gay men from their heterosexual counterparts but also the denial of their fitness to participate in roles symbolic of male strength and competence. The deal that was finally struck—"don't ask, don't tell"—promised freedom from persecution in exchange for invisibility. Heterosexual men are visibly represented in the full range of vocations and professions—the arts, business, politics, athletics, the armed forces, and the police. Gay men are found in all of the same vocations and professions but ironically, the more a given role has been socially identified as masculine, the greater the pressure on gay men to remain invisible in it. This invisibility affects young men who think they might be gay by limiting the range of available role models for them, while it lends credence to stereotypes that undermine their self-esteem. I felt, therefore, that it would be useful, to meet some men in law enforcement—a field that is certainly socially tagged as masculine.

When Zack first came up and told me of his willingness to speak with me, I was struck by his easy smile and the confidence with which he told me about being out on the job, to the extent of introducing his boyfriend to some of his friends on the force. A few weeks later, we had our first meeting. He worked on the ninety-member force of a medium-sized town close to New York City, and so we met on average every four to six weeks for a period of about five years. I learned early on that the ease and confidence I had been initially impressed by had been hard-won, the result of a long and difficult journey.

I have organized the results of my research with Zack into three chapters, each with a primary theme or focus. Chronologically, they correspond roughly to the early, middle, and late periods of our work together. However, there is considerable overlap in the chronology. Where it is important for understanding, I have tried to make the time frame clear. Thematically, there is also overlap in these three chapters since it is impossible to divide a person's life into watertight compartments.

The identities of most of the men in my classes were—and remained—heterosexual. Over the time that we worked together, Clark's became bisexual. Zack's was unambiguously gay. Any study of a gay man in this culture has to be an interactive one—in the sense that it must take into account, not only how others affect him, but also how he affects others. There is the obvious fact that as a boy and as a man he is affected by the rejection of his feelings and often himself by people who mirror the negative attitudes of the institutional culture. The present chapter—"Cultural Confrontations and Identity"—tells the story of the evolution of Zack's awareness of his sexuality, how he dealt with its collision with the institutions of a culture hostile to it, and the eventual self-affirmation that came with the assertion of his identity and its disclosure to his family and on the job.

My research with my students, my work with Clark, and my work with Zack constituted three independent lines of inquiry into men's same-sex feelings. With Zack, these converged on the meaning central to all of them—the emotional and physical fulfillment of the male-to-male bond. With Zack as my collaborator, I was able to explore the depths and dimensions of this bond in men's lives as it unfolded in his own. This exploration constitutes the primary focus of Chapter 11—"The Color Green."

I stated in the opening chapter of this book that it was my intention to turn the spotlight on that place in the mind where sexual emotion rising from within intersects with the life of the individual in culture. Zack's boyhood and adolescent experiences affirm the flexibility of the boundaries of identity during the formative years of boys regardless of their ultimate primary sexual preference. There has, however, been an assumption that, by adulthood, those boundaries lose their flexibility. Obviously, the material in the early chapters of this book contradicts that assumption.

Furthermore, if traditional psychological research has paid little attention to the effects on a gay man of the institutional hostility to his feelings, it has paid virtually none to how a gay man affects men on the other side of the identity boundary. Perhaps because of the stand he took in his life, because of a warm and generous personality, and because both men and women thought him handsome and masculine, Zack seemed to have the capacity to tap, at different levels, the same-sex potential in the feelings of men whose identities were not gay. The third of these chapters then, Chapter 12—"Boundary Crossings"—looks at how Zack, as an adult, seemed to act as a lightning rod that drew down this culture's conflicts about men's bodies, their sexuality, and their emotional relationships to each other.

THE INSTITUTIONAL CULTURE:
EARLY ENCOUNTERS

Early on Zack said about being gay, "It's the nomenclature of my life." He was referring to its function as an affirmation of self. A little later, in another of our sessions, he remarked

> *People* make me "gay." Otherwise I would think I was normal, liking men. That's the way I look at it—society has made me "gay." A book makes me "gay" because it says that a "homosexual" is someone who likes other men. If way back when someone had said it's no problem with men liking men, I'd just exist as I am. History has made it a problem." Intuitively, Zack understood the two faces of identity in this culture. One was the positive face—an affirmative assertion of the sense of self. The other was the negative face—the fact that identity has historically been thrust upon a boy who is suspected of harboring same-sex feelings, an identity that is usually first experienced as pejorative and problematic. Johnny had said, about

that identity, "It wasn't 'gay,' it was people were 'fags' or 'homosexuals.' They were dirty. As soon as it happened, I went right into it. I was dirty, no good, a fag, homosexual. People like that were people you didn't care for. They were sick, demented."

In my first interview session with Zack, the theme that seemed to emerge naturally in our dialogue was the encounter between a child's early sexual stirrings and the cultural institutions organized around hostility to those stirrings. Zack's earliest sexual memory was from about age six or seven with a boy of the same age.

> I remember being in his bedroom and us being under the sheets. We were both very curious about why our "pee-pees" were swollen, that we had a hard-on. I'm sure we both felt excited about what was going on. I don't remember if I touched or sucked his penis. There isn't a very vivid memory of that, though I think something like that did happen. What's more vivid is the feeling of interest about why that was happening. There was no rationale to it. I didn't even think it was wrong or right, none of those feelings. I didn't understand it then.

The innocence of this early experience was not to last. It had taken place when Zack was in second grade, and at the end of that year his family moved to a different town. When he came back to his old playground for a visit the next year, something shocking and inexplicable happened. His friend had apparently told someone about their explorations under the sheets.

> I don't know where they got it from but they said, "Oh, then he's a fag." So when I came back to the playground where I hung out at as a little kid, they all called me "faggot" because I'd sucked his dick. It killed me. I was in shock. All of a sudden they were telling me that something I didn't under-stand was wrong. Now I'm thinking I did something wrong, something terrible.

In a microcosm, this playground incident illustrates the way in which rejection of same-sex feeling is handed down from the top.

Older children, having absorbed it from their elders, pass the sense of condemnation to the upcoming generation. After the move, Zack did not like his new neighborhood or his new school. He had been a good student in first and second grade, and now his grades suffered.

> I didn't get along with anybody in the neighborhood. I hated school; I hated the people I went to school with; I hated everybody. I think it had a lot to do with hating myself too, because I didn't understand myself either. That's one strong thing—looking back, I always knew I was different, and I hated myself for being different from everybody, but there was no comprehension why—I was miserable. Looking back, it was something sexual—though not about the act of sex. I didn't seem to fit in, so I tried to be as nice as I could to everybody, had no opinions, and agreed with everybody so no one would think I was different.

Although Zack said, "I always knew I was different," the memory of this difference didn't appear to predate the playground incident. Much of the sense of childhood difference that gay men sometimes report is, in fact, an imposed sense of difference. Nevertheless, in the third through fifth grades, although Zack felt different, he was not singled out as such, and he had both male and female friends during these years. When he was in fourth grade, he tried some sexual explorations with a male friend, mainly just looking at each other. They were caught by the other boy's mother. They gave the game away when they hastily put on each other's underwear at her approach, but she didn't reprimand them or give Zack the impression that they were doing anything bad. But in sixth, seventh, and eighth grades—late preadolescence to early adolescence—Zack recalled, "I was completely lost. I saw male and female pairing off, thinking they were in love, and I couldn't care less."

EARLY MOVEMENT

Although not finding himself drawn to the kind of male-female pairing he saw around him, he did find himself attracted to things that had about them the aura of maleness. In this period, he recalled,

"I liked the smell of the men's locker room. I just liked sitting there watching the other guys get dressed, or going into the showers. It was a turn-on, but there was no comprehension of what it meant. There was no real sense of wrongness, but I knew I was in my own little world." It was much later in our interviews that Zack mentioned another context for the locker room. In preschool, his father had started him on swimming lessons, which were to provide the basis for the competitive swimming that he would do for the next seven or eight years. And with the memory of the smell there were memories of images of bodies—shoulders, collarbones, nipples— of boys and men. Zack could not put utterance to what was going on emotionally in that "little world" because the culture had no words for it except, as Johnny had understood, for the pejorative one that had been flung at him on the playground. That incident had propelled Zack into a kind of limbo where he both understood and did not understand the connection between his inner feelings and his inner sense of difference from his peers.

EARLY ADOLESCENT EXPLORATIONS

In view of this sense of difference, it may seem paradoxical that in early adolescence Zack became actively involved in sexual exploration with girls. Zack was the middle brother in a family of three boys. They lived across the street from a family that had two girls, and Zack, his younger brother by two years, and the two sisters—who matched them in age—were all very good friends. They also became involved in an ongoing game of sexual discovery. Again, he was knowing and not knowing all at the same time as the two brothers and the two sisters played "doctor" at a rather advanced level. He recalled,

> One of the girls—Gerri—had her legs spread. We had been rolling around with each other and I said, "I'm going to take your temperature now," meaning I was going to stick the dick in. I remember looking at her, at her pussy or whatever, and she had a lot of white fluid around it and I remember touching it. She said, "I don't know if you should stick it in because that's there." I said, "Let me just stick it in a little bit." That's

the most visual and vivid memory I have of the girls, and that's with the one sister. Jean was the other one and I remember she had very fine pubic hair. We were out in the cornfield. I was going in and out of Jean and getting the feeling that I was going to pee. We always paired up—my brother was Gerri's age. We'd get under the covers at the same time and sometimes we'd mix it up, each of us kissing both.

This relationship went on for about two years. But after the first year, Zack began another series of sexual encounters that paralleled and complemented those he and his brother were having with the sisters. These were with a male cousin of about the same age. He recalled the beginning.

One thing happened that started this whole thing with my cousin. There was this swimming hole where we were all swimming around naked. My cousin had a hard-on and I did, and I remember purposely wanting to bump into him with my hard-on. And he had said something like, "Why are you doing that? Do you like that?" It must have been that night that something happened.

Their sexual play gravitated to oral sex and continued over some time. One scene stood out. "This is very funny. We both wanted to suck on each other's dicks at the same time. We were trying to figure out how to do it. You're going to laugh. He did a head-stand on his head and leaned up against the door of the closet and that's how we did it. His legs in the air—and I held on to them, and that's how we did it." Just before this time, the boys had let Zack's younger brother join them. But they kept his brother out of it after that, and Zack remembered his brother pounding on the bedroom door once, wanting to take part in what the older boys were doing. Interestingly, Zack did not come to a climax with the girls or with his cousin. He would stop before he came to an orgasm with the girls because, he said, "I didn't understand what I was about to do." However, his cousin did come to an orgasm with him—just once. "He came in my mouth. I remember because it tasted so different. I just remember saying, 'Now what did you do that for?' I really questioned, 'Why are we doing this? How come we're doing this?'

He said, 'I don't know.' I think that's the last time we had any experiences." In fact, Zack had already been masturbating by this time, but the relation between what he had been doing by himself and what he stopped himself from doing with the girls, and to what his cousin had just done with him, was a little vague. "I remember the exact thought—that he did something in my mouth and it had something to do with coming."

There are a number of striking things about this part of Zack's story. One could say that the early adolescent Zack was an explorer in two complementary realms of human sexuality—male to female and male to male. He felt no aversion to the female body—he felt aroused and interested in what he was doing with the girls—but the male had a greater incandescence for him, although he did not fully understand this at that point. He recalled, "I guess I can say that I preferred holding and touching his body to the girls. With the girls, it was, 'Let's try this,' not so matter of factly, but we knew this could fit or go there. It was more like playing with the girls. With my cousin, it was more sexual. . . . with my cousin, that was *sex.*" He added, *"I'm going to say that I found some type of direction there."*

The questions he asked his cousin and himself reflected his attempt to make sense of what was happening. When his cousin came in his mouth, he had asked, "Now what did you do that for?" Then, questioning more deeply about what this meant, he asked, "How come we're doing this?" "I don't know," was his cousin's poignant reply. Perhaps the question did not need to be asked of the girls because, growing up in a culture that provided ample models for male-female relationships, he had some context for what he was doing with them. But about his cousin, he said, *"Maybe that was not what I was supposed to be doing, even though I liked it."*

THE GUIDE DREAM

Around this period, Zack had a recurring dream that, in retrospect, reflected his differential reaction to these two sets of experiences:

> There was this hairy brown monster that lived up behind all the stuff that hangs up in the attic, and he would come out and

fight with the family once a year. But he would find me first, and we would start fighting. As scary as it was, the fight was—I almost want to say—intimate. I don't want to say sexual, because I don't recall it being sexual, but I recall it being very . . . I almost want to say sexual but it wasn't, it was intimate. I had the same dream a couple of times a year for a couple of years. It happened right around sixth grade, so I guess I was around twelve or thirteen. It's the only recurring dream or specific dream that I will never forget. He was like the orange monster in *Bugs Bunny* that wore sneakers—that kind of shape. But he would always say, "Okay, I'll see you next time" when he went back up to the attic.

I asked Zack if he had any thoughts on the translation of this dream. He said, "Not really," and then added, laughing slightly—"until I just told you right now. I still don't really know, but I just realized—maybe not for the first time—that it was an *intimate* fight with whatever that monster was. But I still can't define what the whole dream meant." I think this was a crucial dream that was telling Zack something very important about himself. Like all dreams, it was a creation of the mind. Western scientific thought makes a sharp distinction in its treatment of perceptions that are created by the mind itself—that come from inside the person—and perceptions that arise from the outside—from external reality. But when neurologist Rodolfo Llinas says, "A person's waking life is a dream guided by the senses . . . . "[1] Cutting-edge neurological theory converges with ancient Buddhist tradition, where the sharp distinction that Western psychology makes between inner and outer reality does not hold. In Tibetan Buddhism, there is a category of deity known as the Yidam. There is an ambiguity in the status of the Yidam, as there is in the status of all the deities. Ultimately, they are all projections of the mind. Nevertheless, they are at first visualized—and related to—as if they were independent realities.

The monster in Zack's dream seems to me to have some of the psychological qualities associated with the idea of the Yidam. It was a projection of his mind, but one that, both in the dream and in his waking recollection, appeared as an independent reality. In Tibetan Buddhism, the person working toward enlightenment adopts, with the help of his or her Lama, a Yidam who will be a mentor and guide in the quest for enlightenment, from an array of deities—each with his or her particular form and associated symbols—depending on which will be most helpful and appropriate to the person's individual needs.[2] More critically, the Yidam represents the person's own basic or innate nature, visualized as a divine or enlightened being in order to use it as a template for the achievement of one's own enlightenment. The figure that appeared in Colin's dreams (Chapter 6) starting with his early childhood was to all intents and purposes Colin's Yidam. It revealed to him something about his nature and, at the same time, was a guide to how Colin would live his life.

Similarly, the monster of Zack's dream was both a personification of his own basic nature and the guide to the path he would have to take for its realization. It seems particularly fitting for a boy just this side of childhood that the "inner I" selected an image that resembled a character from a *Bugs Bunny* cartoon. This dream could be analyzed without resorting to the idea of the Yidam. It could be discussed in a traditional psychodynamic framework—as signifying a boy's conflicted struggle with his sexual feelings toward males. But this explanation, while not untrue, would be incomplete, because this was not primarily a dream of repression, but rather of revelation. For the moment, I feel that the analogy of the Yidam fits Zack's dream monster. It captures its status as a psychological projection that emanates from within the self, but that is experienced as something outside the self. The concept of the Yidam—a psychological projection that serves as a guide—unites the categories of subjective and objective and offers an insight into the workings of emotion and the mind that has been foreign to our intellectual framework.

Like Yidams, monsters are not human and, like Yidams, they are transcendent. Some Yidams have a terrifying aspect—the deities can be wrathful as well as peaceful, but their wrath is always turned against the forces of ignorance and evil. Monsters, also, are not necessarily bad—especially cartoon monsters such as the Cookie Monster of the long-running children's program, *Sesame Street*. Here, the "scariness" of Zack's monster seems to be part of its transcendent, mythological character, and the purpose of myth is to explain, to provide insight. When Zack asked his cousin "How come we're doing this?" his cousin said, "I don't know." The dream gave the answer that neither boy could supply. It revealed something to Zack about himself, not only as he was now, but as he would be in the future—"I'll see you *next time*," the monster said as he went back up to the attic.

DREAM AND MYTH

Freudian psychoanalysis has tended to regard cultural images as resulting from the projection of individual, and often unconscious, meaning onto the larger cultural screen. Jungian thought goes further and asserts that universals are built into the structure of the human mind that shape individual experience and, at the same time, express themselves in myth, art, and religion. In either case, the images that the individual mind creates—whether in waking life or dreams—can share a common set of meanings with the images embodied in myth, art, and religion, and the understanding of one can enhance the understanding of the other. It goes without saying that biological explanations for same-sex feeling ignore inner meaning. Social constructionist explanations have generally failed to see that its continuity over the span of human history and its pervasiveness across different cultures are indications that a profoundly important tendency is built into the structure of human experience. It is this continuity that accounts for the correspondences between the dream of the twentieth-century boy and an ancient myth. This myth is recounted in an epic whose earliest written version is 4,000 years old. In it, Gilgamesh, king of the ancient Mesopotamian city of Uruk, has been troubling his subjects by sexually exploiting their sons and daughters:

> Gilgamesh does not leave a son to his father. . . .
> Gilgamesh does not leave a daughter to her mother.[3]

The gods hear the complaints of the parents and ask one of their number, the goddess Aruru, to create "an equal to Gilgamesh's stormy heart." In response, she creates Enkidu, whose whole body is shaggy with hair and who runs with the animals in primeval comradeship. Gilgamesh has two dreams that he tells to his mother. In the first dream, a "meteorite" falls from the sky. In the second, an axe appears at the entry to his marital chamber. Of both the meteorite and the axe, he says, "I loved it and embraced it as a wife." His mother pronounces the dreams propitious and tells Gilgamesh that both the meteorite and the axe represent a man, a comrade whom Gilgamesh will first compete with and then love. The dreams prove to be prophetic. There is indeed a confrontation in front of a marital chamber—although the context is unclear. Enkidu blocks Gilgamesh from entering. They grapple with each other and Gilgamesh prevails. Enkidu acknowledges him as king, and they kiss each other and became deeply devoted friends.

Although Gilgamesh was an actual historical person—a king of Uruk living about 2700 B.C.E.—the story, of which his relationship to Enkidu is the central element, is mythic in nature. It includes larger-than-life heroes, confrontations with gods and goddesses, and explores the mysteries of death and human mortality. The first encounter between Gilgamesh and Enkidu, a competitive test of strength, has a quintessentially male character. But the test ends in the kiss that marks the establishment of their passionate friendship. In addition to the central theme of male-to-male bonding, two other connected themes run through the story—the threat that female power can pose to male strength and the opposition between male-female love and male-male love.

Near the beginning of the story, Enkidu is drawn to have sex with a beautiful harlot, after which the animals shun him and he loses the primeval quality of strength that allowed him to run with them. Enkidu's blocking Gilgamesh from entering the marital chamber can also be seen as symbolic. Later in the story, after Gilgamesh and Enkidu have returned from their heroic adventures, the goddess of love, Ishtar, falls in love with Gilgamesh—whose beauty is repeatedly extolled throughout the tale. But he spurns her offer of marriage as he recalls the unhappy fate of her previous lovers. In a rage, she persuades her father, Anu, to send the Bull of Heaven to attack Uruk as punishment. However, Gilgamesh and Enkidu kill it, and Enkidu wrenches off the Bull's hindquarters and flings them in Ishtar's face, saying he would do the same to her, if he could. In the end, Enkidu must die, not only for his action in killing the Bull of

Heaven, but also for cutting down the tallest tree in the Cedar Forest and killing Humbaba, its demon-guardian. The grief-stricken Gilgamesh mourns his beloved companion and orders a statue of him to be made, one with a skin of gold and a chest of lapis lazuli. The rest of the epic concerns Gilgamesh's search for the key to immortality and the final recognition that mortality is the lot of humankind.

The hairiness of Zack's monster and Enkidu's body that is "shaggy with hair" are symbols of primeval maleness. Zack's encounter with the monster was in the context of an intimate fight. The fight between Gilgamesh and Enkidu is not only a competition, but also a demonstration of mutually admired and acknowledged strength between men. It is a necessary preamble to the love that springs up between them and binds them to each other. In Zack's life, the two components—the test of male strength and the bond of love—were split. The test of strength went into the dream fight with the monster. The bond of male-to-male love that was also implicit in the "intimate fight" with the monster went into the sexual encounters with his cousin in his waking life. I think the theme of opposition between male-male love and male-female love in the myth is not misogynistic, but rather serves to emphasize the fact that the bond between Gilgamesh and Enkidu is a male-to-male bond. Nonetheless, there are hints of primeval androgyny in Enkidu—he is described as having a full head of hair like a woman's, with locks billowing in profusion like those of Ashnan, the grain goddess. The myth also recognizes that, at the deepest levels, male and female can incorporate and be merged with each other.

The monster of Zack's dream was not only a guide, it also symbolized Zack's own maleness and the male that he would find at the end of his journey—the monster was Zack's Enkidu. This was why Zack said, *"I found some type of direction there."* The hairy brown monster appeared to Zack to guide him to the deepest part of himself, where he would encounter not a female—as the culture in which he lived told him he should—but rather another male like himself. The experience with his cousin was not the beginning—but very near the beginning—of this journey.

Although men and women cross the boundary between their heterosexual identities and the potential for same-sex feeling in dreams, crossing it in waking life is obviously a more dangerous step, as Fred (Chapter 4) understood. What next happened to Zack illustrates why. After Zack and his cousin had let Zack's younger brother join them on one occasion, his brother let the sisters know that the boys had given each other "blow jobs." Looking back, Zack had no idea how they themselves had learned this phrase, but it was unfamiliar to the girls. They took this literally—meaning that the boys were blowing on each other. When they inquired of Zack, he said, "Oh no, that's not a blow job," and offered to show them, saying, "Give me a blow job." The girls passed on this information about what Zack had apparently done with his cousin to a neighbor, who then spread it around. For Zack, the result was catastrophic. He recalled, "Now everybody was saying, 'Zack's a fag,' and that killed me." This was a repetition of the pain of the playground incident. Although there was no cultural context for what they were doing, the boys had not really needed one, because they were still close enough to the innocence of childhood not to think about that too much. But the cultural context had just been supplied for Zack again, with devastating emotional consequences. "I really closed my feelings up inside. I knew I was different all along, but now being different was bad and I hated myself for it, I mean *really, really* hated myself for it. So again, I just tried being nice to everybody no matter what they did. Ninth to twelfth grade was pure hell because I hated myself *so* much." Although he sensed his attraction to men, he didn't fully understand the connection between that and being called "gay"—which at that point came across as meaning "bad, no good," that there was something wrong with him. In an aside that might reveal why, in this culture, some boys who will one day be gay men avoid team sports, Zack recalled, "I didn't do any sports—I regret that now—because if I messed up, I didn't want anyone telling me, 'You're no good.' "[4]

Although the rumors of Zack's being gay followed him to high school, he had no difficulty getting along with his peers. He did not fit into any particular clique or group, but he was generally liked. He dated a few girls, but no sex was involved. Occasionally, the boy who lived down the street would call out "faggot" as Zack rode by on his bike, but he was not usually the target of any such name-calling. Blond-haired and blue-eyed, slender, and above average height, Zack was turning into a handsome young man in his middle and late teens. But his self-image was quite different. He said, "I hated myself so much when I was younger—*I looked in the mirror and hated myself.* When someone said I was a good-looking guy, I didn't know how to handle that because I never felt that." It was ironic that, some years later, a female friend, remembering their high school years, said to him, "Zack, if you only knew how good-looking you were . . . you could have had any girl you wanted." Something else that appears ironic in the light of Zack's experience is the theory that a same-sex orientation results from a sense of inadequacy with respect to a sense of masculinity.[5] That is just the reverse of Zack's experience. Zack did not start off feeling inadequate as a male. The sense of inadequacy came from the outside. It was a social creation, embodied in the epithet "faggot" that was flung at him. The rejection that this label implied did more than undermine his sense of masculinity, it contaminated his whole sense of himself. "I really, really hated *myself* for it," he said.

Zack's cousin did not become gay. In fact, he married not long before Zack and I began our work together. Zack recalled another friend from the swimming hole where they had swum naked. "I remember being there with my friend Don and having a hard-on and us looking at each other and avoiding it. The energy between us was so strong, wanting to do it, and avoiding it." Later, in high school Zack had some near-sexual encounters with friends to whom no suspicion of homosexuality was attached:

> It was in high school, around the tenth grade. I was sleeping over [at] this other guy's house and I felt him breathing right there and his touching me, and me just frozen, and not doing anything about it.
>
> And there was another guy, Mitch, and I had this crush on him, and him on me. We had such a strong attraction to each other. Zack recalled that, mirroring the imagery of the dream, "We would wrestle with each other and several times, in wrestling, it was extremely physical. We had a hard-on. We weren't naked and I remember him saying, "Oh, you've got a hard-on," and me feeling his hard-on. And he gave me a hickey a couple of times, wrestling. *I was so concerned that it was the wrong thing or right thing to do and I just couldn't do it.* One

time, he stayed over and we got really drunk. He tore his clothes off and was running around naked outside and tearing the house apart. I finally got him pinned down in my room and he kept screaming, "Give me a blow job." I was just about to, when my brother walked in. We were just about to get into it for the first time, and my brother walked in, and it never happened again after that.

Mitch, who was just one year behind Zack in school, said that he looked upon Zack as the big brother he had never had. He sent Zack a friendship card, which Zack still had fifteen years later. In it Mitch had wrtten, "I LOVE you and I want us to be best friends for the rest of our life." However, the passion of their friendship—like many adolescent passions—did not survive their high school graduation. Zack could not really explain why they drifted apart. As he read over this manuscript, however, he realized why. He said, "Culture took over." In the course of their tussling, he and Mitch actually gave each other hickeys and, when asked about it at school, acknowledged how they got them. Some of their peers shrugged, "Well, that's Zack and Mitch," but some others said it meant they were gay. In retrospect, he felt it affected their friendship. All in all, he remembered, "It was a painful time." As adults, although they lived in the same town, they had never made any attempt to stay in touch, nor did Zack know if Mitch was gay or not.

With another boy, sex actually occurred.

There was one incident with this boy who invited me to go camping with him. He'd heard rumors that I was gay. We picked up two girls at a party, and were drinking in the woods. It came time to go back to the trailer and mess around, and the two girls chickened out. We were all hot and horny and next thing I knew I was messing around with him and he got off and then he didn't want anything to do with me, saying he was really drunk, and the next morning pretended he didn't remember anything about it. I felt a little used.

THE ROLE OF THE "CARRIER"

In all the sexual encounters between Zack and other boys from the first at age six or seven up through high school, none of them had been labeled as gay except Zack. Why? In a culture at war with itself, someone has to be found to serve as the screen upon which the suppressed feelings are projected. The boy labeled as gay becomes the container—the "designated carrier"—for the repudiated feelings of the group. The incident at the trailer in the woods illustrates this mechanism of repudiation in action. The other boy had sex with Zack and then, under the cover of being drunk, "forgot" about what happened by the next morning. It seems that, under certain conditions, where there is no obvious "carrier" for the repudiated feelings, one must be found.

One of my students did a case study for me on a young man who was gay. However, well before the young man had any conscious sense of sexual attraction to males, he was designated for this role. He remembered the day in the ninth grade when the whole gym class ganged up to taunt him as "queer." He began to cry and the teacher, a kind man, took him aside and asked him, "Son, are you gay?" Quite sincerely, he said that he was not, and that he would admit it if he were. What is of particular interest about this—not uncommon—case is the selection process and its meaning. It is immaterial if the boy selected is or will be gay—he has a role to fulfill for the group.

With adolescence, the emotional ties that bind both boys and girls to friends of the same sex can and do move toward expression through the body. However, as the evidence in this book reveals, this movement is likely to be matched by a need to resist it. The prohibition, although handed down by adults, is internalized in the adolescent subculture and enforced by it. Nevertheless, the energy with which adolescents deny being gay—and sometimes persecute those whom they think are—draws much of its strength from the movement toward same-sex feeling that originates in the self in spite of the cultural prohibition. The boy in gym class was probably picked out as a scapegoat to carry the burden of the rejected sexual feelings of his classmates because he had some of the characteristics the adolescent subculture could identify as stereotypically gay.

However, the lacrosse and football player that he had reciprocal oral sex with in the twelfth grade and who left him for a girl fitted another stereotype—that of the straight jock.

RITES OF PASSAGE

Although the neighborhood rumors about Zack followed him into high school, he was not singled out for the kind of ostracism that the boy in gym class suffered. Perhaps it was because he did not have mannerisms stereotypically identified as gay. His attractiveness to girls—even though he was not aware of it—might have been another factor. When he read this observation in the manuscript, he said it did not matter—the sense of ostracism was already internalized. In any case, at age sixteen, Zack began to engage in one of the group rites through which adolescents mark their passage into the world of adult privilege and hypocrisy—he began to drink.

> I started drinking and hung out with guys that partied—a close-knit group of friends. Drinking was my outlet. I would do wild, crazy things. I only kissed girls—we would give each other hickeys, but otherwise I chickened out because I was scared I could not perform like the other kids—because I was so different. I thought girls would say, "Oh you were terrible, not like so-and-so." I thought everybody else was so much more sexual and masculine than I was.

Our society is impoverished when it comes to initiating either boys or girls into their adult roles as men and women. Adolescents have to find the means to initiate themselves—if they can. In the case studies that my students have done, a recurrent theme is the self-confidence that an adolescent boy gets from feeling sexually successful with girls. In this society, there are few systematic rituals through which boys are ushered into manhood by older men. In their absence, sexual intercourse in particular becomes a symbolic rite of passage. In other words, with no men, including their fathers, to do it for them, adolescent boys are initiated into "manhood" by adolescent girls who are barely this side of childhood themselves.

Drinking is another of the ways—as beer commercials during football games indicate—through which boys can identify with men. But serious alcoholism, although it might masquerade as macho ritual, is about unmet emotional need and pain—and Zack had plenty of both. He began to drink very heavily. By the time he was twenty-one, he would be consuming as many as twelve to fifteen beers, eight shots of whiskey, or some combination of these, in a single night.

After high school, Zack tried college briefly, but he was not emotionally prepared for it and dropped out. However, he got a job at a branch of a major retailer and found some congenial friends there. But he had still not found where he belonged in a larger sense. At around this time, an incident occurred that brought together some of the fragments of what he had been experiencing in an eye-opening way. Zack was still good friends with the cousin with whom he had explored sexually. They were only eighteen, and his cousin wanted to go to New York City. They went to Greenwich Village and inadvertently wound up in a lesbian bar.

> We found this bar—it was a long, thin little bar, with a pool table in back. There were a guy and girl there and we talked to them, and ended up playing pool and buying each other drinks. Being that far in the back and stuck in the corner, we didn't realize what was going on in the bar itself. Just as I'm about to shoot my shot, my cousin goes, "Zack, I think we need to talk." We stepped back and both focused on what was going on in the bar. He said, "Zack, it's a lesbian bar!" I started laughing and he was in shock. I said, "So what, who cares? They're not bothering us." So we stayed for an hour and a half. A couple of girls came over, played pool with us, and bought us drinks. We had a great time. Leaving there we walked past a bar called Uncle Charlie's. I recall looking in the window and saying, "Let's go in here—it looks like a lot of fun." My cousin kept going. I opened the door and looked inside—and realized it was a gay bar. CLICK—the biggest "click" you can imagine went off in my head. "Let's go in here," and my cousin is looking. . . . "Oh, I'm only kidding." We went home and the next week we were in the Village again with all our friends, and we passed by it and I made a good note of where it was.

The following week, Zack went on a date with a girl. They went to the same club he had gone to the week before with the whole crowd.

> We were drinking together, and all of a sudden she jumped across the table and attacked me sexually, kissing me—the table went over, the drinks went over. She got herself wrapped around me. I was like, "*What* are you doing? Get off me." At that point I realized I wanted *nothing* to do with her. She's mad at me; she's drunk—she basically wants to fuck me—I was like, "*Get* away." We're out in the street, it's pouring rain and she met these two guys and said, "I'm going to go with these two guys." I was like, "Do whatever you want." I was drunk, I mean really drunk. I was lucky I could even walk.

Zack found his way to the gay bar whose location he had so carefully noted.

> This kid ended up talking to me and he goes, "Oh, oh, let me guess, this is your first time in this place." I said, 'Yes, I don't even know what I'm doing here.' He was really nice, talked to me for a long time. Needless to say, he got me back into his car and we did all kinds of things that I never thought anyone could do or ever experienced—it was great, a lot of fun. I was in complete shock. He dropped me off at the train station, made sure I got home—he called a couple of times, and could tell I was completely uncomfortable. He said, "I completely understand. Hold onto my number if you ever need anyone to talk to"' That was my first, real, true experience—as far as being, like out in a bar, someone I met and everything. *I told everybody at work that I met this girl. Everything that happened—I said it was a girl.*

Reversing the sexes made it appear to his friends that the eighteen-year-old Zack had "scored" the kind of sexual success that falls into the range of early initiation experiences for a young man in this culture. Whatever the merits of such a do-it-yourself initiation experience in the long run, it could not serve that function for Zack, because he knew the truth—a truth that he could not disclose.

British psychoanalyst D.W. Winnicott coined the term "False Self" to describe a compliant way of being and living that a person constructs—starting in childhood—in order to conform to the needs of his or her caretakers and the demands of the environment.[6] But this False Self does not correspond to the person's own deep inner feelings or authentic potentialities—which are the True Self. For young people whose emotional needs are directed to their own sex, the relationship to the institutional culture is quite similar to a child's relationship to a pathological parent. As Zack stood on the threshold of young adulthood he had begun to construct the kind of social False Self that so many of these young people do when they realize that the True Self is out of sync with the demands of the environment. By falsifying the sex of his partner in order to comply with social expectations, Zack could only alienate himself further from his inner truth.

Not surprisingly, after this incident he began to drink more heavily. "I was a lot of fun when I drank. I was wild and crazy, I made everybody laugh, and I danced with all the girls, but that was it—I had no sexual interest in anyone." Although Zack had gotten a glimpse of another world that *was* of sexual interest to him, he was far from comfortable in that world. So, although he began to go to the gay clubs he had discovered, he would just stand there stony-faced, ignoring everyone who tried to talk to him—and many people did—getting drunk, and returning home at five in the morning, still alone. The False Self could party with the girls, while his True Self had to stand at the sidelines in watchful apprehension at the gay clubs.

Eventually, however, he met a thirty-one year-old-man who became a somewhat steady sexual partner, but in a very limited way.

I don't know why I liked him or anything. He knew I was a heavy drinker and he would make sure I got real drunk. He'd take a room in one of the bathhouses and then he would just give me a blow job. That was it. I would do absolutely nothing, and that's the way it was for years. It was a long time before I let anything else happen. At that point, I realized I liked guys *but I did not understand or accept it.* I belonged in therapy because I was really, really screwed up.

JOINING THE POLICE FORCE

I remarked to Zack, "Somewhere along the line, you got on the police force?" His response to my comment was surprising. "Yes," he said, "which really fucked me up." The cop down the street convinced me to take the police exam and I got in." He was only twenty at the time.

> . . . and lo and behold I got on the fucking police department. *It really destroyed me.* Not only was I trying to deal with who I was, not understanding the whole thing, the whole masculinity part of it, everybody knows—if you're gay, you're a wierdo, strange, you're not normal. And now I'm a police officer, the most masculine job in the fucking world to be—the uniform, the whole thing. Now I just compounded my whole lifestyle that I hated, didn't understand, and I had a severe drinking problem. Compounding the fact that I wasn't out trying to get laid every night, like a lot of cops are trying to do all the time, just to prove they're masculine or one of the guys. I wasn't doing that so, real quick, they picked up on that. All the stuff I just mentioned was still affecting me. I was drinking heavily. I didn't know who I was. I'm surprised I'm even functioning, and here I'm on a job carrying a gun, supposed to be dealing with everybody else's problems—people trying to kill each other, dead babies, dead people—then the in-house stuff in the police department is ten times worse than what's out in the field. So I was a real fucking basket case.
>
> I got out of the academy—I loved the academy. I'd still be happy doing that almost on a full-time basis, maybe teaching. I had a great time, a lot of guys looked up to me. I was in *the* clique in the academy. I was one of *the* people, a squad leader in charge of nine other guys. I could run like an elk—maybe not as strong as some guys—but I was up there, respected, it was a whole new thing. But then you come out of the academy and that doesn't count anymore. You're a zero, a rookie, a shit-on, a piss-on. You've got this whole thing you're expected to play through—write a million tickets your first week. It was not me. I refused to play through it. I hated being a cop for the

first five and a half or six years. *I hated it as much as I hated myself—my job.*

Nonetheless, not long after he joined the force, Zack decided to give a party at his house for his friends and acquaintances on the force. But this event backfired in a very upsetting way. Somehow a rumor got around that some sexual things had happened with prostitutes. The department conducted an informal investigation and confirmed that nothing of that kind had happened. But during the investigation, Zack said, "Someone turned an incident around that happened, making me gay. So, in the investigation, they started questioning other guys about me being gay. 'Do you know anything about Zack's lifestyle?' It went from investigating the party to investigating my sexual preference." As the investigation was ending, the chief spoke with everyone individually, and when Zack went to see him, "The chief mentioned how that was turned around and said, 'I hope you're not into that,' and left it at that." But even raising the question had left its imprint on people's minds.

> Now everyone in the police department thinks I'm gay, and I'm having to deal with the guys I work with all thinking I'm gay—AIDS and everything like that. Talk about compounding everything that happened in the past. Now I'm stuck in this same fucking situation I thought I was getting out of. Everybody thinking I'm gay again and saying it's not right, you're a weirdo, and I have to deal with all that again. And I'm drinking real heavy.

The way the rumor about Zack had gotten started seems significant. At bachelor parties, it is common for the prospective groom to be the object of a good deal of erotic playfulness by the dancer or stripper sometimes hired by his friends for the occasion. Zack had engaged a stripper for this all-male party. She got another man as well as Zack naked, but for some reason, used a dildo to toy with Zack in a particularly suggestive way. Zack was a handsome young man and seeing his body in this symbolically homoerotic context— even though it was orchestrated by a woman—appeared to touch a responsive chord in the man who started the rumor, making Zack the carrier for his own feeling. Nevertheless, in spite of this persistent rumor, Zack continued to be well liked by friends in the department, though it clearly troubled him and emphasized again the disparity between his false social self and the truth of his inner feelings.

About the time he graduated from the academy, Zack met Pat. They began to date, but after a few months, this became a friendship—a very significant one for Zack. "He really helped me understand where I was going. He told me, 'Zack, you're gay, and this is what it's like.' He explained to me about the gay world. He said I was a good-looking guy to whom many people would be attracted. We went to clubs together and Pat would keep people away from me. But he was alcoholic too." About three years after they met, Pat came down with pneumonia. Pat's illness was AIDS related, though Zack did not realize it and Pat did not disclose it at first. The truth of his condition eventually came out as his health deteriorated, and a year and a half later, Pat entered the hospital again. When he did, Zack said,

It really made me a mess. My best friend in the whole world, my mentor, my teacher is telling me he's dying. At the police department everybody liked me. But as far as learning my job, that wasn't happening. I had too much going on inside my mind to worry about them or how to do my job. So they were concerned about my job performance—rightfully so. I was drinking so much that the days I was working were recovery days for me. Pat went into the hospital and I was lost. I was drinking like a fish, waking up in the driveway after sleeping in my truck, or not making it to my bed and pass[ing] out in the hallway. My family was worried about me and I was worried about me, but I couldn't control it. Another friend told me about a program called The Forum. Even though he was a brand-new friend, he was very supportive. He realized I was in bad shape, in the danger zone. Pat was about to die, I was suicidal and wanted to give everything up—*because I still didn't understand or accept that I was gay.*

SUICIDE AND THE FALSE SELF

When Zack spoke of feeling suicidal, this was not a mere figure of speech. But it was not until two years after our first meeting that he told me of a very special place in the wilderness—a place that he loved to go to but that also had darker associations.

> All those years when had I drinking problems—I used to drive there by myself, hike to the top of the mountain and stand on the cliff. I used to sit there and cry and decide—what's worth it, jumping or not jumping? I always ended up climbing back down. My mother would ask, "Where did you go?" I said, "I went hiking." She'd say, "That's the second time this week you went up there." I'd say, "Yeah," but I'd never say why I was going up there—but that was why.

Winnicott said of the False Self:

> The False Self has one very positive and very important function: to hide the True Self, which it does by compliance with environmental demands.[7]

Zack had said, "I hated being a cop for the first five and a half or six years. *I hated it as much as I hated myself—my job.*" The job and everything that went with it seems to have been, up until this point, part of the False Self—the cover Zack had maintained in order to get some part of what he wanted. But although it had been very helpful when Pat told him, "Zack, you're gay, and this is what it's like," even as Pat was dying, Zack said, "I still didn't understand or accept that I was gay."

> The False Self has as its main concern a search for conditions which will make it possible for the True Self to come into its own.[8]

Once, because of his work schedule, Zack happened to have his police semiautomatic handgun with him when he came to our meeting. He was showing me how it worked. It was loaded with a clip, but a single bullet had first to be manually inserted into the firing chamber before the clip was loaded in order for the weapon to fire.

> If conditions cannot be found then there must be reorganized a new defence against exploitation of the True Self, and if there be doubt then the clinical result is suicide.[9]

Suicide by a police officer is, unfortunately, not altogether uncommon. Furthermore, the means to do it—the gun—goes with the job. As he was showing me the gun, a memory came to Zack's mind. He said, "Just before the Forum I was looking at my gun and thinking of killing myself."

> Suicide in this context is the destruction of the total self in avoidance of annihilation of the True Self. When suicide is the only defence left against betrayal of the True Self, then it becomes the lot of the False Self to organize the suicide.[10]

As Pat, his mentor and link to the truth of himself, was about to be taken from him, Zack contemplated suicide by means of his police handgun—an ironic symbol of the False Self and of the job that was part of his "cover." But there was something resilient in Zack, some core of belief in himself—in his True Self—that would not let him act on the self-destructive impulse.

> I had cleaned the gun the night before, and worked that night, but that one bullet you just saw me put in the chamber—I took that out. *I never loaded the gun.* As I was looking at it, playing around with the gun, my eye noticed that something was wrong. I looked—and there was no bullet. If that wasn't a sign . . . . I cried my eyes out and like, "you jerk-off," you know . . . ?

THE TURNING POINT

The scene Zack described took place just before he undertook the two-weekend experience called the Forum. (This was a modification of a program that used to go by the name of EST.) For Zack, this was to be a milestone—a turning point in his life. The first session was Easter weekend. Pat had gone into the hospital the day before his birthday and died that Easter Sunday. Zack said, "I had to deal with all his friends, my family—they thought of him as another

son. The story was that he was dying of cancer." Pat was buried
during the week between the first and second sessions of the program. Zack described what happened next:

I went back and finished the Forum the second weekend.
There were three hundred and sixty people in the class. I
finally stood up and said, "I'm a cop; I'm gay." All the stuff
about the kids finding out and calling me a faggot. The leader
just took me back to all those things, in front of all these
people, standing up—why I am the way I am—the original
things that happened, why I'm such a nice guy and don't stand
up for myself. He took me through all the steps. *As far as I'm
concerned, it goes back to that first incident.* Everybody else is
crying and I still hadn't told him about Pat—I'd buried Pat
over the week, and worked on top of it. I went through the
whole thing. He helped me to realize my "racket," why you
live your life the way you do, how what happened back then
directs the way you are now, what it takes to live your life as
you do. It helps you to start over. He got done with me and I
was in shock. So I started crying and explained that my best
friend in the whole world had passed away while I was here.
The whole place was crying, and we went through that whole
thing. The leader said he'd never gone through anything so
emotional in his whole life.

At the end, there was like graduation day and we all came
back. There were about eight hundred people in the room.
They did a thing called acknowledgment—if anyone wants to
acknowledge how someone else helped them. The leader himself never does this, but he went on and on about this person
who affected more people—and him too—than anyone ever
had. Now I realized he was talking about me. He walked
toward me from the front of room and said, "Zack, stand up." I
cried *so* hard, but for the first time, *the first time in my entire
life, I accepted who I was.* It clicked. It helped me to realize
that it didn't matter what anybody else thinks of me—either
they're going to like me or not, and then there's nothing I can
do about it. And that helped me to accept myself for who I
was. *I liked myself for the first time*—because I'd hated myself

so much, *so* much. I did two follow-up seminars that leveled things off for me. The things I discussed in those seminars—going back to school, stopping drinking, are happening. Everyone saw a difference in me—the guys at work. *It gave me my life back.*

The Forum also enabled Zack to begin to discard the False Self. He no longer needed it to help him live—or die.

The events at the Forum had taken place a couple of months after Zack's twenty-fifth birthday and a little over three years before I met him. For Zack, the experience of the Forum had come at the right time—in fact, at the nick of time. Throughout this book, a major theme has been the effect of the culture—of authority and of the group—on feeling and thought. Zack had suffered from these effects for most of his life, starting with what happened at the playground almost twenty years earlier. *"As far as I'm concerned, it goes back to that first incident."* The Forum was a major corrective to the pathology in our wider culture. He had revealed himself publicly and instead of rejection he had met with acceptance and empathy as people wept for and with him. Paralleling this acceptance, a movement took place within himself—*"I liked myself for the first time."* Having begun to discard the protection of the False Self, he could embrace his True Self. He realized that the time had now come to reveal his inner truth to his family.

SELF-DISCLOSURE—FAMILY

Zack was the second of three boys, younger than the first by four years and older than the third by two. His parents had married young and were only in their fifties. Zack had a good relationship with both of his parents. After the Forum, he wanted to tell his parents the truth about his sexuality because, he said,

Even after the positive things that had happened there I was just not going to be accepting of myself until my parents knew. I had to feel my mother out first. I sat down and started the subject up with my mother. I had the chance to spend the weekend with [a well-known female athlete] a little ways back—with her and her lover and her parents, and it was a wonderful time. I brought that up because she was gay. So I asked, "What do you think about that, Ma?" Boy, did she bust my bubble. She proceeded to say that she thought they were sick, strange, they all belong on an island together, anybody who's gay . . . on and on, very derogatory stuff. My expectation was that it wasn't going to be great, but this was a hundred times worse. I was just about to tell her I'm gay and she thinks that gay people are like that, and belong like that, and think like that? I backed out. I really was committed to do it, so I left a note. I was so upset—you wouldn't believe. . . . I was completely distraught. I left a short, simple, little note and then I disappeared for three days and stayed with a friend.

I called my dad first. He said, "I'm mad at you for what you did to your mother, leaving a note like that—she's been crying for the last three nights." Then he proceeded to tell me, "It's your business. I don't want to hear about it or talk about it." Then I called my mother. She didn't say anything, just, "Are you coming home tonight?" I arrived home at the same time she did. She was crying hysterically. The first words out of her mouth were, "I love you," and the second words were, "Did your friend Pat die of AIDS?" Then she completely went off the deep end.

His mother did not want to accept that Zack was gay and wanted him to see a psychotherapist. At the suggestion of a friend, he agreed to go if she went with him. At the first session, the therapist said to his mother, "There's nothing wrong with your son. I think *you* have to see a therapist to get through this." Although she angrily rejected this, about five months later she did go, and Zack went with her for the first session. After Zack told something of what he had been through, the therapist asked him, "How did you get through this without professional help?" His answer was, "My friends and myself—and the Forum." His mother remained in therapy for herself, and by the time I met Zack, three years later, she was accepting and this acceptance continued to grow. Although Zack's disclosure about his sexuality did not hurt his relationship with his father, it was something that was just not talked about between them. Nevertheless, his father told him "I love you" more frequent-ly over the next several months than he ever had before.

His older brother's reaction was quite different. He said, "The only reason I'm talking to you is because you're my brother." Ironically, his younger brother, who had once wanted to be included in the sexual play between Zack and his cousin, reacted in the same way. His older brother's reaction was also paradoxical because he had been very good friends with Pat—even to the extent of hugging and kissing him. Now, a good many years later, Zack's brothers had come to terms with his sexuality, although the relationship was not particularly close to either one.

SELF-DISCLOSURE—WORK

Two years after the Forum, Zack came out to his department. He said, "There was no doubt in people's minds that I were gay, but it was just never confirmed." It began as a gradual process. At Zack's apartment, "The wife of one of my friends asked me if I were gay. She and I were drunk and for the first time in my life, I said, 'Yes, I am.' We told her husband, who said he didn't care; it didn't bother him." Someone found an article about a week-long event for gay men and women whose dates happened to coincide with Zack's vacation. A friend in the department warned him that others might tack up the article and said to him, "I want you to know that, if you're gay, it makes no difference to me. I like you, I think you're a good cop and a good friend," and he shook Zack's hand. Zack recalled, "I could have cried. It was one of the most dramatic things that ever happened to me. It was a profound thing for that guy to do that, and I told him, 'If you can do that, I can tell you I'm gay.' We've been real close since and talk about a lot of things together."

That summer, Zack went to California and visited family mem-bers in San Francisco. He bought a T-shirt that read, "Too cute to be straight," figuring that if he could wear it anywhere, it was San Francisco. Some of his friends on the force asked him to bring in the pictures he took on his trip. He did, including the ones from San Francisco—wearing the T-shirt. Laughing, he related,

> I was with my family members, my cousin and her kids and all. I saw "pictures, family. . . ." They saw "family, T-shirt."

There were six cops at dinner in the pizza place. They said, "Zack, take your pictures out." I'd shown them to one guy and he'd told everyone else, so they couldn't wait. As I'm taking my pictures out, it hits me like a wrecking ball! I'd realized they were looking at each other and snickering, and at first I hadn't thought anything of it. . . . Then it dawned on me. I almost had a heart attack. What am I going to do now? Nobody said anything, or laughed. All they said was, "Nice pictures, Zack." I called Charlie over and said, "Charlie, Charlie, I don't think anybody realized." He said, "Meet me at this location." When we met, he said, "Zack, I know you've been coming out of the closet, but you didn't have to kick the door down like that!" I said, "What am I going to do, Charlie?" He said, "You *did* it, you kicked your door down. You might as well come out and tell everybody. You know it'll be around to everybody in a second,"—because that grapevine is like a lightning bolt. So I did.

Clearly, something in Zack had decided that it was time to "kick the door down." Maybe he did it in the best possible way—through images, surrounded by family, and wearing a slogan on his chest that was open, funny, and self-affirming. One at a time, Zack spoke to each of the men he worked with over the next three days. He also told his lieutenant and sergeant, first because they were in command over him, and second, because they would be held accountable if anybody harassed him. Neither man had any problem with it. But— also through the grapevine—Zack had heard about some negative remarks about him from several of the department's senior staff. The chief was angry because Zack had not come to him first. Without accusing anyone, Zack wanted the senior staff to know what he had been told and met with the department's second and third in command. He said, "I'm gay—now you know, it's confirmed. I respect any opinion you have, whether you accept it or not, or understand it or not. But in no way am I going to tolerate any derogatory statements aimed at me, as a police officer, or about my lifestyle. If I hear it again I'm going to take action on it, and I want the chief to know it." Zack said that, because of the chief's negative attitude, he felt that he should talk to the mayor as well. The mayor let drop that he had heard something about it but said it was a personal thing, that he assumed that Zack would continue to do his job, and that it did not concern anyone else. He was satisfied that Zack had handled things well and assumed that Zack would prefer that he not intervene. Zack said, "I take it with a grain of salt, but the captain said even though he didn't condone this lifestyle, he respected me for doing what I did, standing up to him, the chief, and everyone else." Perhaps the grain of salt was because the captain assured him, "I won't treat you any differently from the blacks in the department." However, there was no harassment at work and things were going very well. One loose end had been tied just before our first meeting. "The guy who had turned [the] whole thing around at the party—I finally cleared that up last week. He wanted to know why I hated him. I explained it to him. He was reacting out of fear and I understood that and got past it. I cleared it up and I have a true friend now."

In the years between the ages of twenty-five and twenty-eight, a great deal had happened in Zack's life. The False Self that had prevented Zack from accepting the truth about himself, almost as much as it prevented others from knowing it, fell by the wayside, which seemed to make a real difference in the way Zack felt about his work. I think that, as a result of coming out to his department, he could begin to see his professional role as part of his authentic self—the True Self that he valued—instead of as part of the hated front he had put up to the world. Not long after he came out to his department he met Vic, who became his boyfriend. He introduced Vic to his friends, and it meant a great deal to Zack when he and Vic went out as a couple with two other mixed couples—the other men were on the force with Zack. Everyone had a good time, and one of his friends asked, "When are we going to do this again?"

Chapter 11

The Color Green

In an early session, I asked Zack if he could put into words what his feelings were when, in his late teens, he began to allow himself to have sex with a man. He said,

> I can still remember one feeling that has existed through everybody that I've had contact with sexually. I can't put a word on it but I feel a *self* in there. I don't know if it's self-fulfilling—maybe that's the word. I don't know if that expresses what I'm trying to say. I'm being what I want to be when I do that and now it's acknowledging it. Now that I understand and accept it, I look back and say that I felt those same feelings back then, but I was very confused and didn't understand them. The difference is so dramatic—having the puzzle in a million pieces—and now having it all together and I understand it all. *It's to be myself, really, it's a self-being kind of thing.*

Zack's earlier confusion is a dramatic illustration of the power of the institutional prohibitions of the culture to infiltrate the individual mind and throw a veil over the consciousness of a man's inner feelings. This story will be familiar to many gay men. For them, as for Zack, the intensity of those feelings eventually broke through the barriers to consciousness. One can only imagine the numbers of men whose same-sex feelings are not as intense or that exist alongside their feelings for women, for whom the veil is never lifted.

After his early experiences with the girls across the street, Zack had restricted his physical contact with girls and women to kissing. However, he picked up the thread from his adolescent years with

Maria, a close female friend that he had dated and who knew that he was gay. Eventually, they had sex. His body could perform, and he had feeling for her, but something was missing—the "self in there." To experience that self, he had to reach across and close the space between himself and a man. Jeff, whom I discussed in Chapter 4, said about what had happened between him and his best friend in the darkened living room, "Our minds touched." What made this touching a sexual experience was the current of feeling that surged between them. A current can only flow between two points. Zack's knowing that he was gay meant he recognized the strength of the current between himself and another man. It completed a circuit that energized the "self in there." That completion did not occur with a woman because the current did not flow. Perhaps that is why, though he had kissed many girls and women over the years, he said, "There's no comparison between kissing a woman and kissing a man."

I said at the close of the sixth chapter that an examination of the lives of individual men would reveal no fixed path of development that could be said to characterize all heterosexual men or all gay men—or all bisexual men. The only difference is in the emotional bonds that each moves toward strengthening. And this "moving toward" is not a decision of the "I" that thinks in language but is rather a movement of the "inner I"—in Zack's terms, of the self. In Zack's adolescent explorations with his cousin he stood, without realizing it, at the junction of two roads. Zack found himself drawn to take one road, his cousin another. Zack's dream foretold what he would find at the end of it. What started him on that road? And when had the journey begun?

EARLY DIRECTIONS

One of Zack's earliest memories was being a baby on the doctor's table, with the doctor paying attention to his penis. He said, "I remember the crib, the wood paneling, the table that the scale was on that he put me on, very vividly." It seems striking that one of Zack's earliest memories—the male doctor paying attention to his penis—was emblematic of what was to prove to be the direction of his emotional and sexual life. Although the playground incident cast a very long shadow over his life, given how common such experiences are at that age, the sex play with his young friend did not in itself predict that direction. In our sixth session, however, a more significant memory returned from when he was nine years old:

I'd gone to YMCA camp. I was one of those kids in the cabin that everybody looked up to for some reason. There were several and I was one of them, so I had a group of kids that followed me around a lot of the time. One of the kids who was tougher than me came up to me and said, "There's a girl who likes you. Let's go see her." I was like, "No way." I was on the way down this trail to the lake. There was a lifeguard there that was absolutely gorgeous—now I can acknowledge that. Anyway, I refused to go and meet this girl, and I remember this boy saying to me, "What, do you like guys?" He didn't say it very derogatorily though, and I didn't find it upsetting. I made it down to the lake, but I didn't get a chance to talk to the lifeguard. I was sitting by myself and the next thing I knew, there was a group of kids around me and they kidnapped me, dragged [me] from the lake, up this trail, hanging back, to where this girl was, and they literally tossed me in the dirt in front of her, and I was completely aghast. There was a group of girls and guys around. I didn't want to be there. I just wanted to go back and play with my buddies. I could care less about this girl—I don't think it's so unusual at that age.

I remember I always wanted to be with the camp counselors around the campfire at night. I could look out of my bunk on top, over the shutters, and see all the counselors around the campfire. I wanted to be out there so bad, with those camp counselors. And they took me out there one night. I guess they thought the only way they could satisfy this kid's curiosity was to let him sit with [them]. I remember they smoked joints around the campfire—they told me, "No, you're too young to smoke." And they let me sit with them until I fell asleep. Then they picked me up and put me in my bunk.

But the most important thing was that when I came back I found myself missing the camp counselors so much that I cried about it, in front of my mother. Instead of hugging me, and asking me what I was crying about, she yelled at me, "What are you crying about?" I said I missed the camp counselors. I think I used the word *love*—"*I loved them so much. They were so nice to me.*" I remember my mother's reaction. She was very cold about it, like I shouldn't be feeling that way, "get over it" kind of thing.

In these memories from the age of nine it is possible to see two dimensions of experience that had not yet converged in Zack's awareness. One was a child's erotic response to the body of the good-looking lifeguard—but recognized as erotic only in retrospect. In contrast, the dimension of experience with the counselors was deeply emotional—"*I loved them so much.*" I remarked to Zack that we were talking about two things—the imagery of the body, on one hand, and an inner feeling on the other. How could we distinguish between these two? What he said next was very revealing. "Like it's very thrown back and forth between the two. I think there's some type of *inner desire and you can't decipher that until you have some type of visual thing to help you decipher what that feeling is.*" He added modestly, "I don't know if that makes sense." Although I had asked him about a distinction, Zack's answer described a connection. Coming from him spontaneously and intuitively, it was a corrective to the separation between the erotic and the emotional that is so deeply embedded in our cultural frame of reference. Like a dream, the erotic image is a communication—from oneself and to oneself. It is a clue—sometimes the first—that a powerful inner feeling is at work. The attraction to the body of the lifeguard was a clue to an inner feeling that Zack had not yet put into words. It was only when the grief of separation from the counselors overwhelmed him that he found the words for it—"*I loved them so much.*" Subsequently, sex with his male cousin was more exciting than with the girls. Much later, although Zack loved Maria too, the sexual experiences with her were no match for those with men. The reason was that his deepest emotions were embedded in the connection with a male. It was the fulfillment of that emotional connection that gave sex with a man the drive and intensity that was lacking with a woman. All this was already implied at the age of nine, when it was manifestly clear that he much preferred to be close to the lifeguard rather than to the girl who liked him—although it would take many more years for it to be clear to him.

THE COLOR GREEN

As Zack and I continued our dialogues, they became very free-wheeling. Meeting only once a month or so, we got into the habit of talking for an hour and a half or two hours, then going to lunch or—more commonly—dinner, and then returning to talk some more for another hour or so. I taped our sessions because, since we were dealing with emotions that were often so difficult to put into words, it seemed to me important to try to preserve, as much possible, the fragility of their nuances and shades of meaning. Also, as in all the dialogues reported in this book, there was a genuine give-and-take between us, so that sometimes I would find myself putting a thought into words for the first time, and it was helpful to have a record of those as well. Of course, although I did not take my tape recorder there, at dinner we would often pick up the thread of the conversation we had been having in my office earlier. One evening, at dinner, we talked on the theme of love. Zack mused,

> I was thinking about it today. What's love for me? I thought that for me, it's like the color green, a color that I love. It consists of sensations, but there's emotion in it too. I could imagine holding it, even smelling it. I think you could explain what green was even to a blind man—as in grass, its texture, the smell of it, how it moves and bends, the sound of wind passing through it. Love is like a fragile puzzle, in yourself, or between you and somebody else. When part of that puzzle shifts, even if it's only a slight shift, it can change the feelings of love, maybe to another level, maybe to friendship. You might start with attraction, but if a shift occurs, attraction can disappear.

THE DREAM OF THE COLOR GREEN

A few months later, Zack told me a dream that seemed to pick up the thread of that conversation in a revealing way.

We [Zack and I] were on the *Donahue* show. We'd written a book together called *The Color Green.* On the cover there was a circle inside a square. I don't recall for sure, but they might have been the same shade of green. On the set were also the guys from work, as well as the chief, my mother, and another man.

This struck me as a very important dream. He dreamed it about fifteen months from the time of our first meeting. When I first met Zack, I had anticipated a limited number of interviews. But as with Clark, I intuitively felt, after the first few, that something could be learned by letting the process of dialogue unfold over a longer period of time. At the same time, even though he was hard-pressed to say why, Zack found himself quite willing to meet in a fairly open-ended way. The dream told him—and me—what we were doing and, I think, why we were doing it. Zack had used the metaphor of the color green when he tried to explain to me what love felt like to him. In writing a book together called *The Color Green,* Zack and I were, therefore, writing a book about love. But since the focus of our work was on his feelings for men, the dream was saying that love was at the core of those feelings. I felt then and there that "The Color Green" had to be the title for this chapter dealing with the meaning of Zack's same-sex feelings.

Initially, although I noted the circle in the square motif, I didn't make much of it. Out of curiosity, I turned to a copy of Jung's *Man and His Symbols.* In that volume, Aniela Jaffe, in a chapter titled, "Symbolism in the Visual Arts," refers to the circle as a symbol of the self while the square is a symbol of "earthbound matter, the body, and reality."[1] (I think, however that to speak of the body as part of "earthbound matter"—in contradistinction to the self—is to express the split between the spirit and the flesh that is so embedded in our religious history.) In the cosmic system of the ancient Maya, the four directions of the world had a sacred significance, each of these being presided over by an aspect of Chak, the rain god.[2] The square is also one of the forms of the mandala, the Buddhist representation of the cosmos. One could reject the idea that geometric patterns such as the circle and square could be symbols with psychological significance. In that case, one would have to offer another explanation of why they appeared in the dream. But if we are willing to grant the possibility of transcultural symbols for pervasive human experiences, then the book in Zack's dream stood for three interrelated things: green for Zack's feelings of love; the circle for the totality of Zack's self, including his body; and the square for his relation to the world around him. In that case, our task was to inscribe the pages of this book by looking at these three dimensions of his life.

THE IMAGE OF THE DOUBLE

I was struck by the poetic and evanescent imagery of "the color green," but then something occurred that took us down another avenue. Zack had recently been at a club with some friends when a group of men came in. He was immediately struck by one of them. He had broad, square shoulders, dark "buzz-cut hair, a nice nose—almost a German look. Looking at him across the table, it struck me that, except for the hair color, Zack could be describing himself. When we returned to my office, I went back to that part of our conversation. I said that, as he was telling me about the image of his desire, it seemed to me that I was looking at it. Zack, thinking I was speaking metaphorically, said, "You were *feeling* what I was seeing. . . ." "No," I said, "I was *seeing* it as I was looking at you across the table." I said it seemed he was looking for a man who looked like himself. Was he somehow looking for a twin? What then followed was quite striking. Zack laughed and said,

> Oh . . . you're going to find this very funny, because me and Vic were having this conversation the other day. We got into a conversation about brothers. I had an experience with my brother and he came close to having an experience with his. Vic's brother had six or seven friends overnight recently and I was wondering how they would feel about it if they did something—and what would happen if Vic went in there and an orgy-type situation developed. I said, if it were my brother I'd avoid him in the orgy, but not if it was my twin. He said, "Really?" I said if I had a twin and it was an agreed-upon thing, we'd be doing each other all the time. No doubt in my

mind, if that were a possibility that would happen. But if I *really* had a twin, I don't know—but it's a real fantasy. It was a really interesting conversation. I found the whole thing very erotic, exciting. I thought that could really be great, really be wild, if you loved yourself—and in my case I do—and I'm happy with myself and I find myself attractive, and people tell me I'm attractive—and I have a twin just like me, and we're both gay . . . it would be pretty erotic, it would really be this *shared incident.* I don't know what the word is.

"It seems like a powerful thing," I remarked. "Powerful," he echoed, "*that's* the word, and then to be able to sit down with my brother and discuss it. He's looking at me, I'm looking at him, *and we're seeing each other and we're both turned on by it, and we're the same people.* It has this really powerful imagery to it. It's something else, don't you think?"

In fact, this theme had emerged in another context much earlier in our dialogues, when I had asked Zack about fantasies during masturbation. He said that there was usually no fantasy as such. Rather, he focused on himself. He likened it to "a very deep meditation kind of thing, getting into myself." The focus was on his own body, almost always reflected back to him in a mirror. He had said, somewhat apologetically, "It's a little bit narcissistic—in the sense that my stereotype of that 'ultimate' person has always been somebody that really fits my own image. I've always been attracted to guys with blue eyes, buzzed blond hair, and they look like they just stepped out of boot camp. I always found that type of individual extremely, extremely attractive." I said that I did not use the term "narcissistic" very much anymore because it had too much baggage attached to it. He agreed, "It's kind of negative. I guess I just get into myself." Some time later, it emerged that this meditative engagement with his own image began only after the experience of the Forum—that is, only after his self-hatred gave way to self-acceptance.

Zack's fantasy of sex with a twin converges with a theory of the archetype of the "double" Jungian analyst Mitchell Walker has put forward. This is not the place nor am I the person to undertake a critical discussion of Jung's concept of the archetype. My own way of thinking about archetypes is to regard them as powerful themes—often expressed through images—that arise out of the fundamental structure of the human mind and experience. Although an archetype has the quality of universality, how and to what extent it emerges into the consciousness of any given individual depends upon culture and personal life experience. With this in mind, I want to cite a few passages from Walker's article on the archetype of the double:

> The double and the anima/us are equal and complementary, and form a whole, androgynous in nature. For example, the anima [for a man] contains the archetypal images of mother, daughter, sister, lover. The male double, then, contains those of father, son, brother, lover. Just as a woman can serve for projection of the anima, so a man can serve for projection of the male double, and vice versa for a woman.[3]

Walker's idea of the archetype of the double converges with the evidence from men's feelings that I have presented in this book. My students were just beginning to give me the material about their same-sex feelings when Zack and I had the conversation about his twin fantasy. Looking at that fantasy now, in the context of what they said, it appears to focus, in a very intense way, the dominant theme in the same-sex feelings of my male students: the sense of shared ties—of identification—with someone like oneself, the erotic pull toward the best friend, the aura of brotherhood.

Walker points out that the sexual expression of the double can be rejected as a result of cultural prohibitions and thus fall into "shadow"—that is, the repressed unconscious. Not only has the institutional culture explicitly prohibited the expression of sexual love between men, it has—through the "scientific" establishment—tried to deny that such a thing is possible; hence, the attempts to impose a heterosexual model on same-sex relationships. Clark's reactions initially reflected his internalization of this denial—at first, he had to see his male partner as a woman. That denial quickly became transparent, however, and revealed the internalized fear of the image of the double—the man who was "masculine like myself"—that was behind it. It was that internalized fear of the male twin—in Walker's terms, the double—that Clark "conquered" in making love with Alan. When Zack looked at himself in the mirror during sex alone, his own reflection could serve as a stand-in for the spiritual twin he had briefly found in the relationship with his cousin and that emerged as the primeval image of the monster in his dream.

THE DOUBLE IN CONRAD'S THE SECRET SHARER

I think it was after I read Walker's article on the double that I went back to reread Joseph Conrad's story *The Secret Sharer.*[4] When I did so, I realized that it stands, in its brevity and beauty, as one of the purest expressions of the theme of the double in English literature. When I told Zack about it, he immediately sought out a copy to read. He found himself caught up in the intensity of the narrative and immediately grasped the relation of its deeper levels to his own life's story. Like the metaphor of the color green, Conrad's story became a touchstone in our subsequent dialogues. Because Zack felt it was so relevant to his own story, I think an attempt at an analytic reading of it, followed by Zack's comments, is worthwhile.

Three elements combine to cast the story's shimmering spell— the tropics, the ship, and the man from the sea. The story opens in the narrator's voice recalling events that transpired when, as a young man, he had commanded his first ship. As the story, told as a memoir, opens, the captain muses that he and the ship—floating in perfect stillness—share the same fate. "In this breathless threshold of a long passage we seemed to be measuring our fitness for a long and arduous enterprise, *the appointed task of both our existences* to be carried out, far from all human eyes, *with only sky and sea for spectators and judges* [italics added]." Though bound to his ship, the new captain is, to its crew, an outsider. But, he adds, " . . . if all the truth must be told, I was somewhat of a *stranger to myself.*" These lines tell us that the voyage that the young captain is about to embark upon is a voyage of self-discovery.

It begins when he tries to pull up the ladder that had been left hanging over the ship's side and finds a mysterious force resisting his efforts. He looks down and sees the cause—a naked man, clinging to it. "I had somehow the impression that he was on the point of letting go the ladder to swim away beyond my ken—mysterious as he came." Instead, the man climbs the ladder.

> I got a sleeping suit out of my room and, coming back on deck, saw the naked man from the sea sitting on the main hatch, glimmering white in the darkness, his elbows on his knees and his head in his hands. In a moment he had concealed his damp body in a sleeping suit of the same gray-stripe pattern as the one I was wearing and followed me *like my double* on the poop.

The fact that the visitor arrives naked seems important. His nakedness is revealing even as it adds to his mystery. It seems important too that he is young and handsome. It further transpires that he comes from the same region of the country as the captain. The swimmer is a fugitive from a ship anchored a few miles away on which he had been first mate. He was being held under guard because, under the extreme stress of giving orders needed to save the ship in killer seas, he struck a chronically insubordinate seaman who had been surly to him. A fight ensued just as a huge wave crashed over the ship. When the deck became visible again, the mate had his fingers locked around the throat of the now-dead seaman. The captain ordered his mate held for trial when they should reach port. Throughout the story the narrator refers to him as "my double." He takes him to his own cabin, where he will remain hidden.

Even though he says, "He was not a bit like me, really . . ." he continues, "yet as we stood leaning over my bed-place, whispering side by side, with our dark heads together and our backs to the door, anybody bold enough to open it stealthily would have been treated to the uncanny sight of a double captain busy talking in whispers with *his other self.*" As the story proceeds, the emotional bond between the two men grows in circumstances that are both desperate and, because of the necessity for concealment, intimate. "I was extremely tired, in a *peculiarly intimate way,* by the strain of stealthiness, by the effort of whispering and the general *secrecy of this excitement.*" Thus, as the steward tidies up the captain's stateroom, they are together in the bathroom, where now it is the captain's body that is naked—as he bathes—in intimate proximity to his double. They also must share the captain's bed. "I took a bath and did most of my dressing, splashing, and whistling softly for the steward's edification while *the secret sharer of my life* stood drawn bolt upright in that little space. . . . Such was my scheme for keeping my *second self* invisible. . . . At night I would smuggle him into my bed-place, and we would whisper together. . . ." The necessity for concealment makes him give orders about the care of his personal quarters that confuse the routines of the steward who serves his needs. Referring to the ship's chief mate, he says, "There was a sort of curiosity in his eye that I did not like. I don't know whether the steward had told them that I was 'queer' only or downright drunk. . . ."

More and more, the story can be read as a metaphor for an intense emotional and physical bond between two men, of the kind that in the social context of the time, would have had absolutely to be concealed. Once the narrative is looked at from this perspective, the story itself is "doubled."

Looking is important in the story. The captain looks at his double in his place of concealment. "Now and then, glancing over my shoulder, I saw him back there, sitting rigidly on the low stool, his bare feet close together, his arms folded, his head hanging on his breast—and perfectly still. Anybody would have taken him for me. I was fascinated by it myself." When the captain first helps him into his own bed, his double looks at him. "He tumbled in, rolled over on his back, and flung one arm across his eyes. And then, with his face nearly hidden, he must have looked exactly as I used to look in that bed. *I gazed upon my other self for a while* before drawing across carefully the two green serge curtains which ran on a brass rod."

In turn, his double acknowledges having wanted, not merely to be seen, but to be *looked at*. He says, "When I saw a man's head looking over I thought I would swim away presently and leave him shouting—in whatever language it was. I didn't mind being looked at. *I—I liked it.* And then *you speaking to me so quietly—as if you had expected me*—made me hold on a little longer. It had been a confounded lonely time. . . ."

Plans are made for the double to slip overboard and swim to an island near the coast. There is a moment when the captain, fearing for his safety, protests, "Impossible. . . . You can't." Then,

> I felt suddenly ashamed of myself. I may say truly that I understood—and my hesitation in letting that man swim away from my ship's side had been a mere sham sentiment, a sort of cowardice. . . . "As long as I know that you understand," he whispered. "But of course you do. It's a great satisfaction to have got somebody to *understand.* You seem to have been there on purpose." And in the same whisper, as if we two whenever we talked had to say things to each other which were *not fit for the world to hear,* he added, *"It's very wonderful."*

The story works like a multilayered dream. At its uppermost level, it is an exotic tale of adventure surrounded by an aura of mystery. At the next level down it can be read as a metaphor for the sexual love between two men that was not—at that time—"fit for the world to hear." However, at the third and deepest level, it can be seen as giving utterance to an emotional theme that pervades the structure of men's lives and minds—the search for the transforming bond with the "double," the "other self," that, when found, is "very wonderful."

The moment of parting finally comes. Before his double is to slip into the sea once more, the captain insists on giving him some money. "I produced a large old silk handkerchief of mine, and tying the three pieces of gold in a corner, pressed it on him. He was touched, I suppose, because he took it at last and tied it quickly around his waist, under the jacket, on his bare skin." Again, the elements that make up this scene are not accidental. Silk and gold— these are gifts fit for a prince, or for one's beloved. The silk handkerchief is old, which is important because it means that it has been touched by the captain's hand, perhaps used to wipe the perspiration from his face or body. And it seems equally important that the silken token and the gold it contains are tied—not merely around his double's waist—but against his body, "on his bare skin." But there is one last gift.

> A sudden thought struck me. I saw myself wandering bare-
> footed, bareheaded, the sun beating on my dark poll. I
> snatched off my floppy hat and tried hurriedly in the dark to
> ram it on my other self. . . . He understood. . . . Our hands met
> gropingly, lingered united in a steady, motionless clasp for a
> second. . . . No word was breathed by either of us when they
> separated.

The story has a heart-in-the mouth ending. To give his double the
best possible chance of surviving, the captain decides—on the pretext of finding wind—to bring his ship as close as possible to the
shore of the island. The mate and the crew are all terrified at the
prospect that, being so close, the ship would not have sufficient
room to come about without hitting shoals or rocks, and so be lost.
The captain himself is not sure, but to try to ensure the survival of
the man from the sea—his double, his other self—he is prepared to
risk everything—his career, his ship, the crew, himself. "Was she
close enough? Already she was, I won't say in the shadow of the
land, but in the very blackness of it, already swallowed up as it
were, gone too close to be recalled, *gone from me altogether.*" The
outer narrative refers to the ship but the inner narrative—"gone
from me altogether"—is about the loss that is the price of saving the
man whose life he has come to prize above all else.

There is a moment of excruciating uncertainty, when he cannot
tell if the ship is moving. "I swung the mainyard and waited help-
lessly. She was perhaps stopped, and her fate hung in the balance,
with the black mass of Koh-ring like the gate of everlasting night
towering over her taffrail. What would she do now? Had she way on
her yet?" He desperately needs some marker against which the
ship's movement can be gauged.

> All at once my *strained, yearning stare* distinguished a white
> object floating within a yard of the ship's side. . . . I recognized
> my own floppy hat. It must have fallen off his head. . . . Now I
> had what I wanted—the saving mark for my eyes. But I hardly
> thought of my other self, now gone from the ship, to be hidden
> forever from all friendly faces, to be a fugitive and a vagabond
> on the earth, with no brand of the curse on his sane forehead to
> stay a slaying hand . . . too proud to explain. And I watched the

hat—expression of my sudden pity for his mere flesh. It had been meant to save his homeless head from the dangers of the sun. And now—behold—it was saving the ship. . . .

Seeing the hat appear to drift forward, he realizes that the ship has sufficient backward momentum to respond to the helm and be brought around. All are saved. "Already the ship was drawing ahead. And I was alone with her. Nothing! No one in the world should stand now between us, throwing a shadow on the way of silent knowledge and mute affection, the perfect communion of a seaman with his first command."

Once again, the outward narrative speaks of the relationship between captain and ship while its language—*"silent knowledge, mute affection, perfect communion"*—speaks of the relationship between the two men. There is one last glimpse of the hat and with it these thoughts: "I was in time to catch an evanescent glimpse of my white hat left behind to mark the spot where *the secret sharer of my cabin and my thoughts, as though he were my second self,* had lowered himself into the water to take his punishment; a free man, a proud swimmer striking out for a new destiny."

The hat—the object of his "yearning stare"—is the marker symbolizing the relationship that, for the young captain, has given a new direction to his life. In saving the man who briefly wore it he has moved to a new stage—as the confident captain of his ship and as a man on the threshold of the voyage of his life. His double, through which this transformation has been accomplished, though gone from him to seek his own destiny, will live—his soul's twin forever—in memory.

Speaking of the narrator, Zack said,

It seemed like he saw himself as different from everyone around him. Even though he was a good person and deserved to be captain of a ship, he still questioned that. But the question lay in *who* he was rather than in what he was. When this man came to him—that's how it appeared—he *came* to him, he found the missing piece that he'd been longing to understand all the time. This guy represented himself. At the same time it was another man. He realized at that point what he had been searching for all along. He was able to love him at whatever level for that period of time. By saving him he was saving himself. Hiding him in his cabin—in effect, he was hiding himself from the people around him all that time. And the captain from the other ship picked that up instantly. Just like his second mate and all these guys. They were picking up that there was more to this man than just the fact that he was the captain. He drove the entire ship to the edge. Much as they couldn't believe what the captain was doing—he put all their lives on the line—they allowed it. Why? They could have stuck him in the hold, taken control of the ship, and called him a madman. But they all got caught up in what he was doing. They needed to find out where he was going with this. The captain was allowing them to live out something that no captain would do. And they all got out of it.

Joseph Conrad went to sea in 1874, at the age of seventeen, and sailed for twenty years, eventually becoming a captain in the British merchant marine. This was a time of long voyages, when sex aboard ship was a given—as it was on American ships of the period. At the same time, in civilian life a parliament of men had affirmed criminal penalties against "indecency" between men in the law that was eventually used to destroy Oscar Wilde. First as a young seaman, later as an officer and captain, and as a man who was not afraid of exploring the farthest reaches of the human heart, Conrad must have been acquainted with the deep feelings that the necessarily clandestine sexual liaisons—the "secret sharing"—between men could both embody and stir. The tale into which he wove that knowledge—as relevant to the men of Zack's day as it was to his own—touches and evokes the deep stratum of emotional sharing that can move men toward each other even as they find that movement constrained by a culture that fears it.

LOVE IN THE FLESH

Zack had said that when he first began to have sex with a man, all he did was to lie there and let the other man perform oral sex on him, explaining, "As far as my masculinity being affected, that was the most I could handle." When I asked him at what point he began to allow a more complete relationship, Zack interpreted my question as applying to anal intercourse. In our first couple of sessions, we were still groping toward a common language. I was trying to get him to put what he was feeling into the language of emotions, while it was utterly natural to him to use the language of the body. In the discussion that followed, the two came together—a good harbinger for the future of our collaboration. I mentioned earlier that when heterosexually identified men let the inner movement toward a man go far enough, images of reciprocal anal intercourse, as well as oral sex, arose in their minds. That was true for Clark as well.

Zack recalled,

> There was such a long period of time when I didn't have any anal intercourse. I can remember messing around with this guy one night and having such a tremendous urge for him to fuck me. I couldn't explain it. It was something that I wanted to have done *so* bad that it wasn't just a thought. It was a physical thing that had to happen. *Do* it! It was an ache, a body ache.

It was, he said, *"That same aching feeling I can put to 'I want to be with a guy.' "* Ironically, however, virtually every time that he let another man come inside him, his body seemed to rebel. During the second year of our work, he recounted a dramatic instance of this. He was skiing out West, and the other man, Steve, fit the image of the double—a police officer from another part of the country—who was also very handsome and at the center of one of those cliques that arrogate to themselves an air of superiority that somehow manages to make others feel both excluded and envious. When Steve said to Zack, "Let's go," Zack remembered,

> I followed like a puppy dog, and we ended up in bed. That continued all week, the physical, sexual part of it, but during the day you'd never know we were sleeping together. And toward the end of the week we questioned that. 'Why have we acted like we don't even know each other?' I think it has something to do with the cop thing, to be honest with you. I was told by my friend that we were the talk of the town that whole week and didn't know it—very ego building.

He said that to this day, no one knew what was going on. "Everyone was taking bets—'They must both be tops, or if they're both bottoms, what are they doing' Silly stuff."

> It was the second or third time, that we wound up having anal sex. I hadn't let anyone do that to me since I first came out— and I opened up to him. I was honest with him, "I don't do that; I never felt comfortable with it." He was very good about it and didn't push it, just, "Well, is that something you want to do?" Or—"If you don't want to, would you want to fuck me?" There was so much of an attraction to this guy, that it was, "Let's try it." He took his time. It was painful, but at least I relaxed till he was able to do his thing, then I got sick and sat in the bathroom for two hours—sick as a dog. I remember feeling, "God, I let this guy do this," and I was questioning myself, "*What does this mean?* You opened yourself up to this guy; what is that all about?" I probably have a good insight into it now. That whole masculinity thing, "Wait a second, I got fucked; what does this mean now?" I knew I didn't like it and I think I used that as a justification—"I'm still masculine," you know?"

Zack added that he had always associated being on the "bottom" to being less of a man—though he no longer felt that way at all.

When I first met Zack, he was very much in love with Vic. He had had boyfriends before, but his feelings for Vic had an unmatched intensity. Vic was twenty years old and, though very sexual, also somewhat inexperienced. Zack was the first partner he had with whom he could enjoy anal intercourse. However, in our second session, Zack described what happened when Vic—one day not long before—demanded, "When do I get to fuck you?" Zack, who had tried to avoid the issue, said he realized that, "No matter how much he loves me, there's still something not being fulfilled that he needs. So we tried it and I got sick as a dog. But he was all happy—'That was great, now we're going to do this all the time!'" Because Zack did want to make Vic happy, they tried it again, and he said,

I just felt like it loosened my whole insides up. I said, "Stop, Vic, this is just not going to work." This was the same thing that had happened again and again—maybe it was something physical. I got really upset and so did he. I thought, "This guy, no matter how much he loves me, if he doesn't get it from me, he's going to go look for it somewhere else. It's almost fair that we take turns." So he came over, and we started fooling around, and I started fucking him. He stopped in the middle of it, looked right at me, and said, "I want to fuck you."

Zack laughed and said, "The look on his face was, like I didn't have a choice, so 'Okay.' I really can't explain it, but it worked. I relaxed, I didn't feel like my insides were killing me, and it was erotic. For the first time, it was great, the entire thing!" Physically, Zack did nothing different, as far as he knew. But clearly, a mental switch had been thrown, and his body could make the adjustment it needed to. I said to Zack that I thought there was something about the interpenetration of bodies that was very powerful. He agreed.

Sure, it's very meaningful. We talk about this and Vic's question to me was, "Do you think having anal intercourse the way we do is making love?" I didn't give it a whole lot of thought and just answered off the top of my head, and said, "No, I think the relationship part—kissing, caressing, and lying together in bed and holding each other—*that's* love. But the act of having sex is 'sex' and you do it because you love that person. You're having a physical reaction with someone because you love him."

I said to Zack, "You get aroused, get an erection. What gives you that?" He said, "The fact that I'm satisfying him, and the fact that we're joined like that, you know. . . . " I echoed, "*Joined* like that. . . ." Picking up on my emphasis, he added thoughtfully, "Yeah, sure, *it's some type of completion, some type of fulfillment.*"

More than a year later, in looking back over the earlier experience with Steve out West, he said about why he had let Steve have intercourse with him,

Obviously, looking at it now, *there was a real bond there that I wanted to have completed.* In order for me to give into that

after so long, it was really a powerful thing. When I got back
from that trip, I was so depressed that I called out of work for a
whole week. I realized—I did this with this guy—spent a
whole week with him. I had anal sex, then came back to this
big empty apartment that I hated to begin with. I was very
lonely, I didn't want to be there, it was terrible—and not having him call me. Finally I called him. On the phone, I guess I
was fine—I said, "I guess this isn't going to work, huh?" He
said, "Yeah, I was going to call you and tell you, a long-
distance thing isn't going to cut it here." It was like "Okay,"
and I was crushed. Funny thing was, *I held onto him inside.*

His reaction of loss was not because of the kind of sex he and
Steve had. It was about the fracturing of a bond that—though it was
through the body—was not only about the body. Zack was aware
that, at some level, gay culture mimicked the wider culture in regarding the person who was the receiver in anal intercourse—the
"bottom"—as somehow less masculine than the "top." Steve—
whatever his other failings—did not seem to feel that way. And,
intellectually, Zack had come to reject such thinking. Even though
anal intercourse remained an alternative rather than preferred
modality, I think it was his love for Vic that enabled him to overcome the last emotional barriers to allowing another man inside him
in that way. Later, when Zack learned that Vic was not emotionally
equipped to handle monogamy, he understood that it signified Vic's
inability to sustain the one-to-one emotional bond that had enabled
Zack to overcome those barriers. The break, when it finally came,
was emotionally bruising, and recovery took well over a year.

TWO MASCULINITIES

From time to time, the issue of masculinity and femininity came
up in our dialogues. Zack understood that, for many men, same-sex
feelings constituted a threat to their sense of masculinity. He had
long since stopped worrying about it for himself—perhaps he had
overcome the last vestiges of that with Vic. Because I knew that the
concept of masculinity was the subject of a good deal of speculation
and even controversy in the literature, I would sometimes sound out

Zack's feelings about it. I think I was actually more interested in the subject than he was. He said, "I consider myself masculine, and what I appreciate most about myself is that I'm gay, and sensitive, and caring." He said, about masculinity, "It's an aura," adding, "But it's not set in stone. It's like masculinity can almost be an emotion. I can vary my masculinity with the situation I'm involved with—emotions are that flexible." Zack seemed to be talking about something that was both objective and subjective at the same time. The objective side had to do with how men looked, moved, smelled, the structure of their bodies—the things he first recalled responding to at the pool where he had learned to swim. The subjective side had to do with the sense of himself. Both of these elements were brought together in the emotional and physical bonding with another man. At one point, he took a trip to California to visit friends and wound up going to a bar that was neither gay nor straight. Walking by a particularly good looking man who was with a woman, Zack casually tapped him on the arm. As it turned out, Harry had been mostly with women but had recently begun to realize that his attraction to men was greater. He flew east to spend five days with Zack. We had been talking about some of these male-to-male issues around that time, and I asked him how they related to the time he spent with Harry. He said, "I felt I was talking to a man, a masculine man." A little later, he elaborated on what that meant.

> When you're with a man, you're with a *man* . . . you know what I mean? You're sharing every bond possible with a man—you think like him, it's just so special. Being intimate with a man in a way that men are not used to being with each other. And when you experience that, it's a complete turn-on. You know what he's thinking, what he wants, what will make him happy. With women, while you might learn that, with men, it's like that common bond—*two masculinities, two male egos bonding together, it's just explosive.*

The sexual expression of that feeling with Harry had emerged in the imagery of a dream that Zack had while anticipating his arrival:

I was giving him a blow job and there was this overwhelming, great feeling—having him in my mouth was just this complete turn-on.

In another context, Zack had said about having sex with a man in this way, "It's a sense of togetherness with that other person—it kind of creates a bond of togetherness. It's a very strong, masculine kind of feeling about having a penis in your mouth." The dream, then, was very much an experience of the double. But there was another image that was important in Zack's feeling which—while it too might be seen as an expression of that theme—embodied a somewhat different aspect of it.

THE DREAM OF THE YOUNG MAN
IN THE CELLAR

That image first emerged with clarity in a dream in the first six months of our meetings. The dream contained, at one level, intimations of the coming breakup with Vic:

I'm in the cellar of an old house. It's a situation like the old underground railway to free the slaves. People are being helped to escape, two a time. They have to run for it when the signal is given. There's a young guy—more than a boy, but quite young—near me. He's very good-looking. He lets his pants fall and starts stroking himself. He has a beautiful body. I realize that this is a test.

In a psychoanalytic sense, this dream was overdetermined. Several important meanings converged in its imagery. On one hand, the eroticism of the image of the young man "tested" Zack's feelings for Vic, which he realized had begun to shift. But it was also the first appearance of an image that would figure prominently in our subsequent dialogues. The image of the young man in the cellar did not correspond to what Zack had called his "stereotype"—the man with buzz-cut blond hair who looked like he just stepped out of boot camp. Rather, in the dream Zack felt awed by his innocence and beauty, a feeling that existed right alongside the powerful erotic appeal of his image.

It seemed significant that he was a youth just this side of manhood, in contrast to Zack, who had just turned twenty-nine. This image also appeared in the flesh, in the guise of a young man in the neighborhood. Zack said about him,

> He's nineteen and a good-looking kid. He has that very slinky, smooth kind of "cut" body. A boyish kind of body—very broad shoulders but a thirty-inch waist. Funny thing is that there's that eye attraction when we talk to each other, to the point where he even acts bashful about it. He might not think that I'm aware of it, but I am. It wasn't only me but also my straight friend, Ted. He was joking, "Oh, you dog. . . . " I said, "He's a nice kid. I find him attractive and that's it." He said, "But he likes you, Zack; you can see it when he looks at you." That helped to confirm what I already knew. He finds me somehow attractive but I don't know how. I don't know if it's that I'm a police officer or what, but you can obviously see it. He gets flustered once in a while. He was with his girlfriend and he said, "I have to stop by your house." It's not something I try following up.

But twice, during masturbation, Zack found himself thinking about him.

> Not having sex with him, just visualizing what he looked like. Did you ever see *The Jungle Book?* The boy in it reminds me of him. He has that goofy dorkiness about him—just a very cute kid. I visualized him just standing there naked. I'd seen him in shorts and that's it, so I know what he looks like. I visualized his chest—he's very cute. Twice, I found myself doing that.

A month later, the image appeared again, this time with a young man, now twenty-two, whom Zack had known when he was much younger but had not seen in a long time. "When I saw him standing on the dock, I was overwhelmed. I just stood there looking at him. It was just that powerful kind of image. I could see his body under his clothes. He had broad shoulders, a defined—but not cut—smooth chest. He was wearing shorts so I could see his legs. I noticed his hands and fingers." Once again, he remarked on the current of feeling that he sensed had passed between them. "I have no idea if he's gay or not, but there was like a mutual attraction there—I could see it by the way he stood and the smile at the corner of his mouth." Again, Zack's feeling about this young man was not that he would like to have sex with him, but that he would like to get to know him, be his friend.

The idealized image of the youth or young man just this side of manhood figures in one of the most powerful expressions of the male-to-male bond—that between older and younger man. It was especially important in classical civilization. When Antinuous, the young lover of the most power man in the world—Hadrian, Emperor of Rome—drowned in the waters of the Nile, Hadrian declared him to be a god and erected temples to him throughout th empire. Worship in those temples survived well into the Christian era.[5] The difference in ages between Hadrian and the loved young man whom he made a god spanned more than a generation, but the actual age difference in such pairings can vary widely, from that found between older and younger brother to that between father and son, and beyond. I think Zack's three images—the dream image of the boy in the cellar, the boy down the street, and the boy on the dock—reflected this dimension of the male-to-male bond in Zack's feeling.

The image of the young man was not less masculine because of his youth, but his youth seemed to lend the image a special aura. His significance kept coming up in our dialogues, and the following words come from a session several years later:

> You look at someone eighteen to twenty-two, or someone younger than you, and you're seeing in them how you feel inside, almost. You can look in the mirror and know you're older—that's the decay that you see. You're getting lines, losing your hair, or whatever. When you look at someone who is young and beautiful, you're almost projecting their image onto you, as a substitute for how you look on the outside. For whatever that moment is, you feel young again. You're not seeing yourself, but you *are* seeing yourself—young inside and young outside. You know where that person is because

you were there before—almost like you're projecting yourself on them too. Somehow it completes something.

I think that Zack was putting into words another aspect of the double—of the male-to-male bond—that helps to explain its enduring power. It is a power that originates in the relationship between father and son.

However, the idealized image of the youth or young man appears in myth, art, and religion, and has other meanings as well. Those meanings can enter into and deepen the emotions felt between father and son or in the bond between older and younger, but I think they can also stand alone. As I said in Chapter 10, the images that the individual mind creates—whether in waking life or dreams—can share a common set of meanings with mythic images, or with the images found in art or religion.

As it turned out, the image of the young man in the cellar seemed to have another meaning for Zack in addition to that of a partner in the bond between older and younger man. We arrived at this meaning through the circuitous route of an image far removed from our own cultural and religious environment.

THE GOD OF LOVE

In the course of our work together, I often told Zack about some of the things that were turning up in the research with my students, as well as some of the historical or literary connections that were part of my own intellectual background for this book. Among these connections were aspects of Hindu and Tibetan Buddhist thought, because these religious systems contrast with our own in one crucial respect. Rather than setting the erotic and the sacred in opposition, in these religious systems, the erotic can serve as a conduit for the experience of the sacred or transcendent. One evening, about two years after Zack reported the dream of the young man in the cellar, I was reading Zack some passages from a translation of a Sanskrit poem— the "Kumarasambhava," "The Origin of the Young God," by the sixth-century poet Kalidasa.[6] I was telling him about the poet's description of Kama, the god of love. At the opening of the story that the poem recounts, a powerful demon is threatening the universe and the dominion of the gods themselves. The gods approach Brahma, the prime creator, who says that only a hero produced from a union of the great god Shiva and Parvati—the goddess who is the daughter of Himalaya, who is both god and mountain—can defeat the demon. Shiva, however, is deeply engrossed in meditation and ascetic practice after the death of his first wife, who has, in fact, been reincarnated in Parvati. Kama is commissioned by the other gods to let fly one of his flowered arrows at Shiva, so that he will fall in love with Parvati. As Kama passes through the forest to the place where Shiva is meditating, he is accompanied by the goddess Rati, his wife, whose name means "sexual delight," and his beloved companion, the Spring. At their passage, the whole forest is suffused with love. Waiting until Parvati approaches Shiva, Kama takes aim at him, but before he can release the bowstring, Shiva sees him and, in a flash of anger, burns Kama to ashes with fire from his third eye. Rati grieves for her husband, recalling,

> Your body, shining so beautifully
> all women would compare their lovers to you. . . .
> Everyone here is deprived through fate,
> since the pleasure of those who have bodies rests on you.
> Along the streets of cities covered
> with the blackness of the night, who else but you,
> love, can guide the women
> frightened by thunder to their lovers' houses?
> Even if they roll their reddened eyes
> and stumble over words at every step they take,
> the drunkenness through wine of young
> beautiful women is meaningless now without you.
> Your good friend, the moon,
> knowing that your beauty has become only a legend.
> will grow out of darkness sadly,
> O bodiless god, without lovers to welcome his rising.[7]

Love is literally embodied in the form of the god that is both sacred and sensual, "shining so beautifully all women would compare their lovers to you."[8] His body sustains the power of love that pervades the universe. But love's destruction cannot be final. Asceticism cannot triumph at love's expense. Although Kama's arrow did not reach Shiva, Parvati wins his love by other means. Kama's body is restored to life when Shiva and Parvati marry.

> The god who has eight forms took her by the hand
> its fingers painted red, offered him by her father,
> as if it were the first tender shoot of the body
> of Love hidden within Uma and still in fear of Siva.
> At the moment their hands touched, the hair stood up
> on Uma's skin and a sweat broke out on the fingers
> of Siva as if to show that now there had come
> to life the God of Love to be shared between them.[9]

I had read these and other passages from this poem to Zack at my office and later, over dinner, we started talking about the poem, and I asked him if he could describe to me his own vision of the god of love. He said:

> I see him in a field of grass, with a kind of a rail fence stretching down out of sight. He's about fifteen to seventeen. He's wearing no top, maybe kind of ragged pants. He's smiling, with a straw in his mouth. He's so beautiful and pure, you wouldn't think of having sex with him.

This image was very different from Zack's "stereotype." But, I said, suppose he were with someone who fitted that stereotype? Would the god of love be somewhere? He said, *"In his body when I touched him."* This reminded me of the lines in the poem that describe the moment when god and goddess touch hands at their wedding ceremony—*"now there had come to life the God of Love to be shared between them."* This, combined with his saying about his impromptu image of the god of love—"He's so beautiful and pure, you wouldn't think of having sex with him"—indicated that, while it was an erotic image, it didn't represent someone he would literally seek to have sex with.

Rather, this was a symbolic image, and what it 'symbolized, I think, was love itself—as Zack hoped to find it with and through another. At the same time it symbolized a way of loving that, although it had to be experienced in the flesh, went beyond the flesh to touch a deep vein of pure feeling in himself and the other person.

In other words, the image brought together what our religious traditions have so harshly put asunder—flesh and spirit. The dream image of the young man in the cellar—who radiated both innocence and eroticism—and the images of the two young men were incarnations of this same image, and incorporated the same meanings.

They also had a particular meaning in the context of late-twentieth-century American civilization, which is so wracked with ambivalence about adolescent sexuality. Even in our media-hyped culture, there is for many children—and even adolescents—a moment in time when sexual feelings can be experienced with a purity not yet touched by the guilt and the pornographic sensibility that the adult world loads onto them. For Zack, such a moment of innocence occurred twice: The first time with his young friend before the playground incident, and the second with his cousin before word was spread about what they had done. Particularly for young people developing along gay lines, such precious moments might be hard to find, and, even when they are found, prone to being cut brutally short.

A gay man now in his forties told about how, as a young adolescent, he experienced his early sexual feelings as so pure and beautiful. But, he said, as he began to realize how much people hated him because of them, he could never experience them in the same way again. One can see the origins of that hatred in the anguished sexual history of our civilization. The early Christian Fathers held that men's erotic response to the beauty of another man—one of the expressions of divinely ordained love in the ancient world—was so sinful that it paved the road to hell, and they referred to the Olympian gods as "boy molesters."[10]

In striking contrast is a painting at Palmyra that I saw during my travels in Syria a few years ago. Palmyra, situated at an oasis in the desert, grew rich from its position at the crossroads of some of the major trade routes of the ancient world. Its wealthy citizens, who believed in an afterlife, built mausoleums for themselves and their families. A few have survived with some of their sculpture and painting intact. In one of these tombs, a picture on the ceiling is scarcely less vivid than when it was completed almost 2,000 years ago. It shows Ganymede, as a youth, being carried off by Zeus, in the form of an eagle (see Figure 11.1). As the viewer looks up, he sees the naked figure of the young man enfolded by the wings of the

FIGURE 11.1. Zeus in the Form of an Eagle Carrying Ganymede to Heaven: Palmyra, Second Century C.E.

Source: The Hypogeum of the Three Brothers, Palmyra, Syria (photo by E. Tejirian).

305

eagle whose form the god has taken. This image seems very apt in this setting. His love for the young man causes the god to lift him up to the heavens, there to grant him eternal life and eternal youth. But the love of Zeus is emphatically an erotic love. And so, in this image, the consummation of that love becomes the symbol of the aspiration for resurrection and eternal life.

About a year after our conversation on the god of love, Zack met Lucas, a young man just turned nineteen. The circumstances of their meeting are worth relating. Zack spied Lucas waiting for a court hearing on a minor traffic violation. He seemed scared and vulnerable—even though he planned to plead not guilty. Zack, who refused on principle to write traffic tickets except for the most flagrant violations, asked the officer who had cited Lucas if he would be willing to reduce the charges. He agreed and Zack informed Lucas, who was relieved and grateful. Zack also told him where he lived and invited him to drop by if he was ever in the neighborhood. Lucas appeared at his doorstep that evening, bearing coffee.

In describing his reaction to Lucas when he first saw him, Zack reached back to his vision of the god of love, significantly transposing it to the image of an angel. "Like when you said to me—what does an angel look like to you? He looks like that angel, sitting in that field, with that smile and that look. He is that person I described, the angel sitting in that field. He's that image to a T—so innocent and beautiful." Soon after Zack met Lucas, Zack reported this dream:

> I was in the shower—it started off like the shower at the gym, one of those big showers where several people can come in or go out. I was taking a shower and the water was really hot, powerful jets. I love that. I was with Kevin [a young bisexual man] and another guy who, in the dream, was supposed to be straight. Kevin gets out of the shower, and the bathroom at this point becomes the bathroom at my parents' house. It was just a very male bonding kind of shower scene, not sexual at all. Kevin starts blow-drying his hair and says, "Are you going to get out of that damn shower, the two of you?" I say, "I'll be out of here pretty soon, I just have to wash the shampoo out of my hair." I thought to myself that this third person was very, very

attractive. I thought that he was comfortable and secure about himself, so he could take a shower with me and Kevin and that's all that it meant, and not have it be a problem. But this guy was so beautiful. I told Kevin that I just had to rinse the suds out of my hair and I would be out. I got this overwhelming feeling that this other person didn't want me out of the shower. But suds were coming across my face, flowing across it. The next thing I know this person's hands came up through the suds and started rinsing the suds out of my hair. I stood there, frozen in every aspect—I didn't know what to do. Still, it was very warming. Now this person is rinsing the suds out of my hair and is just going on and on and on. I could remember this person looking at me. Suds were coming across my face, but I could see right into this person's eyes. I just cracked the biggest smile and said something like, "Now I thought you were supposed to be straight." And this person's eyes looked even deeper into mine when I said that. He didn't say anything. I remember just staring at his eyes and then got woken up by the telephone.

As Zack told the dream, the image of the person in the shower brought Lucas to mind. Over the many months we had been working together, I shared with Zack some of the material I was collecting from my students that indicated that the boundaries of heterosexual identity were, for many people, more porous than he—or I—had been accustomed to think. Was the dream questioning the rigidity of those boundaries for Lucas? Or was the dream expressing, in the language of the body, a deeper connection that Zack felt existed—or could exist—between them, one that transcended identity? If so, what kind of connection could that be? I think that the answer was in his explanation of what had initially drawn him to Martin, another young man who was the same age as Lucas, but gay. He had said about their meeting, "It was the way he looked at me—we had a real connection through the eyes. I could see his soul through his eyes and I wanted to be a part of that." Lucas, though not gay, looked at him in a way that had a similar effect. I asked Zack what he meant by soul. He thought about it and wrote out this reply:

The soul is the inextricable make-up of one's self—the "self" being emotional, physical, biological, psychological, and environmental. If two people have an attraction toward each other, whether a casual glance or kiss occurs will depend on the make up of the self. If this level is expressed under the right circumstances—whether there's a way for two souls to reach out to each other by eyesight such as the first time Lucas and I met—the door is opened to our souls—a bond is created, the inextricable link to each other.

Culturally, we tend to see sexual attraction as stopping with the body. But Zack, who was intuitively attuned to the relation between inner and outer, put it in his own words—sexual attraction was not just a matter of body, but also of soul. His idea tied in with what some of the heterosexually identified men in earlier chapters said about the deeper meanings of their same-sex feelings.[11]

Obviously, friendship is a very powerful dimension of the male-to-male bond. In one of our early sessions, Zack mentioned that he had slept with most of his good gay friends at least once. Ron, the gay writer about whom I spoke in Chapter 6, said the same thing. When the barriers to sex with another man are lowered, sex becomes another of the ways through which the bond of friendship with him moves toward fulfillment. In fact, that was the primary way in which the heterosexually identified men who revealed their feelings to me first experienced their same-sex feelings. With them, however, concern over identity often impeded the progress of that movement. More than a year after their first meeting, Zack confessed to Lucas—with a wry smile—that when he first saw him, he had "fallen in love" with him. That confession, made without any sense of a demand, seemed to elicit from Lucas an answering reaching out. The resulting bond between them expressed itself, not in a sexual relationship, but in a deepening friendship in which the acknowledged erotic feeling of one appeared—for both—to strengthen the bond between them. Lucas, though handsome and intelligent, was a shy, almost reclusive young man. He, in turn, confessed that Zack was his only true—and best—friend.

THE THIRD MEANING OF THE DREAM
OF THE YOUNG MAN IN THE CELLAR
AND THE DREAM OF THE CAVE

Their friendship across the boundaries of identity reflected yet a third meaning of the dream of the young man in the cellar, which had to do with Zack's relation, as a gay man, to the world around him. The cellar was part of the underground railway. The scene of people being helped to escape two at a time—as couples—expressed Zack's fight to liberate his own need to love from the dungeon in which the institutional culture would have it languish. A year and a half later, in fact, the same evening that Zack described his vision of the god of love, Zack described this dream, which proved to have the same theme:

> I'm in a cave. At first, it's rounded, and then it becomes a square-shaped space. Water is coming in, rippling under the door. It rises to about two feet below the ceiling. Some other guys—they seem to be from work—and I are treading water. None of them have shirts on. They've got well-defined chests and physiques.

In the dream, in spite of the rising water, Zack had no sense of panic. He told me the dream soon after returning home from a long, romantic weekend spent with a man he had just recently met. The dream did not seem to have any relation to that weekend. But Zack said something else in this session that, I think, it did relate to. He said that sometimes he thought it would be easier to describe himself simply as "sleeping with men" instead of as gay. We did not pursue this at the time, but the theme continued to come up. Some time later he put it this way:

> It's frustrating for me. I feel isolated from both things. My appearance is that I'm straight, but when they find out I'm gay, they react to it. There's a lot of positive things attached to that [being gay] but still, I'm no longer "straight," so I'm put into a different category all of a sudden. It's the same thing in the gay world. A lot of people think I'm too "straight-acting," so to speak. I hate to say that, but it's just the way it is.

At this point in his life, Zack saw being gay—loving men—as something affirmative about himself. But having come out of the closet, he did nt want to have to retreat to a ghetto.

Again, I think that the motif of the circle—seen in the round shape of the cave—referred to Zack's self, of which his feelings for men were an essential part. The cave in the dream was a "cave of the heart."[12] It was also an underground, or interior place—with a meaning similar to the cellar in the earlier dream. The theme of swimming harked back to the place where he first began to have an emotional awareness of the male body and its meaning for him— the pool where he learned to swim and later competed. The other men in the pool were, I think, composites. Some reminded him of the men from work. But their bare, defined chests had some associations with gay men as well. In a sense, they combined aspects associated with both the straight and gay worlds. As in the dream of the color green, I think that the square was symbolic of the world outside himself. Trying to lead the men out of the cave where the water is rising reflected Zack's need not to be confined, as a man, to the boundaries of a ghetto and to try to help others—regardless of their identities—to free themselves from its confines as well. This dream and its meaning, then, is the bridge to the next chapter.

Chapter 12

Boundary Crossings

The material in the early chapters of this book makes it clear that it is not only gay men who feel the pressure to hide their feelings from the light of day. Men whose identities are not gay feel it just as much, if not more. Some, of course, go further and succumb to the pressure by locking these feelings away in a secret place to which even they do not have the key. Nevertheless, the emotional need for the double sometimes forces the door ajar.

ZACK AS THE DOUBLE

In fact, as an adult, Zack sometimes found himself the object of the search for the double by men whose identities were not gay. Zack recalled one such instance that occurred several years before we met, and before the experience of the Forum. He was in Florida, visiting Maria, the woman he had once dated steadily but who now knew that he was gay. They were at a club, and Zack spotted a man who matched his own image—"He had buzzed hair, blond, blue eyes, I think, to this day one of the most attractive men." Zack and Maria were sitting at a table behind a railing on a platform raised slightly above the level of the dance floor while the other man was on the dance floor with a woman. Zack recalled,

> He worked his way over and handed the girl over the railing to me! She was pissed off, and I grabbed her because she had no choice at this point. She said, "That guy is a fucking nut." In the meantime, he climbed up over the railing and introduced himself. We started talking—the chemistry between us was so

strong. We ended up partying together and driving around a lot. I was pretty drunk. He said to me, "Zack, you're a real attractive guy and the women were going fucking crazy over you. How come you aren't doing anything about it? Are you a fag?" I remember just wanting to scream, "Yes!" and jump on him, but I sat there frozen and said, "no." My heart went to my stomach and I said to myself, "You idiot, why did you say that?" I still kick myself to this day.

For the next year Zack regretted not having been forthcoming with Don and, when he returned to Florida the next year, he went back to the same club hoping to run into him. Astonishingly, Don was there, but in spite of his eagerness, Zack waited for him to make the first move.

> After an hour, he walked up to me and said, "Zack?" His friend said to me, "Zack, I don't know who you are, but all Don talked about for an entire year was this cop he met in Daytona Beach, and how cool he was, and what a good time he had and how he hoped to run into you. *He planned this trip to be the same night, hoping to run into you,* and you're here, which is unreal."
>
> But the same thing happened. We hung out all night and had a great time. It got to that point where we ended up by ourselves and we both chickened out again. For several years after that, we got in touch and talked on the phone. In 1989, I went to Chicago where he lived, but he blew me off. He knew I was there, he was off that Saturday night, but never showed up. I sent him Christmas cards after that and left one phone message, but I never heard from him.

It is hard to imagine what kind of answer Zack, no matter how conscious he was of his attraction to Don, could have given to the question, "Are you a fag?" Put in such pejorative terms, it would appear to have invited denial rather than disclosure. As such, it probably mirrored the denial of his own powerful feelings of attraction that seeing his double—literally "across a crowded room"—had evoked in Don. Handing off the woman to Zack was a telling gesture—she had become redundant. Yet, his apparently heterosexual identity must have made him back off from the intimate sharing he was secretly hoping for just as he sensed it might be within his grasp.

In the second year of our work together, another incident occurred that threw into even sharper relief the contradictions and paradoxes that can confront men as the emotional sharing they seek runs up against the boundaries of identity. The background for this incident was a landmark experience for Zack. The professor who taught the criminal justice class he was taking as part of the work for his associate's degree asked him if he would talk to the class about his work in the police department as a gay police officer. Zack pondered what it would mean to, in essence, come out to the entire campus but in the end agreed to do it. He started by frankly telling about failing out of college right after high school—though he did not say anything about the severe inner conflict that contributed to it. He then described joining the police department and went on to give a breakdown of the department's composition in terms of sex and race. He added that there was one gay officer in the department. Pausing to catch his breath, he said that he was that officer, adding, "Now you know why I'm so fucking nervous." The explosion of laughter that followed was, however, friendly and reassuring. He said he was not there to promote his culture. It was about combating prejudice, being yourself, and loving yourself—"We're all human but we're all different." For Zack it was a rewarding but also very emotional experience. "It was very, very powerful. The teacher said that for the last twenty minutes of the class, she wanted to cry." The reaction of the class, which was 60 percent male, was almost uniformly positive, with a good deal of admiration for Zack's courage in coming out to them. As he read over their responses later, he found himself moved to the point of tears.

A week or so later, some faculty organized a trip to Washington, DC, for the students in Zack's class, as well as some others. Most of the people on the trip had now heard that Zack was gay. Ironically, the man who wound up being his roommate on this trip had not. Zack's friends felt that if anyone were to tell Dirk that Zack was gay, it should be Zack. At twenty-two, Dirk was younger than Zack by about eight years, and he knew that Zack was a police officer, which Dirk himself was considering trying for. His liking for Zack was immediate and flattering. It was couched in terms that had all the earmarks of someone who had found in Zack, not only the image of the double, but also an ideal that he aspired to emulate. Zack recalled,

> He said, "I'm so glad I have you as a roommate. You're a real man. You drink Jack Daniels, I drink Jack Daniels; I like that shirt you've got; I like those pants you've got. We have a lot in common, we think alike."—all that bonding kind of stuff. He used "faggot" and "queer" and a couple of other names about the other guys in the group. It bothered me, but I let it slide. He said that this was their first time out without Mommy and Daddy around, that they were like bunch of fifth graders on a school trip. One of the guys wanted to come in early one morning and take a picture of me while I was sleeping. Dirk refused to let him come in, and said to me, "Remember, I was looking out for you." All this bonding kind of shit, and I wasn't responding. Throughout the weekend, I'd give him very odd looks. Finally, he said, "Why do you give me this very strange look once in a while?" To respond would be admitting I was gay. I was bothered that he didn't know, and that I didn't tell him. I didn't want to make him feel uncomfortable, but it really, really bothered me that I could come out to the whole class, but I couldn't to this guy who was in the room with me.

On the other hand, although Zack didn't tell him outright, the question came up in Dirk's mind under circumstances that Zack found uncomfortable at the time but amusing in retrospect. A lesbian friend suggested that they—together with two male friends who were not gay but knew Zack was, along with Dirk—go to a gay bar. To Zack's surprise, Dirk readily accepted the invitation.

> I was waiting for him to ask, "Aren't you going to have a problem with this?" or "Why do you want to go to a gay bar with Jeanne?" He said he was tired of getting hit on by guys—it even happened at straight bars—and said, "If I go there with you, *people will think we're together, so they'll leave us alone.*" We were in the back and I was pretty drunk and don't

remember what the conversation was—I was stuck in tunnel vision. All I remember was Dirk looking at me and saying, "Unless you're. . . . " I just looked at him, like "What?" He looked at me and was like, "Nahh, never mind." As if it was "no—no way"—like he didn't want to know the answer.

While Zack recognized the sexual potential in his feelings, he said,

Maybe that's what draws me to him more. I know I can't sleep with him, so I'm going to try to get as intimate with him as I can. He's a very attractive guy and he's my type. *But my attraction to him is that I want him to like me as a person, not to sleep with me.* Why did he make this tremendous push to have this bond with me? When he finds out I'm gay, what will it be for him? For me, I have this tremendous drive to have people *know* I'm gay and to accept that and if they don't, to drive to get them to accept it, *to let them see that I'm no different.* How am I going to feel after I find out how he feels? If he has no problem and wants to be friends, it would be fine. If he doesn't want to be friends there would be some hurt there, even though there shouldn't be. It would be an attack on who I am, rather than just rejecting me because he is not interested in sleeping with a man. It would also be saying that all that bonding stuff he was talking about over the weekend was just bullshit.

At around this same time, Zack had reconnected with Kevin (who appeared in the dream of the shower recounted in the previous chapter), a young and attractive bisexual man he had met two or three years before. They had slept together, which had been very nice. As with his good gay friends, their physical sharing was the affirmation of their friendship, the cementing of a bond—not as lovers, but as friends. With Kevin the sexual experience was "A sense of completion. It didn't go very deep, but it was a completion of something that I'd wanted to have happen." But Dirk had reached Zack a deeper level. As in Conrad's story, each seemed to recognize his double in the other. For Zack, meeting Dirk at that level seemed to be enough—he did not have to have sex with Dirk.

In fact, Zack had not "come on" sexually to him in any way. Dirk, on the other hand, had "come on" to Zack *emotionally*. His saying to Zack, "You're a good-looking guy," was, I think, also a tacit acknowledgment of the movement toward Zack's physical being that was taking place within himself.

I think Zack did not tell Dirk that he was gay for the same reason that he did tell the class. In both instances, it was important that he be recognized for his worth—as a man, a police officer, a friend— whether gay or not. He had said, "I have this tremendous drive to have people *know* I'm gay and to accept that and . . . *to let them see that I'm no different.*" It was important, it seems to me, that the class first be able to react to him as a man and a police officer and then to accept that he was gay. I think the same thing was true with Dirk. With him, the first part had been accomplished. He was waiting, with some urgency now, to see if the second part would be. Zack and he had made a date for Dirk to come over to Zack's house the following week. In the meantime Dirk had learned via the grape- vine that Zack was gay. He appeared very awkward. Although he said it did not matter, it obviously did because, when they subse- quently met on campus, he no longer seemed able to talk to Zack in the free and easy way he had before. I think that Dirk became fearful when he realized that a physical component to their relation- ship could be a possibility even though Zack was in no way imply- ing that he was looking for it. When Will became aware of thinking about his best friend sexually, he had said to himself, "That's crazy. What are you thinking?" I doubt that Dirk's feelings toward Zack had reached that level of awareness. But by cutting off the relation- ship, he was ensuring that they would not.

The incident with Dirk highlighted the importance of the emo- tions of the male-to-male bond for Zack. This was brought home to him forcefully a few months later when he read Andrew Sullivan's *Virtually Normal* after I had mentioned it in one of our sessions.

> One passage really froze me. He was talking about the bond that men have with each other and the tragedy of what being a male homosexual is—because you look to have that bond with men and when they find out that you're gay, it's stripped away from you. And that's so true—and a perfect example of that

was Dirk. It hit me so hard. It really bothered me, and it's been on my mind since. I can't help but say—not that I'm like everybody else, I like being different, being the individual that I am—but I find myself asking, why can't people understand that I can still have that bond with a man and not let it become sexual? That's what bothers me. Straight men just don't understand that. They find out you're gay and all of a sudden, that's why you like them. "Of course I like you—because you're you." They don't understand that. They think you automatically want to sleep with them. They don't understand that it's the same bond they're dealing with, with their friends. It's the exact same thing.

"I FELT I WAS JEWISH"

For a number of years, a group of men in the department had gotten together and organized a wilderness trip to the West. After the last one, Bill, an older man in the department and a very good friend to Zack, asked him if that was the kind of thing he might like to do. When Zack, who had already gone skydiving, assured him that it was right up his alley, Bill said that he would see about getting him invited for the next trip. But when the time came, the invitation was, conspicuously, not forthcoming. Zack was very upset by the fact that neither Bill nor some of the younger men that he had counted among his friends protested the veto by one of the organizers and senior members of the department. It was particularly painful because there could be no question in anyone's mind about the reason for the veto. The pain was slightly mitigated by the fact that most of the group had not been aware of it until the trip began. A couple of men spoke to him later. The man he would have shared a tent with said to him, "I don't understand it, Zack. You're one of the guys." Another friend, Hal, said that it had been talked about on the trip. He said to Zack, "Let's put it this way, it was a very bad decision on whose ever part." Zack said,

I told him I was very hurt and he said, "I don't blame you." But it also was upsetting that he asked me, "What would you do hanging out with a bunch of guys anyway? Would you

really have a good time? You know how they're always talking about tits and ass and all this shit" I looked at him and said,
"I'm a guy. I'm thirty-one years old. I do 'guy' things. What
do you think I've been doing for thirty-one years, sitting in a
closet? I've been partying, hanging out with guys all my life.
What did I do at the PBA convention? I went to a go-go joint
with all those guys. I like guys, you know—that's what I'm
emotionally attached to. But I do all the things a guy does. I'm
not a fucking girl, Hal, I'm a guy." He said, "I feel stupid." I
said, "Good, you should."

This forthrightness on Zack's part was typical of how he dealt with
his colleagues in the department. But inwardly, a storm of feeling
was churning, as the dream he told me graphically expressed:

We were driving on a highway. Craig [a nongay friend who
had gone with Zack and Dirk to the gay club] was with me. We
were trying to get away from a bad storm—roads were flood-
ing out. There was a major highway, eight lanes wide. People
were taking their time, in spite of the wicked storm that was
going to wipe everyone out. I could see a police car coming up
way behind us. I thought, "Those assholes, they never move out
of the way for you. . . . " Me and another car moved over and it
went flying past and instantly disappeared. It was raining so
hard that the road was eroding and collapsing as we were
going across the roadway. If we went any slower we'd get
caught in this decay. There was an accident in front of us. A
whole car of really elderly people ran into the back of another
car. The old people were looking back as if it were our fault,
but we went right around and kept going. There were bicycles
in the back of my truck. We were heading to Provincetown. It
got so bad that we couldn't use the truck anymore and we were
on bicycles now. People ended up joining us, looking to me to
get away from all this. We ended up in a house. Nobody was in
it but it was still standing. We were out of the storm, trying to
get our thoughts together. People were handing a package over
their heads to me. It was a bicycle. They said someone was
going to throw this bicycle out. "We could use this," I said.
"Put it together." They were going to throw the bike out. It

made no sense. Why throw it out when it was something that we needed to get away? They asked me what to do with it. I felt it was so stupid—why do you need me to lead you and tell you why we need this bike?

Then the whole dream changed dramatically. It was just me now. The focus was like tunnel vision. Whatever was occurring just didn't matter anymore. I was standing in my grandmother's house. One of my favorite places to go was the garage. It had old push-button electric switches. I was looking into the garage seeing my grandmother's memorabilia—a sewing kit in an old wooden cabinet with lots of drawers, baskets of peaches. . . . I was looking at them, feeling so relaxed. It was the strangest thing. That was when my grandfather showed up. We were in a hallway kind of room. It was very emotional.

"Actually," he interjected, "I could cry right now, it was that upsetting." Then he continued the narration:

It was about getting old. It was so weird. That day I remember looking in the mirror and saying that I look like my grandfather, with my hair buzzed and everything. I remember [in the dream] saying to him, not that it was time to grow up. . . . I can't quite remember the feeling, but something about I'm growing up and there is nothing I can do about it. I remember thinking in the dream, "Is that what all this is about?" My grandfather was just sitting there, not looking at me. I had to walk up to him to make him realize I was there. I was standing right in front of him and I was crying, hysterical—it was so emotional. I turned to my grandfather and I said to him, "It's all a part of life. It will be my turn soon." And he answered, "Yes I know." I hugged him and I cried so hard. . . .

The raging storm in the first part of the dream and the ground giving way beneath him symbolized the severity of the blow to his equilibrium in his relation to the world. At the same time, there were some positive signs. Craig, the man in the car with him, though not gay, appeared to be sticking by him. Provincetown—their destination—is not exclusively gay, but it is a place where one can be gay and accepted. The bicycle, which he always took with him, also had some reference to Provincetown, and to the gay part of himself that he was not prepared to discard. Once again, as in the dream of the cave, Zack is in a leadership role. I think this indicated an inner conviction that he had to stand up for himself—but not only for himself, because in doing so, he spoke for others as well.

The second part of the dream, however, came from a deeper level. He said,

> I can't help but think that the stress of life was the underlying theme of the dream. Almost like, is there more to life? Is this what it's all about, trying to get by and dealing with all the bullshit that comes at you? Is that it? It must be. I've just got to keep going, I guess. When my grandfather died, I was still kind of young—about twenty-one. It was a very emotional time for me too. I don't remember releasing all that pain about my grandfather dying. I remember saying to myself that I should have felt more upset. He was a wonderful man, a strong man. What life threw at him was unbelievable. He was a very wealthy man before the Depression. It wiped him out, and he struggled to hold onto what he managed to keep thereafter.

Once again, the imagery of Zack's inner life seemed to tap into another aspect of male experience—youth looking to age for comfort, understanding, wisdom, guidance.[1] In the dream, the sorrow that Zack—as the younger of the two—feels for himself converges with the sorrow that he feels for his grandfather, with whom he shares his grief and toward whom he looks for answers in his own life. By the time we met, Zack was over the worst of it. However, he recalled, "A week ago I wouldn't even be able to sit here and talk. I've had about five anxiety attacks. I had two more since I talked to you [about a week before.] I felt so overwhelmed, like I just collapsed or gave up. Other times I just started feeling freezing cold, with shortness of breath. Once, if I had to get out of my police car, I wouldn't have been able to."

This incident caused a radical reassessment of the trust he had placed in some of the people he had believed were his friends.

It's easy enough to say after the fact, "We made a bad decision." Hal was sincere and obviously not telling all that transpired. A week ago, I was pretty scared I didn't have control. It was like a nuclear explosion, and now I'm just trying to pick up the pieces. One thing—where do I hold the people I work with now? A week ago I felt I was Jewish, and they were German and when the Nazis came to the door—as much as they had let me eat in their house, and so forth—they still turned me in. That's how I still feel. People I've been associating with, including Bill, turned me in. That in itself makes you want to cry. I'm not going to say I'm not going to be his friend, because I still have to work with him. You can say, "Look at the position he was put in." I don't know. I came to the conclusion that I have no choice except to let everyone off the hook. The only thing I can hope for is that they all learned from it. I let them know how I felt—"I was Jewish and you turned me over to the Nazis."

The reverberations of this incident extended over the next year in a continuing restatement of the question he had asked himself in his dream—as well as in subsequent dreams where some kind of catastrophe was occurring. He asked himself, what was the meaning of this life? How did his being gay fit into it? On one hand, since his breakup with Vic, two relationships with gay men that seemed promising had not worked out. On the other hand, where nongay men were concerned, he said, "I can't even make a straight friend at this point." In addition, he had been sleeping badly.

I woke up recently and realized that one thing I was doing was trying to make sense of a chaotic world that you just can't make sense out of. I try to rationalize why things are as they are, and I can't. It makes me teeter on the edge of not wanting to deal with it. Like, would I be better off dead?—not that I want to commit suicide, don't get me wrong—but I question, what difference is my life making for anybody? The answer might be in helping others, but how is that helping me? By taking the stand I take—my life in general is taking a stand—is it worth it or not?

At one level, Zack had no question that taking a stand was worth it. Doing it had saved his own life. But it had also challenged the cultural boundaries that circumscribe and limit other men's lives. When he first came out to the department, the reception was largely positive. Interestingly, this was especially true of the older members of the department, a fair number of whom had since retired or left. Bill was one who had stayed on. He seemed very fond of Zack and was among the few who had invited him to his home. Nevertheless, even he sometimes cautioned Zack to keep their off-duty socializing between themselves. Another man had been the boy who, when Zack was in high school, would shout "faggot" at him as he rode his bike down their street. Together with his wife he met Zack for dinner in Provincetown and reminded Zack in the presence of others that he was looking forward to doing it again.

Until the incident of the trip and for a short while thereafter, he and Hal were developing something of a friendship. Like some other men, he seemed interested in talking about gay issues. Zack would give him his copies of *The Advocate*. Hal confided to him that aside from the sexual part, he found little about the women he was dating of interest to him and that he just wished he could find one with a personality like that of his best—male—friend. Around this time, Zack had a dream in which he and Hal were having sex. This dream was revealing in a number of ways. I don't think it was expressing Zack's feelings only. Rather, it was putting into the language of the body the current of feeling that existed between them. My guess is that Hal, like some of the men discussed earlier in this book, had some awareness of his own same-sex feelings and—perhaps consciously, perhaps not—sensed an inner movement toward Zack. In Zack's dream they cut their intimacy short because people could see it. This proved to be an insight into the problematical context in which their friendship was developing. A few months after the dream, he noticed that Hal seemed to be increasingly distant. When he asked Hal about it, he said, "These guys got on me so much about your checking me out, I just felt the pressure," adding, "You hate me, don't you?" Zack's comment was, "It made me sick that they did that to him."

It was ironic that Hal was on the defensive because of something that Zack was supposed to be doing. The assumption was, of course, that Hal was responding to it—that there was a reciprocating current of feeling on Hal's part. In apparent confirmation, another man had remarked to him, "We all wonder about Hal." The group dynamics in the department seemed to reflect, in a microcosm, the dynamics of the larger culture. Most people were cordial to Zack in face-to-face situations, but he could not be sure whom he could count on to stand up for him in a group setting, or in defiance of the contingent who spoke for the values and attitudes of the institutional culture. At least one of this contingent appeared able to control the group dynamic when Zack was frozen out of the trip. Some others seemed to police the boundaries of identity when individuals—like Hal, who felt vulnerable—seemed in danger of straying over those boundaries.

I suspect that, for Hal as for Dirk, the relationship with Zack represented a movement toward the double. But as, under pressure, Hal retreated from the relationship, he had to deny it. Thus, he said to Zack, "You've got to stop getting a haircut like mine." Zack, who for as long as I had known him had worn his hair in more or less the same way, retorted, "As far as I'm concerned, you get a haircut like mine." The man who had said, "We all wonder about Hal," was the same man who had earlier engaged Zack in an earnest and explicit conversation about what men did together sexually. He also came under fire and pulled back. Another friend who had danced with Zack and a woman friend at a departmental event was made to feel the heat. But he eventually rebounded and, at a recent departmental event where people could bring spouses or dates, he suggested he and Zack go together. When someone observed that he had not brought a date, he said emphatically, "Zack's my date."

FIGHTING WITH DESTINY

The incident of the wilderness trip had taken place in the spring of our third year of work together. Afterward, Zack had been assured that he would not be left out the following year. The following year, however, as the time for the trip approached, nothing was mentioned. A friend asked Zack if he wanted him to say something. Zack replied simply, "Please don't. I don't care that I'm not going. I care that I was not even asked after they lied to me last year and said, 'You can go next year'—it's disgusting."

It was around this time that Zack said, "I had the worst anxiety attack—at about three in the morning. I'd just gotten back from work. I was so upset, crying hysterically for ten or fifteen minutes." He had no clear idea of what triggered the attack. But when he had come home that night, he had automatically switched on the television set. Although he did not make the connection, the scene he saw on the screen was reminiscent of the dream that he had after the trip incident the year before. They both had to do with life-threatening catastrophes. He recalled, "The movie *Alive* was on, where a plane carrying a soccer team crashes. They're up there for twenty-eight days and wind up resorting to cannibalism. The plane had just crashed. I didn't really watch more than five minutes of it, and then completely freaked out." He said he had been having trouble sleeping. "Sometimes," he said, "I feel like I'm fighting with destiny."

A little later that year, during the summer, Zack again went to Provincetown for a vacation. It had always been one of his favorite places—but not this year.

> I didn't want to be there. It was beautiful, and I was trying to play the part, but I hated every bit of it. Four days on the beach by myself. All the Boston boys had attitudes beyond belief. On the fourth day, a group of them came up and said, "We've been watching you for the past four days. You're beautiful—what's your problem?" I felt lonely. I just couldn't relax. I felt I didn't have that shallowness to enjoy myself on vacation. Sunday night—the same day the boys came to me on the beach—I had a dinner engagement with friends but I never made it because I had too much to drink. I had a couple of shots, trying to relax, but I realized I was drunk. I got very emotional and I cried—it was uncontrollable—in broad daylight, trying to get back to my place. I got there, sat on the couch, and cried my eyes out for who knows how long. A guy I knew stopped by and asked, "What are you doing?" I remember saying I hated how shallow everyone was here. "You guys from Boston suck—you look right past everybody." He said, "Everybody was wondering why you were by yourself." I said, "That's a perfect exam-

ple—wondering, but nobody came over. Every time I looked over, you guys looked away. It's hard to walk up to a group of people and have them all turn away."

One person had literally ignored him when he said hello! Two years before, he had begun a poem about his feelings in Provincetown with these lines:

I search desperately for an answer
To my emotions in this place where
Feelings only run as shallow
As the salted pools of water left upon
The shore. . . .

Two years later he concluded that, for him, there could be no answer to his emotions in the shallows that he found there. The flood of tears that overwhelmed him in the sun-filled streets of the vacation town was remarkably similar to the one that had overtaken him at home in the dead of night three months before. These were not signs of some clinical depression coming out of nowhere. The cause was identical and identifiable—a sense of loneliness and disconnection as men who should have welcomed him as a brother turned their backs on him instead. In the first instance, even though he was "one of the guys"—as his friend put it—it was not enough because he was gay. In the second instance, even though he was gay, that was not enough because he was not "one of the boys."

COMPASSIONATE RELATIONSHIPS

When he was still trying to recover from the shock of rejection over the wilderness trip, Zack had questioned what difference his life was making for anybody. Part of the answer, he knew, was in helping others. The night he had had an anxiety attack after the movie about the plane crash, he wrote these lines:

I cry so hard that I no longer feel,
Lost in the endless torment of my existence.
Each year that passes I grow stronger,

But less sensitive to the innocence of love.
Lonely I am, but never alone.
I am blessed by his love
Through my compassion for others.

Zack's family was Catholic. Although he was not particularly religious, he felt angry and hurt by the Church's denial of sanctification to same-sex love. In an aside one day, Zack had said that one of his reservations about being a police officer was that it was not his ideal of how to help people. But since he was, nevertheless, in that role he took advantage of it to help them in whatever way he could. One supervising officer who recognized this trait in him preferred to dispatch Zack to handle domestic calls because, he told him, "You're the most compassionate." This compassion expressed itself in the ways that he dealt with young people. Some of these he met informally, though often in uniform, others in the course of duty. Among these young people were "a whole bunch without father figures." One of them, Rick, had been thrown out of his house at age fourteen, and after scraping out a bare existence on his own for a while, was living with an uncle whom Zack described as "virtually psychotic." Zack found him a boarding situation with a kindly landlady. Referring to Zack, Rick said, "He saved my life." About Rick, who had gained ten much-needed pounds thanks to the ministrations of his landlady, Zack said, "I feel like he's my son." Rick was one of three young people whom, at the last minute, Zack invited to have Easter dinner with him and his own family. Another was a young woman whose boyfriend had just broken up with her. The third was a young man of nineteen whose father refused to include him when the family was invited out for Easter. This young man later said to Zack, "I wish you were my father."

Another boy was Gabe, whose sister was killed in a car accident. His parents blamed the boy who was driving the car, while Gabe felt that was unfair, since the other driver was clearly at fault for the accident. That disagreement and the intensity of his parents' grief had made things so tense at home that Gabe moved out and was living with a relative. Zack said,

I've been talking to him a lot. It's the same thing—no direction in his life. He works at a gas station that faces his parents' house but he doesn't talk to them. I said, "Why not send them a card saying you're thinking of them, love them?" Doesn't he realize what they've been going through? But he's a good kid. These parents don't understand. I'd go across the street, grab him by the hair, and drag him back into the house.

Zack had originally met Gabe a few years before when Gabe was sixteen, drunk, and throwing empty beer bottles at Zack's police car. But instead of arresting him, Zack took him home and suggested to his mother that she keep better track of her son. Now, as a young adult, he and Zack had become friends. Soon afterward, Gabe reconciled with his parents and began college.

Zack understood that, for him, a line existed between compassionate and sexual relationships. When Rick, who was eighteen, told Zack about being upset after a much older man had talked him into posing for pictures in bikini briefs, Zack was concerned. He recognized Rick's emotional and even physical vulnerability and strongly advised him to avoid putting himself in that situation again. He said about Rick and these other young men, "I see them as I saw myself at that age, and what they still have to go through, finding out about life and just themselves too. Maybe somehow I feel compelled to help them get through that easier." He recognized that this could also be a component in a romantic relationship with a younger man. But he had come to understand, after his experience with dating Vic and more recently Martin, a young man about to turn twenty, that he had to resist turning his romantic relationships into caretaking ones as well. He needed someone who had enough maturity—whether chronologically or emotionally—to be able to take care of him as well.

BOUNDARY CROSSINGS

In the fourth year of our work together, Zack found himself being drawn into a loose circle of a half dozen to a dozen young men, all of whom were friends with one another. Their ages ranged from twenty to twenty-two or -three. Gabe was more or less the fulcrum of the group. They all knew that Zack was a police officer and also knew that he was gay. They related to Zack as a friend—sometimes an older, more experienced one that they could turn to for advice, but also as someone to relax and have fun with. In turn, Zack enjoyed having, as he put it, "local friends." Some of Zack's best friends had been older men, but the range in his personality could encompass the developing friendships with these younger men as well. Zack's being gay did not appear to be a problem for them. He said, "If they can they get over the fear that I'm going to 'corner' them someday, it's okay. I'd like to," he laughed, "but it's not me. Once they get past that, they're attracted to me, not because I'm gay but because they sense, 'He knows exactly how we're feeling,' whereas they're scared to express that with other men. With me, they feel they can be intimate. They don't know what it all means. But once they get past that, they get very comfortable."

A number of these friends were interested in going with Zack to a local club that drew a mainly gay and bisexual crowd, and enjoyed it. One of them, Jim, was even a bit disappointed that no one tried to "hit on" him when they were there. One day when Zack, Jim, and another friend were together, Jim kept tweaking Zack's nipple through his shirt, saying, "You know, Zack, I'm a nipple man." It was also Jim who left a message on Zack's answering machine, not identifying himself but pretending to be drunk, saying, "I love you. I want you." When Zack played the message for Gabe, he said, pretending to be shocked, "Zack, what are you doing to all my friends?" The next time Zack saw Jim, he said, to Jim's vast amusement, "I got your message and I just want you to know, Jim, that I still like you even though you're gay—I'll still be your friend!"

Another one of the group was even more playfully forward than Jim. Zack related, "One night, we're all out at this bar and Phil jumps across the table and starts kissing me and biting me on my neck. Gabe was terribly embarrassed. I was like, 'Phil, would you please get off me?' And he's like, 'Oh Zack, you're so hot . . . .'" Another time, after they had both stayed over at Gabe's one night, Phil casually sat on Zack's lap at breakfast. And another evening, when he and Phil and a couple of friends were at a bar—not a gay bar—Phil started to playfully kiss him on the lips right in the middle of the floor. When Zack asked, "What would you do if I kissed you back?" Phil only smiled. Taking his cue, Zack led him into the empty ladies' room, held the door shut, pinned Phil against the wall, and kissed him forcefully. Phil responded with energy and enthusiasm. Zack said, "It was like a wrestling match!" Afterward, they arranged themselves, emerged coolly, and the evening went on as before. Phil, it should be noted, was twenty-five and dated women.

These young men seemed to be playing with the boundaries set up by the culture, not respecting them, but rather toying with them in a lighthearted way. Although the underlying erotic intent still could be denied, as it can when the identity of both parties is heterosexual, the fact that Zack was gay implied a more open acknowledgement of the erotic current that underlies this kind of horseplay. Although Zack had no trouble entering into the spirit of it all, it was also stressful in a way. Gabe's pretense of being shocked echoed in his mind.

> I don't know what it all means. I think it bothered me when Gabe said, "Zack, what are you doing to all my friends?" I couldn't help but think, *am* I doing something to them? Am I the cause for them? I don't think that what's happening to them is different from what happens to whole lot of other people that I come into play with. They can't understand why they find themselves attracted to me other than I tend to make people very comfortable when they talk to me. It's no different from the cops who related a lot of stuff to me, but then turned off. That's what I wonder about these friends—when are they going to turn off? When is that level of intimacy going to make it appear that, "I've let myself go too far?"

He was thinking of the department, where the prevailing dynamic in the group created pressure that caused some men to pull back, both from Zack and their own feelings. But that did not appear to be happening in this group of young men. In fact, another kind of dynamic appeared to be operating—one that made them seem open to exploring these feelings in themselves.

One evening, Zack had been out having some drinks with Xavier and because it had gotten very late, he decided to stay at Xavier's. Tony, his roommate, was out.

> Xavier said that the last time I stayed there he'd wanted to come out and curl up on the couch with me. He said he liked

me, and wanted to sleep with me since the day I was over playing cards. I said, "One-night stands are fun and all, but they're not the biggest thing in my life to do." He said, "Oh, okay" I shook his hand good night and went to bed—Tony had said I could sleep in his room. Ten minutes later, he knocks on the door and is standing there. He said, "I just don't know what to say." I said, "Is it that you want to get into bed with me?" He said, "Yeah." I said, "Then why don't you just do that?" So he did. We had our little thing and that was that. I explained to Xavier—I was probably putting my defenses up, and it seemed vain—"Whatever you do, don't fall in love with me because you slept with me once." It sounded stupid, but I know the position he's in—he coaches high school and college soccer. He's not in a position to be out. But that wasn't the end of the story. He has a conversation with Tony—that he slept with somebody we all know and he'll never guess who! So Tony starts going through all these girls and it's like "no . . . no . . ." He's like, "Wait a second, unless it's a guy!"

At first Tony guessed that Xavier was talking about another friend, Nicky. When Xavier acknowledged that he had slept with Nicky as well, but that was not the man he meant, Tony guessed, "Zack!" Then, in quick succession, he said, "Oh my god, I can't believe it," and then, "I've never dismissed the thought of doing that at least once"—that is, sleeping with a man. This was quite a startling statement coming from Tony, who formerly had the reputation of being very homophobic. However, not long before, he had surprised everybody by positively insisting that Zack go out with him and his friends to celebrate his twenty-first birthday. He also told Zack about a recent eye-opening experience in Washington, where he had been working for several weeks. He said, "It's very gay there. I was involved with all these political groups and I was an outsider, being a heterosexual. I felt so isolated and completely understand how you've felt most of your life, just by that simple experience."

It seemed that, in this group of friends, the code of silence that generally surrounds the same-sex feelings of men whose identities are not gay was dissolving. Not only did Tony not recoil from his roommate when he told him he had slept with two mutual friends—it helped to spur an inner movement in Tony, or to acknowledge that it had already taken place. Gabe, to whom Zack was very close, also knew that he and Xavier had slept together. Some time later, after an evening of drinking to celebrate his birthday, Gabe, who was pretty drunk, said to Xavier that he thought that maybe he would like to try "this bisexual thing" and asked to go home with Xavier and Zack and discuss it. Xavier—who did not know that Gabe knew about himself and Zack—was taken aback and had Gabe's other friends take him to his own house.

One can see, in the microcosm of this group of friends, an emerging cultural ethos, so to speak. It was one in which Zack's presence played an important role. In this emerging ethos it appeared that same-sex feeling did not detract from a man's worth as a friend and as a man. Nor did acknowledging it mean that a man had to change identities. When these relationships were first developing, Zack mused, "I guess they're learning that I'm no different from them." I think that it is equally true to say that they were also learning that they were no different from Zack. I think the range of these feelings and reactions in this group reveal what we would find in our society as a whole if we could somehow do away with the "don't ask, don't tell" code of silence around same-sex feeling. In a radically different context, it was reminiscent of what happened in my classes. As with my students, there seemed to be a spectrum encompassing different degrees of intensity of these feelings and different degrees of comfort with them.

Xavier had a girlfriend and had relationships with women, but at this point was finding that his erotic life was increasingly centering itself on men. Tony, and perhaps Gabe, revealed some awareness of the same-sex potential in themselves. Phil was exploring—at once playfully and seriously—the possibilities of male-to-male sensuality. Nicky, who was twenty years old, had actually gone ahead and explored it more fully when he slept with Xavier. He was very drunk during that experience and said to Zack that he now knew that was not what he wanted. Zack was reassuring. He said to Nicky, "If you did that or even do it in the future, it doesn't make you gay, or even bisexual. It means that you have within you the capacity to express yourself with another man—and there's nothing

wrong with that. It's okay." Nevertheless, at this point it seemed to
be more than only a capacity for Nicky. A few weeks later, over a
bottle of wine shared with Zack and Nicky's boss, who was also
gay, Nicky threw open his arms and exclaimed, "Well, we're all
bisexual, aren't we? That's the bottom line, isn't it?" Sober, however, the question of identity troubled him more. Nicky's parents
divorced when he was young and, as with so many young men in
that situation, his relationship with his father had suffered. He said
he looked upon Zack as the older brother he never had, a role that
Zack obviously knew how to play. However, there was a complica-
tion—Nicky was strongly attracted to Zack as well. One night in a
game of Truth or Dare with Xavier and Zack, after several beers,
Nicky said that Zack was the man he would most like to sleep with.
And when dared by Xavier to kiss Zack, he locked his lips onto
Zack's in a deep, lingering kiss.

All this was a dilemma for Zack. Nicky was a very handsome—
one would have to say beautiful—young man. As with Lucas, his
youth and beauty mobilized in Zack all the feelings evoked by the
images of the young man in the cellar and the vision of the angel in
the field. In addition, he was intelligent, masculine, and artistically
talented. Zack knew that even though Nicky was strongly attracted
to him, he was also very conflicted about acting on that attraction
for two reasons. First, unlike some of the other men in the group,
identity was an issue for him, and he was not ready to be seen as
gay. In fact, in spite of what he said after half a bottle of wine, it was
uncertain that, when cold sober, he was ready to be seen as bisexual
either. And second, he had a girlfriend.

In turn, Zack was wary of giving his feelings free rein. Seriously
compounding the problem was uncertainty about the final direction
of Nicky's sexual feelings. If Nicky were on his way to being
gay—which was by no means certain—Zack did not want to be in
the position of being his first—but undoubtedly not last—boyfriend.

When I first began to talk with Zack, I did not have the data from
my students indicating the breadth and depth of same-sex feeling
across the cultural boundaries of identity. In working with Zack, the
first inkling of these feelings was in the recollections of his boyhood and adolescent experiences. These affirmed the more general-

ly acknowledged fluidity of male sexual expression in those years. But as I said earlier, Zack seemed to have the capacity to draw out the generally unacknowledged feelings that adult men who are not identified as gay have about their bodies and their emotional and sexual relationships to each other. Over the years that we spoke together, this seemed to happen with increasing frequency. One day, Zack and I did an informal tally of the number of men—acquaintances and friends—who, in the past year, one way or another, had expressed some degree of same-sex feeling to him—though not in all cases, *about* him. The total turned out to be eight out of sixteen. Even though this was the loosest and most informal of surveys, I'm struck by the coincidence that the proportion was about half—the same as for the men in my classes. Even more significant, I think, is that this happened in a totally different context from the one in which men confided their same-sex feelings to me. It adds further confirmation, from a very different quarter, that same-sex feelings exist in men across the boundaries and categories of sexual identity. Zack knew about some of the findings from my students. Did this alter his awareness of these feelings or in some way enhance his receptiveness to them? Or is it that, in spite—or because—of the "culture wars," the boundaries of self-awareness are being loosened in a younger generation of men? I really do not know, but the pace of these disclosures seemed to be accelerating over the five years that we talked.[2]

Thus, one evening during the fifth year of our work, Zack was out having a drink at a bar with Dave, a twenty-one-year-old aspiring professional baseball player. Dave said, "Can I ask you something? It must be really frustrating for you to go out in an atmosphere like this, because you can't really hit on anybody." Zack said, "Yeah, it's very frustrating." Dave continued, "I can just see that, feel that." Then he said, "You know, I've had thoughts of what it would be like to be with a man. As a matter of fact, I think all men would have to think about it at some point in life, where they would want to have that experience." Zack said, "I totally agree with you. And why people make such a problem of it, I don't know." Dave replied, "I don't know either." He then started to say that he had a best friend—also a ballplayer—in the Midwest, when their conversation was interrupted. At that time, Dave and his girlfriend were in the throes of trying to decide what to do about an accidental pregnancy.

Again and again, Zack seemed to serve as the image of the double that provoked a "moving toward" in men whose identities were not gay. Some, such as Phil and Dave, were comfortable with the idea, but for others, identity or other mixed emotions became a barrier that they could not get past. Jim, a religious young man who appeared to have more inner conflict than he let on, told Zack two of his dreams. In one, a girl was eating some hamburger in the shape of the Eiffel tower. The implications of this—so obvious to Zack—were lost on Jim, as were those of a second dream, which involved twin brothers. Jim had a very close friendship with Arthur, the more conventional of the twins. The other brother, Jared, was more punkish in style and behavior. He also sported a stud in his pierced tongue and once asked Zack, rather wickedly, if he had ever gotten "a blow job" from someone who had one. In Jim's dream, Jared had turned into the devil and was trying to kill Arthur, using some elongated object. The scene then shifted to school, where a third friend was stretched out in front of a building, sunning himself. He was looking at Jim with an inviting smile. Jim said that he couldn't understand why his friend kept smiling and why Jim felt such a strong urge to go to him.

The symbol of the "evil twin" appears in various guises in our culture.[3] One of its meanings—the most important, I think—is that of the double as the forbidden sexual partner. The elongated object with which Jared tries to kill his brother is symbolic of one side of Jim's conflict. The fear of Jim's erotic inner feelings transforms the image of the double—Arthur—into Jared, his demonic, phallic twin. The friend stretched out in the sun, toward whom Jim felt himself wanting to move, is symbolic of the other side—light versus dark—of this inner conflict. Unfortunately, the dark side surfaced one evening when he was out with Zack and Phil. Zack, who had drunk more than he liked to and did not have a clear recollection, said that Jim had accused Phil and Zack of "grabbing his butt." Jim, who used to teasingly tweak Zack's nipples, said he felt "violated" and ended the friendship.

Jim's reaction demonstrates the way in which the institutional culture splits off the potential for same-sex feeling, which is part of the normal spectrum of male feeling, and projects it onto men on the gay side of the identity boundary. Even in dreams sometimes, it is a gay man who is making advances to the dreamer. Within the dream itself, this is a projection of an inner emotional movement onto the image of the other who carries the burden of the dreamer's same-sex feelings. I think this mechanism also operated in the case of Ian, whom Zack met when he was spending time with Gabe and his circle of early-twenty-something friends. One evening, Zack, Xavier, and a few other friends went to a local pub. There, Ian briefly caught Zack's eye. He then came over and joined the game of darts that Zack and the others were playing. He was very interested in the fact that Zack was a police officer and could not believe that he was over thirty. As the night wore on, Xavier invited the dart players to come to his place. Ian accepted immediately. As they were going up the stairs, Martin said to Ian, "You know, we're all homosexuals and we're going to tie you up and rape you when we get you upstairs." Ian continued up the stairs, laughing. After a few beers Zack announced he was leaving and when Ian immediately said the same, Zack offered to drive him home.

What happened next is best described in Zack's own words.

First thing he said to me was, "Are you married?" I said, no, I hadn't found the right person. He goes, "The right *person*," with this cheesy smile on his face. "Who or what is the right person for you?" I thought, "This boy is going somewhere" I told him someone who was as strong as me, who could fit into my life based on my occupation, blah, blah. He goes, "I'm sort of in the same boat. A few of my friends are bisexual." I'm like, "Oh my god, now I definitely know where he's going!" He says, "I've kissed some guys and that's all I've done. It's just something I'm curious about—I don't consider myself bisexual or anything." I said, "I'm gay," and he said, "I know, I figured that out a long time ago. I saw you looking at me in the bar." I said I might have glanced over but not enough to have someone suppose I was interested in them. He said, "Oh no, I could see it in your eyes. I was determined to find out if you were interested, and I wasn't going to give up until I found out."

After Zack drove Ian back to his place, they sat outside and talked in Zack's truck for a long time. Finally, at five in the morning, Zack related, "I said to him, 'How about we do this. I'll give you a kiss goodnight, we'll exchange phone numbers, and call it a night.' He said, 'That sounds fucking great.' He gave me a kiss that fucking whomped me like you wouldn't believe." Zack called Ian the next day and left a message but did not hear from him. When he reached him a couple of days later, Zack invited him to join the darts game at the pub later in the week. Zack said,

> He was hesitating. He said, "I just want to make it very clear— I hope I didn't mislead you the other night." I said, "What do you mean?" He said, "I hope that some of the things I said didn't mislead you into thinking that I had an interest in you. My direction is totally toward women. I just have a curiosity right now, and it's probably going to stay at that level. I hope I didn't mislead you."

Of course, Ian did mislead him, but just as important, he misled himself. Ian had made love to Zack that night—mentally, emotionally, and finally physically. Again, as with Nicky, Zack tried to defuse the identity issue for the other man. "Remember," he said, "just be yourself, because no one can take that away from you." This was good advice, but advice that Ian—still only twenty-two— could not take. Zack told me, I think correctly, "He was using me as a tool to try to understand himself that night—to try to make sense of what he was feeling." Among the things Ian told Zack that night was that he wrote poetry which he rarely showed to anyone. Zack wrote poetry too. Without the benefit of formal literary training, one of his first efforts was nevertheless accepted by his college literary magazine. The brief encounter with Ian and the sense of sudden loss that followed it evoked some wrenching emotions. He wrote the following poem, and sent it to Ian:

> My existence was silent,
> Hidden amongst the masculinity of the room.
> Without warning, I was discovered,
> Unsilenced by a simple stare.
> The room shuddered as I attempted

To restore my presence.
But in my own ignorance lost my way.
He returned my query without hesitation
And a curiosity beyond his own understanding.
It was in that moment that a common stare
Bonded our souls in the darkness around us.
I followed in his discovery
With honesty and utter intrigue.
What seemed like a lifetime
Was only a few hours. And yet
He burned an impression in me
I should never forget.
It came time for us to part
And with a devouring kiss
Sealed his query.
I cried
Silent again.

"My existence was silent"—"Unsilenced by a simple stare"—"Silent again." The sequence is significant. More than a hundred years ago, Oscar Wilde's lover inscribed the words, "The love that dare not speak its name . . ." into the collective consciousness of his time—and ours. As he demanded that Zack speak that name, Ian reached in and opened the door to Zack's soul. When Ian refused to honestly name his own feelings, he closed the door to his own. In his poem, Zack had said, "I cried." Did he, I asked? "Yes," he said, "I cried for myself, but for him too because I know where he's at. And I wish I could take that away from him and help him get through that, without having to deal with the struggle. I didn't cry because I couldn't have him, but just for him."

Even before he met Ian, Zack was wondering why he let himself become emotionally involved with heterosexually identified men. A few months before, Zack took a literature course at college. One of the essays he read dealt with Himmler's persecution of homosexual men during the Nazi era, as well as Himmler's relationship with his own rigid, authoritarian father. It provoked a disturbing dream:

There is a cliff alongside a beach. There are apartments built into the cliff—all abandoned. We were exploring them, weaving through different corridors. Then, there were Nazis on the beach—I was one of them—looking to take people away. They put me in a huge body bag with the other bodies. They threw the bag into the water and it began sinking. It was at the water level and I remember trying to understand why I was part of that. I realized that I could rip the plastic and swim out. I did that and swam to the beach. There was no one around—it was peaceful.

Zack associated this dream with the memory of being excluded from the wilderness trip and with all the feelings it had triggered. Speaking in the metaphorical language of the dream, he said, "Even though I was one of them, they still threw me to the sharks." This was one of the last of a long series of dreams in which Zack was under some kind of threat from human or natural forces. Significantly, however—as in this dream—no matter how dreadful the circumstances, he always lived. But the essay also brought up a complex of feelings about the first important male-to-male bond in Zack's life—that with his father. He said, "My father has never been a part of my life. He's there, but not there. I always looked for affection but never got what I was looking for as a child. These guys can only give so much. The attraction becomes strong, then it's almost like I'm looking for the same sort of rejection from them that I'd gotten from my father."

I avoided starting with Zack's relationship to his father because it would imply yet another attempt to explain a gay man's same-sex feelings as originating with a father-son relationship that he was lacking. But if that were the cause of homosexuality, half the male population of the country would be gay. Over the many years when I had students do case studies on actual people, I usually polled the class by asking how many of the people who were the subjects of their studies had "good enough" mothers or "good enough" fathers. Repeatedly, "good enough" mothers were in the majority—commonly about two-thirds. Repeatedly, "good enough" fathers were in the minority—typically about one-third. These proportions held for both men and women.

Zack had childhood memories of a father who—like so many men—was away much of the time earning a living for his family.

But Zack's memories of him, when he was around, were largely positive. However, one early memory was painful—one of the few times his father hurt him. "One thing that really stands out was when I was involved in a fight in the first or second grade, and the other kid was chasing me around a car. I went back and told my dad and he said, 'Why didn't you stand up for yourself? What do you want me to do, put a dress on you and be a little girl?'" Zack related this in our third session. Much later he said that he dated his feeling of difference from that incident. It is clear from his shocked reaction at the time that his sense of himself was already that of a boy. Nor did his father ever impugn his sense of himself as a male again. I suspect that attributing the sense of difference to this incident is a retrospective projection. One of my students— who was not gay— recalled his father reprimanding him once by saying, "You're crying like a girl." Although this hurt him—and he remembered it years later—it did not leave him with a sense of difference because it was not followed by the attacks on his self-esteem that Zack suffered in the playground incident and subsequently. However, one place where Zack did feel he missed out, in comparison to his brothers, was in not being close to his father by playing in Little League, which his father coached. Although both his brothers played, his father never tried to force him or make him feel bad because he did not want to.

On the other hand, it was his father who started him in competitive swimming and, interestingly, it was in the pool locker room that he had his clearest early memories of sensual responses to male bodies. For the most part, Zack's memories of his father from his middle childhood years were of attachment and identification. He had an indicative memory from the age of eight or nine. His father had been sick. Zack recalled, "He was really laid out on the couch in the TV room, and his eyes were rolled back in his head. I remember being completely whacked out, crying hysterically, 'Daddy is going to die. I know it, my daddy is going to die.' My mother couldn't shut me up." He laughed, saying,

> My dad finally got up off the couch and came over and held me and said, "No, I'm okay, you jerk," and went up to his bed. I remember saying that I wanted to be like my dad, because I

saw how he handled things, how he associated with people. Everyone always likes my dad because he has that same personality that I do. My mother used to scold me, "You're just like your father, do you know that? You're going to grow up just like your father—you're just like him." It was kind of a stupid thing to say, like that's a bad thing. I remember one specific incident where she said that and I was sitting on the couch crying, "I don't want to be like him." But I'm like my dad, I know I'm more like my dad.

His father had also been in the National Guard for a long time and Zack once speculated that what he called "my stereotype," which he was attracted to in others and liked in himself—buzzed hair and clean-cut look—might reflect that.

Where, then, was his nagging sense of dissatisfaction about the relationship with his father lodged? At one of our meetings, he related that he overheard his father tell his mother that he had tickets to a Mets game, and he asked her if Zack's brother was off that day. Zack said, "I was right there, but he did't ask me." He told his father that he could get free tickets to Mets games anytime he wanted to go. He added, "I think if he ever asked me about my life he'd know that one of my ex-lovers worked for the Mets. When my father comes over, he says he stopped in to see the cat, not me. It's a way of trying to connect with me, but it's a pretty pathetic way." About why he did not ask Zack to go the game, Zack said, "Maybe he thinks I wouldn't be interested, or maybe he's afraid he'd have to have a longer conversation than, 'How's the cat?' " Yet, when Zack had lived in his own apartment some time before, his father would stop over on the pretext of tinkering with his antique clock. While Zack and I were working together, Zack bought a house, and his father helped him with the carpentry. He was also a skillful mechanic and worked with Zack on his truck. Some years before, when Zack's police car had been hit by another car and Zack was severely hurt, he knew his father had been distraught. It seems to me that, although Zack's father was "good enough," and Zack knew that they had a bond of love, he needed more from him emotionally. He needed to have his father reach out and initiate emotional contact through a more tangible expression of that bond—sometimes, as in the case of the ball game, in shared comradeship, but especially in words. When Zack first told his parents he was gay, his father said, "It's your business. I don't want to hear about it or talk about it." So, without meaning to hurt him, his father effectively closed a door that communicated with the deepest sources of his son's being. Nevertheless, especially over the last two years of our work, there seemed to be a growing and conscious sense of emotional closeness on both their parts.

I do think that relationships with heterosexually identified men might have held one special meaning for Zack that relationship with gay men did not. The turning point in his life had been the experience of the Forum, where, "The leader just took me back to all those things, all the stuff about the kids finding out and calling me a faggot. . . . As far as I'm, concerned, it goes back to that first incident." As heterosexually identifed men moved to bond with him—at whatever level—it was a natural continuation of the process of undoing the sense of difference imposed on him by that first incident, one that had been interrupted for a while by the episode of the wilderness trip. But, in the end, neither Zack nor they needed any justification to meet as equals and friends—and even more—at a place beyond the categories of identity. I said in an earlier chapter that once people understood that half of the human race did not have to be off-limits for emotional and physical closeness, they could experience their same-sex feelings as a worthwhile part of themselves. I think something similar happened for some of the men on the other side of the identity boundary who came to know Zack as a friend. It was a process from which both sides emerged changed for the better.

Although Zack might have wondered about his own motivations in relationships with heterosexually identified men, they were never one-sided and, in fact, were just as often initiated by the other man. That was virtually always the case where any sexual component was concerned, as it was for Perry, the last man discussed in this chapter other than Zack. Although it was Zack who 'made the first overtures of friendship when they met at the gym, it was Perry who introduced an overt sexual meaning to their relationship. The friendship began to develop as the loosely knit group of young twenty-some-things around Gabe began going their separate ways. Perry was about ten years younger, but since he was not gay, Zack did not see a boyfriend relationship developing. He frankly recognized the attraction, however. Perry was about Zack's height and general build and had served in the military. He had a girlfriend. And although their friendship got off to a somewhat tentative start after their meeting at the gym, a strong emotional bond soon developed, nurtured as much on Perry's part as Zack's. Further, in contrast to Dirk, who had to withdraw as soon as he learned that Zack was gay, this knowledge seemed to have the opposite effect on Perry. In fact, he openly expressed his attraction to Zack. One night at a bar with his girlfriend, Zack, and Xavier, Perry was saying about Zack, "Look at this guy—he's so fucking beautiful." Zack said, "I was a little drunk, but Xavier remembered every bit. He said, 'The boy is obviously in love with you. It upset his girlfriend.' I asked him how he knew and he said, 'She told me.'" Although Gwen was very accepting of their friendship, she did confide to Zack that she was a bit worried: "He grabbed your butt and kept hugging you, and not leaving you alone. It was all about you—'Zack this and Zack that'—I was really upset that night."

When they were alone together, Perry would say things such as, "You want me, just admit it already." Once, Zack remembered that when Perry caught him looking at a very handsome, well-built man, Perry said, "Oh, cut it out." Zack replied, "But he's gorgeous," and then, teasingly, "He puts you in the shade." Perry retorted, "Would you just admit you're in love with me?" Their relationship was also very physical, with wrestling and nipple pinching on both sides.

But the relationship also went beyond the physical. Zack recognized that Perry struck the chord in him that was searching for the other who could be, in an emotional if not sexual sense, the other half of himself that the double represented. Elements of that clearly existed for Perry as well. In jest, he said things such as, "If Gwen and I break up, I can move in with you," adding with just enough deniability, "and get used to it." At a party at Zack's, Perry quipped, in relation to a job search he was engaged in, "I'll wait until I get hired, then drop Gwen and marry Zack." He also wanted to be Zack's best friend—about that he was serious. Once, when he met Carey, a married friend at whose wedding Zack had been best man, he said, "I understand you're Zack's best friend. I'm his best friend too." Carey said, "I don't mind sharing Zack." Perry shot back, "But I do." When Zack was going to be in another friend's wedding party, he asked Perry if he would like to go with him. Perry asked, "Do I have to wear a dress or dance with you?" Zack reassured him on both counts. But then, at the last dance—a slow one—Perry suggested dancing together and they did. Zack recalled, "Everyone thought we were boyfriends and asked, 'How long have you two been together?'" After the wedding, they went back to Perry's, picked up Gwen, and went as a threesome to a local bar. As Gwen was occupied at the jukebox and Perry and Zack were sitting at the bar together, Perry said to Zack, "You know you love me." Zack replied "How about you, Perry?" Perry, who had turned away and was looking down, slowly turned his head and, looking up at Zack, said seriously, "Yeah, I love you."

The irony that Perry—who was presumably heterosexual—had been much freer in taking the initiative with Zack than vice versa was not lost on Zack. The next morning, over breakfast, Zack said to Perry, "You said a lot of things last night that scared me." Perry, knowing that Zack was responding to the overt romantic mood he had created and the sexual subtext that implied, said, "That's not a part of me." But then, he paused and added, "But I guess it is." When I asked Zack what Perry said that scared him, he said, "He crossed the line of understanding that I was gay and he was straight." Yet, it was Perry who insisted on approaching that line and Zack who—self-protectively, he acknowledged—gently put on the brakes, but not, I think, with the intention of stopping the movement altogether. I suspect, rather, that he wanted to give Perry the space he needed to figure out which direction he wanted to go.

Zack had earlier said, "I have attraction for these straight guys in one sense, and I end up not expressing it to them, even though they are expressing things to me that I almost should be saying to them! They're telling me and I'm not saying anything." I don't think that Zack was looking for rejection from heterosexually identified men any more than he was from gay men—and he certainly was not looking for it from Perry. I think there were several dimensions to what Zack wanted from men, which had nothing to do with sexual identity—his or theirs. He wanted to feel included as a man in the circle of male solidarity, to feel he could have friends and be a friend. In this he was no different from most men. But he also wanted something more—a connection of the soul—that would ultimately be expressed through the body as well. In many ways, Perry signaled to Zack that he wanted such a connection with him too. As Zack pondered the complexities of his relationship with Perry and the meaning that it held for them both, he wrote these words:

> When I look in a mirror, what I see are the souls of all those that my path has crossed. Who I am is not a singular form, but an array of those whose souls have been passed on to me. I am a mirror of them. The mirror is me. My reflection is the other. Perry, when he looks at me, sees the other. He doesn't know it yet, but when he sees his reflection, he will find himself. I am a soul that is giving him his other.

Even as he wrote these words, he sensed that Perry might have gone as far as he could in finding his other, and himself, through and with Zack. He knew Perry loved him—he had told him so—but he feared that Perry was in that place that so many men in our culture are: a kind of emotional limbo where the forms for the expression of love between men are inadequate to encompass its breadth and depth. Although Perry did not want to share Zack with anyone else, it was himself that he had to find a way to share—with Gwen, who was the woman in his life, and with Zack, who was the most important man.

By the time the manuscript deadline for this book drew near, Zack found himself coming to terms with the situation in the police department. He recognized that some there were genuine friends and that some had to keep their distance. His ability in the area of human relations had been acknowledged through his assignment to the community policing division and to a program that aimed at teaching children about drugs and their dangers. Zack had no illusions that his work with fifth and sixth grade children would ensure that they would never try drugs. His aim was broader—to teach self-acceptance and respect for others. He took his job seriously and was respected by principals, teachers, and parents, and was popular with the children, to whom he was "Officer Zack."

My work with Zack was not intended as therapy—by the time I met Zack, he had begun the process of healing himself. But we had come a long way together since our first meeting at the Gay Officers Action League. As I tried to understand the nature of his experience and its meaning for the research in which I was engaged, he tried to understand the relation between his inner feelings and his place in the world. I had come to feel, after many years as a therapist, that the process of therapy is about movement in a person's life—akin to trying to find the path to the top of a mountain. At the beginning, neither therapist nor patient knows where the path lies, or what the view from the top will be like. But the therapist has some experience with mountains and so can help the patient find the way. Not every expedition reaches the top, but when one does, both patient and therapist know it. Zack was, of course, in the midst of life's journey when I first met him. It seems fitting, then, that the last dream I will report in his story ends on a mountaintop:

> I was in a stagecoach, but it also was like a skiing gondola. I was hanging onto a pole looking out a window over a valley. Behind, there were really high mountains, in front a valley, with mountains in the distance. It was frustrating because there was no communication going on. I remember saying, "I've had enough." I ended up on a mountain edge. It was not really scary, but it was like going up a ladder—where you know the ladder will not fall, but you still think about it. I was climbing to the top. I came to a very plushy, very green strip of lawn, and then I got to the top. It was the highest point of wherever I was. I was looking out over the valley, and wishing I had someone to share this moment with. Then Perry appeared and lay down beside me. I had my arm across his chest and we snuggled there together, looking out over the valley.

I think that frustration over communication not going on, in the first part of the dream, referred to the fact that not only did Perry have a very hard time expressing his feelings, he had an equally hard time reaching out to Zack to listen to his. I think he did want to be Zack's best friend, but as with some of the men in the earlier chapters, the intensity of his feeling for Zack moved toward expressing itself through the body as well. That movement took him to a place somewhere between best friend and lover and, as for so many men in our culture, he could not figure out what step to take next.

Nonetheless, in the dream Zack and Perry are alone together at the mountaintop. Why? I think the climb up the mountain was, in fact, symbolic of one of the more dangerous aspects of life's journey. It was reminiscent, too, Zack said, of the climb in the wilderness where, many years before, he would go to ask himself if his life was worth living. The color green tells us what this dangerous undertaking is about—the search for love that he could not accept then but understood now. As he reaches his goal, Perry is waiting for him. As they lie together, looking out over the valley and the far mountains, the words of the young captain in Conrad's *The Secret Sharer* come to mind to describe what they are feeling—"silent knowledge, mute affection, perfect communion." Perry was there because, for a time, that was what he and Zack had shared. And he was there because his presence was a symbol of what Zack still hoped to find.

Conclusion

Identity and Beyond

Identity has two faces, one subjective, one objective. At the subjective level, it can be an affirmation of self, as it was for Zack when he said about being gay, "It's the nomenclature of my life." But at the objective level, it is a construct—a label and a set of assumptions imposed on someone by others, as he also realized. In this sense heterosexuality, as well as homosexuality, is a construct that exists outside the self. In Greek legend, Procrustes, an outlaw living on the road to Athens, invited travelers who stopped with him to use a special bed. Those who were too short were stretched on a rack to fit it, and those who were too long had their legs chopped off to the appropriate length. Each construct—heterosexuality as well as homosexuality—functions as a Procrustean bed on which people are stretched or shrunk to fit. The difference is that the man who is gay has to resist being stretched or shrunk to fit the stereotype of "the homosexual," whereas the man who is not gay may have to stretch or shrink the truth about himself to fit the stereotype of "the heterosexual."

Nevertheless, having taken on the appearance of objectivity, the categories remain unquestioned in much of the research on male sexuality, even as they distort the reality of what men are actually like. I think the evidence in this book demonstrates that when the voices of individual men are no longer marginalized, ignored, or suppressed, the hollowness of the stereotypes that the institutional culture imposes on them is exposed. And as the hollowness of "heterosexuality" is exposed, so is that of "homosexuality." We can then see that men's emotional and physical feelings for each other are not confined to any single category of men. And as we listen to men and ask what their feelings about each other mean to them, we can see something else that the institutions of this culture have been organized to deny. This is that the identity that really counts—that constitutes the deepest source from which men's sexual feelings for each other spring—is not a gay or heterosexual identity. That source is, rather, a *male* identity, and—beyond that—a human identity.

Appendix

David and Jonathan

The prohibitions against homosexuality that are such a corrosive element in our religious traditions rely on two main sources. The first, and more important, was introduced into the early Christian church by Paul. In his letter to the Romans of his day, he says: "For this reason God gave them up to dishonorable passions. Their women exchanged *natural* relations for *unnatural,* and the men likewise gave up *natural* relations with women and were consumed with passion for one another, men committing shameless acts with men and receiving in their own persons the due penalty for their error" (italics added, Romans 1:26-27).[1]

The other source, one often cited by the religious right, consisted of the prohibition laid down in Leviticus 18:22: "You shall not lie with a male as a with a woman; it is an abomination." The penalty for this is prescribed in Leviticus 20:13: "If a man lies with a male as with a woman, both of them have committed an abomination; they shall be put to death, their blood is upon them."

In his discussion of the place of the prohibition against homosexuality in the evolution of Jewish religious law, Saul Olyan points out that the two references to sex between males found in Leviticus are the only ones in the Hebrew Bible. Nowhere else are such prohibitions referred to, a fact that he points out is not generally acknowledged by scholars. Olyan also cites philological evidence that indicates that the prohibition in Leviticus 18:22 refers to the active or penetrating partner in anal intercourse, and can be understood to apply to anal intercourse only. The restatement of the prohibition in Leviticus 20:13 begins in the same way but then switches in midstream to include both penetrating and receptive partners, suggesting a later editorial revision, probably by a different author. The force of the prohibition and the original intent of the penalty is, then, aimed at the partner taking what is generally regarded in our current culture as the characteristic "male" role.[2]

The Holiness Code of Leviticus was probably formulated during or after the period of the destruction of the first temple and the Babylonian exile.[3] The relation of its codes to the range of sexual practices that prevailed at the dawn of the monarchy four or more centuries earlier might be quite remote. Leviticus 18:11 says, "You shall not uncover the nakedness of your father's wife's daughter, begotten by your father; she is your sister." Leviticus 20:17 repeats this prohibition, adding that if "she sees his nakedness, it is a shameful thing, and they shall be cut off in the sight of the children of their people. . . . " However, the book of Samuel, which is the epic of the founding of the monarchy and the establishment of the Davidic dynasty, re-counts events that took place hundreds of years before the Holiness Code was set down. In that ancient period, marriage between half siblings was not yet forbidden. 2 Samuel 13 tells of the desire of King David's son Amnon for Tamar, his half sister. After he reveals his desire to her, she replies, "No, my brother, do not force me; for such a thing is not done in Israel. . . . Now, therefore, I pray you, speak to the king; for he will not withhold me from you." This plea would indicate that a union between a brother and sister of the same father but different mothers—forbidden in the later Holiness Code—was conceivable in those ancient times.

The first book of Samuel tells the story of the relationship between Jonathan, the son of Saul, the first king of Israel, and David, the future king. It forms part of the ancient chronicles of the Israelites. In it, human passion and political intrigue intertwine in an epoch when prophets made kings and kingship itself was still untested. It is agreed that the text is not the product of a single author. There is evidence for an older layer that is closer to tradition and legend and some later editorial reworking to support the legitimacy of the dynasty established by David. Furthermore, there is no single definitive text. A summary of the critical commentary on 1 Samuel, including the relationship between Jonathan and David, can be found in the Anchor Bible series, with a translation and further commentary by P. Kyle McCarter Jr.[4] In the excerpts that follow, I cite the translation appearing in the latter volume first, followed by the equivalent in the Revised Standard Version—in indented format—where the two differ in some important emphasis.

In 1 Samuel itself there are two different versions of how the young David is introduced to Saul the king. In one version he is brought to the court because he is expert at playing the lyre, whose music has the power to bring the king out of the evil fits of brooding to which he is prey. Another version has Saul meeting David after he has slain the Philistine champion, Goliath, and brought his head to Saul. It is in this version that Jonathan and David first meet. The king asks, "Whose son are you, lad?" And David answers, "The son of your servant Jesse the Bethlehemite" (1 Samuel 17:58). "By the time [David] finished speaking with Saul, Jonathan found himself bound up with David. Jonathan loved David like himself! Saul took [David] at that time and would not let him return to his father's house, and Jonathan and David made a covenant, because [Jonathan] loved him like himself. Jonathan took off the robe he had on and gave it to David along with his uniform, his sword, his bow and his belt" (1 Samuel 18:1-4).

In the Revised Standard Version of the Bible, these verses read:

> When he had finished speaking to Saul, the soul of Jonathan was knit to the soul of David, and Jonathan loved him as his own soul. And Saul took him that day, and would not let him return to his father's house. Then Jonathan made a covenant with David, because he loved him as his own soul. And Jonathan stripped himself of the robe that was upon him, and gave it to David, and his armor, and even his sword and his bow and his girdle.

As the story unfolds, David's military prowess kindles Saul's jealousy, and he determines to kill the young man. Jonathan swears to protect David and when his father understands this, he upbraids his son in the following terms: "You son of a rebellious servant girl! Do I not know that to your own disgrace and to the disgrace of your mother's nakedness you are in league with the son of Jesse?" (1 Samuel 20:30).

In the Revised Standard Version, Saul's angry accusation is translated,

> You son of a perverse, rebellious woman, do I not know that you have chosen the son of Jesse to your own shame, and to the shame of your mother's nakedness?

The confrontation between father and son continues. "For as long as the son of Jesse is alive upon the earth, you will not establish your kingship! Now then, have him brought to me, for he is a dead man! 'Why should he be killed?' replied Jonathan to Saul. 'What has he done?' But when Saul raised his spear to strike him, [he] realized that his father was so intent upon evil that he would kill David, and he sprang from the table in a burning rage and would eat no food on the second day of the New Moon, because his father had humiliated him so" (1 Samuel 20:31-34). Recognizing that his father is determined to kill David, Jonathan helps him to escape and at their parting, "David arose . . . fell on his face, and did obeisance three times. Then they kissed each another and wept over each . . . (1 Samuel 20:41). Eventually, Jonathan and his father are killed fighting the Philistines. David mourns him in the famous lament (2 Samuel 1:26-27):

> I am distressed for you, my
> brother Jonathan;
> very pleasant have you been to me;
> your love to me was wonderful,
> passing the love of women.
> How are the mighty fallen,
> and the weapons of war perished.[5]

That Jonathan loves David is unambiguously clear and that David is responsive to that love also seems clear. Could this have been a love relationship in the sense that we would now understand it—that is, one that included sexuality? The way the story is told recalls in many ways the *erastes-eromenos* relationships of the Greek classical period, with Jonathan the *erastes,* the passionate lover, and David the *eromenos,* the beloved who responds to Jonathan's passion with gratitude and deep affection. Sex between males was certainly part of the ancient Near East. In fact, the prohibitions of the Holiness Code testify to its existence. Could a sexual relationship between two heroes of Jewish history have existed in contravention of this code? Why not? If a sexual relationship between half siblings which was declared incestuous in that code had been conceivable in this more ancient era, why could the sexual expression of a powerful love between two young men not have been?[6]

McCarter points out that later editorial revisions of the primary story might be responsible for some lines that make Jonathan appear to acquiesce to the inevitability of David's succession to the kingship. In an exchange that might reflect this later editorial revision, Jonathan is made to hint at the inevitability of David's succession to the kingship—still in the context of a declaration of love. "If I remain alive, deal loyally with me; but if I die, never cut off your loyalty from my house. . . . So again Jonathan swore to David out of his love for him, for he loved him as he loved himself" (1 Samuel 20:14-17). McCarter proposes that the word "love" in this story hints at a political meaning, as well as deep friendship. He cites the command of loyalty given to vassals of the Assyrian king Ashurbanipal, "You must love him as you love yourselves."[7] I think this suggestion reflects our civilization's wish to deny the sexual implications in this relationship. We are familiar with the use of "love" to mean political loyalty in Shakespeare also, but context leaves no doubt about which meaning of the word is intended. That Jonathan's love for David might have political consequences is one thing, but the narration depicts the inspiration of this love as unambiguously emotional and not political—in fact, Jonathan has no political motive that could make any sense. He cannot be ordered to "love" David, because Jonathan is clearly the social superior. In 1 Samuel 20:8-9 David says to Jonathan, "Now deal loyally with your servant, for you have brought your servant into a covenant of Yahweh with you. If there were any guilt in me, you could kill me yourself! So why should you turn me over to your father?" Jonathan replies, "Heaven forbid! If I learn that my father intends that evil should come upon you . . . I shall inform you."

In this exchange, David refers to himself as a subject of a king's son—"your servant"—even though their relationship is deeply emotional. The Anchor Bible version has Saul say to Jonathan, "You son of a rebellious servant girl! Do I not know that to your own disgrace and to the disgrace of your mother's nakedness you are *in league with* the son of Jesse?" In the Revised Standard Version, Saul's angry accusation is translated, "You son of a perverse, rebellious woman, do I not know that you have *chosen* the son of Jesse to your own shame, and to the shame of your mother's nakedness?" The phrase "in league with" is translated from the Septua-

gint—the early Greek version of the Hebrew Bible—while "chosen" is closer to the most intact Hebrew text. The former translation
connotes a possible political conspiracy, the latter an overriding
emotional bond. Earlier, the young David has been introduced to
the reader as follows: "He was ruddy and attractive, handsome to
the eye and of good appearance" (1 Samuel 16: 12). Recalling the
narrative's context for their first meeting, Jonathan's actions and
feelings seem like those of a man who has fallen in love at first
sight. There is no hint anywhere that Jonathan is aware at this first
meeting that David has been or will be chosen by God to succeed
Saul. This is not, as with John the Baptist meeting Jesus, a recognition on Jonathan's part that David is the future king. Whatever the
historical facts might have been, the traditional story depicts Jonathan's feelings as personal and emotional. The covenant that Jonathan makes with David—a "covenant of Yahweh"—brings their
relationship into a circle of sanctity, but that relationship on Jonathan's part is one of personal and not political loyalty. When Saul
upbraids Jonathan for defending David, he charges him with favoring "the son of Jesse *to your own shame, and to the shame of your
mother's nakedness. . . .*"

The phrase "the shame of your mother's nakedness" seems important. In the Holiness Code, a prohibited sexual relationship between two people "uncovers the nakedness" of a third, related person. "You shall not uncover the nakedness of your father, which is
the nakedness of your mother; she is your mother, you shall not
uncover her nakedness. *You shall not uncover the nakedness of your
father's wife; it is your father's nakedness*" (Leviticus 18:7-8).[8]
Although the events recorded here date from a much earlier period
of history, much if not all of the actual text which sets down the
ancient traditions is unquestionably much later, and its language
and even some of its concepts might reflect those of the later era.
When the narrator has Saul charging Jonathan with shaming himself and his mother by metaphorically uncovering her "nakedness,"
the charge adds the implication of a sexual bond—perhaps no longer deemed licit but nevertheless tacitly understood to have been
possible in the earlier era. The paranoid suspicions of a king whose
doom Yahweh has sealed are merged with the sarcasm of a father
who informs his son that his affair is an open secret. "Do you think

I don't know what's going on between you two?" Nevertheless, there is no reason to think it is the sexual relationship that Saul objects to—rather, it is his belief that Jonathan is so blind that he is willing to jeopardize his own succession to the kingship. The narrator in turn seems to accept the tradition of the relationship between the king's son and the young hero as a deeply emotional bond with a possible sexual dimension. This dimension is nevertheless not condemned. When, in mourning Jonathan, David is recorded as saying about him,

> your love to me was wonderful,
> passing the love of women

the intensity of their emotional bond is explicitly acknowledged, while the sexual bond is implied.

In the worldview of classical civilization it was understood that it was part of divine—as well as human—nature to express the emotion of love through the body. When love passes a certain threshold of intensity, expression through the body becomes more and more difficult to resist. In a culture prohibiting the sexual expression of love between men, resistance can take the form of the mind dividing itself. The loving feeling remains in consciousness, but since culture—like identity—sets boundaries on thought, the imagery of the body expressing that love may have to split off and go underground, perhaps surfacing in dreams, where the culturally determined boundaries of the imagination are loosened. I think the perplexity many feel when they try to imagine a sexual relationship between Jonathan and David is inevitable because the culture in which they have grown up has set limits to the imagination when it comes to sex between men, except for those who fit the category of gay. On the other hand, the Greeks would not have imagined David's saying "your love to me was wonderful, passing the love of women" to be anything *except* a confirmation of its sexual nature, because in their culture's terms it would not be comprehensible that such an intense emotional bond would *not* be expressed through the body. In our own cultural climate, the uncertainty about the sexual nature of this relationship probably cannot be resolved, short of unearthing a lost document that explicitly confirms it.

Notes

Preface

1. John P. De Cecco and John P. Elia, eds., *If You Seduce a Straight Person, Can You Make Them Gay? Issues in Biological Essentialism versus Social Constructionism in Gay and Lesbian Identities.* Binghamton, New York: Harrington Park Press, 1993.

2. David Greenberg has pointed out that the question of what factors shape individual sexual desire is analytically distinct from the question of what *categories* are used to conceptualize sexuality. See his discussion of the interaction of essentialist and constructionist approaches in: Greenberg, *The Construction of Homosexuality.* Chicago: University of Chicago Press, 1988, pp. 482-493.

3. An interesting, though unintended, acknowledgment of the way in which the use of a statistical test of inference can create and sustain stereotypes is the comment by the author of an article on sex differences in intelligence that appeared in *American Psychologist,* the organ of the American Psychological Association. The writer says, "Those opposed to research on sex differences fear that it will increase prejudice and discrimination by legitimizing false stereotypes. . . ." However, she continues, "Stereotypes do not result from research on the ways in which females and males differ; they arise inductively through experience (e.g., secretaries are usually female), they are 'carefully taught.' . . . Research is the only way in which psychologists can distinguish between those stereotypes that have a basis in fact (i.e., are statistically associated with one group more than another) and those that do not." The irony is that while the writer will have no truck with "false stereotypes," she fails to see that even a stereotype that is statistically associated with one group more than another—and therefore presumably "true" (?)—remains *false* for all the members of the group to whom it does not apply. I do not think psychology should be in the business of peddling half-truths any more than outright falsehoods. (Diane F. Halpern, "Sex Differences in Intelligence: Implications for Education." *American Psychologist,* 1997, v. 52, No. 10, 1091-1102).

4. De Cecco and Elia further point out that, although research on the "causes" of homosexuality uses quantitative measures of sexuality, both research and press reports continue to place people in discrete categories as either homosexuals or heterosexuals, with a nod in the direction of bisexuals who "muddy the otherwise tidy conceptual waters" (De Cecco and Elia, p. 4). Most psychologists who have earned their doctorates doing quantitative research have not been trained as statisticians or mathematical logicians. To put it bluntly, they have applied cookbook

formulas. However, a movement is afoot—as seen in the pages of *American Psychologist*—to question the inappropriate interpretations of statistical tests of significance that give uncertain probabilities the appearance of unqualified certainties. (See Jacob Cohen, "The World Is Round (p < .05)." *American Psychologist*, 1994, v. 49, No. 12, pp. 997-1003. A more recent discussion by several different writers can be found in *American Psychologist*, 1998, v. 53, No. 7, pp. 796-803.) If the pace of educational change follows the usual pattern, however, it will be at least a decade—if not two—before any changes are made in doctoral training programs in psychology.

5. Gilbert Herdt and Robert Stoller used the dialogue method for their interviews in *Intimate Communications: Erotics and the Study of Culture* (New York: Columbia University Press, 1990). Blending ethnographic and psychoanalytic perspectives, they explored the subjective meanings of people's sexual feelings in another culture. Although they used this method in the context of a cross-cultural study, I believe that this method and the same combination of perspectives is necessary for the study of sexuality in the context of our own culture.

6. Edward J. Tejirian, *Sexuality and the Devil: Symbols of Love, Power, and Fear in Male Psychology.* New York: Routledge, 1990.

Chapter 1: The Inner Boundary

1. Edward J. Tejirian, *Sexuality and the Devil: Symbols of Love, Power, and Fear in Male Psychology.* New York: Routledge, 1990.

2. David F. Greenberg's *The Construction of Homosexuality* (Chicago: The University of Chicago Press, 1988) provides voluminous historical and cross-cultural evidence for the normality of male same-sex feeling.

3. Alfred C. Kinsey, Wardell B. Pomeroy, and Clyde E. Martin, *Sexual Behavior in the Human Male.* Philadelphia: W. B. Saunders & Co., 1949.

4. Alfred C. Kinsey, Wardell B. Pomeroy, Clyde E. Martin, and Paul H. Gebhardt, Paul H. *Sexual Behavior in the Human Female.* New York: Pocket Books, 1965, pp. 474-475. Original edition published 1953.

5. Randall L. Sell, James A. Wells, and David Wypij, "The Prevalence of Homosexual Behavior and Attraction in the United States, the United Kingdom and France: Results of National Population-Based Samples." *Archives of Sexual Behavior*, V. 24, No. 3, 1995, pp. 235-248.

6. Martin S. Weinberg, Colin J. Williams, and Douglas W. Pryor, *Dual Attraction: Understanding Bisexuality.* New York: Oxford University Press, 1994.

7. Ibid., pp. 148-151.

8. Two excellent sources for reproductions of erotic scenes from Pompeii as well as other examples of erotic art of Greek and Roman antiquity are: *Eros in Antiquity,* New York: The Erotic Art Book Society, 1973. Also, Catherine Johns, *Sex or Symbol: Erotic Images of Greece and Rome.* Austin: University of Texas Press, 1982.

9. See *The Theodosian Code and Novels,* translated by Clyde Pharr, in collaboration with Theresa Sherrer Davidson and Mary Pharr. New York: Greenwood

Press, 1969. These edicts are chronologically presented in Book 16: Title 10: *Pagans, Sacrifices, and Temples,* edicts 1-25. They are an early example of the incremental approach to the destruction of a culture. In 435 C.E., the following edict was proclaimed: "We interdict all persons of criminal pagan mind from the accursed immolation of victims, from damnable sacrifices, and from all other such practices that are prohibited by the authority of the more ancient sanctions. We command that all their fanes, temples and shrines, if even now any remain entire, shall be destroyed by the command of the magistrates, and shall be purified by the erection of the sign of the venerable Christian religion. All men shall know it should appear, by suitable proof before a competent judge, that any person has mocked this law, he shall be punished with death" (16:10:25).

10. N.Q. King traces the graduated series of steps by which a succession of Christian emperors throttled the ancient religion of their ancestors. (N.Q. King, *The Emperor Theodosius and the Establishment of Christianity.* London: SCM Press Ltd, 1961.) King cites Libanus, a pagan and contemporary of Theodosius, as testifying that mobs led by Christian monks would charge that sacrifices (which had been declared illegal) were taking place in a temple, which would then be attacked and plundered. In 391 C.E., the temple of Serapis in Alexandria, which King notes was, after the great temples in Rome itself, the premier pagan shrine of the empire, was razed to the ground. The Bishop of Alexandria was thought to be the prime mover behind this attack (pp. 75-77 ff.).

11. Jeffrey Weeks, *Sexuality and Its Discontents: Meanings, Myths, and Modern Sexualities.* London: Routledge & Kegan Paul, 1985, p. 198.

12. Steven Zeeland, *Sailors and Sexual Identity: Crossing the Line Between "Straight" and "Gay" in the U.S. Navy.* Binghamton, NY: Harrington Park Press, 1995, pp. 7, 9.

Chapter 2: Women at the Boundary

1. Sandra Blakeslee, "How the Brain Might Work: A New Theory of Consciousness." *The New York Times,* March 21, 1995, pp. C1, C10.

2. David Freedberg, *The Power of Images.* Chicago: University of Chicago Press, 1989, p. 438.

3. My thanks to Joy Grasso Krebs, the "Julia" of this chapter, for this sensitive and revealing reminiscence.

4. Antonio M. Damasio, *Decartes' Error.* New York: G. P. Putnam's Sons, 1994.

5. Richard Cytowic, *The Man Who Tasted Shapes.* New York: G. P. Putnam's Sons, 1993, p. 8.

6. Damasio, *Descartes' Error,* p. xiv.

7. Joseph Ledoux, in *The Emotional Brain,* remarks: "Freud was right on the mark when he described consciousness as the tip of the mental iceberg." (Joseph Ledoux, *The Emotional Brain: The Mysterious Underpinnings of Emotional Life.* New York: Simon & Schuster, 1996, p. 17.)

Chapter 3: "Moving Toward" and Resistance

1. Howard Eilberg-Schwartz cites numerous biblical references to God's body, thus refuting the later idea that Jewish thought from the beginning conceptualized God as an incorporeal spirit. On the other hand, the inability or refusal to dwell on the sexual attribute of God reflected, he proposes, the fear of the homoerotic potential in men's relationship to a phallic deity, a meaning incompatible with a central tenet in ancient Hebraic culture—the obligation to procreate. He points out that, as rabbinical thought became the main conduit for the dissemination and preservation of Jewish religion and culture, Jewish men were increasingly "feminized" in their relation to God. Eventually, this culminated in a paradox—Jewish men are enjoined to cover the penis in prayer, even though it bears the mark of God's covenant with the Jewish people—circumcision. Thus, men's maleness and sexuality become further and further removed from their relationship to God. As for the possibility that the relationship between David and Jonathan might have been sexual, he feels it to be dubious. But I think the judgment of its doubtfulness is heavily influenced by the very fear of homoeroticism and the reactive demasculinization of men that his book persuasively argues for (Howard Eilberg-Schwartz, *God's Phallus: And Other Problems for Men and Monotheism.* Boston: Beacon Press, 1994).

2. One of Zeeland's informants reminisced about it:

"Then there's all these men with . . . just boots on and short shorts or frayed cut-off shorts, and no shirt at all. And then they had like a pirate's handerkerchief. They were just screaming at us. . . . I was sitting there smiling. . . . these guys, they'd fucking pick you up, and get in your face, and go, "You think it's funny, wog?" I was looking up [from all fours] and I seen three guys' dicks just dangling out of their shorts. A lot of them didn't wear underwear. I noticed some hard-ons on some guys. And they were spanking us with these shillelaghs. . . . In the hangar bay they made us fuck each other. They said, "Get on him and fuck him and suck his dick!" They would fuckin' shove your head in some guy's crotch.

(Steve Zeeland, *Sailors and Sexual Identity: Crossing the Line Between "Straight" and "Gay" in the U.S. Navy.* Binghamton, NY: Harrington Park Press, 1995, pp. 281-282.)

3. B.R. Burg, the editor of these diaries, commented: "Already aware of homoerotic relations among seafarers, he [Van Buskirk] claimed that all his acquaintances on board the *Plymouth* engaged in sexual contacts with other men, and that no one saw much harm in it" (B.R. Burg, *An American Seafarer in the Age of Sail: The Erotic Diaries of Philip C. Van Buskirk, 1851-1870.* New Haven, CT: Yale University Press, 1994, p. 74).

4. Guy Trebay, "Good Order and Discipline: The Killing of Allen Schindler." *The Village Voice,* June 1, 1993, pp. 21-26.

5. Nick Ravo, "For Gay Legislator, Bill Is End of Long Journey." *The New York Times,* April 23, 1991, p. B4

6. Frank, the man I wrote about in *Sexuality and the Devil,* had a similar anxiety. The devil symbolized the man he unconsciously desired sexually, but also feared. His conscious associations to what the devil would do to him if he should possess him were that he would dominate him, make him his slave, and humiliate him. Frank was reflecting the fact that one of the unconscious meanings of the devil symbol—and one of the sources of homophobia and "homosexual panic" in our culture—is that of the powerful, phallic male capable of sexually dominating other men and destroying their masculinity. (See *Sexuality and the Devil,* where Chapter 7, "The Symbol of the Devil" and Chapter 8, "Symbolism, Culture, and Sexuality" present evidence for this cultural meaning of the devil symbol.)

7. Bernard E. Trainor and Eric L. Chase, "Keep Gays Out." *The New York Times,* March 29, 1993, p. A15.

8. Even the most casual look at the sociology of prisons in this country reveals that a very large percentage of men whose identities are heterosexual engage in sex while in prison, frequently initiating it themselves.

9. "Little Trouble in Canada When Its Gay Ban Ended." *The New York Times,* January 31, 1993, p. 22. On the same page on which this report appeared, *The Times* printed a long feature story by James Sterngold, headlined: "Death of a Gay Sailor: A Lethal Beating Overseas Brings Questions and Fears. " It gave details of the brutal beating and murder in Japan of the twenty-two-year-old naval radioman, Allen Schindler, by some of his shipmates. I daresay that Trainor and Chase would fail to see any connection between their attitudes and this act of murderous homophobia.

10. Bernard E. Trainor, "The Answer to a Chaplain's Prayer." *The New York Times,* August 13, 1993, p. A27.

11. In *The Symposium,* written around 416 B.C.E., Plato has Phaedrus utter the following:

> If then one could contrive that a state or an army should entirely consist of lover and loved, it would be impossible for it to have a better organization than that which it would then enjoy through their avoidance of all dishonour and their mutual emulation; moreover, a handful of such men, fighting side by side, would defeat practically the whole world. A lover would rather be seen by all his comrades leaving his post or throwing away his arms than by his beloved; rather than that, he would prefer a thousand times to die. And if it were a question of deserting his beloved or not standing by him in danger, no one is so base as not to be inspired on such an occasion by Love himself with a spirit which would make him the equal of men with the best natural endowment of courage. In short, When Homer spoke of God "breathing might" into some of the heroes, he described exactly the effect which Love, of his very nature, produces in men who are in love.

(Plato, *The Symposium,* Walter Hamilton, translator. London: Penguin Books, 1951).

In fact, such a fighting force existed roughly contemporary with Plato. History knows it as the Sacred Band of Thebes, composed of 150 pairs of friends. They were sworn to protect each other and their city. Under the Theban general and statesman Epaminondas, they served as both spearhead and rallying point in battle. They were drawn from noble Theban families, and their courage was legendary. And they were not only friends—they were also lovers.

Chapter 4: Men on Men: Image, Emotion, and Meaning

1. Suzanna Andrews, "She's Bare. He's Covered. Is There a Problem?" *The New York Times,* November 1, 1992, Section 2, "Arts and Leisure," pp. 13-14.

2. Fred was referring to the statement in *Sexuality and the Devil:* "When Freud uses the phrase homosexual libido he is linking loving a man and having sex with a man together in an essentially seamless continuum of emotional and sexual'energy'" (p. 234).

3. Eve Kosofsky Sedgwick, *Between Men: English Literature and Male Homosocial Desire.* New York: Columbia University Press, 1985, p. 35.

4. From a scholarly vantage point, Christine Downing has brought together the stories and legends of same-sex love among the gods and goddesses of the Greeks in her *Myths and Mysteries of Same-Sex Love* (New York: Continuum, 1989).

5. In his book on Latino gay men, Rafael Diaz notes, "Mutuality and nurturance in sexual behavior is often interpreted as non-masculine, taking away the erotic charge for those men who have accepted the gender definition of homosexuality" (Rafael M. Diaz, *Latino Gay Men and HIV: Culture, Sexuality, and Risk Behavior.* New York: Routledge, 1998, p. 77). In other words, both partners have internalized the cultural defense that protects the masculine self-esteem of the one at the expense of the other.

6. My thanks to Caroll Hunter for this information.

7. Irving Bieber, Harvey J. Dain, Paul R. Dince, Marvin Drellich, Henry G. Grand, Ralph H. Gundlach, Malvina W. Kremer, Alfred H. Rifkin, Cornelia B. Wilbur, and Toby B. Bieber, *Homosexuality.* New York: Random House, 1962.

8. Weinberg, Williams, and Pryor, *Dual Attraction,* pp. 139-141.

9. Craig Williams, "Brothers, Friends, and Lovers in Roman Literature." Paper presented at the Columbia University Seminar on the Homosexualities, March 3, 1994.

10. As it appeared that publication of this book might be nearing, I contacted—among others—both Brad and Gary. Several years had gone by and I wanted them to read what I had written about what they had told me and make sure that they were comfortable with it. It was in the spring of the year, and they both revealed that—coincidentally—each was planning a July wedding, Gary with a young woman who was in my class in the same semester that he was.

Chapter 5: Heterosexuality versus Moving Toward Women

1. Biological or genetic explanations have tended to be assimilated into the paradigm of "gender nonconformity," whether defined behaviorally, as a lack of sufficient interest in activities socially typed as masculine or an excessive interest in those typed as feminine, or psychologically, as a failure to develop a fully formed male identity. Consider the recent and widely publicized study by Dean Hamer and his associates that was aimed at demonstrating a genetic basis for homosexuality. The book's title was *The Science of Desire: The Search for the Gay Gene.* In a book remarkable for its insensitivity to any cultural or even emotional issues, the following statement—as deeply homophobic as it is casually flippant—stands out: "Most sissies will grow up to be homosexuals, and most gay men were sissies as children. Despite the provocative and politically incorrect nature of that statement, it fits the evidence. In fact, it may be the most consistent, well-documented, and significant finding in the entire field of sexual-orientation research and *perhaps in all of human psychology*" [italics added]. (Dean Hamer and Peter Copeland, *The Science of Desire: The Search for the Gay Gene and the Biology of Behavior.* New York: Simon & Schuster, 1994, p. 166.)

2. The "masculine identification" of a man who is thought to be heterosexual, no matter what his appearance or interests might be, is hardly ever questioned. If a man's sexual partners are women, this issue is moot. The section of personal ads in an alternative weekly newspaper published in western Massachusetts (*The Valley Advocate,* September 19-26, 1996) neatly illustrated this. In the "Men Seeking Men" section, the word "masculine" or the phrase "straight-acting" appeared in twenty out of sixty-nine ads. In fourteen cases, these were self-descriptions. On the other hand, "masculine" did not appear as a self-description in *any* of the ads appearing under the heading of "Men Seeking Women." Of fifty "Women Seeking Women" ads, ten mentioned the word "feminine." Three of these were self-descriptions; the others specified this as a quality they were seeking in a partner. In addition, one woman described herself as a tomboy, one as "butch," and one as "semi-feminine." Of men looking for men, only one said that he was looking for a "feminine" man, but no one described himself as "feminine." Of ninety-four "Women Seeking Men," only one referred to herself as "feminine." I doubt that the men and women looking for opposite-sex partners were identifiably different from those seeking partners of the same sex. Rather, their identification as men or women has not been challenged in the way that it often is for gay men and lesbian women, and so did not require comment.

3. Eve Kosofsky Sedgwick, *Between Men: English Literature and Male Homosocial Desire.* New York: Columbia University Press, 1985, p. 24.

4. Sigmund Freud, *Civilization and Its Discontents.* New York: W.W. Norton, 1961, p. 13.

5. The very title of a book reporting the results of an expensive, time-consuming, and potentially very useful longitudinal study headed by psychiatrist Richard Green—*The Sissy-Boy Syndrome and the Development of Homosexuality* (New Haven, CT: Yale University Press, 1987)—is a stunningly succinct expression of

the assumptions that have guided both the questions asked and the conclusions reached in "gender" research on homosexuality. The study followed boys who either explicitly wanted to be girls in childhood or who so thoroughly preferred culturally sterotyped female activities that they were thought to be implicitly rejecting a sense of themselves as male. Follow-up data were available for forty-four out of the sixty-six boys originally seen. At last follow-up, they were in their teens or early twenties. To his credit, Green, in his own final thoughts on the study's results, seems to acknowledge the complexity and diversity of human feeling and is less than confident about fully explaining it. Nevertheless, cultural biases are evident in the questions asked and the analysis of the data. The Kinsey rating scales were used to place the participants, as young men, on a spectrum from: exclusively heterosexual or "incidentally" homosexual (0-1); more than incidentally homosexual (2-4), a category that corresponded with "bisexual"; and predominantly homosexual (5-6). The group of forty-four young men broke down into: twelve heterosexual; fourteen bisexuals, and eighteen homosexual. Referring to these results, Green says, "Three-fourths of them are homosexual or bisexual." The study included a matching group of boys who were not "feminine" in childhood and therefore were classified as "masculine" (these are the author's quotation marks). Of the twenty-five "masculine" boys on whom there were follow-up data, twenty-four were rated as heterosexual or only "incidentally homosexual." Only one was rated as more than incidentally homosexual.

A matching, or control, group is thought be be necessary in most well-designed research. But the way it is used reflects the assumptions underlying the research. The use of the control group in this study confirms that "feminine" boys are more likely to become gay than "masculine" boys. But it leaves unexplored all the other questions surrounding this finding. Although Green says, of the men who had been "feminine" boys, that "three-fourths of them are homosexual or bisexual," he could have said with equal accuracy that, "three-fifths of them are heterosexual or bisexual." This would have recognized that bisexuality is as close to heterosexuality as it is to homosexuality. In fact, one-quarter of the boys became exclusively heterosexual adults. Another third were heterosexual as well as homosexual—a reality that the term "bisexual" masks. Therapy seemed to have no systematic influence on outcomes. If this book had been titled *The "Sissy Boy Syndrome" and the Development of Heterosexuality* it would have focused on very different questions and maybe offered a whole new perspective on the relationship between concepts of masculinity and feminity and sexual orientation. But to do that would mean moving beyond the constructs of the institutional gender system, where only "opposites" attract.

"Incidental homosexuality" (1 on the Kinsey scale) was grouped in a single category with "exclusively heterosexual" (0 on the scale) and ignored, so that we have no figures on how many men were assigned a 1. However, Weinberg, Williams, and Pryor in *Dual Attraction* make the interesting observation that increments on the Kinsey scale can be far from uniform in their meaning, and moving from 0 to 1 may be a bigger step than moving from 2 to 4. Shifting the anchor from an exclusive sexual preference, they say, can have more profound implications for one's sexual identity. I think the material I cited in the previous chapter bears out their observation. The conclusions in the Green study ignore the meaning of "incidental homosexuality" and its relation to the homosexuality of "homosexual orientation," as well as ignoring the meaning of the fact that 60 percent of the "feminine" boys were sexually attracted to women in their adult lives. Thus, the data that could have served to challenge the categories of sexual orientation and gender identity of the institutional culture were instead interpreted in a way that shores them up.

Chapter 6: Emotional Paths

1. Andrew Sullivan, *Virtually Normal: An Argument About Homosexuality.* New York: Alfred A. Knopf, 1995, p. 4.

2. Ibid., pp. 4-5.

3. Ibid., p. 6.

4. Ibid., p. 9.

5. Patrick Merla, ed., *Boys Like Us: Gay Writers Tell Their Coming Out Stories.* New York: Avon Books, 1996. Ron Caldwell's story is titled "Out-Takes."

6. Frederick Suppe, in an article on "explaining" homosexuality, remarked, "after nearly 1,000 studies of homosexuality, we really haven't established much of anything positive about the cause of homosexuality." Frederick Suppe, "Explaining Homosexuality: Philosophical Issues and Who Cares Anyhow?" *Journal of Homosexuality,* v. 27, No. 3/4, 1994, pp. 223-268.

Chapter 7: Identity Crises

1. I met Johnny at the same institution where I met Clark. My interviews with Johnny touched on the issues of rape, but not very extensively. Those issues are taken up in much more detail in the chapters on Clark.

2. The late John Boswell produced evidence for the existence of ceremonies of same-sex unions in both Western and Eastern churches. (John Boswell, *Same-Sex Unions in Premodern Europe.* New York: Villard Books, 1994.) That such ceremonies existed is not in doubt, since manuscripts in monastery and church archives document them. Rather, their meaning is questioned. What kinds of unions were these? Certainly, love was understood to be one of their components, but what kind of love? A prototype for these unions and frequently invoked in these ceremonies were Saints Serge and Bacchus, two Christian officers between whom there were powerful bonds of friendship and love. They had enjoyed the personal favor of the Emperor Maximian, who ruled in the late third and early fourth centuries, but were tortured and executed for refusing to participate in the worship of the gods. The following passage is from a ceremony dating from the eleventh or twelfth century:

Lord God omnipotent who didst fashion humankind after thine image and likeness and gavest unto them life eternal, whom it hath pleased that thy

holy and glorious apostles Peter and Paul, and Philip and Bartholomew be
joined together not by the bond of blood but of fidelity and love, who didst
deem it meet for the holy martyrs Serge and Bacchus to be united together,
bless Thou also these thy servants . . . joined together not of birth, but of
faith and love. Grant them to love one another, let them continue without
envy and without temptation all the days of their lives, through the power of
thy Holy Spirit and the prayers of the Holy Mother of God and all thy saints
who have pleased Thee throughout the ages. (pp. 303-304)

Chapter 9: Movement into New Territory

1. In *Sexuality and the Devil,* I dwelt at length on the way that, in our cultural
history, the symbol of ultimate cosmic evil—the devil—came to be associated
with human sexuality in general and, especially later, with male same-sex feeling.
See Chapter 7 of *Sexuality and the Devil,* "The Symbol of the Devil."
2. Gert Hekma, " 'A Female Soul in a Male Body.': Sexual Inversion As Gen-
der-Inversion in Nineteenth-Century Sexology. " In: Gilbert Herdt, ed., *Third Sex,
Third Gender: Beyond Dimorphism in Culture and History.* New York: Zone
Books, 1994, p. 234.

Chapter 10: Cultural Confrontations and Identity

1. Sandra Blakeslee, "How the Brain Might Work: A New Theory of Consciousness." *The New York Times,* March 21, 1995, pp. C1, C10.
2. For a fuller discussion of these issues see: John Blofeld, *The Tantric Mysticism of Tibet.* New York: Penguin Books, 1992, pp. 111ff.
3. *The Epic of Gilgamesh.* Translated with an Introduction and Notes by Maureen Gallery Kovacs. Stanford, CA: Stanford University Press, 1989. These lines
are from Tablet 1, lines 57 and 62, on p. 5 of this edition. There is some ambiguity
about the meaning of these lines, but according to David Greenberg, the Assyrian
rescension contains an episode which makes clear that Gilgamesh was using both
males and females sexually. Greenberg's own translation of the old Babylonian
version that appears on the Pennsylvania tablet appears in: Will Roscoe, *Queer
Spirits.* Boston: Beacon Press, 1995, pp. 169-182, in a section titled, "He Is an
Equal to You (Gilgamesh and Enkidu)." Greenberg's translation makes the homoerotic content of the first dream explicit when Gilgamesh says to his mother,
"Mother, this very night I was a male prostitute, walking around in the midst of
youths" (p. 174).
4. In his book *Jocks: True Stories of Gay Male Athletes* (New York: Alyson
Books, 1998) Dan Woog recounts stories of men who were both athletes and gay.
Overall, however, the stories in this book counteract the cliché that same-sex feeling and interest in athletics are somehow antithetical. It should be borne in mind,
too, that one of the most homosexual civilizations the world has known—Greece
of the classical period—gave us the apotheosis of athleticism in the Olympic

Games. Further, William Armstrong Percy points out that in Greece of the classical period, the sexual expression of the male-to-male theme was closely intertwined with athletics and the world of the *gymnasion.* (See William Armstrong Percy III, *Pederasty and Pedagogy in Archaic Greece.* Urbana and Chicago: University of Illinois Press, 1996, pp. 97ff.) In an interesting and recent return to their psychological and cultural roots, gay men have been using the gym as a place where they can work to reclaim the pride in their male bodies that so many were denied in their formative years. The association between athletics and, not masculinity but rather, heterosexuality, seems to be a cultural artifact of this century. However, one of the men in Woog's book recalled how, although he was an excellent baseball player, his sense of being different meant he had to be better than anyone else, for fear that people might call him the "f word" and undermine his team's spirit. As a result, he dropped out of competition altogether.

5. In a book that purported to take an enlightened psychoanalytic approach to explaining male homosexuality, Richard C. Friedman proposed that prehomosexual boys enter puberty with, at the very least, an "unmasculine" self-representation. Unmasculine does not necessarily mean feminine. It is sufficient that it be *felt* as inadequate with respect to masculinity. As the biological changes of early adolescence usher in a greatly amplified potential for erotic feeling, accompanied by sexual imagery, the fantasies of the boy with this kind of inadequate self-representation emerge as homoerotic. Once differentiation of fantasy has occurred during the critical period of early adolescence it is "imprinted" and not subject to change, although the inadequate self-representation eventually gives way to positive masculine self-regard in a great many adult gay men. For men who come through the sexual differentiation phase as exclusively heterosexual, no "meaningful homoerotic fantasy option" is presumably available during adulthood. This conclusion is flatly contradicted by the testimonies of a great many men in this book. Although Friedman says that the reasons for the connection are unknown, he leaves room for only one conclusion: that "gender disturbance" is *the cause* of homosexual preference. And yet, the research data the author himself cites indicate that a great many boys whose self-images are not "gender disturbed" also become gay men. But these data are discarded because they demonstrate a similarity rather than a difference between gay and heterosexual men. No parallel theory explains why "gender normality" (if that is the opposite of "gender disturbance") is also associated with same-sex attraction. The role of culture is not discussed in this theory. Nor is the fact that a sense of inadequacy as a male is the result rather than a cause of the sense of same-sex attraction that violates the definitions of the institutional gender system. Finally, the theory does not take into account the fact that the definition of masculine adequacy in this culture is a powerful motivation for the suppression of homosexual behavior or imagery from childhood onward. Failing to take into account the role of culture, the theory ends up a victim of its stereotypes. (Richard C. Friedman, *Male Homosexuality: A Contemporary Psychoanalytic Perspective.* New Haven, CT: Yale University Press, 1988.)

6. D. W. Winnicott, *The Maturational Processes and the Facilitating Environment.* Madison: International Universities Press, 1965, pp. 140-153.

7. Ibid., pp. 146-147.
8. Ibid., p. 143.
9. Ibid.
10. Ibid.

Chapter 11: The Color Green

1. Aniela Jaffe, "Symbolism in the Visual Arts." In: Carl G. Jung and M.L. von Franz, eds., *Man and His Symbols.* Garden City, NY: Doubleday, 1964, pp. 240ff.
2. In their book *Maya Cosmos: Three Thousand Years on the Shaman's Path* (New York: William Morrow, 1995) David Freidel, Linda Schele, and Joy Parker tell about a modern-day Mayan ceremony to induce the gods to send rain:

> Pitching his voice into a higher octave to show the proper respect, Don Pablo spoke softly to the Chak Lords, the rain gods. He circled around the tall, thin cross made of sticks that stood behind the altar and the four young men stationed at its four corners. These men were making the roaring sounds of thunder. . . . They were clapping small wooden sabers and pistols together, and sprinkling fresh, clean water from little gourds onto the boys who crouched at their feet beside the corn plants of the arbor. The men embodied the Chakob, and the boys were the frogs of the rainstorm. (p. 32)

3. Mitchell Walker, "The Double: An Archetypal Configuration." *Spring,* 1976, p. 165.
4. Joseph Conrad, *Heart of Darkness and The Secret Sharer.* New York: Barnes and Noble Books, 1994.
5. See Royston Lambert, *Beloved and God: The Story of Hadrian and Antinuous.* New York: Meadowland Books, 1988.
6. *The Origin of the Young God: Kalidasa's Kumarasambhava.* Translation, introduction, and annotation by Hank Heifetz. Berkeley, CA: University of California Press, 1985.
7. Ibid., pp. 59-60.
8. Kama, the name of the Hindu god of love, is also the word for love, as is Eros in Greek.
9. *The Origin of the Young God,* 7: pp. 76-77. In this passage, "Siva" is the transliteration—the one preferred in scholarly writing—for the name of the god. However, it is pronounced "Shiva"—the spelling I have used elsewhere in this book when referring to the deity. Uma is another name for Parvati—or vice versa, since all the goddesses can also be seen ultimately as manifestations of the one Goddess.
10. Professor Eugene Rice, personal communication.
11. The eyes and the image of the body act as conduits to a higher—or deeper—plane of feeling in Hindu worship, where the act of looking has devotional or sacred significance. In looking upon the image of a god or goddess, the essence of contact is not with the image but through it to the deity beyond the image. In her

book *Darshan: Seeing the Divine Image in India,* Diana Eck points out that in looking at the image of the deity, the worshipper is, in fact, looking through it and seeing the god or goddess whose presence imbues it. In turn, the worshipper is seen by the deity. (Chambersburg, PA: Anima Books, 1985, p. 3). From our own cultural tradition come the following words: "The Icon is voiceless yet speaks. You unite with him, you discover him. You encounter him with the lips, with the eyes, with the heart. Icons . . . should be venerated and kissed with eyes, lips, and heart" (St. John of Damascus, *On Icons,* eighth century).

12. "Cave of the Heart" is a title of a dance work by Martha Graham that suggests to me that this was one of the symbolic meanings of the cave in Zack's dream.

Chapter 12: Boundary Crossings

1. In the dream, Zack's grandfather appears to capture some aspects of the image—or archetype—of the "Wise Old Man." Jungian analyst Robert Hopcke says of this image, "Though fatherly and heroic in certain ways, the Wise Old Man is also symbolic of a certain quality of masculine spirit unrelated to Father or Hero—a quietness, a hermitlike secretiveness, a force expressed not in the phallic thrustings of the Hero or in the procreativity of the Father but a force that comes from within, a magical strength that guides and fortifies one in one's inner struggles" (Robert Hopcke, *A Guided Tour of the Collected Works of C.G. Jung.* Boston and London: Shambhala, 1992, p. 117).

2. It is possible that a cultural shift is taking place among a younger generation of men that is enabling them to acknowledge and act on their same-sex feelings more readily than in the recent past, regardless of identity. In a study that had to do with health needs among this population in the Canadian city of Calgary, 13 percent of young adult males in a random survey appeared to be homosexual or bisexual. The sample was from outside Calgary's center, where the gay population tends to be concentrated. Respondents punched in their answers anonymously on a laptop computer. The results showed that 4.9 percent had at least one male *and* one female partner in the past six months. A total of 7.7 percent were classified (by the researchers) as bisexual on basis of having one partner of each sex in the previous six months or self-identifying as bisexual. A total of 6.0 percent were classified as homosexual on the basis of being currently exclusively homosexual or self-identifying as such. Only 43 percent of homosexual men and 48 percent of bisexual men had become homosexually active by their eighteenth birthday. The authors note that this contrasts with studies of established gay communities. On the other hand, with respect to the bisexual men, it is consistent with the mean age of first same-sex awareness in the study by Weinberg, Williams, and Pryor.. It is also consistent with the fact that most of my heterosexually identified male students reported their first same-sex feelings in the first year of college or afterward (Christopher Bagley and Pierre Tremblay, "On the Prevalence of Homosexuality and Bisexuality in a Random Community Survey of 750 Men Aged 18 to 27." *Journal of Homosexuality,* v. 36, No. 2, 1998, pp. 1-18).

3. In modern cinematic treatments, the really intense relationship is between an evil, demonic figure and the male protagonist. The relationship has unmistakable hints of eroticism, as the "good"—and heterosexual—hero becomes the target of an amoral counterpart who is the object of the hero's fascination, even as the hero almost succumbs to being corrupted by him.

Appendix: David and Jonathan

1. In *The Gnostic Paul: Gnostic Exegesis of the Pauline Letters* (Philadelphia: Trinity Press International, 1975) Elaine Pagels notes that the Gnostics—especially Valentinus and his followers—would have interpreted this passage metaphorically and, hence, in a radically different way. While appearing to deal with the alienation of one sex from the other, it actually referred to the separation between the spiritually initiated minority—the "pneumatics"—who understood the inner mysteries hinted at in the parables and story of Jesus, and the uninitiated majority—the "psychics"—who, lacking this understanding, took them literally (pp. 17-18). The Valentinians claimed Paul as one of their own and respected him as a great Gnostic teacher. When Paul spoke of sexual relations, they understood him to be speaking of spiritual relations (p. 68) since, for the initiated, observance of sexual prohibitions was irrelevant. However, the literalists—or orthodox—won out in the end and it was their literal reading of Paul and their version of Christianity that became the state religion of the Roman Empire. (See also Pagels' *The Gnostic Gospels* [New York: Vintage Books, 1979] for a fuller discussion of the Gnostic movement and its relation to the religious system that we know as Christianity today.)

2. Saul M. Olyan, "And with a Male You Shall not Lie the Lying Down of a Woman." *Journal of the History of Sexuality,* v. 5, October 1994, 179-206. Olyan does not give a definitive translation of the Hebrew *to'eba,* which is translated as "abomination" in the Revised Standard Version. Olyan says that the meaning of *to'eba* is not altogether clear and may not mean exactly the same things in all circles (see Olyan, p. 180, note 18). He says that the conventional translation "abomination" suggests only what is abhorrent, without suggesting the violation of a conventional social boundary that is also established by the deity. Howard Eilberg-Schwartz in his own translation of the Leviticus verses (see *God's Phallus,* p. 93) gives "abhorrence" as equivalent to *to'eba.*

3. David F. Greenberg notes that the final editing of Leviticus probably occurred in the sixth or fifth century B.C.E. See his discussion of its prohibitions of homosexuality in *The Construction of Homosexuality.* (Chicago: The University of Chicago Press, 1988, pp. 190ff.)

4. *The Anchor Bible: 1 Samuel,* with translation and commentary by P. Kyle McCarter Jr. New York: Doubleday, 1980.

5. Revised Standard Version.

6. In his study of the problem of homoeroticism in Jewish religious thought, Howard Eilberg-Schwartz regards the sexual component of this relationship as dubious. He cites the political dimensions of the story in which David is being

portrayed as the legitimate successor to Saul, Jonathan's father. He remarks that the loving relationship is also about David's right to claim Johnathan's position as Saul's successor. The two themes do not appear to me to be incompatible.

7. McCarter, *The Anchor Bible,* note to 1 Samuel 20:17, p. 342.

8. Revised Standard Version.

Bibliography

Andrews, Suzanna, "She's Bare. He's Covered. Is There a Problem?" *The New York Times*, November 1, 1992, Section 2, "Arts and Leisure," pp. 13-14.

Bagley, Christopher and Pierre Tremblay, "On the Prevalence of Homosexuality and Bisexuality in a Random Community Survey of 750 Men Aged 18 to 27." *Journal of Homosexuality,* 1998, v. 36, No. 2, pp. 1-18.

Bieber, Irving, Harvey J. Dain, Paul R. Dince, Marvin Drellich, Henry G. Grand, Ralph H. Gundlach, Malvina W. Kremer, Alfred H. Rifkin, Cornelia B. Wilbur, and Toby B. Bierber, *Homosexuality*. New York: Random House, 1962.

Blakeslee, Sandra, "How the Brain Might Work: A New Theory of Consciousness." *The New York Times,* March 21, 1995, pp. C1, C10.

Blofeld, John, *The Tantric Mysticism of Tibet*. New York: Penguin Books, 1992.

Boswell, John, *Same-Sex Unions in Premodern Europe*. New York: Villard Books, 1994.

Burg, B.R., *An American Seafarer in the Age of Sail: The Erotic Diaries of Philip C. Van Buskirk, 1851-1870*. New Haven, CT: Yale University Press, 1994.

Caldwell, Ron, "Out-Takes." In: Patrick Merla, ed., *Boys Like Us: Gay Writers Tell Their Coming Out Stories*. New York: Avon Books, 1996.

Cohen, Jacob, "The World Is Round (p < .05)." *American Psychologist*, December, 1994, v. 49, No. 12, pp. 997-1003. See also: "Comment," *American Psychologist*, July, 1998, v. 53, No. 7, pp. 796-803, for letters from readers on the interpretation of tests of statistical inference.

Conrad, Joseph, *Heart of Darkness and the Secret Sharer.* New York: Barnes and Noble Books, 1994.

Cytowic, Richard, *The Man Who Tasted Shapes*. New York: G.P. Putnam's Sons, 1993.

Damasio, Antonio M., *Decartes' Error.* New York: G.P. Putnam's Sons, 1994.

De Cecco, John P. and John P. Elia, eds., *If You Seduce a Straight Person, Can You Make Them Gay? Issues in Biological Essentialism versus Social Constructionism in Gay and Lesbian Identities*. Binghamton, NY: Harrington Park Press, 1993.

"Death of a Gay Sailor: A Lethal Beating Overseas Brings Questions and Fear." *The New York Times*, January 31, 1993, p. 22.

Diaz, Rafael M., *Latino Gay Men and HIV: Culture, Sexuality, and Risk Behavior.* New York: Routledge, 1998.

Downing, Christine, *Myths and Mysteries of Same-Sex Love*. New York: Continuum, 1989.

Eck, Diane L., *Darshan: Seeing the Divine Image in India*. Chambersburg, PA: Anima Books, 1985.

Eilberg-Schwartz, Howard, *God's Phallus: And Other Problems for Men and Monotheism.* Boston: Beacon Press, 1994.

The Epic of Gilgamesh. Translated with an Introduction and Notes by Maureen Gallery Kovacs. Stanford, CA: Stanford University Press, 1989.

Epstein, Steven, "Gay Politics, Ethnic Identity: The Limits of Social Constructionism." In: Edward Stein, ed., *Forms of Desire: Sexual Orientation and the Social Constructionist Controversy.* New York: Routledge, 1992.

Freedberg, David, *The Power of Images.* Chicago: University of Chicago Press, 1989.

Freidel, David, Linda Schele, and Joy Parker, *Maya Cosmos: Three Thousand Years on the Shaman's Path.* New York: William Morrow, 1995.

Freud, Sigmund, *Civilization and Its Discontents.* New York: W.W. Norton, 1961.

Friedman, Richard C., *Male Homosexuality: A Contemporary Psychoanalytic Perspective.* New Haven, CT: Yale University Press, 1988.

Green, Richard, *The Sissy Boy Syndrome and the Development of Homosexuality.* New Haven, CT: Yale University Press, 1987.

Greenberg, David F., *The Construction of Homosexuality.* Chicago: The University of Chicago Press, 1988.

Halpern, Diane F. "Sex Differences in Intelligence: Implications for Education." *American Psychologist*, 1997, v. 52, No. 10, pp. 1091-1102.

Hamer, Dean and Peter Copeland, *The Science of Desire: The Search for the Gay Gene and the Biology of Behavior.* New York: Simon & Schuster, 1994.

Hekma, Gert, " 'A Female Soul in a Male Body' " Sexual Inversion As Gender Inversion in Nineteenth-Century Sexology. In Gilbert Herdt, ed., *Third Sex, Third Gender: Beyond Dimorphism in Culture and History.* New York: Zone Books, 1994.

Herdt, Gilbert and Robert J. Stoller, *Intimate Communications: Erotics and the Study of Culture.* New York: Columbia University Press, 1990.

Hopcke, Robert, *A Guided Tour of the Collected Works of C.G. Jung.* Boston and London: Shambhala, 1992.

Jaffe, Aniela, "Symbolism in the Visual Arts." In Carl G. Jung and M.-L. von Franz, eds., *Man and His Symbols.* Garden City, NY: Doubleday, 1964, pp. 240ff.

Kalidasa, *The Origin of the Young God: Kalidasa's Kumarasambhava.* Translation, introduction, and annotation by Hank Heifetz. Berkeley, CA: University of California Press, 1985.

King, N.Q., *The Emperor Theodosius and the Establishment of Christianity.* London: SCM Press Ltd, 1961.

Kinsey, Alfred C., Wardell B. Pomeroy, and Clyde E. Martin, *Sexual Behavior in the Human Male.* Philadelphia: W.B. Saunders & Co., 1949.

Kinsey, Alfred C., Wardell B. Pomeroy, Clyde E. Martin, and Paul H. Gebhardt, *Sexual Behavior in the Human Female.* New York: Pocket Books, 1965. Original edition published in 1953..

Lambert, Royston, *Beloved and God: The Story of Hadrian and Antinuous.* New York: Meadowland Books, 1988.

"Little Trouble in Canada When Its Gay Ban Ended." *The New York Times*, January 31, 1993, p. 22.

Pagels, Elaine, *The Gnostic Gospels.* New York: Vintage Books, 1979.

Pagels, Elaine, *The Gnostic Paul: Gnostic Exegesis of the Pauline Letters.* Philadelphia: Trinity Press Internationa, 1975.

Percy, William Armstrong III, *Pederasty and Pedagogy in Archaic Greece.* Urbana and Chicago: University of Illinois Press, 1996.

Plato, *The Symposium,* translated by Walter Hamilton. London: Penguin Books, 1951.

Popol Vuh: The Mayan Book of the Dawn of Life. Translated by Dennis Tedlock. New York: Simon and Schuster, 1985.

Ravo, Nick, "For Gay Legislator, Bill Is End of Long Journey." *The New York Times,* April 23, 1991, p. B4.

Sedgwick, Eve Kosofsky, *Between Men: English Literature and Male Homosocial Desire.* New York: Columbia University Press, 1985.

Sell, Randall, L., James A. Wells, and David Wypij, "The Prevalence of Homosexual Behavior and Attraction in the United States, the United Kingdom and France: Results of National Population-Based Samples." *Archives of Sexual Behavior,* 1995, v. 24, No. 3, pp. 235-248.

Sterngold, James, "Death of a Gay Sailor: A Lethal Beating Overseas Brings Questions and Fear." *The New York Times,* January 31, 1993, p. 22.

Sullivan, Andrew, *Virtually Normal: An Argument About Homosexuality.* New York: Alfred A. Knopf, 1995.

Suppe, Frederick, "Explaining Homosexuality: Philosophical Issues and Who Cares Anyhow?" *Journal of Homosexuality,* 1994, v. 27, No. 3/4, pp. 223-268.

Tejirian, Edward J., *Sexuality and the Devil: Symbols of Love, Power, and Fear in Male Psychology.* New York: Routledge, 1990.

The Theodosian Code and Novels. Translated by Clyde Pharr, in collaboration with Theresa Sherrer Davidson and Mary Pharr. New York: Greenwood Press, 1969.

Trainor, Bernard E., "The Answer to a Marine Chaplain's Prayer." *The New York Times,* August 13, 1993, p. A27.

Trainor, Bernard E. and Eric L. Chase, "Keep Gays Out." *The New York Times,* March 29, 1993, p. A15.

Trebay, Guy, "Good Order and Discipline: The Killing of Allen Schindler." *The Village Voice,* June 1, 1993, pp. 21-26.

Walker, Mitchell, "The Double: An Archetypal Configuration." *Spring,* 1976, pp. 165-175.

Weeks, Jeffrey, *Sexuality and Its Discontents: Meanings, Myths, and Modern Sexualities.* London: Routledge & Kegan Paul, 1985.

Weinberg, Martin S., Colin J. Williams, and Douglas W. Pryor, *Dual Attraction: Understanding Bisexuality.* New York: Oxford University Press, 1994.

Winnicott, D.W., *The Maturational Processes and the Facilitating Environment.* Madison, WI: International Universities Press, 1965.

Woog, Dan, *Jocks: True Stories of Gay Male Athletes.* New York: Alyson Books, 1998.

Zeeland, Steven, *Sailors and Sexual Identity: Crossing the Line Between "Straight" and "Gay" in the U.S. Navy.* Binghamton, NY: Harrington Park Press, 1995.

Index

Page numbers followed by the letter "f" indicate figures; the letter "n" indicates a note.

Order Your Own Copy of This Important Book for Your Personal Library!

MALE TO MALE
Sexual Feeling Across the Boundaries of Identity

_____ in hardbound at $49.95 (ISBN: 1-56023-975-1)

_____ in softbound at $24.95 (ISBN: 1-56023-976-X)

COST OF BOOKS _____	☐ **BILL ME LATER:** ($5 service charge will be added) (Bill-me option is good on US/Canada/Mexico orders only; not good to jobbers, wholesalers, or subscription agencies.)
OUTSIDE USA/CANADA/ MEXICO: ADD 20% _____	
POSTAGE & HANDLING _____ *(US: $4.00 for first book & $1.50 for each additional book* *Outside US: $5.00 for first book & $2.00 for each additional book)*	☐ Check here if billing address is different from shipping address and attach purchase order and billing address information.
	Signature _____
SUBTOTAL _____	☐ **PAYMENT ENCLOSED: $** _____
IN CANADA: ADD 7% GST _____	☐ **PLEASE CHARGE TO MY CREDIT CARD.**
STATE TAX _____ *(NY, OH & MN residents, please add appropriate local sales tax)*	☐ Visa ☐ MasterCard ☐ AmEx ☐ Discover ☐ Diner's Club ☐ Eurocard ☐ JCB
FINAL TOTAL _____ *(If paying in Canadian funds, convert using the current exchange rate. UNESCO coupons welcome.)*	Account # _____ Exp. Date _____ Signature _____

Prices in US dollars and subject to change without notice.

NAME _____

INSTITUTION _____

ADDRESS _____

CITY _____

STATE/ZIP _____

COUNTRY _____ COUNTY (NY residents only) _____

TEL _____ FAX _____

E-MAIL _____

May we use your e-mail address for confirmations and other types of information? ☐ Yes ☐ No
We appreciate receiving your e-mail address and fax number. Haworth would like to e-mail or fax special discount offers to you, as a preferred customer. **We will never share, rent, or exchange your e-mail address or fax number.** We regard such actions as an invasion of your privacy.

Order From Your Local Bookstore or Directly From
The Haworth Press, Inc.
10 Alice Street, Binghamton, New York 13904-1580 • USA
TELEPHONE: 1-800-HAWORTH (1-800-429-6784) / Outside US/Canada: (607) 722-5857
FAX: 1-800-895-0582 / Outside US/Canada: (607) 772-6362
E-mail: getinfo@haworthpressinc.com
PLEASE PHOTOCOPY THIS FORM FOR YOUR PERSONAL USE.
www.HaworthPress.com

BOF00